Ernest Arthur Gardner, And Others

Authority and Archaeology, Sacred and Profane

Essays on the Relation of Monuments to Biblical and classical Literature

Ernest Arthur Gardner, And Others

Authority and Archaeology, Sacred and Profane
Essays on the Relation of Monuments to Biblical and classical Literature

ISBN/EAN: 9783337177454

Printed in Europe, USA, Canada, Australia, Japan

Cover: Foto ©ninafisch / pixelio.de

More available books at **www.hansebooks.com**

AUTHORITY AND ARCHAEOLOGY
SACRED AND PROFANE

ESSAYS ON THE RELATION OF MONUMENTS
TO BIBLICAL AND CLASSICAL LITERATURE

BY S. R. DRIVER, D.D.   ERNEST A. GARDNER, M.A.
F. LL. GRIFFITH, M.A.   F. HAVERFIELD, M.A.
A. C. HEADLAM, B.D.   D. G. HOGARTH, M.A.

WITH AN INTRODUCTORY CHAPTER ON THE NATURE OF
ARCHAEOLOGY BY THE EDITOR

EDITED BY

DAVID G. HOGARTH

Fellow of Magdalen College, Oxford; Director of the British School at Athens

SECOND EDITION

LONDON
JOHN MURRAY, ALBEMARLE STREET
1899

PRINTED BY
HAZELL, WATSON, AND VINEY, LD.,
LONDON AND AYLESBURY.

PREFATORY

It is hoped that these Essays will shew in what ways and to what degree the results of archaeological research may legitimately affect the views of those who, without special archaeological knowledge, concern themselves with the antiquity of civilization. Evidence and hypotheses, which have not been subjected to an adequate test, do not come within the proper scope of this volume, which, it is hoped, may not be open to the reproach, often brought against summaries, that they resume work which has not yet been done. The impossibility of containing even a rapid survey of all archaeologies within a volume of reasonable bulk has caused the purview of the essayists to be confined to the geographical area from which the culture of Christian Europe has directly sprung, namely, that debatable land of the Near East, where the energetic nature disputes possession with the contemplative, and where have originated the great ideas but not the great institutions of humanity.

The views, contained in this volume, regarding both Archaeology in general and its special departments, have not been arrived at by any common understanding. Each essayist is responsible for his own views, and the Editor for no more than those expressed in his own contributions.

In regard to Archaeology in general a word must be said by way of preface, since the connotation of the term has come to be ambiguous in ordinary thought and speech; and, in fact, it is not used in the same sense at all times by the contributors to this volume. In common parlance it has nowadays three connotations. With one of these, "Archaeology" signifying the propaedeutic training of the aesthetic faculty by the study of style in antique art—a frequent connotation of the term in universities and other places of education,—we are not here concerned, though we hold it in all honour. The remaining connotations are mutually related as whole and part. Both must be allowed to be legitimate enough; and harm is done only when the part is mistaken for, or put in place of, the whole.

Half a century ago one of the greatest exponents of Archaeology, the late Sir Charles Newton, defined his study to be *the science of all the human past*. On this definition all documents, literary or material, all products of man, all things on which he has set his impress, and even all things which have set their impress on him—all alike are to be the archaeologist's *materia*. His end being to reconstitute in imagination the society of the past, his only limitation will be such an arbitrary line as must somewhere be drawn between modern and ancient, not clean cut through time, but rather (since man of to-day may be as ancient in development as man of forty centuries bygone) wavering in *isopolitic* curves across the chart of history. This, then, is the Greater Archaeology.

The sense, however, of our own generation seems to find Newton's definition too wide, and to object to it especially that it leaves too small a function to History. If the archaeologist is to have for his part, not only the seeking, examining, and ordering of all the documents of the human past, but also the reconstitution of the picture, what shall the historian do? It will be his, indeed, to apply the result to the life of man in the present and future; and to many historians that supreme function, the true end of all investigation of antiquity, seems a sufficient reason of existence. But more appear to hold that the historian himself should also reconstitute the picture, and these have pushed the frontier of Archaeology back to that point where the ordering of the documents in evidence has been fully achieved. And, furthermore, since on the one hand the *literary* documents of the human past need the less seeking, examining, and ordering, and on the other all sciences with the increase of material tend to restrict their scope, the general opinion has come to identify Archaeology with the study of *material* documents in chief, and to confine the connotation of the term within some such definition as this, that it is *the science of the treatment of the material remains of the human past*.

This, then, is the Lesser Archaeology, a science clearly outlined and not unduly extensive. The limits of its field, however, must be clearly understood. This sort of archaeology stops short of any possibility of truly reconstituting the picture of the human past; for to that end the literary documents are all essential. Let any one compare for a moment a history of the past which has to be compiled from material documents only, however abundant and complete, with a history whose basis is literary—the history of ancient Egypt, for instance, with the history of classic Greece. The desert sands have given us specimens of almost every product of the ancient life of the Nile valley, as readily to be recognized as on the day they were first buried. We have all the material and circumstance of its life; only the life itself is wanting. Those "histories" of Egypt that have been written sincerely and candidly from the monuments will speak for themselves to the truth of this.

Materials for a picture of the Egyptian past they contain; but there is no picture. Unaided by any record of contemporary human intelligence which may inform him, not so much of what was, but of what seemed, the student of antiquity occupies a position not less external to the object of his studies than an astronomer observing a star. For the relation of the circumstances of life to life itself he can draw only on his subjective experience acquired beyond a gulf of time or space. Change the analogy, and he is an algebraist, confronted by a formula of many terms, all depending for their value on the value of one, and that unknown.

Very different is the case of the student of ancient Greece. With a wealth of literary documents at command, he can take almost the position of a contemporary in regard to the past. Though he need depend less than the student of any other ancient society on material documents, no one can make more or better use of these; for they fall into their places as soon as they are duly examined. Being almost inevitably related in some way to our knowledge, they can seldom or never long remain enigmas, stimulating those rank growths of speculation that cumber the ground of prehistoric archaeology. It is hardly too much to say that there are very few material remains of classic Hellas that are not as intelligible now as when they expressed an existing civilization.

Obvious as is this appreciation of literary documents as evidence for the human past, it is not unseasonable to repeat it now; for depreciation is often in the mouth of the professed student of the Lesser Archaeology. "An inch of potsherd is worth all Herodotus!" Why should the professed archaeologist compare these at all—he whose science deals with the potsherd, but not with Herodotus, except as illustrated by or illustrating potsherds? It is rather for him to compare to whose end the end of Archaeology is always relative: Herodotus will have all due honour from the historian. And short of this obvious exaggeration we may often hear an invidious comparison between the sound objective evidence of material documents and the unsound subjective evidence of literature. Yet neither is the latter any less objective than the former, nor is the former less open to subjective falsification than the latter. *Exempli gratiâ*, on the one hand behind the personal and subjective standpoint of an Aristophanes, easily enough discounted, lies a mass of objective circumstance more informing as to society in fifth-century Athens than all the contents of her museums. On the other hand, the material documents of antiquity are often coloured by a subjectivity that will mislead,—those inscriptions of kings and cities that were expressly intended to deceive contemporaries and posterity; those even not so intended, which may as easily deceive us, not knowing from other evidence the circumstances of their erection. Literature sometimes warns us in time; the name of Melos appears engraved on an Athenian assessment list some years before the date at which Thucydides records that the Republic actually brought that island over to herself, and we are not deceived, recognizing on the marble an example of a world-wide practice of imperial states, prone to swell the public lists of their tributaries with drafts on the bank of hope. But in how many similar cases, with no Thucydides at our elbow, have we been led by material documents to falsify the picture of a past society?

In its proper place, however, this study of the Lesser Archaeology has fairly established a claim to be a science of firstrate importance to the end of history. It is young, for the impulse towards scientific method operated upon it only after the events of the first quarter of this century which opened the Levant and Egypt to scholars. It suffers from the impossibility of verifying many of its hypotheses, especially in dealing with periods before written history, which are at once its opportunity and its occasion of falling. But at least the processes and methods by which it fulfils its three functions in regard to the material documents of the human past—seeking, examining, and ordering—have steadily grown more scientific and sound.

No seeker after antiquities to-day can claim *flair* or fortune superior to the great finders of a past generation, Mariette, Layard, Newton, or Schliemann; but the methods of search at present in vogue are better than theirs. The spade remains the spade, and excavation is still carried on for the most part with local and often primitive tools, found by experience to suit native workmen and to conduce to greater minuteness of search. Among the modern apparatus of excavation a Décauville light railway or a few hydraulic jacks will probably alone represent the nineteenth century, and these are not conspicuously in advance of the devices of Pharaoh's overseers. But the excavator, from being a random hunter for treasure, has become a methodical collector of evidence, conscious of responsibility to the study of every specialist, and not to his own predilection merely, trained to observe everything that his spade disturbs ere the information which its relative position would convey be lost for ever, and to note it in a way which scholars of all nationalities can understand. The modern science of excavation—the science not only of finding with the spade, but of not destroying with the spade—has no better exponents of its principles than Mr. Flinders Petrie and his school, who observe and record on a rigid system which admits no personal preference for one class of antiquities over another. And even the most careless of official "gangers," who, clearing out Egyptian temples, throw unsifted earth by the unsupervised truckload over precipices or into the Nile, admit the principle which in execution their instructions, their impatience, or their sloth prompt them to disregard. There are of course divers peculiar gifts, qualities, and items of knowledge which go to give one excavator success and another ill-success,—eyes compared to which other eyes are not eyes; character which will secure intelligence, strenuousness, and honesty in workmen where another's instruments retain all their vices and acquire new ones; experience which can open out in a week a foundation-deposit or the treasure-chamber of a tumulus which many would seek for long months and never find at all. But these are individual prerogatives. All explorers can be thorough, careful, unprejudiced, systematic—and therein lies the root of the matter! To treat no item of evidence as not worth observation and record, and to leave as little as may be for the man who may come after —in these things is all the law of scientific search for the material documents of antiquity. And those not only underground, but aboveground; for the principles which Mr. Petrie by demonstration in the sands of Egypt has taught excavators to observe, Mr. Ramsay has impressed on travellers also by the example of his early journeys on the hills and plains of Asia Minor.

In the examination of the material documents when found we can claim to be better than our fathers in virtue not only of greater knowledge derived from experience in a wider field, but rather of those mechanical extensions of our physical powers in the invention of which this century has so greatly surpassed all before it. For example, the part played by photography in assisting the eye, hand, and brain of the archaeologist in both the field and the museum needs only to be recalled, and every year its use becomes more easy, and more generally to be applied. The field-glass, the *chambre-claire*, improved instruments for surveying, more appropriate chemical detergents—with these and many other discoveries adopted from alien sciences the science of Archaeology has vastly increased its power to examine its documents. But also in other methods more subjective there has been immense improvement. From the famous decypherment of the Egyptian hieroglyphs and the Achaemenid wedge-characters by regular process of hypothesis, experiment, and verification has resulted a special science of dealing with written documents in an unknown script or tongue; and the tendency now is to lay increasing stress in this matter on systematic experimental methods to the elimination of the element of ingenious conjecture which marked earlier stages. Thus, to take one example of a case where verification is as yet impossible, the careful comparisons made independently by MM. Jensen and Menant of the relative positions of single symbols and of groups of symbols in the various "Hittite" texts has advanced the solution of the yet insoluble problem of their decypherment by a distinct stage, which will not have to be traversed again. Not less in the study of artistic documents also there is a tendency to insist on experimental and almost mechanical methods of examination which, compared to those of the dilettante period, denote a great advance in system. As Mr. Penrose, by laboriously measuring the Parthenon, advanced definitely the whole study of Greek architectural proportion, so students of sculpture now rely more on the measurements of statues in their several parts to arrive at the canons of the divers schools, and to relate works of art to their true influences and true authors, than on any general impression or even detailed observation of style.

Concerning the third function of Archaeology—the ordering of the material documents, whether actually in the show-cases of a museum, or by representation on the plates or in the letter-press of an archaeological publication —less need be said, for the advance in the two preliminary processes entails a corresponding advance in the third. The root-principle of this function of ordering is comparison. The improvement in the methods of search supplies nowadays a far more numerous and varied material than formerly, and the improvement in all methods of examination makes comparison far more easy and sound. How scientific this final function of Archaeology may be brought to be will be learned from the numismatists. How near an approach can be made to similar certainty in classification of a less homogeneous class of documents the catalogues of ceramic will shew. How students of the most erratic and individualistic documents, that are subject of the archaeologist's study, the products of Grand Art, strive after similar ordering by similar processes, may be discerned in such treatises on Greek sculpture as the recent writings of Dr. Furtwängler.

With the ceaseless progress of discovery the documents for the human past have been so quickly and so greatly increased that specialism has become inevitable where it was once possible to take a wider view. Labour must be divided, and each worker in the field, taking his peculiar corner, will achieve perhaps a more useful result than if he were to range over the whole area as it is to-day. Therefore, observing that as Archaeology has narrowed its connotation it has come to denote a more scientific study, we do not seek to insist on the term being used only in that wider sense in which Sir Charles Newton understood his science. But the continual reference to literary documents, which will be noted in the essays that follow, is designed to keep in view the great fact that Archaeology, understood thus as the science of the treatment of the material documents of the human past, is concerned with only one, and (if comparison need be instituted) not the most important, class of documents from which the life of past society is to be reconstituted. If all the material documents of antiquity had vanished off the earth, we could still construct a living and just, though imperfect, picture of antiquity. But were it, on the other hand, literature that had perished utterly, while the material remains of all past civilizations survived everywhere in soils as fecund and as preservative as the sands of Egypt, nothing of that picture could be drawn beyond the most nebulous outline. As things stand at this day, material monuments take a place, important or unimportant, in the historian's reconstruction of the past according as they can be interpreted well or ill by comparison of the monuments of letters.

CONTENTS

PART FIRST

HEBREW AUTHORITY

		PAGE
I. INTRODUCTORY	. . . . .	3
II. THE PENTATEUCH	. . . .	9
III. THE KINGS AND AFTER	. . . .	80

PART SECOND

CLASSICAL AUTHORITY

I. EGYPT AND ASSYRIA	. . . .	155
II. PREHISTORIC GREECE	. . .	220
III. HISTORIC GREECE	. . . .	254
IV. THE ROMAN WORLD	. , . .	. 296

PART THIRD

CHRISTIAN AUTHORITY

I. THE EARLY CHURCH	. . . . .	. 335
II. REMAINS IN PHRYGIA	. , . .	. 363
III. THE CATACOMBS AT ROME	. . .	. 396

PART FIRST
HEBREW AUTHORITY

BY

S. R. DRIVER, D.D.

CANON OF CHRISTCHURCH, REGIUS PROFESSOR OF HEBREW IN THE
UNIVERSITY OF OXFORD

CHRONOLOGICAL TABLE.

BABYLONIA.	ASSYRIA.	EGYPT.[3]
B.C.	B.C.	B.C.
7-6000.[1] Temple of Bel at Nippur founded.		
c. 4000.[1] Lugal-zaggisi, king of Uruk (Erech).		4777. Menes, the first historical king of Egypt.
		3998-3721. *Fourth* Dynasty.
3800.[2] Sargon, of Agadè.		3969-3908. Cheops. Great Pyramid built.
3750.[2] Narâm-Sin, his son.		
c. 2800. Gudea, king of Lagash.		
c. 2800. Ur-bau and Dungi, kings of Ur.		
c. 2800. Singashid, king of Uruk.		
		2778-2565. *Twelfth* Dynasty.
2478-2174.[2] First Dynasty of Babylon.		
c. 2400-2200. Kings of Larsa.		
2376-2333.[2] Khammurabi.		
		2098-1587. Period of Hyksos rule.
1786-1211.[2] The Cassite Dynasty.	c. 1820. Ishmi-dagan, *patesi*, or priest-king, of Nineveh.	
		1587-1327. *Eighteenth*Dynasty.
		1587-1562. Aahmes I.
	c. 1450. Asshurbelnishèshu, first king of Assyria, at present known.	1503-1449. Thothmes III.
		1414-1383. Amenôphis III.
1400. Burnaburiash II.		1383-1365. Amenôphis IV.
		1327-1181. *Nineteenth*Dynasty.
	c. 1300. Shalmaneser I. (builder of Calach, Gen. x. 11).	1327-1275. Seti I.
		1275-1208. Ramses II.
		1208-1187. Merenptah (probably the Pharaoh of the Exodus).
		1181-1060. *Twentieth* Dynasty.
		1180-1148. Ramses III.
c. 1140. Nebuchadrezzar I.	c. 1100. Tiglath-pileser I.	
		960-810. *Twenty - second* Dynasty.
	885-860. Asshurnâṣirabal.	960-939. Shishak.
	860-825. Shalmaneser II.	
	812-783. Rammân-nirâri III.	
747-733. Nabonassar.	745-727. Tiglath-pileser III.	
728-727. Tiglath-pileser (Pul).	727-722. Shalmaneser IV.	
	722-705. Sargon.	
721-709. Merodach-baladan.	722. Sargon captures Samaria.	
		715-664. *Twenty-fifth*Dynasty.
		715-702. Sabako.
709-705. Sargon.		
	705-681. Sennacherib.	690-664 Tirhaka.
	681-668. Esarhaddon.	
	668-626. Asshurbanipal.	
		664-525. *Twenty-sixth*Dynasty.
		664-610. Psammetichus I.
625-604. Nabopolassar.		
	607. Nineveh destroyed by the Umman-manda.	
604-561. Nebuchadrezzar II.		
555-538. Nabo-na'id, last king of Babylon.		
538. Capture of Babylon by Cyrus		

[1] Hilprecht's dates.   [2] Sayce dates (*Early Israel*, 1897, pp. 280 f.)   [3] Petrie's dates (till Shishak).

PART FIRST

HEBREW AUTHORITY

I. Introductory

JUST fifty years have elapsed since Mr. (afterwards Sir Henry) Layard published two volumes entitled *Nineveh and its Remains*. The work created a profound sensation. It contained an account of excavations carried on at, or near, the site of the ancient Nineveh, and of the surprising discoveries which resulted. Previously, as was observed by the author in his Introduction (p. xxv), with the exception of a few cylinders and gems, preserved elsewhere, "a case hardly three feet square" in the British Museum "enclosed all that remained, not only of the great city, Nineveh, but of Babylon itself!" Now, however, palace after palace disclosed itself from beneath the mounds of Nimroud; and Mr. Layard's graphic narrative told of the bas-reliefs, gigantic sculptures, paintings, and inscriptions which in almost countless numbers met the astonished eyes of the explorers, and revealed the life and manners, the institutions and history, of a long-buried but once magnificent and imposing civilization. Certainly, few of the inscriptions could as yet be read; but the architecture and art of ancient Assyria spoke to the eye with a distinctness that could not be misunderstood, and were eloquent of the greatness of an empire which had passed away.

The peculiar cuneiform character in which the inscriptions

of Assyria and Babylon were written presented a formidable problem to the decypherer; and the process of wresting from them their secret was a long one. The story of its accomplishment is told elsewhere in the present volume. Here it may suffice to say that, building upon the labours of Grotefend and Major (afterwards Sir Henry) Rawlinson, a succession of skilful and indefatigable scholars, working partly upon the texts discovered by Layard, partly upon those which in great numbers have been brought to light since, have constructed since 1851 the grammar and lexicon of the language; so that now, though naturally uncertainties sometimes occur, Assyrian and Babylonian texts can be read, as a rule, without difficulty. Nor is this the only discovery of the kind which the past century has witnessed. The hieroglyphics of Egypt, those weird sphinx-like symbols which impress the eye even more strongly than the wedge-shaped characters of Assyria, have also yielded up their secrets. Here the most important step had been taken, as early as 1821, by Jean François Champollion: by the help of the clues which he then discovered progress was rapidly made. Champollion himself brought to Europe a large number of additional inscriptions; and ere long, the grammar and lexicon of a second language, very different from Assyrian, and entirely unknown at the beginning of the century, were, in great measure, recovered by scholars.

Babylonia and Assyria on the one side, Egypt on the other,—these are the countries which have yielded during the last half-century the most surprising archaeological results. In both, exploration has been actively carried on: Germany and France, England and America, have alternately vied with one another in their search for the treasures buried under the mounds of Babylonia and Assyria, or the sands of Egypt. And the texts obtained from both countries have engaged the attention of a series of scholars, in most cases men of marked ability and power, who have devoted their lives to analysing more accurately the language, to studying the antiquities, and to piecing together the history of two great nations. Much, it is certain, remains still to be discovered ; but even now it may be said that the two last generations have seen exhumed and re-constructed two entire civilizations, each beginning in an almost incalculable antiquity, each presenting a highly organized society, possessing well-developed institutions, literature, and art, and each capable of being followed with much circumstantiality of detail through a long and eventful history. And thus, whereas fifty or sixty years ago little was known of either nation beyond what was stated incidentally in the Bible or classical writers, now voluminous works descriptive of both are being constantly written, and are quickly left behind by the progress of discovery. Nor is this all. Though the discoveries made in Babylonia and Assyria, and in Egypt, eclipse in interest all made elsewhere, they do not by any means stand alone. From Phoenicia and the Phoenician colonies, from the land of Moab, from Palmyra and other parts of the north and north-east of Palestine once thickly covered with Aramaic-speaking populations, from districts in the north-west and the south of Arabia, inscriptions written in different Semitic dialects have been discovered, which throw valuable light on the antiquities of the countries in which they are found, and often illustrate in a most welcome manner different passages of the Old Testament. The discovery and utilization of material from these sources have also been chiefly the work of the last half-century. Gesenius, in his *Monumenta Phoenicia*, published in 1837, collected, and explained with great success, the Phoenician inscriptions then known ; and many additional ones, including some of great interest, have been discovered since. De Vogué published a large number of inscriptions from Palmyra in

1868. The very valuable inscription of Mesha, king of Moab (translated below), was discovered in the same year. In 1884 and 1885 there were published a number of Nabataean inscriptions found at Medā'in Ṣāliḥ, in North-west Arabia. A much larger number, chiefly of the type called *Sabaean* and *Minaean*, some from the same neighbourhood in North-west Arabia, others from South Arabia, have been copied at different times during the past century, especially by Halévy (1869-70), Euting (1883-4), and Ed. Glaser (in a series of journeys undertaken between 1883 and 1894). And quite recently, in 1888-91, the excavation of a huge mound at Zinjirli, in Syria, about seventy miles north of Aleppo, brought to light some inscriptions, written in a previously unknown Aramaic dialect, and dating from the eighth century B.C.,—the age of Amos, Hosea, and Isaiah.

It will be the object of the following pages to explain, so far as the available limits permit, the bearing of the new facts brought to light from these various sources upon the Old Testament. Naturally it will be impossible to notice every illustration which might be adduced; many incidental illustrations of words, or customs, or names, for instance, though they might prove interesting to the special student, must of necessity be passed over; but the writer hopes to be able to include notices of all the great and important historical illustrations of the Old Testament which the monuments have supplied, as well as to offer examples of the manner in which, in other cases, words or allusions have had light thrown upon them from the same sources.

The general result of the archaeological and anthropological researches of the past half-century has been to take the Hebrews out of the isolated position which, as a nation, they seemed previously to hold, and to demonstrate their affinities with, and often their dependence upon, the civilizations by which they were surrounded. Tribes more or less closely akin to themselves in both language and race were their neighbours alike on the north, on the east, and on the south; in addition to this, on each side there towered above them an ancient and imposing civilization,— that of Babylonia, from the earliest times active, enterprising, and full of life, and that of Egypt, hardly, if at all, less remarkable than that of Babylonia, though more self-contained and less expansive. The civilization which, in spite of the long residence of the Israelites in Egypt, left its mark, however, most distinctly upon the culture and literature of the Hebrews was that of Babylonia. It was in the East that the Hebrew traditions placed both the cradle of humanity and the more immediate home of their own ancestors; and it was Babylonia which, as we now know, exerted during many centuries an influence, once unsuspected, over Palestine itself. It is true, the facts thus disclosed do not in any degree detract from that religious pre-eminence which has always been deemed the inalienable characteristic of the Hebrew race: the spiritual intuitions and experiences of its great teachers retain still their uniqueness; but the secular institutions of the nation, and even the material elements upon which the religious system of the Israelites was itself constructed, are seen now to have been in many cases common to them with their neighbours. Thus their beliefs about the origin and early history of the world, their social usages, their code of civil and criminal law, their religious institutions, can no longer be viewed, as was once possible, as differing in kind from those of other nations, and determined in every feature by a direct revelation from Heaven; all, it is now known, have substantial analogies among other peoples, the distinctive character which they exhibit among the Hebrews consisting in the spirit with which they are infused and the higher principles of which they are made the exponent. Their literature, moreover, it is now apparent, was not exempt from the conditions to which the literature of other nations was subject; it embraces, for instance, narratives relating to what we should term the pre-historic age, similar in character and scope to those occurring in the literature of other countries. There are many representations and statements in the Old Testament which only appear in their proper perspective when viewed in the light thrown upon them by archaeology. And in some cases, as will be seen, it is not possible to resist the conclusion that they must be interpreted in a different sense from that in which past generations have commonly understood them.[1]

[1] In the Rev. C. J. Ball's *Light from the East* (which has appeared since the first edition of the present work was published) the reader will find an interesting collection of pictorial illustrations of many of the subjects and persons referred to in the following pages; for instance, cherubic figures, standing or kneeling before the sacred tree (pp. 28-30, 32); portrait of Hammurabi (p. 65); head of mummy of Ramses II. (p. 108); statue of Merenptah (p. 128); Sargon and his "Tartan" (p. 186), etc.

II. The Pentateuch

THE Book of Genesis opens with a Cosmogony (i. 1—ii. 4a), which for sublimity alike of conception and expression stands unique in the literature of the world. While for long this cosmogony was regarded as a literally true description of the manner in which the earth was gradually adapted to become the habitation of man, the progress of science during recent years has shewn this view of it to be no longer tenable; the order in which the several creative acts are represented as having taken place conflicting too seriously with the clearest teachings of astronomy and geology for it to be regarded as possessing any value as a scientific exposition of the past history of the earth. And hardly had science established this conclusion, when archaeology opportunely disclosed the source from which the Hebrew cosmogony was derived. As long ago as 1872, Mr. George Smith, on the strength of what he had already observed on the tablets preserved in the British Museum, expressed his conviction "that all the earlier narratives of Genesis would receive new light from the inscriptions so long buried in the Chaldaean and Assyrian mounds"; and in 1876, after his expeditions to Assyria in 1873 and 1874, he published all the inscriptions relating to the Creation which had been found by him, in his *Chaldaean Genesis*. Since that date other tablets have come to light; and though the series relating to the Creation is unfortunately incomplete and in parts fragmentary, enough remains not only to exhibit clearly the general scheme of the

Cosmogony, but also to make it evident that the Cosmogony of the Bible is dependent upon it. who says so?

The inscriptions preserved on these tablets are written in a rhythmical form; and constitute in fact a kind of epic poem, the theme of which is the triumph of Marduk (Merodach), the supreme god of Babylon, over the powers of confusion and disorder, and the sovereignty thus secured by him over the other gods. The first tablet (of which 13 lines and fragments of some others are preserved) describes how, before what we term earth or heaven had come into being, there existed a primaeval watery chaos (*Tiâmat*, corresponding to the Hebrew *tĕhōm*, the "deep," of Gen. i. 2), out of which the Babylonian gods were evolved :—

> When [1] the heaven above | was not yet named,
> And the land beneath | yet bare no name,—
> (While) the abyss, the primaeval, | their begetter,
> Mummu-tiâmat,[2] | the mother of them all,
> [5] Streamed with their waters | commingled together,
> (When) no field had yet been formed, | no marsh-reed
>   was yet to be seen,—
> When of the gods | still none had come forth,
> No name had yet been named, | no destiny yet fixed,
> Then were born | the gods [altogether?],
> [10] Lachmu and Lachamu | came forth.
> Long ages passed, ...
> Anshar and Kishar | were born ;
> Long were the days, ...
> The gods Anu, [Inlil (*i.e.* Bel), and Ea were born].

Different Babylonian deities thus gradually came into being. Tiâmat, or the deep, is the representative of chaos and disorder; and is personified in the sequel as a huge

---

[1] The translations from the Creation-tablets are based upon those of Zimmern, in Gunkel's *Schöpfung und Chaos* (1893), pp. 401 ff., and of Friedr. Delitzsch in *Das Bab. Weltschöpfungsepos* (1896), pp. 92 ff. See also the excellent chapter on the Cosmology of the Babylonians (pp. 407 ff.) in Jastrow's *Religion of Babylonia and Assyria* (Boston, U.S.A.), which reached the writer only after the following pages were in type.

[2] *I.e.* the surging, chaotic deep.

dragon. The following tablets shew that the parts of the first which are lost must have told how Tiâmat, jealous of her domain being invaded by the new gods, declared her intention of contesting their supremacy.

The second tablet is likewise imperfect, only 19 lines and some fragments being preserved; but its contents can be recovered with tolerable certainty from the narratives of the subsequent tablets: it must have told, namely, how Tiâmat attacked the other gods, how some of these, especially Lachmu and Lachamu, took her side, and how the rest rallied round Anshar (the prototype of Asshur, who became afterwards the supreme god of Assyria). In the extant lines (towards the end of the tablet), Anshar commissions Marduk (the Merodach of Jer. l. 2) to be the champion of the gods against Tiâmat, and the latter undertakes the task laid upon him.

In the third tablet (138 lines) Anshar is introduced speaking. He relates Tiâmat's preparations for the coming contest: how she had prepared a brood of formidable monsters to be her allies; how he had invited Anu and Ea to enter the lists against her, and how both had declined the unequal contest. In Marduk's prowess, however, the gods feel confidence; and the tablet closes with a picture of the feast held by them in anticipation of his victory.

The fourth tablet, consisting of 146 lines, is preserved almost intact. The narrative contained in it is told with dramatic force and vividness. First, the gods equip Marduk with weapons for the combat with Tiâmat, and send him with their blessing upon his way. The power of Marduk's *word* is illustrated: a garment is placed in the midst; he speaks, and it vanishes; he speaks again, and it reappears. Next Marduk advances to the fray: he seizes Tiâmat in a huge net, and transfixes her with his spear. The carcase of the monster he split into two halves, one of which he fixed on high, to form a firmament supporting the waters above it [1] :—

[137] He cleft her like a fish | into two parts,
With one half he made | and covered the heaven,
Set bars before it, | stationed guardians,
[140] Commanded them not | to let its waters come out.
He marched through the heaven, | surveyed the places (below),
Prepared in front of the abyss | the abode of Ea.
Then Bel [2] measured | the compass of the abyss,
A great house like to that | he established E-shara,
[145] The great house E-shara, | which he built like heaven.

The "abyss" was the huge body of waters on which the earth was supposed to rest: E-shara is a poetical designation of the earth, which was conceived by the Babylonians as a hollow hemisphere, similar in appearance to the vault of heaven, but placed beneath it (with its convex side upwards), and supported upon the "abyss" of waters underneath.

The fifth tablet (24 lines preserved, some imperfectly) describes the formation of the sun and moon, and afterwards the appointment of years and months :—

[1] He [3] formed the stations | for the great gods,
As stars resembling them | he fixed the *lumâsi*,[4]
He ordained the year, | defined divisions,
Twelve months with stars, | three each, he appointed.
[5] From the day when the year begins | even to its close,
He fixed the station of Nibir (Jupiter), | to determine their limits,
That none (of the days) might err, | none commit a mistake.
The station of Bel and Ea, | he fixed by his (Jupiter's) side.

. . . .

[12] He caused the moon-god to shine forth, | and subjected to him the night.
Appointed him as a night-body, to determine the days.

---

[1] In Berosus' account of the Babylonian cosmogony, the other half of the monster's carcase was made into the earth. However, that is not stated in the present tablet.

[2] *I.e.* the lord, a title of Marduk.

[3] From Delitzsch's translation (pp. 108 f.), which, however, is admitted by him to be in parts, especially lines 2-4, very uncertain.

[4] According to Zimmern, the stars of the zodiac.

The sixth tablet is lost; but Hommel and Delitzsch agree that it must have narrated the formation of dry land, the appearance of vegetation, and the creation of animals. That the creation of man followed is also regarded by the same scholars as unquestionable; for the last tablet, which celebrates the deeds and attributes of Marduk, expressly names him as one who "created men," and utters the wish that "his command may continually remain unforgotten in the mouth of the black-headed ones, *whom his hands have formed.*" After the account of the formation of man, Delitzsch (p. 111) places a fragment of 13 lines, assigning his duties to the newly formed being:—

Towards thy God, thou shouldest be of pure heart: that is dearest to the Deity. Prayers, supplications, prostration of face, thou shouldest offer Him early every morning. Mercy becomes the fear of God; sacrifice enhances life; prayer absolves from sin. Against friend and neighbour speak not [evil (?)]. . . . When thou promisest, give, and [fail (?)] not.

What seems to have been the last tablet consists of a hymn of 64 lines (with a few *lacunae*), celebrating (as has just been said) the deeds and attributes of Marduk, and representing him as powerful, beneficent, compassionate, and just.

There are also two other texts, descriptive of creation, though one probably, and the other certainly, do not belong to the poem just described. The first (which consists of 14 very fragmentary lines) begins thus in Delitzsch's translation (p. 110):—

At the time when the gods altogether had created [the heaven (?)], (and) formed the splendid (?) constellations (?), they caused living beings to come forth altogether, cattle of the field, wild beasts of the field, and creeping things of the field, etc.

The other text, a Sumerian[1] (not a Semitic) one, with interlinear Semitic translation, which was first brought to

[1] Before the Semites gained power in Babylonia, the country was in the possession of a different, non-Semitic race, called *Sumerian*. Most of the oldest Babylonian inscriptions are written in Sumerian.

light by Mr. Pinches in 1890, consists of 60 lines, nearly complete.[1] It is too long to translate *verbatim*: but it describes how, when as yet no reed or tree had been created, no house or city built, Nippur and Erech, with their temples, not yet founded, and when all the lands were yet sea, a movement arose in the sea, Babylon, with its temple E-sagil, was built, and the gods, the Anunnaki (subordinate divine beings), were created: how then Marduk "created men," made beasts of the field, living things of the land, the Tigris and the Euphrates in their places, the herbage of the field, lands, marshes, reeds, the wild-ox, the sheep with its young, meadows and forests, etc., constructed houses, and built the [cities and] temples of Nippur and Erech. These texts shew that different representations of the course of creation were current in Babylonia: on the second, see below, pp. 18 f.

The differences between the Babylonian epic and the first chapter of Genesis are sufficiently wide: in the one, we have an exuberant and grotesque polytheism; in the other, a severe and dignified monotheism: in the one, chaos is anterior to Deity, the gods are made, or produced—we know not whence or how—and they only gradually and with difficulty rise superior to the state of darkness and disorder in which they find themselves; in the other, the supremacy of the one Creator is absolute, and His word alone suffices to bring about each stage in the work of creation. But, in spite of these profound *theological* differences, there are *material* resemblances between the two representations, which are too marked and too numerous to be explained as mere chance coincidences. The outline, or general course of events, is similar in the two narratives. There are in both, moreover, the same abyss of waters at the beginning, denoted almost by the same word, the

---

[1] See *Records of the Past*, 2nd series (cited hereafter as *RP.*), vi. 109 ff.; also Zimmern, *l.c.*, pp. 419 f.

separation afterwards of this abyss into an upper and a lower ocean, the upper ocean being retained in its place by a celestial vault or "firmament,"[1] the formation of heavenly bodies and their appointment as measures of time, and the creation of man. In estimating these similarities, it must further be remembered that they do not stand alone: in the narratives of the Deluge (as will shortly appear) we find traits borrowed unmistakably from a Babylonian source; so that the antecedent difficulty which might otherwise have been felt in supposing elements in the Creation-narrative to be traceable ultimately to the same quarter is considerably lessened. In fact, no archaeologist questions that the Biblical cosmogony is, in its main outline, derived from Babylonia. Thus Professor Sayce writes: "The Biblical writer, it is plain, is acquainted, either directly or indirectly, with the Assyrian and Babylonian tradition": it is true, it is "stripped in his hands of all that was distinctively Babylonian and polytheistic," and "breathes a spirit of the purest and most exalted monotheism"; but "this ought not to blind us to the fact that the narrative is ultimately of Babylonian origin."

The only questions open are, At what time, and through what channel, did the Babylonian elements which the Cosmogony presents find their way into Hebrew literature? These are questions which the materials at our disposal do not enable us to answer positively: the most that we can do is to propound more or less probable hypotheses. Only one thing may be assumed as certain; viz. that these elements were not derived *directly* from any known Babylonian source: it is incredible that the monotheistic author of Gen. i., at whatever date he lived, could have borrowed any detail, however slight, from the crassly polytheistic epic of the conflict of Marduk and Tiâmat; the Babylonian

---

[1] The Hebrew "firmament," it will be remembered, was not an "expanse" of air, but a solid vault.

myth must have been for long years transplanted into Israel, it must there have been gradually divested of its polytheistic features, and gradually reduced more and more to a simple, unadorned narrative of the origin of the world, until parts of it (we cannot at present positively say more) were capable of adoption—or adaptation—by the author of Gen. i. as elements of his cosmogony. In other words, the narrative of Gen. i. comes at the end of a long process of gradual elimination of heathen elements, and of gradual assimilation to the purer teachings of Israelitish theology, carried on under the spiritual influences of the religion of Israel. At what time, however, was the Babylonian myth transplanted into Israel? According to some it is derived from the time when the ancestors of the Hebrews lived side by side with the Babylonians in Ur of the Kasdim. According to others, it was brought into Israel in the age of Ahaz, or shortly afterwards, when there are traces in the Old Testament of intercourse taking place between Judah and Assyria. Since, however, the Tel el-Amarna tablets have shewn how strong Babylonian influence must have been in Canaan, even before the immigration of the Israelites, this has been thought by many[1] to have been the channel by which Babylonian ideas penetrated into Israel: they were first, according to this view, naturalized among the Canaanites, and afterwards—as the Israelites came gradually to have intercourse with the Canaanites—they were transmitted to the Israelites as well. This is not impossible, though it must be remembered that it is consistent only with a critical view of the authorship of the Pentateuch, not with the traditional view; for that Moses, who, if the testimony of the Pentateuch is of any value, set his face sternly and consistently against all intercourse with the Canaanites and all compromises with polytheism, should

[1] *E.g.* by Sayce, Gunkel, Winckler.

have gone to Canaan for his cosmogony, is in the last degree improbable. The cosmogony of Gen. i. presupposes a long period of naturalization in Israel itself, during which "the old legend was stripped of its pagan deformities. Its shape and outline survived. But its spirit was changed, its religious teaching and significance was transfigured, in the light of revelation." And thus in its new form, it became the divinely appointed means for declaring to all time some of those eternal spiritual realities which, though invisible to the eye of sense, are nevertheless implicit in the material cosmos.[1]

The *sabbath* (Gen. ii. 2, 3) is further in all probability an institution ultimately of Babylonian origin. In a lexicographical tablet, published in the second volume of Rawlinson's *Inscriptions of Western Asia*, the " šabattum " is defined as *ûm nûḫ libbi*, or " day of rest of the heart " ; *i.e.* not, as was formerly supposed, a day of rest for man, but (as parallel occurrences of the same phrase shew) a day when the gods rested from their anger, or a day for the pacification of a deity's anger.[2] Further, in a religious calendar for two months (the second Elul, and Marcheshvan) which we possess, prescribing duties for the king, the 7th, 14th, 19th, 21st, and 28th are entered as " favourable day, evil day," while the others are simply " favourable " days. On the five specified days certain acts are forbidden : the king is not, for instance, to eat meat roasted at the fire, not to put on fineries or offer sacrifice, not to mount his chariot or to sit in state, not to enter the sacred chamber where the gods dwell, not to call in a physician, not to invoke curses on his enemies ; on the other hand, as soon as the day is over, sacrifices

[1] See more fully, on the theological aspects of the narrative, Ryle's *Early Narratives of Genesis* (1892), chaps. i., ii. ; or the present writer's *Sermons on the Old Testament*, pp. 4 ff., 163 ff.

[2] See Morris Jastrow, " The Original Character of the Hebrew Sabbath," in the *American Journal of Theology*, April, 1898.

may be offered, and the king's prayer will be favourably accepted. The days, it is evident, are viewed superstitiously: certain things are not to be done on them, in order not to arouse the jealousy or anger of the gods. *Seven* was a mystical number among the Babylonians; and the ancient syllabaries preserve to us the names of the seven planetary deities, from whom afterwards the days of the week were named. It is difficult not to agree with Schrader, Sayce, and other Assyriologists in regarding the week of seven days, ended by a sabbath, as an institution of Babylonian origin. The sabbath, it is true, assumed a new character among the Hebrews; it was divested of its heathen associations, and made subservient to ethical and religious ends: but it originated in Babylonia. If, however, this explanation of its origin be correct, then it is plain that in the Book of Genesis its sanctity is explained unhistorically, and ante-dated. Instead of the sabbath, closing the week, being sacred, because God rested upon it after His six days' work of Creation, the work of Creation was distributed among six days, followed by a day of rest, *because* the week, ended by the Sabbath, already existed as an institution, and the writer wished to adjust artificially the work of Creation to it. In other words, the week determined the "days" of Creation, not the days of Creation the week.

The section Gen. ii. 4*b*—iii. 24, embracing the story of Paradise and the Fall, exhibits also points of contact with Babylonia, though not so definite or complete as those presented by chap. i. 1—ii. 4*a*. The general order of Creation (which differs from that in chap. i. in that the formation of man *precedes* that of plants and animals) is in accordance with that described in the Babylonian text referred to at the top of p. 13. That text (which is bilingual, one of the versions being written in the pre-Semitic Sumerian) presents a narrative of great antiquity,

—according to Professor Hommel, as old as the fourth millennium B.C.; which originated perhaps at the famous temple of Eridu, on the Persian Gulf, to be mentioned directly. Professor Sayce, in view of the antiquity of this narrative, does not hesitate to see in it "the earliest starting-point yet known to us of that form of the story of creation, which we find in the second chapter of Genesis." "Eden," though to Hebrew readers it no doubt suggested the Hebrew word *'eden*, "pleasure," has been explained with great plausibility as being in reality the Babylonian word *edinu*, "plain," or "field," applied especially to the great alluvial plain of Babylonia, watered by the Euphrates and Tigris. The *shôham*, or onyx stone, may be the *sâmtu* of the Assyrians. Two of the four rivers, into which the stream which arose in Eden was parted after it left the garden, are Babylonian, the *Ḥiddeḳel* (Ass. *Idiglat*, the Tigris) and the *Pĕrāth* (Ass. *Purat*, the Euphrates).[1] The irrigation of a tract of country by a river (with, it is to be understood, cross-canals) is Babylonian. A sacred palm is alluded to in old Babylonian hymns, and often depicted on Assyrian monuments. The *cherubim* (iii. 24)—those composite, emblematic figures, described more particularly in the first chapter of Ezekiel—are clearly no native Hebrew conception, and point in all probability in the same direction. An inscription which has been often cited in illustration of this section of the Book of Genesis deserves to be here quoted:—

At Eridu a palm-stalk grew overshadowing; in a holy place did it become green;
Its root was of bright lapis which stretched towards the abyss;
[Before] the god Ea was its growth at Eridu, teeming with fertility;
Its seat was the (central) place of the earth;
Its foliage (?) was the couch of Bahu the (primaeval) mother.
Into the heart of its holy house which spread its shade like a forest hath no man entered.

---

[1] On the names of the other two rivers, the Pishon and the Gihon, no light has at present been thrown by archaeology.

In its interior is the sun-god, Tammuz,
Between the mouths of the rivers (which are) on both sides.

Eridu was a very ancient sacred city of the people of Babylonia: once, when the Persian Gulf extended further inland than it does now, it stood upon its south shore; now its site (Abu-Shahrein) is on the right bank of the Euphrates, about fifty miles from its mouth.[1] There is no doubt, in Mr. Pinches' opinion,[2] that the place described in these lines is the Babylonian paradise. Professor Sayce writes of it as follows: " In the neighbourhood of Eridu was a garden, 'a holy place,' wherein grew the sacred palm-tree—the tree of life—whose roots of bright lapis lazuli were planted in the cosmic abyss, whose position marked the centre of the world, and whose foliage was the couch of the goddess Bahu, while the god Tammuz dwelt in the shrine under the shadow of its branches, within which no mortal had ever entered. An oracle was attached to 'the holy tree of Eridu,' and Eri-aku (Arioch) calls himself its 'executor.' This tree of life is frequently represented in the Assyrian sculptures, where it is depicted with two guardian spirits, kneeling or standing on either side of it. They are winged, with the heads sometimes of eagles, sometimes of men."[3] It is possible that these figures are the prototypes of the Biblical "cherubim"; though Lenormant's statement that he had read the word on an Assyrian gem does not appear to have been confirmed by other Assyriologists. Future exploration may very probably throw fresh light upon this question.[4]

[1] Maspero, *Dawn of Civilization*, pp. 561, 563, 6141.
[2] *Transactions of the Victoria Institute*, xxix. (1897), p. 44.
[3] Hastings, *Dictionary of the Bible*, vol. i. (1898), s.v. EDEN.
[4] The passage quoted by Sayce, *Verdict of the Monuments*, p. 104 (cf. p. 65 *note*), from the description in the third tablet of the Creation-epic (lines 132-138) of the feast held by the gods does not really allude to the Fall: see the translations of Delitzsch, p. 103; Zimmern, p. 410; Jastrow, p. 424.

Thus, though no complete Babylonian parallel to the story of Paradise is at present known, there are parallels with parts of it, sufficient in the light of the known fact that other features in the early chapters of Genesis are derived from Babylonia to support the inference that the framework of this representation is derived from it likewise. Of course, it must not be supposed that the Hebrew narrator gives us exact transcripts of what was believed in Babylonia: what rather happened was that echoes of Babylonian beliefs reached Palestine, and supplied materials upon the basis of which he constructed his narrative. A consideration of the theological aspects of this narrative does not fall within the scope of the present volume: it must suffice therefore to remark briefly that it teaches a variety of ethical and theological truths respecting human nature,—such as its relation to God, its moral and spiritual capabilities, the relations subsisting between the sexes, the psychology of temptation, how man awoke to consciousness of a moral law, and how, almost as soon as he became conscious of it, he broke it—in a figurative or allegorical form, the details not being true in a literal sense, but being profoundly true in a *symbolical* sense, *i.e.* as representing in a symbolical or pictorial form real facts of human nature and real stages through which human nature actually passed. If the view here advocated be correct, the *materials* upon which this figurative or symbolical representation was constructed were derived, at least largely, from Babylonia. Babylonia possessed an ancient and many-sided civilization, far more impressive and far more influential than that which the Hebrews could boast of; it possessed a copious and varied literature, and a mythology describing, among other things, how the poets and sages of Babylonia pictured to themselves the creation of the earth and its living inhabitants, and the early fortunes of man upon it. Echoes of these myths and traditions reached Palestine, and impressed

themselves upon the Hebrew mind. Stripped of their
polytheism, and accommodated to the spirit of Israelitish
religion, the Hebrew narrator adapted them for the purpose
of exhibiting, vividly and pictorially, some of those deep
spiritual truths which the teachers of Israel were inspired
to discern.

The fourth and fifth chapters of Genesis span the interval
between the Creation and the Deluge. Chap. iv. traces
the line of Adam's descendants, through Cain, for seven
generations, and records the beliefs current among the
Hebrews respecting the progress of civilization, and also
the development of the power of sin. Chap. v. exhibits
the line of Adam's descendants, through Seth, for ten
generations, to Noah, with dates, adapted to give a
picture of the increasing population of the earth, and to
convey an idea of the length of the first period of the
history of humanity, as it was pictured by the narrator.
Very little light has been thrown hitherto upon these
names by archaeology :[1] the Babylonians (as we learn from
Berosus) enumerated ten kings, who lived before the
Deluge (and reigned, it should be added, four hundred and
thirty-two thousand years !); but the names are very different, and the attempts which have been made to explain
the Hebrew names as translations or equivalents of the
Babylonian names, though plausible in one or two instances,
are, taken as a whole, <u>more ingenious than convincing.</u> →

Chaps. vi.–ix. of Genesis contain the story of the
Flood. Here we have a direct and interesting parallel
from Babylonia, which was discovered by George Smith
in 1872, and translated by him in 1876 in his *Chaldaean
Genesis* (chap. xvi.). The story forms an episode in
the great Babylonian Epic which narrates the exploits

---

[1] The name Methushael (iv. 18), "man of God," is, however,
Babylonian in form.

of Gilgamesh,[1] the hero of Uruk (the Erech of Gen. x. 10). The epic is divided into twelve cantos, each describing a distinct episode in the hero's career; and the story of the Deluge forms the eleventh of these cantos. Erech has been besieged for three years by Ḫumbaba, king of Elam. Gilgamesh, with the help of Shamash, the sun-god, delivers it from its foes, slays Ḫumbaba, and becomes its king. But Eabani—a kind of divine satyr, endowed with preternatural intelligence and power—who had been created by Aruru, the mother of Gilgamesh, to assist and advise her son in his contests, dies. Smitten himself with leprosy, and prostrated by the death of Eabani, Gilgamesh determines to visit his ancestor Pâr-napishtim (who was reputed to have been endowed with perpetual youth), in the hope both of having his dead friend restored to life, and of being cured himself from his disease. After many adventures, he arrives at the ocean which encircles the world; he crosses it, and afterwards passes the Waters of Death: there the happy island rises in front of him, and he sees Pâr-napishtim, his figure unchanged by age, standing upon its shores. Gilgamesh declares to him the object of his visit: he desires to know the secret by which he and his wife had received immortality. Pâr-napishtim in reply describes how, in consequence of his piety, he had been preserved from destruction at the time of the great Flood, and had afterwards been made immortal by Bel.

Pâr-napishtim's story occupies some 200 lines, and only a few characteristic extracts can be given here.[2] He begins (lines 8–31) by narrating how the gods, Anu, Bel, Adar, and Ennugi, had determined to bring a flood upon the earth, and how Ea, " lord of wisdom," had warned him to escape it by building a ship :—

[1] The name was formerly read by Assyriologists (as by George Smith) *Izdubar*, or *Gisdubar*.
[2] See more fully Jastrow, *Religion of Bab. and Ass.*, pp. 467–517.

²¹ O ¹ man of Shuripak,² son of Ubaratutu:
Frame a house, build a ship;
²⁵ Forsake (thy) possessions, seek (to save) life;
Abandon (thy) goods, and cause (thy) soul to live:
Bring up into the midst of the ship the seed of life of every sort.
As for the ship, which thou shalt build,
Let its form be long;
³⁰ And its breadth and its height shall be of the same measure.
Upon the deep then launch it.

There follows (lines 32 ff.) the excuse which he is to make, if asked by the men of his place what he is doing. After a *lacuna* of seven or eight lines, Pâr-napishtim proceeds to relate how he carried out these instructions:—

⁵⁷ On the fifth day I began to construct the frame of the ship.
In its hull its sides were 120 cubits high.
And its deck was likewise 120 cubits in breadth:
⁶⁰ I built on the bow, and fastened all firmly together.
Then I built six decks in it,
So that it was divided into seven storeys.
The interior (of each storey) I divided into nine compartments;
I drove in plugs (to fill up crevices).
⁶⁵ I looked out a mast, and added all that was needful.
Six *sars* of bitumen I spread over it for caulking:
Three *sars* of naphtha [I took] on board.

When he had finished it, he entered it with all his belongings:—

⁸¹ With all that I possessed, I laded it:
With all the silver that I possessed, I laded it;
With all the gold that I possessed, I laded it;
With the seed of life of every kind that I possessed, I laded it.
⁸⁵ I took on board all my family and my servants;
Cattle of the field, beasts of the field, craftsmen also, all of them, did I take on board.
Shamash (the sun-god) had appointed the time, (saying,)
"When the lord of the whirlwind sendeth at even a destructive rain,
"Enter into thy ship, and close thy door."

---

¹ The translations are based upon those of Professor P. Haupt in the (forthcoming) third edition of Schrader's *Cuneiform Inscriptions and the Old Testament*, advance-sheets of which have been kindly lent to the writer by the translator.

² A city on the Euphrates.

The arrival of the fated day filled Pâr-napishtim with alarm :—

> [93] I feared to look upon the earth :
> I entered within the ship, and closed my door.

The storm which then began is finely described (lines 97-132). Rammân (the storm-god) thundered in heaven ; the Anunnaki brought lightnings : other gods joined in the fray : the waves mounted to the sky ; "light was turned to darkness" :—

> [112] Brother looked not after brother,
> Men cared not for one another.

Even the gods were in consternation : they took refuge in heaven, "cowering like dogs" ; and Ishtar "cried like a woman in travail" :—

> [125] Six days and nights
> Raged wind, deluge, and storm upon the earth.
> [130] When the seventh day arrived, the storm and deluge ceased,
> Which had fought like a host of men ;
> The sea was calm, hurricane and deluge ceased.
> I beheld the land, and cried aloud :
> For the whole of mankind were turned to mud ;
> [135] Hedged fields had become marshes.
> I opened a window, and the light fell upon my face.

The ship grounded on Nizir,—a mountain east of the Tigris, across the Little Zab,—and remained there for six days :—

> [146] When the seventh day arrived,
> I brought forth a *dove*, and let it go :
> The dove went to and fro ;
> As there was no resting-place, it turned back.
> [150] I brought forth a swallow, and let it go :
> The swallow went to and fro ;
> As there was no resting-place, it turned back.
> I brought forth a *raven*, and let it go :
> The raven went, and saw the decrease of the waters ;
> [155] It ate, it waded, it croaked (?), it turned not back.

After this Pâr-napishtim leaves the ark, and, like Noah, offers sacrifice :—

[156] Then I sent forth (everything) towards the four winds (of heaven):
I offered sacrifice:
I prepared an offering on the summit of the mountain.
I set Adagur-vases, seven by seven,
Underneath them I cast down reeds, cedar-wood, and incense.
[159] The gods smelt the savour,
The gods smelt the goodly savour;
The gods gathered like flies over the sacrificer.

Bel is at first incensed at the rescue of Pâr-napishtim, and the frustration of his plan; but afterwards he is pacified by Ea, and acquiesces in his suggestion to be in future more discriminating, and not again to punish all without distinction by a flood. Ea says to him:—

[183] How wast thou so ill-advised as to cause a deluge?
Let the sinner bear his own sin,
[185] Let the evil-doer bear his own evil-doing.
Be indulgent, that (all) be not cut off; be merciful, that (all) be not destroyed.
Instead of causing a deluge,
Let lions come, and minish mankind:
Instead of causing a deluge,
[190] Let tigers come, and minish mankind:
Instead of causing a deluge,
Let a famine arise, and smite the land:
Instead of causing a deluge,
Let pestilence come, and desolate the land.

In the end Bel accepts Pâr-napishtim favourably, and takes him and his wife away to immortality:—

[201] He turned to us, he stepped between us, and blessed us (, saying):
" Hitherto Pâr-napishtim has been a (mortal) man, but
" Henceforth Pâr-napishtim and his wife shall be like unto the gods, even unto us, and
" Pâr-napishtim shall dwell afar at the confluence of the rivers."
Then he took me, and far away at the confluence of the rivers he made me to dwell.

The resemblances with the Biblical narrative are patent; and there is no occasion to point them out in detail. There are, of course, differences; the Biblical account of the Deluge was not, any more than the Biblical account of Creation, transcribed directly from a Babylonian source;

but by some channel or other—we can but speculate by what—the Babylonian story found its way into Israel: details were forgotten or modified; it assumed, of course, a Hebrew complexion, being adapted to the spirit of Hebrew monotheism, and made a vehicle for the higher teaching of the Hebrew religion: but the main outline remained the same, and the substantial identity of the two narratives is unquestionable.[1] It should be added that fragments of two different versions of what is manifestly the same story have been found, one being of extreme antiquity, the tablet on which it is written being dated in the reign of Ammi-zaduga (2245-2223 B.C.), the fourth successor of Khammurabi (see p. 29).[2]

Chap. x. contains the "Table of Nations," an ethnological chart of the principal nations known to the Hebrews at the time when the chapter was composed. The nations are grouped in it genealogically, being exhibited as the members of a great family, more or less closely related to each other, according to circumstances. Whatever the intention of the compiler of the Table

[1] The literary criticism of the Biblical account shews that it consists in fact of a combination of *two* narratives, which have been united together by a later compiler: in reality, therefore, two different Israelitish authors, writing at different times, cast the story of the Flood into a written form, each version possessing characteristic features of its own, and exhibiting slight divergences from the other. It would have been interesting to point out in detail in what respects each of these versions resembled in turn the Babylonian narrative; but for our present purpose the question of the distinction of sources in the Biblical account is unimportant.
[2] Sayce, *Monuments*, pp. 108 f.; and J. A. Selbie in the *Expository Times*, May, 1898, pp. 377 f. (from the *Revue Biblique*, Jan. 1898, pp. 1 ff.). Professor Sayce is in error in saying (*Early Hist. of the Hebrews*, pp. vii, viii) that the text of the latter fragment is identical with that published by George Smith: it is, in fact, entirely different.

It may be worth adding that recent geologists consider the basis of the Flood-story to be an actual extraordinary inundation of the Euphrates: see Huxley, *Essays on Controverted Questions*, pp. 583-91, 605.

may have been, the principle of arrangement followed in it is not, however, as a fact, purely ethnological, in our sense of the word; the tribes, or peoples, represented in it as closely related by blood, being in several instances not so related in reality,—the Canaanites, for instance, were not racially connected with Egypt (*v.* 6), nor the Hittites with the Canaanites (*v.* 15), nor Elam with the Assyrians (*v.* 22). It is thus clear that the purely ethnological principle of arrangement was superseded sometimes by geographical considerations, sometimes by considerations of a historical or political nature. There is no ground for supposing that the particulars contained in this Table were derived from a Babylonian source; but the Babylonian and Assyrian inscriptions abound with the names of tribes and peoples; and they illustrate accordingly many of the names contained in the Table. A few examples may be briefly referred to. Gomer (*v.* 2) are the *Gimirrai*, a people mentioned frequently by Esarhaddon and Asshurbanipal (seventh century B.C.), and settled at that time in or near the later Cappadocia: Mādai, in the same verse, are the *Madâ* of the inscriptions, often mentioned from about 800 B.C. as living in the mountains south-west of the Caspian Sea: Tubal and Meshech are the *Tabali* and *Musku*, the former mentioned first by Shalmaneser II. (860-825), the latter by Tiglath-pileser I. (*c.* 1100 B.C.), and both dwelling to the south of the Gimirrai. Yavan ('Ιάϝονες) is the name by which the Greeks were known to Sargon (722-705 B.C.): Cush (*v.* 6) are the *Kash*, or *Kesh*, of the Egyptian monuments, a people dwelling on the south of Egypt, beyond the First Cataract, and repeatedly mentioned in the Egyptian inscriptions. It is, however, not impossible that (as has been widely held by Assyriologists) the "Cush" of *v.* 8 is not the same as the "Cush" of *vv.* 6, 7; the compiler of the chapter (who attached *vv.* 8-11 to *v.* 7) seems to have been misled by the similarity of name; and Cush in v. 8 represents the *Kasshu* of the Assyrian inscriptions, a predatory and warlike tribe, whose home was in the mountains across the Tigris, north-east of Babylon, and who furnished Babylon with a dynasty (the "Cassite kings") which continued in power for five hundred and seventy-six years (1786–1211 B.C.). Upon Nimrod (v. 8) archaeology has at present thrown no light: speculation has been busy with him; but his name has not hitherto been found on the monuments.[1] Nor does archaeology know of any one name which it can connect, as vv. 10, 11 connect Nimrod, both with the foundation of Babylonian civilization and with its extension to Nineveh. Babylon, as we know from a dynastic list discovered by Mr. T. G. Pinches in 1880 among the treasures of the British Museum, possessed a line of eleven kings—of one of whom, Khammurabi, we shall hear more anon—ruling 2376–2333 B.C.; and the contract-tablets from this period, which have been published by Meissner, and which relate to sales, loans, the letting of houses, fields, and gardens, adoption, marriage, inheritance, etc., shew that society was already highly organized, and that legal formalities were habitually observed. Erech (named in Gen. x. 10 as one of the cities of Nimrod's kingdom)—now Warka, about a hundred miles south-east of Babylon—has been shewn, by the recent excavations of Mr. Hilprecht, to have been the capital of a powerful monarch, Lugal-zaggisi, who has left inscriptions of himself, and who claims to have ruled as far as the Mediterranean Sea, at a date even earlier than 4000 B.C.[2] Nineveh, on the other hand, which became

[1] See the present writer's paper in the *Guardian*, May 20, 1896. It is a plausible suggestion that Nimrod corresponds to Gilgamesh, the hero of Erech (above, p. 23); but the conjecture has not at present received confirmation from the monuments.

[2] Of Accad and Calneh nothing certain is known. The same may be said of Rehoboth-Ir and Resen in vv. 11, 12.

afterwards the famous capital of Sennacherib, Esarhaddon, and Asshurbanipal, is first mentioned about 1800 B.C.: it was then under the rule of *patêsi*'s, or priest-kings. The earliest Assyrian king whose name has been handed down to us lived about 1450 B.C. Calach (Gen. x. 12), some twenty miles south-east of Nineveh—now Nimroud—beautified afterwards by the palaces of Sargon, Esarhaddon, and other Assyrian kings, was built (as we know from a statement made by one of his successors) by Shalmaneser I., about 1300 B.C. This was the site first excavated by Mr. Layard, and described by him in the volumes mentioned above (p. 1). The oldest capital of Assyria was, however, neither Nineveh nor Calach, but a city called Asshur, about sixty miles south of Nineveh, on the west bank of the Tigris—now Kal'at-Sherkat: this, though not mentioned in Gen. x. 11, is often named in the inscriptions of the Assyrian kings, and was not permanently superseded by Nineveh till the ninth century B.C. In the light of all these facts, it becomes impossible to place the beginnings of imperial power at Babylon and Nineveh within the lifetime of a single man. But the two broad facts which Gen. x. 10, 11 express, *viz.* that Babylon was an older seat of civilization than Nineveh, and that Nineveh was, as we might say, a younger colony, founded from it, are unquestionably correct: not only did Assyria acquire political importance much later than Babylon, but, as the monuments also shew, it was moreover dependent socially and materially upon the older state. The Hittites (x. 15, "Heth"), Elam (x. 22), and Sheba (x. 28) are all nations of whom we now know much, through the progress of archaeology, and who will be referred to again in the following pages. Asshur (x. 22) is, of course, Assyria.

Of the narrative of the Tower of Babel, and confusion of tongues (Gen. xi. 1-9), no direct illustration has as yet been

furnished by the inscriptions. The tower referred to has
often been supposed to be the *ziggurat*,[1] the ruined remains
of which form the huge mound, now called *Birs Nimroud*.
Birs Nimroud stands within the site of the ancient Borsippa,
a city almost contiguous to Babylon on the south-west, and
in the inscriptions called sometimes the "second Babylon."
This *ziggurat*, we are told by Nebuchadnezzar, had been
built partially by a former king of Babylon, but not completed; its "head," or top, had not been set up; it had
also fallen into disrepair, so that the unbaked bricks
forming the interior had been reduced by the rain to a
mass of ruins; and Nebuchadnezzar states that he restored
and completed it. It has been conjectured that this huge,
unfinished pile, close to Babylon, taken in connexion with
the known antiquity of the city, and the fact that it was
the chief centre of a region in which the Hebrews placed
the earliest home of the human race, gave rise to the story
told in Genesis; but no actual Babylonian parallel to the
Biblical narrative has at present been discovered.[2] The
object of the narrative is, no doubt, as Professor Ryle points
out, to supply an explanation, "suited to the comprehension
of a primitive time, of the two great phenomena of
human society, the distinction of races and the diversity
of language. How these originated must have seemed
one of the greatest mysteries to the men of the ancient
world. But in the language of popular tradition we must
not look for the teaching of modern science. It should
be enough for us if the Hebrew version of the narrative
emphasizes the supremacy of the one God over all the
inhabitants of the world," and teaches that distribution

[1] A *ziggurat* (or *zikkurat*, from the verb *zukkuru*, to elevate) is a
massive pyramidal tower, ascending in stage-like terraces, with a temple
at the top. Cf. Jastrow, in the work cited above, pp. 615 ff.

[2] The reference in the fragmentary inscription translated by G.
Smith, *Chald. Gen.*, pp. 160 ff., and mentioned by Sayce, *Monuments*,
p. 153, is very uncertain.

into languages and nations is an element in His providential plan for the development and progress of the human race. It may be added that the inscriptions have proved the incorrectness of the etymology assigned in *v.* 9 for the name "Babel": the name of Babylon is written in the inscriptions in a manner which shews clearly that it signifies "gate of God," and that it cannot be derived from the Hebrew word *bālal*, to confound.

Before proceeding to the period of Abraham, we may pause for a moment in order to point out a conclusion, resulting directly from archaeology, which is of some importance on account of its bearing on the historical character of Gen. i.–xi. The *dates* of all important events recorded in the Pentateuch are carefully noted; and it is a matter of very simple calculation to ascertain, in the case of each, how many years it happened after the creation of man, and also (with the help of the date given in 1 Kings vi. 1) to correlate the Pentateuchal dates with those of the monarchy, and so to reduce them to years B.C. The date of the creation of man is thus fixed to 4219 B.C., and that of the Deluge to 2564 B.C.[1] That these dates, however, or even the dates according to the text of the Septuagint,[2] of 5408 and 3166 B.C., respectively, are unhistorical is proved by the testimony of the monuments. The excavations carried on within the last ten years at Nippur—now Niffer, or, more correctly, Nuffar—about fifty miles southeast of Babylon, by the expeditions organized by the American University of Pennsylvania, have shewn that a civilization existed at this spot of an antiquity previously

---

[1] Ussher's dates are 4004 and 2349 B.C.; but he treats the four hundred and thirty years of Exod. xii. 40 as including the sojourn of the patriarchs in Canaan, whereas by the terms of the text they are manifestly limited to the sojourn in Egypt. (The text of the Septuagint adds "in the land of Canaan.")

[2] Which assigns a greater age to several of the patriarchs at the birth of their firstborn son.

ANTIQUITY OF NIPPUR

quite unsuspected. Some thirty-five feet below the present surface of the soil there was found a platform composed of bricks stamped with the names of Sargon and his son Narâm-Sin (whose dates are known independently to be 3800–3750 B.C.);[1] but Mr. Haynes, the leader of the expedition, excavating in 1893–6 below this platform through the *débris* of older buildings, only reached the virgin soil at a depth of some thirty feet more, leading to the inference that the buildings constructed upon it could not date from a later period than 7000–6000 B.C. The vases, bearing long inscriptions, presented to the sanctuary of Nippur at about 4000 B.C., by the Lugal-zaggisi, mentioned above, and the numerous sculptured stones, with inscriptions, recording their public buildings, their victories, and their votive offerings, which have come down to us from the kings of Lagash—now Telloh, about eighty miles south-east of Nippur—and which must belong substantially to the same age, afford conclusive evidence that the actual beginnings of art and civilization in Babylonia precede 4000 B.C. by many centuries, not to say by many millennia. It is particularly observable that the art of writing, though the characters are archaic in type, and decidedly ruder than those which appear at a later age, is already, at the date just mentioned, familiarly practised.

The same lesson has been taught by exploration in Egypt. The latest and most careful chronologer of Egypt, Professor Petrie, fixes the date of Menes, the first historical king of Egypt, at 4777 B.C. ("with a possible error of a century").[2] But in 1897 the tomb of Menes[3] was discovered by M. de Morgan at Nagada, a little north of Thebes; and the objects of art, and the hieroglyphics, found in it shew that civilization in Egypt was already far advanced. The pyramids of the fourth dynasty (beginning, according

---

[1] So Sayce, Hilprecht, and others. See, however, below, p. 213.
[2] Cf., however, below, p. 215.   [3] Cf. p. 165.

to Petrie, 3998 B.C.), and the remarkable finish and *technique* displayed by the sculptures and paintings of the same period, support the same conclusion. Quite recently, also, the new and startling fact has been disclosed that before the time of Menes the Valley of the Nile was inhabited by a race entirely different from that generally known as Egyptian, and probably of Libyan origin, having a white skin, and dolichocephalous skull, and possessing a very different type of civilization. Egypt thus agrees with Babylonia in shewing equally that the beginnings of man upon earth must date from a period very considerably more remote than that assigned by the Biblical chronology for his creation.[1] Nor is this all. We possess inscriptions written in three entirely distinct languages, Sumerian, Babylonian, and Egyptian, all belonging to an age very much earlier than the date—whether 2564 or 3166 B.C. —assigned by the Biblical narrative for the confusion of tongues, an age, in fact, when, according to the same narrative, "the whole earth was of one language and of one speech." The progress of Babylonian and Egyptological research has strikingly confirmed the results obtained by anthropologists upon other *data* respecting the immense antiquity of man upon this earth. The chronology of the Book of Genesis forms, however, it is evident, a carefully constructed scheme: it coheres intimately, especially in the earlier chapters, with the lives and persons of the characters mentioned: and, if it deviates from the reality, not (as is the case in parts of the chronology of the Kings) by a matter of twenty or thirty years only, but by whole centuries, it materially confirms the conclusion, reached in the first instance upon other considerations, respecting the symbolical character of the narrative to which it is attached.

---

[1] Cf. pp. 209 f. (where, however, Menes is not assigned to an earlier date than *c.* 3800 B.C.), 218.

FIRST]   BIBLICAL CHRONOLOGY   35

The fact that these early narratives of Genesis are not, in our sense of the term, historical, does not, of course, if rightly understood, detract from their theological value. Their theological value does not consist in their outward form; it consists in the moral and spiritual truths of which they are the expression. They are, from this point of view, analogous to allegory and parable. In their outward form they relate to that prehistoric age which the Israelites, like other nations, imagined as preceding the period to which actual recollections reached back. They thus preserve to us the popular conceptions prevalent among the Hebrews "as to the origin of the universe and the foundations of human society. Inspiration did not *infuse* into the mind of a writer accurate scientific knowledge of things unknown. But the Israelite writer, gifted by the Holy Spirit, was overruled to draw, here from one source and there from another, the materials for a consecutive account, which, while it embodied the fulness and variety of Hebrew tradition, was itself the appointed medium of Divine instruction."[1]

In Gen. xi. 28, 31 we read that Abraham left his native home in "Ur of the Kasdim," with his father Terah, for the purpose of journeying to Canaan; and that he came as far as Ḥaran, and dwelt there. No confirmation of these statements has been furnished hitherto by the inscriptions (for, so far as is at present known, they contain no mention either of Abraham, or of any other ancestor of the Hebrews); but a good deal is known about the two places, Ur and Ḥaran.[2] The site of Ur[3] was identified in the

---

[1] Ryle, *Early Narratives of Genesis*, pp. 135 f.
[2] To be pronounced *Khārān* (or *Kharrān*), and to be carefully distinguished from *Hārān* (with the soft aspirate), the name of the brother of Abraham.
[3] In the expression "Ur of the Kasdim," the last three words are not part of the native name, but must be an addition of Palestinian origin. *Kasdim* is the Hebrew form of the Babylonian and Assyrian

early days of Assyriological study. A huge mound, about six miles south of the Euphrates, on its right bank, and a hundred and twenty-five miles from its present mouth, was excavated by Colonel Taylor in 1854; and it proved to conceal the ruins of the venerable "Ziggurat" (p. 31) of the moon-god, Sin, the bricks in the lowest storey of which were all stamped with the words "Ur-bau, king of Ur, builder of the temple of Nannar."[1] There are other ruined remains in the neighbourhood of the temple, covering an oval of about a thousand yards long by eight hundred broad; and this must have been the site of the ancient town. Ur-bau, and his son Dungi, have left many monuments of themselves,—engraved cylinders, and other works of art, besides numerous buildings, not only in Ur itself, but also in Larsa, Uruk, Nippur, and elsewhere. Here are two of their inscriptions:—

To Nannar, his king, Ur-bau, king of Ur, has built his temple. He built the wall of Ur.

Dungi, the mighty, king of Ur, and king of the four quarters of the world, builder of I-Shidlam, the temple of Nergal, his lord, in Kuta.[2]

The date of these two kings was probably about 2800 B.C. —long before Babylon became the capital of what was afterwards known as Babylonia, and five hundred years before the time of Abraham (if Amraphel in Gen. xiv. 1 be rightly identified with Khammurabi: see below). Although few of its rulers are known to us by name, Ur was already an important city. Its position gave it advantages both commercial and political. The Euphrates anciently flowed

, *Kaldû* (Chaldaeans), a tribe (according to Winckler) first alluded to in the inscriptions about 1100 B.C., and named repeatedly from 880 B.C.: they lived then in Lower Babylonia, towards the sea-coast: afterwards, as they increased in power, they gradually advanced inland: in 721 B.C.
· Merodach-baladan, "king of the land of the Kaldû," made himself king of Babylon; and, ultimately, under Nabopolassar and Nebuchadnezzar,
ᵛ the Kaldû became the ruling caste in Babylonia.

[1] The name by which the moon-god, Sin, was known in Ur.
[2] The *Cuthah* or *Cuth* of 2 Kings xvii. 24, 30; cf. below, p. 102.

almost by its gates, and ensured easy transport for the products of Upper Syria, while in the opposite direction the Wady Rummein brought gold and odoriferous resins from Arabia, and a caravan-route, marked out by wells, led across the desert to Southern Syria and the Sinaitic Peninsula. Trade was already active in these early times : Gudea, king of Lagash—some seventy miles north of Ur —about 2800 B.C., states, for instance, that when engaged in the construction of a temple, he obtained cedars from Lebanon and Amanus, as well as many other materials from other places.[1]

At a point some five hundred miles north-west of Ur, a tributary from the north, called the Belikh, flows into the Euphrates ; and on the left bank of this tributary, about sixty miles from the confluence, lay the ancient city of Haran (or Kharran). From Gen. xxiv. 10, compared with xxvii. 43, it appears that Kharran was in " Mesopotamia," in the Hebrew, " Aram-Naharaim," *i.e.* " Aram (or Syria) of the two Rivers." The Egyptian inscriptions mention this region under the name *Naharina*; and the Tel el-Amarna letters (*c.* 1400 B.C.) under the names *Nachrima* and *Narima*. The Hebrew designation is clearer than the English : the region north-east of Palestine was inhabited largely by Aramaean (or Syrian) tribes ; and " Aram of Naharaim " denotes that part of this region which lay between the " two Rivers,"—whether the rivers meant be the Euphrates and the Tigris, in the upper part of their courses, or, as others think more probable, the Euphrates in its upper course, and the Habor (2 Kings xvii. 6, xviii. 11), now the *Khabour*, a river flowing into the Euphrates from the north, some distance to the east of the Belikh. At present, the remains of a mediaeval castle, and a few mounds, are all that mark the site of Kharran ; but for many centuries, and even millennia, it was a well-known

[1] *R.P.*², ii. 78–93. Cf. Maspero, *Dawn of Civilization*, pp. 610–19.

and important place. It is often mentioned in the Assyrian inscriptions. Like Ur, Kharran was, in a special degree, devoted to the worship of the moon-god; an ancient and celebrated temple of the moon-god stood there : by a remarkable coincidence, Nabo-na'id, the last king of Babylon (555–538 B.C.), as he tells us himself in two of his inscriptions, restored the temples of Sin in both Ur and Kharran.

In the statement that Abraham's home was in Ur, and that he migrated thence into Canaan, there is naturally, in the abstract, no difficulty. A difficulty does, however, arise when it is observed that, whereas Gen. xi. 28 speaks of Ur as the "land of" Abraham's "nativity," in Gen. xxiv. 7 precisely the same expression is applied (as appears from a comparison of *v.* 4, and xxvii. 43) to Kharran ; and that other passages in the Book of Genesis create strongly the impression that the writers thought of Kharran as the home of Abraham's kindred.[1] In other words, two traditions seem to have been current respecting the primitive home of the Hebrews, one connecting them with Ur, in South Babylonia, the other connecting them with Kharran, in North-west Mesopotamia. Contract-tablets and other contemporary inscriptions, recently discovered, bear witness to the fact that in, or even before, the age of Abraham persons bearing Hebrew (or Canaanitish) names resided in Babylonia, and shew that intercourse between Babylonia and the West was more active than was once supposed to be the case : but nothing sufficiently direct has hitherto been discovered to shew definitely that the ancestors of the Hebrews migrated from Ur. It is, however, not impossible

---

[1] The expression "beyond the river," in Josh. xxiv. 2, 3, 15, points to the same conclusion : Kharran (from a standpoint in Palestine) was "beyond" the Euphrates, but Ur was on the same side as Palestine. Hommel's explanation (*Anc. Heb. Tradition*, pp. 323 ff.) of the way in which the expression might have come to be used of Ur is very unconvincing.

that future discoveries may throw further light upon the question.

We pass to Gen. xiv., the chapter which narrates the expedition of the four kings from the East against the five kings of the Jordan-valley, their defeat of the latter in the mysterious "vale of Siddim," their capture of Lot, and Abraham's pursuit of the victors as far as Hobah, on the north of Damascus, where he recovered Lot and the other captives. Let us take in order the names mentioned in *v.* 1, and consider in what respects they have each been illustrated by archaeology.

1. Amraphel, king of Shin'ar. "Shin'ar" (also Gen. x. 10, xi. 2, and elsewhere) is a Hebrew name for Babylonia: it has not, however, been found certainly on the monuments; and its origin remains matter of conjecture. Amraphel, there is little doubt, is a corrupt representation of Khammurabi, the name of the sixth king in the dynastic list mentioned above (p. 29). Khammurabi, according to a nearly contemporary chronological register of part of this dynasty, reigned for forty-three years (2376–2333 B.C.):[1] as his own inscriptions testify,[2] he was a powerful and successful ruler, who did much both for the material and for the political welfare of his country; in fact, by his skill in organizing and consolidating its resources, he laid the foundation of its future greatness. In one of his inscriptions he is styled "king of *Martu*," or the West land,—an expression denoting generally Syria, Phoenicia, and Palestine, and indicating that he claimed to rule as far as the Mediterranean Sea. In illustration of this claim of Khammurabi, it deserves mention not only that his great-

---

[1] Cf. below, p. 212. The date is Professor Sayce's (*Early Israel*, 1899, p. 281). His former date (based on the slightly different figures of the dynastic list) was 2346–2291 B.C. (Winckler, 2314–2258 B.C.; Maspero, 2304–2249).

[2] *K. B.*, iii. 1, pp. 107 ff.; Maspero, *Struggle of the Nations*, pp. 40 ff.

great-grandson, Ammisatana, bears nearly the same title, "king of the wide West land," but also that similar claims are made on behalf of much earlier rulers of Babylonia: Lugal-zaggisi (above, p. 29) claims in his inscriptions to have been invested with a domain extending from the Persian Gulf to the Mediterranean Sea; Sargon of Agadè[1]—a powerful ruler, reigning about 3800 B.C.,[2] the temple built by whom at Nippur has been excavated recently by the Pennsylvania expedition—is stated in a contemporary inscription to have subjugated "the land of Amurru" (the Amorites), on the north of Canaan;[3] and Sargon's son Narâm-Sin (who built huge fortifications at Nippur) styles himself on his bricks "king of the four quarters (of the earth)."[4]

2. Arioch, king of Ellasar. In all probability Eriaku (or Riaku), king of Larsa—now Senkereh, about midway between Babylon and the mouth of the Euphrates—whose name is mentioned in many inscriptions,[5] and who was contemporary with Khammurabi. Here are two inscriptions, dating from his reign:—

> To Nana, daughter of Sin [the moon-god], their mistress, Kudurmabuk, the *adda* ["father," *i.e.* ruler] of Jamutbal, and Eriaku his son, the mighty shepherd of Nippur, the defender of Ur, king of Larsa, king of Sumer and Akkad, have built the temple which she loves, etc.

> To Nannar, his king, Kudurmabuk, the *adda* of Martu (the West land), when Nannar heard his prayer, built the temple I-Nun-mach, for his own life, and for the life of Eriaku, king of Larsa.

---

[1] A place near Babylon, but not at present certainly identified.

[2] Cf. the note on p. 33.

[3] M. de Sarzec found at Telloh (the site of the ancient Lagash) contract-tablets, dated "In the year in which Sargon conquered the land of Amurru": see Thureau-Dangin, in the *Comptes Rendus de l'Acad. d'Inscriptions*, 1896, pp. 357 f.

[4] The magniloquent title borne regularly in later times by the kings of both Babylonia and Assyria.

[5] *K. B.*, iii. 1, pp. 93 ff. The reading of the name, it should be added, has been disputed; and some Assyriologists prefer still to read it *Rim-Sin*; but there has been latterly a growing consensus in favour of *Riaku* or *Eriaku*.

Eriaku was thus ruler of Larsa, Nippur, and Ur; and in other similar inscriptions he is described further as conquering Eridu (above, p. 20) and Nisin. The conquest of Nisin must have been an important event in Eriaku's reign; for contract-tablets are dated by it: there is one which shews that Eriaku must have continued in power at least twenty-eight years after it. All the places mentioned are in South Babylonia, Nippur being the most northerly; and this therefore is the region in which we must picture the kingdom of Eriaku as situated. Further, Eriaku is said to be the son of Kudurmabuk, *adda* of Jamutbal. Kudurmabuk, now, is not a Babylonian, but an Elamitish name,[1]—Elam being the region, largely mountainous, across the Tigris, to the east of Babylonia, often mentioned in the inscriptions; and Jamutbal appears from other notices to have been a province in the eastern part of South Babylonia, bordering on Elam, and at this time (as the name Kudurmabuk shews) under Elamite dominion. These inscriptions thus shew that at the time to which they relate, the Elamite power had obtained a footing in South Babylonia: Kudurmabuk, we may suppose, ruled himself in Jamutbal, or, as we might call it, West Elam, and, supported by him, his son, Eriaku, maintained himself in Larsa and the surrounding parts of South Babylonia. The title "*adda* of Martu,*"* or the West land, if the expression, as seems natural, is to have the same meaning which it bears elsewhere in the inscriptions, will imply that Kudurmabuk claimed—whether it was really exercised, or not, we do not know—the same kind of authority over Syria and the West which we have seen was claimed by Khammurabi.

Eventually, however, the Elamite rule in South Babylonia was brought to an end through the subjugation of Eriaku, as well as of his father Kudurmabuk, by the Babylonian

---

[1] Kudur (meaning perhaps "servant") occurs in other names known to belong to Elam.

king Khammurabi. We read, *viz.*, in another inscription belonging to the same period :—

> On the 23rd day of Shebat, in the year when Khammurabi, through the might of Anu and Bel, established his possessions, [and] his hand overthrew (?) the *ad*(?)-*da* of Jamutbal, and King Eriaku.

It may be conjectured that it was after this victory, which secured Khammurabi's power throughout Babylonia, that he assumed the title " king of *Martu*," quoted above.

3. Chedorlaomer, king of Elam. Elam is a well-known name ; but until lately no trace of Chedorlaomer had been found on the monuments. The component parts of the name had indeed been found : Kudur, as has just been remarked, was known independently to be an Elamitish word ; and La'omer—or, as it might be pronounced, Lagomer (LXX. Λογομμορ)—was evidently the same as Lagamar, the name of an Elamite god, mentioned by Asshurbanipal (about 640 B.C.) : but the name itself had not been met with. In 1895, however, Mr. T. G. Pinches discovered in the British Museum three inscribed clay tablets, which proved to relate to this period, and to contain what can hardly be doubted to be the name Chedorlagomer. It is true, these tablets are of very late date (*c.* 300 B.C.), and are written in a florid, poetical style, so that they have not the value of contemporary testimony ; at the same time, it is reasonable to suppose that they are based upon more ancient materials, and preserve the memory of genuine historical facts. The tablets are unhappily, in parts, much mutilated ; but enough remains to indicate the general character of the events recorded. A few extracts may be quoted (in Mr. Pinches' translation)[1] :—

> The gods . . . . in their faithful counsel to Kudurlachgumal, king of the land of Elam, said (?) " Descend," and the thing that unto them

---

[1] *Transactions of the Victoria Institute*, xxix. (1897), pp. 56, 65.

was good [they performed, and] he exercised sovereignty in Babylon, the city of Kardunias,[1] [and] he placed [his throne?] in Babylon, the city of the king of the gods, Merodach .... Dur-mach-i-lāni, the son of Eri-êkua, who [had carried off?] the spoil, sat [on] the throne of dominion.

One of the other inscriptions, after several (mutilated) allusions to the " Elamite enemy," and his doings, continues :—

> Who is Kudurlachgu[mal], the maker of the evils? He has gathered also the Umman-man[da];[2] .... he has laid in ruins ....

After this it states that the Elamite enemy "set his face to go towards Borsippa"; and finally, after subduing the nobles of .... with the sword and pillaging the temples, that he returned with their spoil to Elam.

The gist of these inscriptions is thus to describe how Kudurlachgumal—or, as the name is read by Hommel and Zimmern, Kudurdugmal—invaded Babylonia with his troops, plundering its cities and temples, and exercising sovereignty in Babylon itself. If, now, Kudurlachgumal be rightly identified with Chedorlaomer, the Eri-êkua mentioned in the same inscriptions can hardly be different from the Eriaku, king of Larsa, who has just been referred to. And the third inscription names in addition one "Tudchula, son of Gazza," who, though the connexion in which he is mentioned is obscure (through the mutilation of the tablet), may well be identical with the fourth king, "Tid'al, king of Goyim," named in Gen. xiv. 1.[3]

The inscriptions do not explain the relative positions of Kudurlachgumal and Kudurmabuk; but it may be conjectured that Kudurlachgumal was over-lord of Kudur-

[1] The district surrounding Babylon.
[2] A term denoting generally hordes from the North.
[3] It ought to be mentioned that Mr. L. W. King, in his recently published *Letters and Inscriptions of Ḥammurabi* (1898), questions the correctness of these three identifications. In particular, he observes, neither Eri-êkua nor Tudchula is styled "king," and the reading of the middle part of the name Kudurlachgumal is still conjectural. Mr. Ball also questions the identifications (*Light from the East*, p. 70.)

mabuk (who is called only "*adda* of Jamutbal," not "king of Elam"), and of his son Eriaku, king of Larsa. Kudur-lachgumal's victories in Babylonia will naturally have preceded Khammurabi's final and successful endeavour to shake off the Elamite supremacy, and bring to an end the kingdom of Eriaku. Numerous letters and despatches of Khammurabi have recently been discovered; and in one of these, now at Constantinople, as translated by Father Scheil in 1896, there occurred the name Kudurnuchgamar, which was supposed for a while to correspond likewise to Chedorla'omer.[1] Mr. King has, however, now shewn, by means of a photograph of the inscription in question, that the name had been transcribed incorrectly, and that it is in reality that of an officer of Khammurabi, named *Inuḫsamar*.[2]

4. Tid'al, king of Goyim. Probably the Tudchula, just mentioned. "*Goyim*" is the ordinary Hebrew word for "nations" (hence Auth. Vers. "king of nations"); but as this yields no satisfactory sense, the term is rendered in the Revised Version as a proper name. No people called *Goyim* is, however, known from the monuments; and hence Sir H. Rawlinson's conjecture has been widely accepted, that the name is a corruption of *Gutim*, the *Guti* of the inscriptions, a people whose home was to the north of Babylon, in the mountainous district on the east of the Little Zab, corresponding to the eastern part of the present Kurdistan.

Let us sum up what the monuments have taught us respecting Gen. xiv. They have brought the four kings from the East, who were previously but mere names, into the light of history, and have told us many interesting particulars about three of them, especially about Amraphel

---

[1] See Scheil, *ap.* Sayce, *Early Hist. of the Hebrews*, pp. 27 f.

[2] King, *l.c.*, pp. xxxiv–xxxvi. Professor Sayce agrees (*Expos. Times* March 1899, p. 267) that Father Scheil's reading is incorrect.

(Khammurabi). They have shewn further that these four kings were really contemporaries, and that at least three of them really ruled over the countries which they are said in Gen. xiv. to have ruled,—two facts which may be taken as an indication that the author of the narrative derived his names from some trustworthy source, in which (probably) they were mentioned together. And they have shewn, thirdly, that several rulers of Babylonia, as well as one Elamite ruler (Kudurmabuk), claimed authority over the "West land," and that an invasion of Palestine and neighbouring countries on the part, at least, of a ruler of Babylonia (Sargon), was, in the abstract, within the military possibilities of the age. The monuments have not shewn more than this. They make no mention of the *particular* expedition into Canaan, which forms the principal subject of Gen. xiv.; and they name neither Abraham, nor Melchizedek, nor any one of the five Canaanite kings (*v.* 2), against whom the expedition was directed. Their "confirmation" of the Biblical narrative is thus limited to the statements respecting the four kings contained in *v.* 1. The historical character of the four kings themselves has never been seriously questioned. On the other hand, the narrative which follows has been felt by many to contain, at least in some of its details, historical improbabilities; but whether that is the case or not, the inscriptions which have been hitherto found do not remove them; for not one of the details of the expedition has received any corroboration from them. The inferences which these inscriptions authorize respecting the historical accuracy of the narrative in Gen. xiv. have been much exaggerated. The evidence that the campaign described in this chapter was historical is for the present confined to that which is supplied by the Biblical narrative itself.[1]

[1] See further two papers by the present writer in the *Guardian*, March 11 and April 8, 1896; or G. B. Gray in the *Expositor*, May,

The chapters of Genesis which now follow receive little light from archaeology, only an occasional word or name being capable of illustration from monumental sources. A few examples will be sufficient. The mention of the *Philistines* in xxi. 32, 34, xxvi. 1, 8, 14, 15, 18—if not in Exod. xiii. 17 as well—is very probably an anachronism: Hebrew tradition knew that the Philistines were immigrants, and declared that they came from Caphtor (Amos ix. 7, Jer. xlvii. 4), *i.e.* (probably) Crete; and there are at least substantial reasons for identifying them (with W. Max Müller, Maspero, and Sayce) with the Purasati, a piratical people, who, with other sea-faring tribes from the coasts of Asia Minor or the Aegean isles, made a descent upon Egypt in the time of Ramses III. (*after* the Exodus), and who appear to have subsequently established themselves on the south-west coast of Canaan, in the five cities, so often mentioned in the Old Testament (*e.g.* 1 Sam. vi. 17) as the strongholds of the Philistines. If this view be correct, the Philistines will evidently not yet have been settled in Canaan in the age of Abraham. The Buz and Ḥāzō of Gen. xxii. 21, 22 (sons of Naḥor) are not improbably the tribes of Bāzu and Ḥazū, mentioned by Esarhaddon, who dwelt apparently somewhere on the eastern border of Gilead. 'Ephah (xxv. 4; see also Isa. lx. 6), a son of Abraham by Ḳeṭurah, is probably the Arabian tribe Khayâpâ, whom Tiglath-pileser III. and Sargon speak of subduing; and the Ishmaelite tribe Ḳedar (xxv. 13; also Isa. lx. 6,

---

1898, pp. 342-6. *Jerusalem* is not mentioned in the inscriptions at present known till *c.* 1400 B.C., some nine centuries after the date of Khammurabi: see p. 73.

The reader will probably have noticed that the inscriptions speak of Kudurlachgumal and Khammurabi, not as allies, but as *foes*: there is, however, nothing unreasonable in the conjecture, that until Khammurabi succeeded in freeing himself from the Elamite supremacy, he was obliged by Kudurlachgumal to take part with him in his campaigns.

and elsewhere) is unquestionably the Ḳidrai, whose territory was invaded by Asshurbanipal. "Gad" (xxx. 11) is known, from Phoenician and Aramaic inscriptions, to have been an old Semitic god of fortune (cf. Isa. lxv. 11). Mr. Tomkins and Professor Sayce may be right in explaining the name Beth-lehem (xxxv. 19, and elsewhere) as meaning "House (*i.e.* Temple) of Lachmu," and as preserving a recollection of Babylonian influence in Canaan (see p. 72), Lachmu being the name of a Babylonian god (above, p. 10). A few other illustrations similar to these could be instanced; but they are not of sufficient general interest to be particularized here. Chap. xxxvi. is valuable historically, on account of the information respecting Edom contained in it: the country is frequently mentioned in the Assyrian inscriptions; but unfortunately, no native Edomite inscriptions have been hitherto discovered. We may pass on therefore to the chapters (Gen. xxxix.-l.) dealing with the history of Joseph.

These chapters, as has long been observed, display, in certain parts, a marked familiarity with Egypt; and many interesting illustrations of statements or allusions contained in the narrative have been supplied by the monuments.[1] Although the position of authority assigned to Joseph in Potiphar's house (Gen. xxxix. 4-6) can hardly be said to be distinctively Egyptian, yet it agrees with what we learn from the monuments respecting the organization of great establishments in Egypt: mention is frequently made in them of the superintendents of different departments, as the slaves, the fields, the cattle, etc., and in particular of the *mer-per*, or "master of the house." To the story of Joseph and his master's

---

[1] See more fully, on the subject of the following pages, the writer's article JOSEPH in Hastings' *Dictionary of the Bible*, where references to authorities are also more completely given.

wife there is a curious parallel in the popular Egyptian romance, called the *Tale of the Two Brothers*, written under the nineteenth dynasty.[1] The tomb of Ramses III. (of the twentieth dynasty), at Thebes, furnishes an illustration of a royal bakery:[2] in it we see a number of figures engaged in different processes of bread-making, and among them one carrying a tray containing rolls of bread upon his head (Gen. xl. 16): mention is also made in the inscriptions of a "superintendent of the bakery," corresponding to the "chief of the bakers" in Genesis. "Butlers" or "cup-bearers,"—the word for both in Hebrew is the same, meaning literally "the one giving to drink"—though, naturally, not an institution peculiar to Egypt, being found in Persia (Neh. i. 11), and elsewhere,—are represented in the tomb of Paheri, at El Kab, in the act of offering wine to the guests: the "chief of the butlers" is considered by Chabas and Ebers to correspond to the "conducteur des contrôleurs qui goûtent le vin," mentioned in a list of Egyptian court-officials; and Ebers has even illustrated from a text found in the temple at Edfu, and published by M. Naville, the custom of squeezing grapes into water (Gen. xl. 11), for the purpose of producing a refreshing beverage. The birthday of the Pharaoh (Gen. xl. 20), at least in the Ptolemaic period, as we learn from the Canopus and Rosetta decrees (239 B.C. and 195 B.C.), was celebrated with festivities, and the granting of amnesties to prisoners.

Pharaoh's dreams, both in themselves, and in their subject-matter, are appropriate to the country. In Egypt, as in Babylon, much weight was attached to dreams; and the monarchs of both countries are not unfrequently

---

[1] It is translated in Petrie's *Egyptian Tales* (1895), ii., pp. 36 ff.
[2] Wilkinson-Birch, *Ancient Egyptians*, ed. 1878, ii. 34; or Erman, *Life in Ancient Egypt* (1894), p. 191.

represented as taking important steps at the suggestion of a dream.¹ The fertility of the soil of Egypt is dependent upon the Nile; and Hat-hor, and Isis more especially, seem at times to represent the land which it fertilizes. The cow being sacred to both these goddesses, kine emerging from the Nile would be a natural emblem of fruitful seasons, and might moreover appear naturally in a dream relating to the fertility of the soil. The Egyptian hierarchy was highly organized; and among the priestly classes were "sacred scribes" ($\iota\epsilon\rho o\gamma\rho\alpha\mu\mu\alpha\tau\epsilon\hat{\iota}s$, in the Greek text of the Canopus inscription), or "knowers of things," as they are termed in the Egyptian text, the possessors of esoteric lore, whom the Pharaoh was wont to consult in any difficulty (Gen. xli. 8). Joseph's shaving himself before appearing in the presence of Pharaoh (Gen. xli. 14) is in accordance with Egyptian custom: upon the monuments, only foreigners, or Egyptians of inferior rank, are represented as growing beards. The practice of decorating a court-official with ornaments of gold, including chains (Gen. xli. 42), as a mark of royal favour, is thoroughly Egyptian.² The inscriptions also supply examples of foreigners rising to posts of political importance in Egypt, and adopting then a change of name.³

Joseph's plan of laying up corn in store-houses is in agreement with Egyptian institutions: in all important cities granaries were established, partly for the reception of the corn-tax (an important item in the Egyptian revenue), partly to provide maintenance for soldiers and other public officials: the "superintendent of the granaries" was an important officer of state, whose duty it was to take care that they were properly filled, and who also had to furnish

---

[1] Cf. Wiedemann, *Religion of the Ancient Egyptians*, p. 266.
[2] Erman, pp. 118 f., with the illustrations on pp. 120, 208; cf. p. 108.
[3] Erman, pp. 105 f., 517 f., 518 *note*.

the king annually with an "account of the harvests of the south and of the north."[1] Famines of long duration, due to the Nile failing to overflow, are not unknown in Egypt : not to mention the late and questionable testimony of the inscription, of the third century B.C., copied by Mr. Wilbour at Sehêl (an island in the First Cataract), which mentions a seven-years' famine under King Toser (?) of the third dynasty (*c.* 4400 B.C.),[2] or the famine attested by the Arabian historian El Makrizi for A.D. 1064-1071, the sepulchral inscription of one Baba, found at El Kab, in Upper Egypt, represents the deceased, in the course of an enumeration of his virtues and charitable deeds, as saying : " I collected corn, as a friend of the harvest-god ; I was watchful at the time of sowing. And *when a famine arose, lasting many years, I distributed corn to the city each year of famine.*"[3] The age of Baba (latter half of the middle kingdom) would coincide approximately with that of Joseph ; and it has been conjectured that the famine referred to may even be the same. In illustration of the measures said to have been adopted by Joseph, there may be quoted the words in which Ameni, governor of the "nome of the Gazelle," under Usertesen I., of the twelfth dynasty, states that he discharged his office: "In my time there were no poor, and none were hungry in my day. When the years of famine came, I ploughed all the fields of the nome; I kept the inhabitants alive, and gave them food, so that not one was hungry." The statement (Gen. xlvi. 34) that "every shepherd is an abomination to the Egyptians" is not directly supported by the monuments : but the keepers of oxen and swine were considered in Egypt to follow a degrading occupa-

---

[1] Erman, p. 108; cf. pp. 81, 86, 89, 95.
[2] Brugsch, *Steininschrift und Bibelwort* (1891), pp. 88-97; Sayce, *Monuments*, pp. 217 f.
[3] Brugsch, *Hist. of Egypt* (ed. 1891), p. 121.

tion. They are depicted as dirty, unshaven, poorly clad, and even as dwarfs and deformed; and the shepherds seem here to be treated similarly. There are parallels for parties of foreigners, such as were Jacob and his sons, receiving permission to settle in Egypt. Under Hor-em-heb, of the eighteenth dynasty, a troop of *Mentiu*, or nomads, whose lands had been ravaged by their enemies, appeal to the Pharaoh, and receive from him permission to settle in a prescribed locality; and an instance is cited below (p. 58) of a similar permission being granted to a body of Shasu, or Bedawin, under Merenptah, of the nineteenth dynasty. The peculiar system of land-tenure (xlvii. 26), according to which all land in Egypt, excepting the priests', belonged to the Pharaohs, and was rented by individuals from the crown upon an annual payment of one-fifth of the produce, and which is said to have been originated by Joseph, must have prevailed in the narrator's day; and it is so far in accordance with the testimony of the monuments that, in the New Empire (which arose after the expulsion of the Hyksos[1]), "the old aristocracy" is found to have "made way for royal officials; and the landed property has passed out of the hands of the old families into the possession of the crown and of the great temples."[2] The inscriptions at present known do not, however, mention particulars respecting the system of land-tenure, or state by whom it was introduced.

The monuments do not help us, except indirectly, to fix the date of Joseph. As in the Book of Exodus, the name of the Pharaoh is not mentioned; and, in view of the fixity of Egyptian institutions, the allusions in his biography to Egyptian manners and customs are not sufficiently distinctive to furnish a clue to the age in which he lived.

---

[1] A race of foreign invaders, who held Egypt, according to Manetho, for 511 years (2098–1587 B.C., Petrie).

[2] Erman, p. 102.

There are, however, as will appear more fully below, strong reasons for supposing Ramses II. to be the Pharaoh of the Oppression ; and if we argue back from this *datum*, it becomes probable that Joseph's elevation is to be placed under one of the later Hyksos kings. And this, in fact, is the date adopted by the majority of modern Egyptologists.

The Egyptian *names* occurring in the history of Joseph have all been explained on the basis of *data* supplied by the monuments. Brugsch[1] and Ebers both agree with Steindorff[2] that Potiphar (of which Poti-phera, Gen. xli. 50, is generally considered to be only a Hebrew variant), means *Gift of Ra*, the sun-god, and that Zaphenath-pa'aneach, the Egyptian name given to Joseph (Gen. xli. 45), means *God speaks, and he lives* ; while Ebers and Steindorff agree in explaining Asenath as *Dedicated to Neith*. Names formed after all these types are common in the Egyptian inscriptions ; but, singularly enough, not till long after the age to which (upon any view of the chronology) Joseph must be placed : names of the first two types (though there is one of the type Potiphar, known earlier, borne by a foreigner) appear otherwise first in the twenty-second dynasty (that of Shishak, in the time of Rehoboam) ; those of the type Asenath are met with occasionally in earlier times, but only become frequent at about the same period. The *combination*, in a single narrative, of names, all otherwise either rare or unknown at an early period, is remarkable ; and though future discoveries may correct the inference, it is impossible not to feel that it creates a presumption against their being historical.

The situation of the land of Goshen (Gen. xlv. 10, etc.), though a very probable determination was afforded by the rendering of the Septuagint, has been fixed more closely by the discoveries of M. Naville. This clever and successful

---

[1] *Steininschrift*, p. 83.
[2] *Zeitschr. für Aeg. Sprache*, xxxii. (1892), pp. 50-2.

explorer, at the end of 1884, came accidentally upon a large village about forty miles north-north-east of Cairo, called Saft el-Henneh, where he observed a monument bearing the name of Nectanebo, the last of the Pharaohs (367–350 B.C.), and which he perceived at once to be the site of a large ancient city. Excavating on this spot in the following year, he found the remains of a shrine erected by Nectanebo to the god Sopt, with inscriptions which shewed, among other things, that the place on which the shrine stood bore the name of *Kes*. Now, ancient hieroglyphic lists of the "nomes," or administrative districts, of Egypt mention *Kesem* as the twentieth nome of Lower Egypt, and state that its religious capital was *Pa-sopt*: *Kesem*, however, is simply the older and fuller form of *Kes*, while the name *Sopt* is manifestly preserved in the modern *Saft*. It follows that Kesem was the ancient name of the district surrounding Saft. Assuming now, as we may do, the identity of *Kesem* with the Hebrew *Goshen* (or, as it might be vocalized, *Geshen*), we obtain the situation of the "land of Goshen"; it must have been the district around Saft, "within the triangle lying between the villages of Saft, Belbeis, and Tel el-Kebir."[1] In the age of Joseph, however, Kesem did not yet exist as an independent nome. From texts of the nineteenth and twentieth dynasties it is inferred by M. Naville that "it was not an organized province occupied by an agricultural population; it was part of the marshland called *the water of Ra*, in which the city of" Bairest,—elsewhere called Per-Bairest, and believed to be the modern Belbeis,—"was situate. It could be given by the king to foreigners, without despoiling the native population. It must have been something

---

[1] The same locality is indicated by the rendering of the Septuagint, "Gesem of Arabia"; for "Arabia," as we learn from the geographer Ptolemy, was the name of a nome situated in the same direction, and having as its capital a place called *Phakusa*,—which is just *Kes*, with the Egyptian article *Pa*.

very like the borders of the present Sharḳiyeh, north of Fakoos, where the Bedawin have their camps of black tents and graze their large flocks of cattle." The expression "land of Rameses" (Gen. xlvii. 11) has not been illustrated from the monuments: it is considered by M. Naville to denote a larger area than the "land of Goshen," and to include that part of the Delta which lies to the east of the Tanitic branch of the Nile, a region which Ramses II. enriched with numerous works of architecture. If this be the true origin of the name, it is plain that the writer of Gen. xlvii. 11 must have transferred to the age of Joseph relations which did not begin to exist till long subsequently.

We may pass now to the Book of Exodus.

About thirty miles east of Saft lies a mound bearing the name of Tell el-Maskhuta, the "mound of the statue," so called from the statue of a king sitting between two gods, which has long existed there. The inscription on the statue shews that the king is Ramses II., and that the two gods are Ra and Tum, both forms of the solar-deity. It was on this spot that M. Naville in 1883 first began his excavations for the Egypt Exploration Fund. He soon met with inscriptions making it evident that the ancient name of the place was *Pi-Tum*, the "abode of Tum," evidently the Pithom of Exod. i. 11, one of the two store-cities built by the Israelites for the Egyptian king. Proceeding further, he found that Pithom was a city forming a square of about 220 yards each way, enclosed by enormous brick walls, and containing store-chambers, built likewise of bricks, and a temple. Inscriptions found within the area covered by the city shewed that it had been founded by Ramses II.,—in all probability, partly as a store-house for supplying provisions to Egyptian armies about to cross the desert, and partly as a fortress for the protection of the exposed eastern frontier of Egypt. Other inscriptions brought to light at the same spot shewed that Pithom had been enlarged, or beautified, by later kings; but no notice was found of the Israelites, as its builders. The other store-city, stated to have been built by the Israelites, was Raamses. Pa-Ramessu Meriamun (*i.e.* "the Place of Ramses II.") is a name often given in the papyri to Zoan, *i.e.* Tanis, a place on one of the branches of the Nile, about thirty miles north-north-west of Pithom, which, though built at least as early as the time of Amenemhet I., of the twelfth dynasty, was so much added to by Ramses II. that he is called by M. Naville its "second founder"; and Brugsch and Ebers both consider that Zoan is the place here meant. Zoan is, however, mentioned elsewhere in the Old Testament under its proper name; and as Ramses built largely at many different places in the Eastern Delta, others[1] think that one of these, not at present identified, is the Raamses built by the Israelites. In addition to the interest attaching independently to M. Naville's discoveries at Pithom, one fact fixed by him is important historically: for if Ramses be its founder, and it was built as narrated in Exod. i. 11, it follows that Ramses II. (1275-1208 B.C., Petrie) was the Pharaoh of the Oppression (Exod. i. 8—ii. 23), and that consequently the Exodus could not have taken place until (Exod. ii. 23) the reign of his successor had begun.

The *corvée* was a familiar institution in ancient Egypt: if stone had to be procured from the quarries, if a temple or palace had to be built, or a gigantic statue hauled to its place, if dykes or canals needed repairing,—all these works were carried out by gangs of men working compulsorily under overseers, who were not sparing in their choice of means for curing idleness. The native peasants were not exempt from the painful necessity of serving in the

[1] So, in particular, Maspero, *Rev. Archéol.*, xxxiv. (1879), pp. 323 f.

corvée; but criminals and prisoners of war were naturally those most frequently employed in it.¹ Representations of captives so employed for the purpose of making bricks have been found on the monuments. In the sepulchral chamber of Rekhmara at Thebes there is a graphic illustration of a body of men busily engaged in the work: a superscription over the scene states that the labourers are "prisoners whom Thothmes III. brought home for the works in the temple of his father Amen" in Thebes:² and taskmasters carrying wands are seen standing over them.³ An inscription, forming evidently part of a foreman's report, which has been translated by Brugsch and Chabas, is also worth quoting in the same connexion:—

> Number of builders, 12, besides men for moulding the bricks in their own towns (?), brought to work on the house. They are making the due number of bricks every day: they are not remiss in their labours for the new house. I have thus obeyed the command given by my master.

But no representation of the Israelites as thus employed —or, indeed, as resident in Egypt at all—has been found hitherto.⁴

¹ The *corvée* was introduced into Israel by Solomon, if not by David, for the construction of his buildings, though the fact is obscured in the English versions by inadequate renderings of the Hebrew word employed: it is what is really meant by the "tribute" of 2 Sam. xx. 24, and the "levy" of 1 Kings iv. 6, v. 13, xii. 18. The Hebrew word in these passages is the same as that which is used in Exod. i. 11.

² The writer is indebted to Mr. F. Ll. Griffith for many valuable improvements on pp. 56–61, partly in the text, and partly in the translations (especially those on pp. 59, 60).

³ See Wilkinson-Birch, i. 344, or Erman, pp. 417 f.

⁴ In two papyri, belonging to the reign of Ramses II., the writer, an officer of the commissariat-department, reports to the Pharaoh that he has executed his orders to "give corn to the Egyptian soldiers and to the *Aperiu* who are engaged in drawing stones to the great *bechen*, or fortified enclosure, of Pa-Ramses." It was supposed by Chabas that these *Aperiu* were the *Hebrews*; but the identification has not been generally accepted by other Egyptologists, partly on the ground that the Egyptian word does not correspond to "Hebrew" as it should do, and partly because a body of Aperiu is mentioned as settled at Heliopolis in the time of Ramses III., and another body is mentioned

In the account of the route taken by the Israelites at the Exodus, it is stated that after leaving Rameses, the places next passed by them were Succoth, and Etham "in the edge of the wilderness," after which they turned back, and encamped at Pi-haḥiroth, between Migdol and the sea, in front of Baal-zephon (Exod. xii. 37, xiii. 20, xiv. 2, 9).

There are several inscriptions known which throw light upon the topography of the region here in question.

The natural defences of Egypt on its north-eastern frontier were strong, but the almost waterless desert of the peninsula of Suez was threaded by two routes. One of these ran along the outlying coast of the Levant, where a series of wells afforded a scanty living to the Bedawin, and provided travellers with the means of continuing their journey; the other was connected with the valleys of Sinai, and entered Egypt by the fertile and marshy Wady Tumîlat. Some believe that a wall was carried right across the Isthmus of Suez in ancient times to prevent on the one hand the inroads of Bedawin, and on the other the escape of deserters or other fugitives from Egypt. In a description written by Sinuhit, a political exile from Egypt, in the reign of Usertesen I. (2758–2714 B.C., Petrie), of the adventures which befell him on his flight, there is an interesting allusion to these defences, and to the manner in which they were guarded :—

<small>Then [1] I fled on foot, northward, and reached the "Walls" (*anbu*) of the Ruler, built to repel the Sati. I crouched in a bush for fear of being seen by the guards, changed each day, who watch on the top. At nightfall I set forth, and at the lighting of the day I reached Peten, and skirted the lake of Kemur, etc.</small>

The name Kemur is applied apparently at all times to the Bitter Lakes; but in the Pyramid Texts of the Old

<small>as engaged in the quarries at Hamamat in the time of Ramses IV.,—both being long after the period of the Exodus (see Brugsch, *Hist.*, pp. 318 f.; Maspero, *Struggle of the Nations*, p. 443 *note*).</small>

<small>[1] Petrie, *Egyptian Tales*, i. 100 f. Cf. Erman, pp. 537 f.</small>

Kingdom it is the name of a great wall or fort, implying that in a remote period the region of the Lakes had been guarded by a wall.

In the New Kingdom we find each of the two routes to Egypt guarded on the frontier by an important fortress, called a *khetem*, "closed place," "fortress," "castle." On the northern route was the "Castle in Zaru," on the southern the "Castle in Theku." The northern route was by far the more important, as being the direct road to and from Syria. The southern route led only to the mines of Sinai. Besides the two great *khetems* on the eastern frontier, there were also towers (*bekhen*), watch-towers (*migdols*), etc., probably outposts along the route. The exact sites of the "Khetems" of Zaru and Theku are still uncertain, but undoubtedly they both lay very near the line of the present Suez Canal, on the edge of the cultivable land. Zaru was a great place under the Hyksos domination. Through it, in the eighteenth dynasty, Thothmes III. led his conquering hosts; and on the walls of Karnak the castle in Zaru is pictured in the scene of the triumphant return of Seti I. (father of Ramses II.) from his Syrian conquest. The primary occasion of Seti's expedition had been the rebellion of the Shasu nomads between Egypt and Syria against the authority of Egypt, and their stirring up of the Syrians to participate in their venture. As the result of this expedition we read that—

> In the first year of King Seti there took place by the strong arm of Pharaoh the annihilation of the miserable Shasu, from the castle (*khetem*) of Zaru as far as Pa-Kan'ana.

Pa-Kan'ana has been identified with a ruined site Kanâan, a little south of Hebron.[1]

About a century after Seti's expedition, in the eighth year of Merenptah (the successor of Ramses II., and in

---

[1] Maspero, *l.c.*, p. 370 *note*; cf. on Zaru pp. 122, 123.

all probability the Pharaoh of the Exodus), the Shasu appear in a different *rôle*. They now ask and obtain permission to pass the southern border-fortress, in order to find food and pasture for themselves and their herds in the rich pasture-land about Pithom. An Egyptian officer reports to the Pharaoh on the subject as follows:—

> Another matter for the satisfaction of my master's heart. We have allowed the tribes of the Shasu of Atuma to pass the castle (*khetem*) of King Merenptah which is in Theku, towards the lakes of Pithom of King Merenptah which is in Theku, in order to obtain a living for themselves and their cattle in the great estate of Pharaoh, who is the beneficent sun in every land, in the year 8 . . . .

Another inscription, belonging to Merenptah's reign, has been supposed, in its references to foreigners established in the Delta, to preserve an allusion to the Israelites; but its terms, when carefully examined, leave it doubtful whether that is really the case. The inscription, which is inscribed on one of the walls of the temple of Karnak, recounts in high-flown language Merenptah's overthrow of the invading Libyans in his fifth year. After the heading we have a description of the Pharaoh as protector of On (Heliopolis) and Memphis: the inscription then continues (if we may supply from the context some words, which are here missing):—

> [7] [foreigners of some kind had entered the land, setting up] tents in front of the city of Per-Bairest, making a dwelling-place (?) on the arable land (*shedt*) of Atiu; [8] [for the district] was without protection, it was left as pasture-land (*sha*) for cattle because of the nine bows (*i.e.* the foreigners), it was abandoned in the times of the ancestors. The kings of Upper Egypt sat with their councillors, [9]. . . . . the kings of Lower Egypt at the helm of their city, surrounded by the diwan of the two lands, (helpless) for want of soldiers, having no warriors to oppose to them. Then it came to pass that [10] [Merenptah (?)] arose on the throne of Horus, to give life to men, etc.

After this, we read, the king collected his forces, and prepared to meet the invaders.

Heliopolis (seven miles north-east of the modern Cairo) was about thirty miles south-west of the region identified above (p. 53) with Goshen; and Atiu was the river of Heliopolis, *i.e.* the Pelusiac branch of the Nile (which, a little lower down its course, passed through Goshen). Per-Bairest, as has been already remarked (*ibid.*), is thought to be the modern Belbeis, on the southern border of Goshen. The description of the helpless condition of the kings of Upper and Lower Egypt is not to be taken *au pied de la lettre*: the glorious age of Ramses II. was only just past. It is unfortunate that the inscription is mutilated at a crucial point (line 7); but judging from the parts which remain, the reference seems to be to a vacant district in front of Per-Bairest, which had been occupied recently by invaders, rather than to one which had been given up by previous kings to a body of foreign settlers.

From the same reign a happy chance has also preserved for us some of the entries made by Paembasa, a scribe stationed (apparently) at Zaru, respecting persons crossing the frontier. Here are two of them:—

In the 3rd year, on the 15th of Pachon. There went out the servant of Ba'al-....., son of Zapur, of Gaza, who had for Syria two letters as follows:—to Chay, the superintendent of the peasantry,[1] one letter, to Ba'al- . . . . , the prince of Tyre, one letter.

In the 3rd year, on the 17th of Pachon. There came the chiefs of the mercenaries at the Well of Merenptah, in the sand hills (?), in order to hold an inspection in the castle (*khetem*) which is in Zaru.

From the reign of Merenptah's successor, Seti II., we have the report of a scribe, who had been sent out to overtake two fugitive servants of the Egyptian king:—

I started from the court of the palace (at Tanis or Memphis?) on the 9th of Epiphi [July], in the evening, in pursuit of the two slaves. Now I arrived at the *sgr* of Theku on the 10th of Epiphi, and was told that they spoke of (*or* purposed) the south (*i.e.* of taking the southern route?)—they passed on on the 9th of Epiphi. I went to the castle (*khetem*) (*i.e.* of Theku); and was told, " The horseman (or groom), who

---

[1] According to Brugsch and Erman (pp. 538 f.), colonies of Egyptian workmen, resident in Palestine.

comes from abroad (or rather, perhaps, who travels to and from Egypt), [says] that they passed the *anb.t* (enclosure ?) north of the watch-tower (*migdol*) of Seti Merenptah."

Manifestly, these extracts place us in the same neighbourhood as the opening stages of the Exodus: the Shasu pass from the desert into Egypt, the officer of Seti II. passes from Egypt into the desert, by the same route, approximately, as that which, according to the Pentateuch, was taken by the Israelites. But whether the places named are the same is still uncertain. Succoth may be the Theku of the inscriptions, Hebraized so as to agree with the Hebrew word for "booths" (Gen. xxxiii. 17); but this identification is open to the objection that, according to the geographical lists, Theku was the name of a district connected with Pithom, whereas the Hebrew narrative appears to require a definite station on the route. Succoth was perhaps the *khetem* of Theku, otherwise this *khetem* may be Etham.[1] M. Naville identified Atuma with Etham; but the passage in the flight of Sinuhit to which he appeals seems to require a locality further from Egypt, and is moreover read differently by other Egyptologists: hence those authorities are probably right who identify Atuma with Edom. Migdol, Baal-zephon, and Pi-haḥiroth are all quite uncertain. Migdol is a Hebrew word signifying "tower," and in the Egyptian form *Maktl* occurs frequently in the inscriptions; but we have no means of knowing what "Migdol" is here meant. A "Migdol" of Merenptah is mentioned in the report of Seti II.'s officer; and it is possible that that is the same as the Migdol of Exod. xiv. 2: but nothing more definite can be said. Mention is also made in a papyrus of a (Phoenician) deity called Bali-zapuna, whence Brugsch and Ebers derive the name Baal-zephon; but the situation of this place remains

[1] Though a stronger guttural, corresponding to the Egyptian *kh*, would have been expected, had Etham been the Hebrew transcription of *khetem*. Maspero (*Rev. Arch.*, p. 324) questions the identification.

conjectural. Archaeological research has not as yet succeeded in making clear the route of the Exodus.[1]

The date of the Exodus cannot be determined precisely by means of the Egyptian monuments, as they contain no unambiguous reference to it; but there are strong reasons (cf. p. 55) for holding Ramses II., of the nineteenth dynasty (1275-1208 B.C.), to be the Pharaoh of the Oppression (Exod. i. 8—ii. 22); and hence his successor (cf. Exod. ii. 23), Merenptah, has been generally considered to be the Pharaoh of the Exodus (Exod. v.-xv.). Until 1896 no mention whatever of the Israelites had been found upon the Egyptian monuments; but in that year Professor Petrie made the interesting discovery, in the course of his excavations at Thebes, of a large stelè, which, upon examination, proved to contain a notice of them.[2] It had been long known that Merenptah in his fifth year had gained at Prosopis a great victory over the Libyans, who had invaded the Delta with a formidable body of allies: the narrative of his success, inscribed at Karnak, may be read at length in Brugsch's *History of Egypt*, pp. 311-5. The inscription found by Professor Petrie consists, for the greater part, of a grandiloquent description of the same occurrence: no longer, says the author, is the land disturbed with preparations for repelling the invader; Egypt is again at peace:—

The[3] villages are again settled. He who prepares his harvest will eat it. Ra has turned himself (favourably) to Egypt. He is born for the purpose of avenging it, the King Merenptah. Chiefs are prostrate, saying "Peace!"[4] Not one among the nine bows (the

---

[1] Cf. p. 9 of the *Atlas of Ancient Egypt*, published by the Egypt Exploration Fund: "Up to the present time, none of the various theories can claim sufficient proof to warrant an exclusive acceptance."

[2] Petrie, *Contemporary Review*, May, 1896, pp. 617 ff.

[3] The translation is based in the main upon that of Spiegelberg, in the *Zeitschr. für Aeg. Sprache*, xxxiv. (1896), pp. 14, 23 f., compared with Breasted's in the *Biblical World*, 1897, pp. 63 f.

[4] A token of submission to the victor.

barbarians) raises his head. Vanquished are the Tehennu (Libyans); the Khita (Hittites) are pacified; Pa-Kan'ana (Canaan) is prisoner in every evil; Askalni (Ashkelon) is carried away; Gezer[1] is taken; Yenoam[2] is annihilated; *Ysiraal is desolated, its seed* (or *fruit*) *is not*;[3] Charu[4] has become as widows for Egypt;[5] all lands together are in peace. Every one that was a marauder hath been subdued by the King Merenptah, who gives life like the sun every day.

The terms in which Israel is mentioned are not sufficiently explicit to make it certain what is referred to: but the important point to observe is that, whereas the other places (or peoples) named in the inscription have all the determinative for "country," Ysiraal has the determinative for "men": it follows that the reference is not to the *land* of Israel, but to Israel as a *tribe* or *people*,—whether migratory, or on the march. From the position in which Israel is mentioned—in close proximity to towns or districts of Palestine—it is inferred by Steindorff and Breasted that it was already in Canaan, and had sustained a defeat there at the hands of Merenptah,—whether the Israelites meant be, as Professor Petrie was inclined to conjecture, the descendants of individual Hebrews, who had been left behind in Canaan, when the body of the nation migrated into Egypt,[6] or who had returned thither after the end of the famine; or whether (Steindorff) the Israelites left

[1] About half-way between Joppa and Jerusalem.

[2] Generally identified with *Yânûḥ*, a village seven miles east of Tyre; but according to Naville (*Recueil de Travaux*, xx. 34 f.) *Jamneia* in Judah.

[3] *I.e.* its crops, or supplies of produce, are destroyed. Others understand "seed" in the sense of *posterity*; but the parallels quoted by Spiegelberg and Breasted certainly support the other interpretation, which is also that of Maspero, *Struggle of the Nations*, pp. 436, 443 ("n'a plus de graine").

[4] A people in the south or south-east of Palestine, perhaps the Horites (Gen. xxxvi. 20–30) of Edom (Maspero, Hommel, Naville).

[5] Fig. for, are helpless before the attacks of Egypt. The expression, as Mr. Griffith remarks, is no doubt chosen for the sake of the play on Charu, the word for "widows" being *char.ôt*.

[6] So Maspero, p. 444 (alternatively), "un clan oublié aux monts de Canaan."

Egypt earlier than is commonly supposed, perhaps under Amenôphis IV. (*c.* 1400 B.C.),[1] and so had by 1200 B.C. (the date of the inscription) obtained possession of part of Western Palestine. Others, on the contrary, think that it is equally consonant with the terms of the inscription to suppose that the Israelites were in the wilderness on the south of Canaan: the Libyan attack on Egypt (though not mentioned in the Book of Exodus) might have seemed to afford them a favourable opportunity for escaping from bondage; and the disappearance of a subject-people in the desert may well have been described in the high-flown phraseology of the inscription as its ruin or desolation.[2] In point of fact, the statement in the inscription is too indefinite to enable us to pronounce confidently on the nature of the occurrences to which it alludes. But it must be owned that the inference which would naturally be drawn from it is that expressed by Mr. Crum[3]; *viz.* "that Israel, or a part of that people, was already in some part of Syria, and had been in hostile contact with Egypt." At the same time, though obviously a statement which describes a nation as "desolated" cannot be regarded as "confirming" an account which tells of its triumphant deliverance, the opinion that the inscription gives the Egyptian version of the Exodus is one which may not unreasonably be held by those who are satisfied, on *independent* grounds, of the substantial correctness of the Biblical narrative. Even this opinion, however, can only be adopted provisionally: and it must be clearly understood that either this, or any other explanation which may be proposed, may be shewn any day to be untenable by the discovery of a fresh inscription

---

[1] In this case, however,—unless, indeed, they left Egypt in more than one detachment,—they cannot have built Pithom and Raamses (Exod. i. 11), which, as was shewn above, could not have been founded before the time of Ramses II.

[2] Naville; Maspero, *l.c.* (alternatively).

[3] In Hastings' *Dictionary of the Bible*, i. 665 *b*.

speaking more explicitly, or mentioning facts about the Israelites at present unknown.

The site of Pithom has been fixed by archaeology; that of Etham is still doubtful, though no doubt it may be fixed approximately: on the rest of the forty stations passed by the Israelites, according to Numb. xxxiii., on their journey to Canaan, very little light has been shed by archaeology. Two or three sites, still retaining their ancient names, have been recovered by travellers (the most notable being Kadesh): some others may be fixed approximately; but of the position of the majority, we are quite ignorant. Even the site of Sinai itself is disputed. The oldest known tradition identifies it with Jebel Serbâl, but this tradition cannot be traced back with certainty beyond the third century A.D.; a somewhat later tradition (sixth century) identifies it with Jebel Mûsa (about thirty miles east of Jebel Serbâl). Professor Sayce argues that it was not in the Sinaitic peninsula at all, but on the east side of the Gulf of Akaba: in the days of the Exodus, he points out, the western side of the Sinaitic peninsula was an Egyptian province: there were in it valuable mines of copper and malachite,[1] which were worked for the Egyptian kings, and the workmen engaged in these mines were protected by Egyptian soldiers: hence "to have gone into the province of Mafka would have been not only to return to Egypt, but to an Egypt more strictly garrisoned, and more hostile to the wandering tribes of Asia, than Egypt itself"; the Israelites, like Sinuhit, if they wished to place themselves beyond the power of the Pharaoh, would naturally make their way at once to the land of Edom.[2]

Let us endeavour to estimate the bearing of what has

---

[1] Cf. Maspero, *Dawn of Civilization*, pp. 349-58 (with plans and illustrations).
[2] Sayce, *Monuments*, pp. 265 f.

been adduced from the Egyptian inscriptions upon the narratives of Joseph, of Israel in Egypt, and of the Exodus. The first thing to notice is that there is no mention whatever in the inscriptions of any *person* named in these narratives, and only indirect and uncertain allusions to any *event* named in them : there is a passage (p. 59) which *may* refer to the Israelites in Goshen, and there is another passage (p. 63) which, though it says actually that Israel is "desolated," *may* be understood as giving the Egyptian version of the Exodus. Otherwise, it is exclusively *customs, institutions*, and *places*, mentioned or alluded to in the Biblical narratives, which receive elucidation from Egyptian sources. The fact that the illustrations furnished by the monuments relate not to historical events, but to subjects such as these, considerably diminishes their value as evidence of the historical character of the events narrated. Customs and institutions, especially in Egypt, and names of places generally in the ancient world, rarely varied from age to age: the allusions to the former are moreover mostly of a general kind, being seldom or never so precise and technical as to imply personal cognizance of the facts described ; while the places mentioned are few in number, and all such as might be readily known to Israelites travelling from Palestine into Egypt. The indirect circumstantial evidence, in other words, is neither large enough nor minute enough to take the place of the direct historical corroboration which at present the inscriptions do not supply for these parts of the Biblical narrative.

There is, however, a critical consideration which deserves to be taken into account. The narratives respecting Joseph are held by critics to consist in the main of a combination of two narratives, originally distinct, *both* of which display that familiarity with Egypt which has been referred to. This fact tends to shew that it was inherent in the common tradition, which (with slight differences in detail) both the narratives represent, and increases the probability that that tradition rests ultimately upon a foundation in fact. The question of the credibility of the Pentateuchal narratives cannot, it must be remembered, be either discussed or settled *solely* upon the basis of archaeology. The credibility of a narrative depends in part upon such questions as whether or not it is the work of a contemporary hand, and whether or not it contains intrinsic improbabilities; and these are questions which cannot be answered by archaeology alone. The Egyptian colouring of the Pentateuchal narratives is certainly insufficient to shew that they were committed to writing by a contemporary hand. And in some of the details, for instance, of the narrative of Joseph, there are unquestionably improbabilities, though this is not the place to consider their nature, or the precise weight that they may possess. On the other hand, the *general* course of Joseph's career (apart from particular details) cannot be said to be improbable: the Egyptian monuments supply examples of foreigners rising to positions of distinction at the court of the Pharaohs; while, as has been just remarked, the general congruity of the narrative with what is known independently of ancient Egyptian institutions may be regarded as supporting the opinion that the traditions underlying it are based upon a foundation of fact. On the whole, therefore, it may be said that, while not definite enough to be conclusive, and while affording no guarantee for the historical character of particular details, the Egyptian inscriptions tend to shew that the Biblical traditions respecting Joseph embody a genuine nucleus of historical fact.

Not so much can be said of the testimony of the inscriptions to the Oppression and the Exodus. Of course, those who accept these facts as narrated in the Book of Exodus, will find in the inscriptions interesting antiquarian and topographical illustrations of them: but those who seek *corroboration* of the facts from the monuments will be disappointed. There is certainly no sufficient reason for questioning that the Israelites were long resident in Egypt, that they built there the two cities Pithom and Raamses, and that afterwards, under the leadership of Moses, they successfully escaped from the land of bondage: but none of these facts are vouched for by the inscriptions at present known. The discovery of the site of Pithom, for instance, valuable as it is archaeologically, is not evidence that the Israelites built the town. The mention in inscriptions of other persons passing to and fro by Succoth and Etham is not evidence that the Israelites left Egypt by that route, —or indeed that they left Egypt at all. What we know about "Goshen" is consistent with the residence there of a comparatively small band of foreign settlers, but not (as Professor Sayce has pointed out [1]) with the numbers which, according to the Pentateuch, resided in it at the time of the Exodus. The utmost that can be said is that, from the fact of the topography of the first two or three stations of the Exodus being in agreement with what the monuments attest for the age of the nineteenth dynasty, a presumption arises that the tradition was a well-founded one which brought the Israelites by that route.[2]

The Asiatic campaigns of the Egyptian kings of the eighteenth and nineteenth dynasties made Palestine and

[1] *Early History of the Hebrews*, p. 212.

[2] The non-mention of the *name* of either of the Pharaohs in the Book of Exodus, as also of the *place* at which they held their court, is strong archaeological evidence that the narrative is not the work of a contemporary hand. On the former point, comp. Sayce, *Monuments*, p. 228, who observes that in native and contemporaneous documents, though the term "Pharaoh" (*i.e.* "Per-âa," great house) is often employed, it is only *after* the king's personal name has been already specified. The absence, also, in the narrative of the Exodus, of any notice of the line of border-forts, and of the troops by which they were guarded, points in the same direction.

Syria known to the Egyptians; and it is interesting to find, from the Egyptian records of this period, that many places bear already the same names by which they are known in Biblical times. Thothmes III. (1503-1449 B.C.) has left, inscribed on the walls of his temple at Karnak, a list of three hundred and fifty places in these countries owning his suzerainty, the first hundred and nineteen of which are within, or near, the borders of Canaan.¹ It must be admitted that the identifications of many of these places are uncertain, and others seem to have been exceedingly unimportant places, mentioned only incidentally in the Old Testament; but a few are better known. We may instance No. 2 Megiddo,² 28 Astr-tu (Ashteroth-karnaim, Gen. xiv. 5; or Ashtaroth, Deut. i. 4), 42 Taanach (Judg. v. 19), 43 Ibleam (Josh. xvii. 11), 47 Acco (Judg. i. 31), 58 Sharuchen (Josh. xix. 6), 62 Joppa, 65 Ono (Ezra ii. 33), 87 Rehob (Josh. xix. 28), 104 Gezer (Judg. i. 29), 111 Beth-anath in Naphtali (Judg. i. 33): two names, also, which transliterated into Hebrew would become Joseph-el and Jacob-el (Nos. 78 and 102), are remarkable, as including the names of two patriarchs. The inscriptions of Seti I. and Ramses II. (of the nineteenth dynasty), and of Ramses III. (of the twentieth dynasty), furnish similar lists.³ There exists, further, a curious and interesting papyrus, called *The Travels of a Mohar*,⁴ written during the reign of Ramses II. (1275-1208 B.C.), the author of which, a *littérateur* of the age, draws an imaginative sketch of a

---

¹ The list has been studied most thoroughly by Maspero, *Trans. of the Victoria Institute*, 1886, pp. 297 ff., 1888, pp. 53 ff.; and W. Max Müller, *Asien und Europa nach altaegyptischen Denkmälern* (1893), pp. 157 ff. See also Tomkins, in *RP.²*, v., pp. 25 f., 43 ff.; Sayce, *Patriarchal Palestine*, pp. 225 ff.
² The names are cited here, as a rule, in their familiar English forms.
³ See W. Max Müller, pp. 191 ff., for that of Seti I.: and for those of Ramses II. and III., *RP.²*, vi., 24 ff., 31 ff.; W. Max Müller, pp. 164-6 227 ff.; Sayce, *l.c.*, pp. 235-40.
⁴ An Assyrian official title.

tour through Palestine.[1] Among the places mentioned by him are Gebal (Josh. xiii. 5, Ezek. xxvii. 9), Biruti (Beyrout), Zidon, Zarephath, and Tyre, in Phoenicia; Achshaph (Josh. xi. 1); the "mountain of User"—a name which has been supposed to indicate that the tribe of Asher was already in pre-Mosaic times settled in its home in the north of Canaan; the "mountain of Sakama" (Shechem); Hazor in Naphtali (Josh. xi. 1, etc.); Kiriath-anab and Beth-sopher—as W. Max Müller has pointed out, scribal errors for *Beth*-anab (Anab in Judah, Josh. xv. 50) and *Kiriath*-sopher (the Kiriath-sepher of Josh. xv. 15, Judg. i. 11—previously, it is there stated, called "Děbir," the *adyton*, or inmost sanctuary of a temple); Beth-sha-el (*i.e.* as it seems, a Babylonian equivalent of Beth-el[2]); Megiddo, Joppa, and Gaza. "Kiriath-sopher" means "city of the scribe," for which "Kiriath-sepher" of the Old Testament—*i.e.* "city of book(s)"—is probably an incorrect vocalization. The place may have been the residence of a family or guild of scribes; but the name forms a slender basis on which to found far-reaching inferences respecting the literary culture of the ancient inhabitants of Palestine.[3]

On the condition of Canaan before the Hebrew occupation new and surprising light has recently been thrown by the discoveries now commonly associated with the name of Tel el-Amarna. Tel el-Amarna is a spot about 170 miles south of Cairo, the site of a new capital built by Amenôphis IV., of the eighteenth dynasty, as a centre for the worship of the sun-god, which he sought to encourage

[1] The Papyrus Anastasi I. See Erman, *Life in Ancient Egypt*, pp. 380 ff.; W. Max Müller, pp. 57, 172-5, 184-7, 394; Sayce, *l.c.*, pp. 204 f., 209-24.

[2] Erman, as cited by Müller, pp. 153, 192 f. The *sha* is Babylonian (cf. Methu-sha-el, above, p. 22). The Bethel meant cannot, however, be the well-known Bethel in Benjamin, but must be one not mentioned in the Old Testament, in or near the plain of the Kishon

[3] Sayce, *Monuments*, p. 54.

and his devotion to which led him to assume the title of *Khu-n-Aten,* or " Light of the Solar Disk." Some *fellahin,* digging here in 1887, came across a collection of more than three hundred clay tablets, written in the cuneiform characters of Babylonia, which, after examination, turned out to be a part of the official archives of Amenôphis III. and Amenôphis IV., and to consist of letters and reports addressed to these kings by their officials, and by Eastern rulers having relations with Egypt. The latter, about forty in number, are chiefly from kings of the Hittites (on the north of Palestine), of the Mitanni (in the north of Mesopotamia), of Assyria, and of Babylonia ; the former, which constitute the bulk of the correspondence, and are also the richer in historical interest, are principally from governors stationed by the Egyptian kings at various places in Palestine, Phoenicia, and Syria. It had long been known that the Pharaohs of this age, especially Thothmes I. and II., shortly before Amenôphis III., and Seti I. and Ramses II., shortly afterwards, had led their victorious armies over Western Asia, as far even as Mesopotamia :[1] but it was not known before by what means the Egyptians sought to organize and maintain the power which they had thus acquired. The correspondence discovered at Tel el-Amarna shews that, at about 1400 B.C., Palestine and the neighbouring countries formed an Egyptian province, under the rule of Egyptian governors, stationed in the principal towns, and (what is more remarkable) communicating with their superiors in the *Babylonian* language. This last-named circumstance is particularly noticeable. It affords,

[1] Thothmes I. erected a stelè on the middle course of the Euphrates, near Carchemish, to mark the limit which his arms had reached (Maspero, *Struggle of the Nations,* p. 210). Another interesting monument of the same successes is the monolith known as "Job's Stone," at Sa'diyeh (in the ancient Bashan), with an inscription proving, as Erman has shewn, that it was erected in honour of Ramses II. (See the article ASHTAROTH, in Hastings' *Dictionary of the Bible,* with the references.)

namely, conclusive evidence that for long previously Canaan had been under Babylonian influence. When, or how, this influence began we do not, indeed, know: we are hardly in a position to affirm that it had been continuous since those early days when Lugal-zaggisi, Sargon, Khammurabi, and Ammisatana claimed authority over the "land of Martu," or the West land;[1] but at all events Canaan had remained subject to it so long, that, at least for official purposes, the practice of using the language and writing of Babylonia continued to prevail, even after Canaan had become a province of the Egyptian empire. The Babylonian king who corresponds with Amenôphis IV. is Burnaburiash (II.), one of the kings of that Cassite dynasty which (p. 29) ruled in Babylon for five hundred and seventy-six years (1786-1211 B.C.): and it was perhaps under this dynasty that the influence of Babylonia become stronger in Palestine than it had been before. Primarily, no doubt, the influence was political; but it would naturally bring with it elements of civilization, of arts and sciences, and of religious belief.

We learn from these letters that the Egyptians had at the time considerable difficulty in maintaining their authority in Syria and Palestine: their power was threatened, namely, partly by the Hittites and other powerful neighbours, partly by the native population, partly by intrigues and rivalries between the Egyptian governors themselves: accordingly the writers of the reports frequently dilate upon the dangers to which they are exposed, beg urgently for assistance, bring charges of disloyalty against other governors, and protest emphatically their own fidelity.[2] The principal districts and

---

[1] See above, pp. 29, 39, 40.
[2] See the luminous summary of the Tel el-Amarna letters, and of the political movements disclosed by them, in Professor Petrie's *Syria and Egypt in the Tell el Amarna Letters* (1898).

places mentioned are, in the north, the land of Amurru (the Amorites), Birutu (Beyrout), Ziduna (Zidon), Zurru (Tyre), Zumur (Zemar, Gen. x. 18); the city of Ziribashani, no doubt some place in Bashan, on the east of Jordan; in the centre of Palestine, Acco and Megiddo; in the south, Joppa, Gezer, Urusalim (Jerusalem), Ashkelon, Lachish, and Gaza: all these are under Egyptian governors. Seven of the letters are from Abdi-khîba, governor of Jerusalem. He, too, like many of the other governors, is in difficulties. He is hard-pressed by formidable foes, termed the Chabiri: the neighbouring cities of Gezer, Lachish, and Ashkelon are aiding the enemy: he has been slandered to the king, and accused of disloyalty. But he protests emphatically his innocence: he owes his position, not to his father or his mother, but to the king:[1] gratitude alone therefore would have preserved him from the thought of plotting against him. He is beset by foes, and prays earnestly for troops: if they are not sent, the country is lost to Egypt.[2]

The position occupied by the Amorites is noticeable. In the Hebrew traditions of the conquest of Canaan, they are represented as occupying partly a region on the east of Jordan, ruled by Sihon, partly a considerable portion of the territory west of Jordan; but in the age of the Tel el-Amarna letters, as is clear from the manner

[1] "Behold, neither my father nor my mother has established me in this place: the arm of the mighty king has caused me to enter the house of my father." See Ball, *Light from the East,* p. 89.

[2] The letters of Abdi-khîba have been supposed to throw light upon the figure of Melchizedek, "king of Salem," and "priest of 'El 'Elyōn (God Most High)," in Gen. xiv. But the inference is not justified: there is no indication in the letters either that an "'El 'Elyōn" was worshipped in Jerusalem, or that Abdi-khîba was his "priest"; moreover, the letters relate to a period (if Amraphel in Gen. xiv. 1 is rightly identified with Khammurabi) *nine hundred years* subsequent to the age of Melchizedek. See the writer's paper in the *Guardian,* April 8, 1896.

in which they are mentioned, they are exclusively on the *north* of Canaan, and in fact occupy a particular district at the back of Phoenicia, on the Orontes. They appear in the same locality in the inscriptions of Seti I., and Ramses II., of the nineteenth dynasty, and even later, in those of Ramses III., of the twentieth dynasty, after the time of the Exodus.[1] It may be conjectured that, while the district north of Phoenicia continued to retain the name of "land of Amar," branches of the nation gradually pushed forward, and gained a footing on the territory, upon both sides of Jordan, afterwards occupied by the Israelites.[2]

Two other interesting illustrations of the condition of Canaan before the Hebrew occupation may be here conveniently noticed. The first is afforded by the one spot in Palestine, besides Jerusalem, which has been systematically excavated. Mr. (now Dr.) F. J. Bliss, following in the steps of Professor Flinders Petrie, and excavating in 1891 in the south-west of Judah, discovered, buried under the huge mound called Tell el-Ḥesy, the remains of no less than *eleven* different cities, superimposed one on the top of another, shewing that when one city had been burnt, or otherwise destroyed, another, after no long interval of time, had arisen in its place. A cuneiform tablet, found in the *débris* of the fourth city, and shewn by its character and contents to belong to the same age as the tablets discovered at Tel el-Amarna,[3] fixes the date of that city to about 1450 B.C.: the pottery, Egyptian scarabs, and other remains, found in the other strata of the mound, make it probable that the earliest city is not later than 1700 B.C., and that the latest dates from about 400 B.C.[4] It is

---

[1] W. Max Müller, *Asien und Europa*, pp. 217 ff.

[2] The use of the term in Gen. xiv. 7, 13, xv. 16, xlviii. 22, must be proleptic.

[3] Petrie, *Syria and Egypt*, No. 235; in Winckler's edition, No. 219.

[4] See F. J. Bliss, *A Mound of Many Cities* (1894).

highly probable that Tell el-Hesy stands on the site of the ancient Lachish, a city mentioned in the Tel el-Amarna letters, stated in Josh. x. 32 to have been captured by the Israelites, according to 2 Chron. xi. 9 fortified by Rehoboam, and known, from one of his own inscriptions (see p. 108), to have been taken by Sennacherib. The place was evidently an old Canaanite stronghold, such as were, no doubt, most or all of the towns mentioned in the Tel el-Amarna correspondence, and of a kind of which, we may be sure, there were many examples in the age when the Egyptian Pharaohs of the eighteenth and nineteenth dynasties were in the habit of marching their armies through Palestine. The Israelites also had traditions of the fortified cities (Numb. xiii. 28), described rhetorically as "fenced up to heaven" (Deut. i. 28, ix. 1), which their forefathers, when entering Canaan, had to storm.[1] The history of Lachish, as told by the mound which now marks its site, testifies to the indomitable perseverance of its inhabitants, who, one generation after another, never neglected to rebuild their ruined fortress. The valuable results obtained at Tell el-Hesy make it almost certain that, if only the means were forthcoming for similar excavations to be carried on at other favourable spots in Palestine, such as the eye of an expert could readily indicate, discoveries of equal, if not of greater interest, would reward the labours of the explorer.

The other illustration of the condition of Canaan before

[1] It should, however, be explained, to avoid misunderstanding, that there is no archaeological evidence that the original builders of Lachish were specifically *Amorites*. It is true, the place is sometimes described popularly as an "Amorite" stronghold, and the pottery found in the *débris* of the two earliest cities is called by Dr. Bliss "Amorite"; but Dr. Bliss distinctly explains (p. 41) that he does not use this word in an ethnological sense, but simply in the sense of "pre-Israelitish," for the purpose of distinguishing the oldest types of pottery found on the site from the definitely "Phoenician" pottery found in the strata representing the cities next following.

the Israelite occupation is furnished by the Tel el-Amarna letters. These letters, as stated above, are written in the language of Babylonia (which is allied to Hebrew, though by no means identical with it); but from time to time Canaanite words are used, either independently, or for the purpose of glossing or explaining a Babylonian expression in the more familiar dialect of the scribe who was writing the despatch ; and these Canaanite words are hardly distinguishable from Hebrew.[1] These letters thus shew that the pre-Israelitish inhabitants of Canaan were closely akin to the Hebrews, and that they spoke substantially the same language.[2] The same fact follows from many of the names of places preserved to us from a period later than that of the Tel el-Amarna letters, but earlier than the Hebrew immigration into Canaan, in the inscriptions of the Egyptian kings of the eighteenth and nineteenth dynasties (above, pp. 69 f.) : the names have in many cases evidently Hebrew etymologies. Divided religiously, the Hebrews and the Canaanites were in language and civilization closely allied.

An interesting illustration of the sacrificial laws in Leviticus is afforded by the Carthaginian inscription, now at Marseilles, prescribing the dues payable to the priests by the persons offering certain sacrifices. The inscription contains some words of doubtful or unknown meaning, and is also in parts imperfect ; but the general sense is sufficiently clear, and the missing parts can in some cases be supplied partly from parallel passages in the same inscription, partly from fragments of inscriptions, of similar import, and couched in similar phraseology, which have been

---

[1] The fact was pointed out by Zimmern in the *Zeitschrift des Deutschen Palästina-Vereins*, 1890, pp. 146 f.; and has often been noticed since, *e.g.*, by Sayce, *Monuments*, p. 356.

[2] Isaiah calls Hebrew " the language of Canaan " (xix. 18).

discovered in the neighbourhood of the ancient Carthage. The following is a translation of it [a] :—

¹ Temple of Baal[-   ]. Tari[ff of pay]ments,[b] e[rected by the superintendents of the pay]ments in the time of [   ]baal, the suffete,[c] son of Bodtanit, son of Bod[eshmun, and of Ḥalaẓbaal] ² the suffete, son of Bodeshmun, son of Ḥalaẓbaal, and their colleagues.

³ For an ox, whether it be a whole-offering, or a prayer(?)-offering, or a whole thank-offering, the priests shall have 10 (shekels) of silver for each; and if it be a whole-offering, they shall have, besides this payment, [300 shekels of fle]sh; ⁴ and if it be a prayer(?)-offering, the . . . . (?)[d] and the . . . . . (?)[d]; but the skin, and the . . . . (?),[d] and the feet, and the rest of the flesh, shall belong to the person offering the sacrifice.

⁵ For a calf whose horns are imperfect (?) . . . . (?), or for a hart,[e] whether it be a whole-offering, or a prayer(?)-offering, or a whole thank-offering, the priests shall have 5 (shekels) of silver [for each; and if it be a whole-offering, they shall have, be]sides ⁶ this payment, 150 shekels of flesh; and if it be a prayer(?)-offering, the . . . . . . (?) and the . . . . . (?); but the skin, and the . . . . . (?), and the fee[t, and the rest of the flesh, shall belong to the person offering the sacrifice].

⁷ For a ram, or for a goat, whether it be a whole-offering, or a prayer(?)-offering, or a whole thank-offering, the priests shall have 1 shekel, and 2 zars, of silver for each; and if it be a prayer(?)-offering, they shall [have, besides this payment, the . . . . . (?)], ⁸ and the . . . . . (?); but the skin, and the . . . . . . (?), and the feet, and the rest of the flesh, shall belong to the person offering the sacrifice.

⁹ For a lamb, or for a kid, or for the young (?) of a hart, whether it be a whole-offering, or a prayer(?)-offering, or a whole thank-offering, the priests shall have three-fourths (of a shekel), and [   ] zars, of silver [for each; and if it be a prayer(?)-offering, they shall have, besides] ¹⁰ this payment, the . . . . . (?), and the . . . . . (?); but the skin, and the . . . . . . (?), and the feet, and the rest of the flesh, shall belong to the person offer[ing the sacrifice].

---

[a] Professor Nöldeke, of Strassburg, who is generally recognized as the leading living authority on the Semitic languages, and whom the writer consulted on the feasibility of reducing the uncertainties in the translation, gave it as his opinion that, with our present knowledge, it was not possible to do so.

[b] Or *imposts, dues* (the word rendered "tax" in 2 Chron. xxiv. 6, 9).

[c] The title of the chief magistrate at Carthage; lit. *judge*.

[d] Terms of unknown meaning, denoting parts of the animals offered.

[e] Or (the word being differently vocalized) *a ram*; but this rendering leads to difficulties in lines 7 and 9.

¹¹ For a bird, whether domestic (?) or wild (?), whether it be a whole thank-offering, or a ...... (?), or a ...... (?), the priests shall have three-fourths (of a shekel), and 2 *zars*, of silver for each; but the fl[esh] shall belong [to the person offering the sacrifice].

¹² For a bird (?), or sacred first-fruits, or a sacrifice of game (?), or a sacrifice of oil, the priests shall have 10 a[*gŏrāhs*?ᵃ] for each.

¹³ In every prayer(?)-offering, which is presented before the gods, the priests shall have the ..... (?), and the ..... (?); and in the prayer(?)-offering [   ].

¹⁴ For a cake,ᵇ and for milk, and for fat, and for every sacrifice which a man may offer for a meal-offering, [the priests] shall [have   ].

¹⁵ For every sacrifice which a man may offer who is poor in cattle or birds, the priests shall have [nothing].

¹⁶ Every ...... (?), and every ..... (?), and every ...... (?), and all men who may sacrifice [,] ¹⁷these men [shall give] as payment for each sacrifice, according as is prescribed in the regulations [.

¹⁸ Every payment which is not prescribed in this table shall be made according to the regulations which [were drawn up by the superintendents of the payments in the time of [   ]baal son of Bodtan]it, ¹⁹ and Ḥalaẓbaal son of Bodeshmun, and their colleagues.

²⁰ Every priest who may accept a payment other than that which is prescribed in this table, shall be fin[ed   ].

²¹ Every person offering a sacrifice who shall not give   ] for the payment which [   ].

The tablet is not probably earlier than the fifth or fourth century B.C.; but it affords, nevertheless, a welcome illustration of the sacrificial institutions of the Phoenicians. Of course the regulations are not *identical* with those laid down in Leviticus; but there is a general resemblance between them: several of the technical terms are the same; and both are manifestly expressions of the same general religious ideas. The word rendered *whole-offering* (meaning an animal of which the whole was offered upon the altar) is one which is used in Deut. xxxiii. 10 and Ps. li. 19 of the burnt-offering: the word for "thank-

---

ᵃ See 1 Sam. ii. 36 Heb. ("an *agŏrah* of silver"). Perhaps the same coin as the *gērāh*, the twentieth part of a shekel (Exod. xxx. 13, and elsewhere).

ᵇ Properly, *something moistened* or *mixed*: the corresponding verb occurs, also of the "meal-offering," in Lev. ii. 4, 5, and elsewhere.

offering" is the one which regularly stands in Hebrew for the "peace-" or "thank-offering" (Lev. iii. 1, 6, etc.); and the "meal-offering" of line 14 is verbally the same as the "meal-offering" of Lev. ii. 1, etc. The animals, and other objects, offered as sacrifices are largely the same as those which were offered by the Hebrews. The regulations assigning certain specified parts of the sacrifice to the priests, and to the worshipper, respectively, are analogous to those in Lev. vi. 26, vii. 8, 31-4, Deut. xviii. 3, 4, etc. With the consideration shewn for the poor in line 15 may be compared Lev. v. 7, 11, xii. 8, xiv. 21 (in the last of which passages the word for "poor" is the same [1]).

[1] On the difficulties of the text the curious reader may consult the notes in the *Corpus Inscriptionum Semiticarum*, Pars I. Tom. i. No. 165; or (more briefly) Ball's *Light from the East*, p. 250 ff. There are elements, it may be remarked, in Mr. Ball's translation of the Inscription, including even some of the expressions resembling those occurring in the Old Testament, which are far from certain.

III. The Kings and After

WE may pass now to the Books of Kings. The intermediate books, though the inscriptions furnish some elucidations of the names of deities, or places, or foreign tribes occurring in them from time to time,[1] supply no examples of really important light being thrown upon the narrative by archaeology. During the whole period from Merenptah to the division of the kingdom under Rehoboam, there is no mention, upon the monuments at present known, either of the Israelites in general, or of individual leaders or kings, or of any of the foreign wars or invasions by which, during this period, the Old Testament describes them as being assailed : so far as the inscriptions are concerned, the history of Israel during this entire period is a blank. But when we come to the period embraced by the Books of Kings, there is a change. Omri and Ahab are named in a contemporary Moabite inscription. In particular, Assyria, from the ninth century B.C., enters into more direct relations with Israel and Judah than (so far as we know) she had done previously. It was the most brilliant period of Assyrian history ; and the kings of Nineveh, in their almost annual military expeditions, often came into hostile contact with the peoples of Western Asia : they had thus in their inscriptions frequent occasion to mention by name the kings of Israel or Judah, or to notice public events recorded in the Old Testament. More than this, the

[1] Some instances will be found below, pp. 139 ff.

information which the monuments supply of the movements and policy of the Assyrian kings not unfrequently sheds a valuable light upon the writings of the prophets, and throws a new meaning into their words. The writer regrets that the limits of space at his disposal do not permit him to illustrate the last-mentioned subject as fully as he would wish. Before, however, we proceed to the Assyrian inscriptions, some monuments of a different kind deserve to be noticed.

In 1 Kings x. we read of the visit of the Queen of Sheba to Solomon, bringing with her "spices, and very much gold, and precious stones." Shĕbā occurs also elsewhere in the Old Testament as the name of a distant and wealthy nation, whose caravans, trading in the articles just named, might often be seen journeying through the deserts on the south-east of Palestine (Ps. lxxii. 10, 15, Ezek. xxvii. 22, Jer. vi. 20, Isa. lx. 6, Job vi. 19). The home of Sheba was known to be in the extreme south of Arabia, partly from Gen. x. 28, partly from Strabo's description of the *Sabaeans*, who were evidently the same people. Until recently, however, little beyond this was known of Sheba, as indeed our knowledge of ancient Arabia generally, prior to about A.D. 600, until the present century was virtually a blank. But within recent years the south of Arabia has been visited by Europeans,—Wellsted (1834–5), Arnaud (1843), Halévy (1869–70), and especially Ed. Glaser, who in four journeys, made at different times between 1883 and 1894, copied more than a thousand inscriptions, being those who have increased most materially our knowledge of the country. The inscriptions obtained by these scholars have not yet been studied as fully as they deserve, nor indeed have they at present been all published: but they already enable us to form an idea of the ancient civilization and history of Sheba, and some of the neighbouring peoples. The dialects in which the inscriptions from these parts are written are most nearly allied to Arabic, but present at the same time many peculiarities of their own. The country inhabited by the ancient Sheba lay about two hundred miles north of the modern Aden; its capital was Marib, the Mariaba of Strabo. The inscriptions, and other antiquities found in the country, shew that its inhabitants had attained a high degree of civilization: "they build fortresses, and live in walled cities; they raise massive temples, and construct works of irrigation on a large scale." The history of Sheba cannot at present be written continuously; but the inscriptions, so far as they have been examined, seem to shew that it was at first under the government of a succession of *mukarribs* (plural, *makârib*), lit. "blessers," *i.e.* priest-kings, who were afterwards followed by kings, properly so called. The names of many both of the *Makârib*, and of the kings, are preserved in the inscriptions. Two of the early *Makârib* constructed at Marib a great reservoir, with connecting sluices, the remains of which are still visible, for the purpose of retaining the water flowing down from the neighbouring mountains. The chronology is difficult to determine with precision; but a fixed point is secured by the fact that Sargon, in 715 B.C., mentions receiving tribute of "gold, precious stones, ivory, spices of all kinds, horses, and camels," from Itamara, king of Sheba; and Glaser, arguing back from this date, thinks it probable that the *Makârib* ruled from about 1050 to 820 B.C., and that they were then succeeded by the "kings." The *data* being incomplete, it is quite possible that these dates are too low: but though the inscriptions have taught us much about Sheba that was not previously known, they do not, unfortunately (so far as they have been hitherto read), mention the Queen who was Solomon's contemporary (*c.* 950 B.C.), or corroborate in any way the Biblical account of her visit to him.

Twice in the Books of Kings mention is made of "kings of the Hittites." In 1 Kings x. 29 allusion is made to the export of chariots and horses from Egypt for "the *kings of the Hittites*, and the kings of Syria"; and in 2 Kings vii. 6 the Syrians, who were besieging Samaria in the reign of Jehoram, exclaimed in a panic, " Lo, the king of Israel hath hired against us the *kings of the Hittites*, and the kings of the Egyptians, to come upon us." The Hittites are also mentioned elsewhere in the Old Testament, though rarely, if ever, in terms from which anything definite could be inferred respecting their character or home. In Gen. xxiii., for instance, Abraham buys the field containing the cave of Machpelah from the "children of Heth" (*i.e.* the Hittites) in Hebron. Two of David's warriors were Hittites, Ahimelech (1 Sam. xxvi. 6) and Uriah (2 Sam. xi. 3, etc.). The Hittites are also regularly mentioned in the rhetorical lists of the nations of Canaan, dispossessed by the Israelites (Exod. iii. 8, 17, xiii. 5, etc.); though Judg. i. 26 speaks of the "land of the Hittites" in terms implying that it was outside Canaan. But the information furnished both by these and by all other passages in which the Hittites are mentioned was meagre and vague. Considerably more is known now. When the Egyptian monuments came to be decyphered, the Hittites were found to be frequently mentioned in them. Thothmes III., of the eighteenth dynasty, who, as has been already remarked, had extended his conquests through Palestine and Syria as far as Carchemish, the great fortress on the Upper Euphrates, received presents from the kings of the "great land of the Khâti." In the Tel el-Amarna tablets the Hittites are frequently mentioned as intriguing against the Egyptian power in the north of Palestine. Seti I. and Ramses II., of the nineteenth dynasty, waged long war with the Hittites,—for the possession, as it seems, of the neutral "land of Amar," or the Amorites (p. 74), which lay between the Hittites and the territory claimed by Egypt. Ramses II., on account of the prowess displayed by him in an engagement with the Hittites at Kadesh on the Orontes, in his fifth year, became the hero of a short epic, written by a contemporary poet, Pentaur. In Ramses II.'s twenty-first year a treaty—the most ancient example of the kind known—was concluded between Egypt and the Hittites, in which each recognized the other as a power equal in rank to itself, and agreed to help it in case of need—a striking testimony to the position which the Hittite empire enjoyed at the time.[1] A century or so afterwards, under Ramses III. (twentieth dynasty), the Hittites, with their neighbours the Mitanni, of Naharina (the "Aram-Naharaim," or Syria of the two rivers, *i.e.* Mesopotamia, of the Old Testament[2]), are found advancing against Egypt, and being defeated, somewhere probably on the coast of Palestine, by the Egyptian king.[3] More is not heard of the Hittites from the Egyptian inscriptions; but the Assyrian kings, Tiglath-pileser I. (*c.* 1100 B.C.), Asshurnâṣirabal (885-860 B.C.), and Shalmaneser II. (860-825 B.C.), all speak of victorious invasions of their territory. After the successes of Shalmaneser II. the power of the Hittites seems to have been considerably broken; and in the end Carchemish, their capital on the Euphrates, was captured by Sargon, the contemporary of Isaiah (cf. Isa. x. 9), 717 B.C. So well known were the Hittites to the Assyrians, that Shalmaneser and the following kings often use the expression "land of the Hittites" as a general term for Western Asia, including Phoenicia, Palestine, and the adjoining countries.

The monuments of the Hittites themselves have hardly been known for more than a quarter of a century. The

---

[1] See the text of the treaty in Brugsch, *Hist.*, pp. 281-6; and cf. Maspero, *Struggle of the Nations*, pp. 390-8.
[2] Gen. xxiv. 10, Judg. iii. 8. Cf. above, p. 37.
[3] Maspero, pp. 465 ff.

traveller Burckhardt had indeed in 1812 noticed in the corner of a house in Hamah, on the Orontes (about a hundred and twenty miles north of Damascus—the Hamath of the Old Testament), a block of black basalt engraved with strange hieroglyphic signs; but he was unable to decypher them; and the discovery was forgotten. In 1870 and 1871, interest in the subject was reawakened by the discovery at Hamah of other stones of the same character; and in 1872 Dr. W. Wright, then missionary in Damascus, obtained casts of five of the inscriptions. Afterwards, also, monuments of the same kind were found at Aleppo, and at Jerabis, on the Euphrates, about a hundred miles north-east of Aleppo, the site (as has since been proved by excavation) of the ancient Carchemish.

It was Professor Sayce who, while studying these inscriptions, and the figures accompanying them, was struck by the resemblance of the latter to certain sculptures, which had been observed and copied by previous travellers, carved upon the rocks in different parts of Asia Minor, particularly in the Karabel, a little east of Smyrna, at Ghiaur Kalessi, in what was the ancient Phrygia, at Boghaz Keui and Eyuk, in the ancient Cappadocia, and at Ivrîz, in the ancient Lycaonia. Subsequent investigation confirmed the conclusions to which these resemblances pointed; and shewed that the region north of Phoenicia and the " land of the Amorites " had once been the seat of a great Hittite civilization, which continued to exist for many centuries. It is thought by many that the original home of this civilization was in Northern Cappadocia, and that it radiated thence partly south-eastwards, where Carchemish, the most important strategic and commercial point on the Upper Euphrates, became its principal city, partly westwards, as it seems by a series of colonies, along the chief commercial routes over a large part of Asia Minor, and partly southwards, where its emissaries pressed upon the "land of the Amorites," and at the beginning of the nineteenth Egyptian dynasty acquired some kind of supremacy over its capital, Kadesh on the Orontes. Whether, however, this distinctive civilization, with its peculiar art and system of writing, was spread by the conquests of one great people, or was borrowed and developed by a number of small peoples, perhaps united by federation, is still uncertain. The somewhat wide and confident conclusions as to the type, habits, and polity of the "Hittites," drawn on the first discovery of a few of their monuments, tend to become less assured as the number of those monuments increases. The Hittite inscriptions present a problem of exceptional difficulty to the decypherer: but a brilliant, and, in the opinion of some scholars, a partially successful endeavour to extort from them their secret has been made by the eminent Assyriologist, P. Jensen.[1]

Who the "kings of the Hittites" were, that are alluded to in the two passages quoted above from the Books of Kings, will now be plain. The situation of the "land of the Hittites," mentioned in Judg. i. 26, is now also seen to have been on the north of Palestine. The inclusion of the Hittites in the lists of tribes dispossessed by the Israelites is probably to be explained by the fact that as the Hittites pressed southwards, and drove the Amorites before them, offshoots, or colonies, established themselves in the extreme north of Canaan: in Josh. xi. 3, the Septuagint, in all probability rightly, reads, "*the Hittite* (for *the Hivite*) under Hermon"; and there is little doubt that in Judg. iii. 3 we should read similarly, "*the Hittites* (for *the Hivites*) that dwelt in Mount Lebanon." Of the presence of Hittites in the *south* of Palestine, in Hebron (Gen. xxiii.), however, archaeology offers no satisfactory explanation; and it is very possible that in the passages

---

[1] Comp. further, on the Hittites, Maspero, *l.c.*, pp. 351 ff.

implying this,[1] the term is used, by an inexact extension of its proper sense, to denote the pre-Israelitish population of Canaan generally.

During the reign of Rehoboam, we read (1 Kings xiv. 25, 26), Shishak, king of Egypt, invaded Judah, and carried away a considerable amount of treasure from Jerusalem. Shishak is manifestly the Egyptian Shashanq, a Libyan, the founder of the twenty-second dynasty. No detailed account of this expedition has come down to us,—perhaps because only fragments of the annals of Shashanq have been preserved : but there exists an interesting relief on the outer southern wall of the temple of Amen at Karnak, representing the colossal figure of Shashanq dealing out blows to his conquered foes, while behind him are paraded in long rows the names of a hundred and fifty-six subjugated towns and districts, each enclosed in a *cartouche* surmounted by the head of a captive. The first nine names are those of various foreign peoples, which conventionally head the lists of Egyptian conquests. Of the names which follow,[2] some are destroyed and of the rest the identifications are in many cases uncertain, the places referred to being often, it seems, insignificant ones, not named in the Old Testament. A tolerable number, however, are clear, as 11 Gaza, 13 Rabbith in Issachar (Josh. xix. 20), 14 Taanach, 15 Shunem (2 Kings iv. 8), 18 Hapharaim in Issachar (Josh. xix. 19), 22 Mahanaim on the east of Jordan, 23 Gibeon, 24 Beth-horon, 26 Aijalon, 27 Makkedah (Josh. x. 10), 29 Iaoudhammelouk, "Yehud of the king," in Dan (Josh. xix. 45,—now *el-Yahudîyeh*), 37 Keilah and 38

---

[1] Which all occur in the document of the Pentateuch called by critics the *priestly narrative*.
[2] See Maspero in the *Transactions of the Victoria Institute*, xxvii. (1894), pp. 63 ff. ; W. Max Müller, *Asien und Europa*, pp. 166 ff.

Socho, both in the lowland of Judah (Josh. xv. 44, 35, 1 Sam. xvii. 1), 65 Ezem (Josh. xv. 29), 108 Arad, about sixteen miles south of Hebron (Numb. xxi. 1), 124 Beth-anoth (Josh. xv. 59). The list, it will be noticed, after Gaza, the border-fortress of Palestine, on the Egyptian side, passes to places in the north and centre of Canaan; from 37 and 38 the places mentioned are chiefly, if not entirely, in Judah and the south. Jerusalem, and other important places, may have been mentioned in parts of the list that are now destroyed. The Book of Kings says nothing about Shishak's invading *Northern* Israel; and it is commonly supposed that his attack upon Judah was due to the suggestion of Jeroboam (who had taken refuge in Egypt, 1 Kings xi. 40, xii. 2): if this supposition be correct, the mention, in Shishak's list, of places north of Judah must be explained, with Maspero,[1] from the practice of the Egyptian kings to count as conquests places which merely owned their suzerainty, or paid them tribute.

In 2 Kings iii. 4, 5 we read that Mesha, king of Moab, was a sheep-master, who paid the king of Israel an annual tribute consisting of the wool of a hundred thousand lambs and a hundred thousand rams, but that after the death of Ahab (*c.* 850 B.C.) he rebelled. In 1868, Dr. Klein, a German missionary in Jerusalem, was fortunate enough to discover at Dhibân, on the east side of the Dead Sea, the site of the ancient Dibon (Isa. xv. 2), a slab of black basalt, bearing an inscription which proved to contain Mesha's own account of the circumstances of the revolt. Through some misunderstanding, in the course of the negotiations for the acquisition of the stone, the suspicions and cupidity of the native Arabs were aroused: they imagined that they

---

[1] *Struggle of the Nations*, p. 774.

were about to be deprived of some valuable talisman; they therefore put fire under it, poured cold water over it, and being then able to break it in pieces, they distributed fragments of it as charms among the people of their tribe. Happily, however, a squeeze of the inscription had already been secured: many of the fragments also were afterwards recovered; so that, although occasionally a letter or two is uncertain, and parts of the last few lines are missing, the inscription is in the main quite intelligible and clear. The language in which it is written resembles closely the Hebrew of the Old Testament. The following is a translation of the inscription:—

¹ I am Mesha', son of Chemoshmelek, king of Moab, the Daibonite.
² My father reigned over Moab for 30 years, and I reigned ³after my father. And I made this high place for Chĕmôsh in ḲRḤH,* a high place of salvation, ⁴because he had saved me from all the kings (?), and because he had let me see (my desire) upon all them that hated me.
Omri ⁵ was king over Israel, and he afflicted Moab for many days, because Chemosh was angry with his land. ⁶ And his son succeeded him; and he also said, I will afflict Moab. In my days said he th[us]; ⁷ but I saw (my desire) upon him, and upon his house, and Israel perished with an everlasting destruction.
Omri took possession of the [la]nd ⁸ of Mĕhĕdeba, and it (*i.e.* Israel) dwelt therein, during his days, and half his son's days, forty years; but Chemosh [resto]red ⁹ it in my days.
And I built Ba'al-Me'on, and I made in it the reservoir (?); and I built ¹⁰ Ḳiryathên.
And the men of Gad had dwelt in the land of 'Aṭaroth from of old; and the king of Israel ¹¹ had built for himself 'Aṭaroth. And I fought against the city, and took it. And I slew all the [people of] ¹² the city, a gazingstock unto Chemosh, and unto Moab. And I brought back (*or,* took captive) thence the altar-hearth of Dawdoh (?), and I dragged ¹³ it before Chemosh in Ḳeriyyoth. And I settled therein the men of SHRN,* and the men of ¹⁴ MḤRTH.*
And Chemosh said unto me, Go, take Nebo against Israel. And I ¹⁵ went by night, and fought against it from the break of dawn until noon. And I took ¹⁶ it, and slew the whole of it, 7,000 men and....., and women, and...., ¹⁷ and maid-servants: for I

---

* The vocalization of these names is uncertain

had devoted it to 'Ashtor-Chĕmōsh. And I took thence the [ves]sels [18] of YAHWEH, and I dragged them before Chemosh. And the king of Israel had built [19] Yahaẓ, and abode in it, while he fought against me. But Chemosh drave him out from before me; and [20] I took of Moab 200 men, even all its chiefs; and I led them up against Yahaẓ, and took it [21] to add it unto Daibon. I built ḲRḤH,[a] the wall of Ye'arim (or, of the Woods), and the wall of [22] the Mound. And I built its gates, and I built its towers. And [23] I built the king's palace, and I made the two reser[voirs (?) for wa]ter in the midst of [24] the city. And there was no cistern in the midst of the city, in ḲRḤH.[a] And I said to all the people, Make [25] you every man a cistern in his house. And I cut out the cutting for ḲRḤH[a] with the help of prisoner[s [26] of] Israel. I built 'Aro'er, and I made the highway by the Arnon. [27] I built Beth-Bamoth, for it was pulled down. I built Beẓer, for ruins [28] [had it become. And the chie]fs of Daibon were fifty, for all Daibon was obedient (to me). And I reigned [29] [over] an hundred [chiefs] in the cities which I added to the land. And I built [30] Mehĕdĕ[b]a, and Beth-Diblathĕn, and Beth-Ba'al-Me'on; and I took thither the naḳad [b]-keepers (?), [31]............ sheep of the land. And as for Ḥoronĕn, there dwelt therein ...... and .... [32] .... Chemosh said unto me, Go down, fight against Ḥoronĕn. And I went down .... [33] .... [and] Chemosh [resto]red it in my days. And I went up thence to ..... [34] .... And I ....

The inscription is of great interest, both historically and linguistically. In the Book of Kings, the revolt of Mesha is said to have taken place after the death of Ahab; but from line 8 of the inscription it is evident that this date is too late, and that it must in fact have been completed by the middle of Ahab's reign. The territory on the east of Jordan and the Dead Sea, north of the Arnon, belonged ostensibly to Reuben and (contiguous to it on the north) Gad; but these tribes were not able to hold it permanently against the Moabites. David reduced the Moabites to the condition of tributaries (2 Sam. viii. 2); but we infer from the inscription that this relation was

[a] The vocalization of these names is uncertain.
[b] The name of a choice breed of sheep. The word is partly obliterated: if restored correctly, it will be the one which is used of Mesha in 2 Kings iii. 4 (A.V. "sheep-master").

not maintained. Omri, however, determined to reassert the power of Israel, and gained possession of at least the district around Medeba, which was retained by Israel for forty years, till the middle of Ahab's reign, when Mesha revolted. The inscription names the principal cities which had been occupied by the Israelites, but were now recovered for Moab, and states further how Mesha was careful to rebuild and fortify them, in the event of a siege. Most of the places named are mentioned in the Old Testament, in the passages which describe the territory of Reuben (Josh. xiii. 15-23) or Gad (Josh. xiii. 24-8), or allude to the country occupied by Moab (Isa. xv. 2, 4, 5, Jer. xlviii. 1, 3, 18, 19, 21-4, 34, 41).

The inscription furnishes many interesting illustrations of the ideas and language of the Old Testament, though only a few can be noticed there. "High places" (line 3) are often mentioned as places at which the worship both of Jehovah and of other gods was carried on (*e.g.* 1 Kings iii. 2, 3, 4, xi. 7, Isa. xvi. 12). Chemosh is several times named as the national god of Moab; and the Moabites are called his "people" in Jer. xlviii. 46, and his "sons" and "daughters" in Numb. xxi. 29. The phrase in line 4, lit. "let me look upon them that hated me" (*viz.* in triumph), is verbally the same as that which occurs in Ps. cxviii. 7 (cf. lix. 10). The terms in which Chemosh is spoken of are singularly parallel to those used with reference to Jehovah in the Old Testament: Chemosh is, for instance, "angry" with his people (cf. Deut. ix. 8, 2 Kings xvii. 18): he says to Mesha, "Go, take Nebo," or "Go down, fight against Ḥoronên," just as we read, for instance, in 1 Sam. xxiii. 4, "Arise, go down to Keilah," or in 2 Sam. xxiv. 1, "Go, number Israel and Judah": he "drives out" Mesha's foes before him, just as Jehovah "drives out" (the same word) the foes of Israel (Deut. xxxiii. 27, Josh. xxiv. 18). The expression "gazingstock" (line 12) is used similarly by Nahum (iii. 6). The custom of "devoting" (or "banning") captives to a deity (line 17) is one to which there are repeated references in the Old Testament: see, for instance, Deut. vii. 2, "When Jehovah thy God shall deliver them up before thee, and thou shalt smite them, then thou shalt *devote* them" (A.V. "utterly destroy them"), 1 Sam. xv. 2, "Now go, and smite Amalek, and *devote* (A.V. "utterly destroy") all that they have," v. 8, "And he *devoted* (A.V. "utterly destroyed") all the people with the edge of the sword." Ashtor-Chemosh, in the same line, must be a compound deity, of a type of which there are other examples in Semitic mythology: Ashtor would be a male deity, corresponding to the female Phoenician deity, Ashtoreth. It is interesting to learn from lines 17 and 18 that there was a sanctuary of Jehovah in Nebo, with "vessels," implying an altar, and the other requisites for performing sacrifice. The word rendered "obedient" in line 28 (lit. *obedience*) is exactly the same as that which occurs in Isa. xi. 14, lit. " and the children of Ammon (shall be) *their obedience*." Linguistically, the idiom in which the inscription is written differs from Hebrew only dialectically; small idiomatic differences are observable; but on the other hand, it shares with it several *distinctive* features, so that, on the whole, it resembles Hebrew more closely than any other Semitic language at present known. In point of style, the inscription reads almost like a page from one of the earlier historical books of the Old Testament. Its finished literary form combines with its contents in shewing that the civilization of Moab, in the ninth century B.C., was hardly inferior to that of its more celebrated neighbours, Israel and Judah.

We may now proceed to the Assyrian monuments, which, as was remarked above, make frequent mention of the kings of Israel and Judah, and often supplement the Biblical narratives in a most welcome manner.

The earliest Israelitish king whose doings, so far as is at present known, are thus alluded to is Ahab. Shalmaneser II. (860–825 B.C.), in the course of a long inscription on a monolith, now in the British Museum, describes his expedition in his sixth year against Irchulini, king of Hamath: after setting out from Nineveh, and receiving tribute from various places, he advanced to Khalman (Aleppo), and then proceeded to invade the territory of Irchulini [a]:—

[90] Karkar, his royal city, I destroyed, I laid waste, I burnt with fire. 1,200 chariots, 1,200 horsemen, 20,000 soldiers of Dad'idri (Hadadezer) [91] of Damascus, 700 chariots, 700 horsemen, 10,000 soldiers of Irchulini of Hamath, 2,000 chariots, 10,000 soldiers of Ahab of [92] *the land of Israel*, 500 soldiers of the Guaeans, 1,000 soldiers from the land of Muṣri (Egypt), 10 chariots, 10,000 soldiers from the land of Irkanat, [93] 200 soldiers of Matinubaal of Arvad [b] . . . . . . 1,000 soldiers of [95] the Ammonite Ba'sa, son of Rukhubi—these 12 kings he (*i.e.* Irchulini) took to his assistance; for [96] battle and combat they advanced against me. With the exalted succour which Asshur, the lord, rendered, with the mighty power which Nergal, who marched before me, [97] bestowed, I fought with them . . . .; 14,000 [98] of their troops I slew, like Rammân (the storm-god) I rained down a flood upon them, I scattered their corpses . . . . ; [101] the river Orontes I took in possession.

Karkar will have lain somewhere between Aleppo and Hamath. Dad'idri of Damascus must be Ben-hadad [c] (II.), king of Syria, mentioned in 1 Kings xx. We read in that chapter that Ben-hadad, having in two successive years invaded Israel, and having been defeated each time with great loss, succeeded ultimately in obtaining terms from

[a] The translations of the following inscriptions are based upon the transliterations and translations in Schrader's *Cuneiform Inscriptions and the Old Testament*, compared with those published in his *Keilinschriftliche Bibliothek*, vols. i.–iii., 1889–1892. The last-named work possesses the advantage of enabling the reader to study the inscriptions *in extenso*.

[b] In Phoenicia (Gen. x. 18).

[c] The Biblical writer, as Schrader and Sayce have pointed out, seems to have confused Dad'idri (*i.e.* Hadadezer) with his father Ben-hadad (1 Kings xv. 18).

Ahab, and a treaty was concluded between them (*v.* 34)
In the inscription Ben-hadad and Ahab both appear among
the allies of Irchulini of Hamath, who, it may be presumed,
were called out for the purpose of making common cause
against the formidable encroachments of the Assyrians.
They were, however, defeated with great loss. The defeat
broke up the alliance: hostilities again arose between
Israel and Syria; and Ahab induced Jehoshaphat to
embark with him in an endeavour to recover Ramoth in
Gilead from the Syrians, and was wounded mortally in
the attempt (1 Kings xxii.). The inscription, apart from
its direct historical interest, is also important chronologically; for it shews that Ahab was still on the throne
at a date equivalent to 854 B.C.[1]

Jehu, who overthrew the dynasty founded by Omri
(2 Kings ix., x.), is mentioned twice by Shalmaneser II.
The first passage occurs on the famous Black Obelisk,
found at Nimroud (the site of the ancient Calach) by
Sir Henry Layard, and now a conspicuous object in the
Nimroud Central Saloon of the British Museum. This
obelisk, in its upper part, is decorated with five tiers
of bas-reliefs, and in its lower part is covered with a
cuneiform inscription of 190 lines, recounting the chief
events of thirty-one years of Shalmaneser's reign. Each
tier of bas-reliefs represents the tribute brought to the
Assyrian king by nations whom he had either subjugated or who sought his favour. The second tier
depicts a prince or deputy prostrating himself before
Shalmaneser, and followed by attendants bearing offerings.
The superscription reads:—

Tribute of Jehu, son of Khumri (Omri): silver, gold, a golden bowl, a golden ladle, golden goblets, golden pitchers, lead, a staff for the hand of the king, shafts of spears, I received.

---

[1] See below, p. 118. Shalmaneser mentions other defeats of Ben-hadad in his eleventh and fourteenth years (Schrader, pp. 202 f.).

The tribute-bearers are bearded, and wear long-fringed robes : their strongly marked Jewish physiognomy is very noticeable.

The title "Jehu, son of *Omri*," is remarkable. Jehu, in point of fact, overthrew the dynasty (Omri, Ahab, Ahaziah, Jehoram), which Omri had founded : but Omri seems to have been a more important ruler than the brief notice of his reign in the Book of Kings (1 Kings xvi. 23, 24) would lead us to suspect : his choice of Samaria as his capital (*ibid.*) shews that he had the eye of a military leader : and that he (or his dynasty) enjoyed, from whatever cause, a reputation abroad, appears clearly from the fact that "the land of the house of Omri," or "the land Omri," is the standing Assyrian designation of the Northern Kingdom (see pp. 96, 98, 101). The mistake of the Assyrian scribe in calling Jehu Omri's son is thus readily explained.

Jehu is mentioned again in another inscription of Shalmaneser's, in which he writes :—

⁴⁰ In the eighteenth year of my reign (= 842 B.C.) I crossed the Euphrates the sixteenth time. ⁴¹ Hazael of Damascus ⁴² trusted in the multitude of his troops, assembled his hosts in numbers, ⁴⁵ and made Mount Sanir,* the summit of the mountains, ⁴⁶ which are opposite the mountain of Lebanon, his fortress. ⁴⁷ With him I contended, ⁴⁸ I effected his overthrow ; 16,000 of his warriors I slew with weapons, 1,121 of his chariots, 470 of his horsemen, together with his stores, ⁵² I took from him ; to save ⁵³ his life, he betook himself off. I pursued after him. ⁵⁴ In Damascus, his royal city, I besieged him ; ⁵⁵ his plantations I cut down. To the mountains ⁵⁶ of Haurân I marched, cities ⁵⁷ without number I destroyed, I laid waste, I burnt with fire ; their prisoners ⁵⁹ without number I carried away. . . . At that time ⁶³ I received the tribute of the Tyrians, of the Sidonians, and of *Jehu*, ⁶⁴ *the son of Omri*.

The mention of Hazael as ruling in Damascus twelve years after Dad'idri (p. 93) agrees with the Biblical statement that Ben-hadad was smothered to death by his general Hazael, who then succeeded him on the throne (2 Kings viii. 15). The tribute rendered by Jehu to the

* The *Senir*, which according to Deut. iii. 9 was the Amorite name of Hermon.

Assyrians is not alluded to in the Old Testament. It may be conjectured that, as in the case of the Phoenician cities mentioned, it was offered partly with the view of conciliating the Assyrians, whose advances in the West were now becoming yearly more alarming, and partly in the hope of securing their help against the Syrians, who, though disabled for the time, might nevertheless be expected to take the first opportunity of injuring the Israelites, and encroaching upon their territory (cf. 2 Kings x. 32 f.).

About half a century later, we again read of Israel being tributary to the Assyrians. Rammân-nirâri III. (812–783 B.C.), after enumerating other countries subjugated by him, writes :—

[11] From the Euphrates to the land Ḥatti (the Hittites),[a] the West country in its entire compass, [12] (namely) Tyre, Zidon, *the land Omri*, Edom, Philistia, [13] as far as the great sea [b] of the sun-setting, I subjected to my yoke; [14] payment of tribute I imposed upon them. Against [15] Syria of Damascus I marched; Mari, the king of Syria, [16] in Damascus, his royal city, I besieged. [17] The terror of the majesty of Asshur, his lord, cast him to the ground, my feet he embraced, [18] allegiance he offered, 2,300 talents of silver, 20 talents of gold, [19] 3,000 talents of copper, 5,000 talents of iron, variegated garments, clothing, [20] a couch of ivory,[c] a bed (or litter) inlaid with ivory, his possessions, his belongings [21] without number, at Damascus, his royal city, in the midst of his palace, I received.

The reign of Rammân-nirâri synchronized with the reign of Jehoash (*c.* 802–786) and the early part of the reign of Jeroboam II. in Israel (*c.* 786–746); and the facts mentioned in this inscription enable us to understand the successes gained by these two kings against Damascus (2 Kings xiii. 14–9, 25, xiv. 28): the Syrians were at the time weakened by the victories of Rammân-nirâri.

We pass to the second half of the same century,—a period when the relations between Assyria and Israel become

---

[a] The expression is used in the wider sense explained above, p. 84.
[b] The Mediterranean Sea: cf. Josh i. 4, ix. 1, etc.
[c] Cf. Amos vi. 4.

closer, and are fraught with grave consequences for both the Northern and the Southern Kingdoms. The allusions in the Book of Hosea (c. 746-736) make it evident that at this time the Northern Kingdom was a prey to opposing factions which sought to strengthen themselves by invoking the aid of Assyria and Egypt respectively: the prophet foresaw the consequences which would ultimately ensue; but his warnings were in vain.[1] Shallum had assassinated Zechariah, son of Jeroboam II., after a brief reign of six months; and a month later Shallum himself was assassinated by Menahem. Menahem, to secure his throne, gave Pul, king of Assyria, a thousand talents of silver, which he exacted of the wealthy men of his kingdom. For long, no Assyrian king bearing the name of Pul was known; but Schrader had argued with great cogency that the king meant must really be Tiglath-pileser (2 Kings xv. 29, etc.), who reigned 745-727 B.C.; and two documents, published by Mr. Pinches in 1884, *viz.* a second dynastic list similar to the one mentioned above (p. 29), and an inscription usually known as the "Babylonian Chronicle," have made Schrader's conclusion a certainty. The dynastic list, namely, mentions as reigning in Babylon at this time, *Ukinzir* (three years), and *Pulu* (two years); while the Chronicle says:—

[19] In the third year ot Ukinzir Tiglath-pileser marched [20] against Akkad, [21] laid waste Bit-Amûkani, and took Ukinzir captive. [22] Ukinzir reigned three years in Babylon.
[23] Tiglath-pileser ascended the throne in Babylon.
[24] In the second year of Tiglath-pileser, he died in the month of Tebet.

The identity of Pulu with Tiglath-pileser follows at once from these parallel statements. It has been conjectured that Pulu was not the rightful heir to the crown, but a usurper, whose personal name was Pulu, but who as king of Assyria assumed the name of one of his predecessors, the great conqueror Tiglath-pileser I. (*c.* 1100 B.C.). It

[1] Hosea v. 13, vii. 11, viii. 9 f., x. 4-6, xii. 1.

is in harmony with the statement of the Book of Kings respecting the tribute paid by Menahem to Pul, that in an inscription relating to 738 B.C. Tiglath-pileser mentions "Menahem of Samaria" among other tributary princes of Western Asia.

Uzziah, or, as he is called in 2 Kings, Azariah, was on the throne of Judah at this time; and Tiglath-pileser mentions him, probably about 740 B.C. :—

> Nineteen districts [31] of the city of Hamath, together with the towns round about them, which are by the sea of the sun-setting, which in their faithlessness had made revolt to *Azriyâu* (Azariah), [32] to the territory of Assyria I annexed: my officers as prefects I appointed over them.

Hamath was an important town, about 150 miles north of Palestine, often mentioned both in the Old Testament and in the Assyrian inscriptions. Uzziah, it seems, had formed an alliance with its king, in the hope, it may be conjectured, of offering effectual resistance to the advances of the Assyrians. Tiglath-pileser describes, with sufficient plainness, the fate of Hamath: Uzziah was fortunate in escaping the punishment meted out to his ally.

The age was one in which almost every year the Assyrian kings were organizing expeditions in the direction of Syria or Palestine. In 734 Tiglath-pileser advanced as far as Gaza, on the south-western border of Canaan. He writes (the inscription is in parts mutilated):—

> ". . . . the city of Gal-[ed ?] . . . . [A]bel- [Beth-Maacah ?] which was above the land of the House of Omri . . . . . the broad, in its whole extent to the territory of Assyria I annexed; my [officers] as prefects I appointed over it. Hanno of Gaza, who fled before my arms, to the land of Egypt escaped. Gaza [I captured]; his possessions, his gods, I carried away, and my royal effigy I erected." "The land of the House of Omri, ... the whole of its inhabitants, together with their possessions, to Assyria I deported. *Pekah, their king, I slew. Hoshea [to rule] over them I appointed.* Ten [talents of gold, 1,000 talents of silver, together with . . . .]. I received from them."

Though there must be some exaggeration in the statement that "the whole" of the inhabitants of the "land of the House of Omri" were deported to Assyria, the rest of this notice is in evident agreement with 2 Kings xv. 29, 30: "In the days of Pekah, king of Israel, came Tiglath-pileser, king of Assyria, and took Ijon, and Abel-beth-maacah, and Janoah, and Kedesh, and Hazor, and Gilead, and Galilee, all the land of Naphtali"—all places or districts in the north or north-east of Israel—" and carried their [inhabitants] into exile to Assyria. And Hoshea, the son of Elah, made a conspiracy against Pekah, the son of Remaliah, and slew him, and reigned in his stead." The inscription mentions, however, a point not stated in the Old Testament—*viz.* that the conspiracy in Samaria, which cost Pekah his throne and life, was carried through with the aid of the Assyrians, and that Hoshea's elevation to the throne was due to his recognition of Assyrian supremacy. Pekah, it will be remembered, had been in alliance with Rezin, king of Damascus, and had with him invaded Judah,—with the object, it is commonly supposed, of forcing Ahaz to take part with them in a coalition against Assyria,—on an occasion which has been rendered famous by a celebrated prophecy of Isaiah's (2 Kings xv. 37, xvi. 5; Isa. vii. 1-16). Ahaz, however, was Assyrian in his sympathies, and invoked the assistance of Tiglath-pileser —of course at the cost of his independence—to rid him of his invaders (2 Kings xvi. 7, 8). Tiglath-pileser accepted the terms offered by Ahaz: he invaded the territory of Damascus and Israel in the rear, thereby necessitating the withdrawal of the allied forces from Judah: he also, as the inscription just quoted shews, carried into exile the inhabitants of a large part of Northern Israel, and slew Pekah. In the following two years, 733 and 732, he also led expeditions against Damascus. The inscription describing these expeditions is, unhappily, mutilated; but it speaks plainly of severe losses sustained by the country; and there is no reason to doubt that the final result is correctly described in 2 Kings xvi. 9: "And the king of Assyria hearkened unto him: and the king of Assyria went up against Damascus, and took it, and carried it (*i.e.* its people) into exile to Kir, and slew Rezin."[1] Both Judah and many neighbouring peoples were now tributaries of Assyria: an inscription of Tiglath-pileser's last year but one (728 B.C.) speaks of him as receiving tribute, not only from various countries on the north of Palestine (as Gebal and Hamath), but also from "Sanibu of Ammon, Salaman of Moab, Mitinti of Ashkelon, *Jauḥazi* (i.e. *Joaḥaz*, the fuller form of *Aḥaz*) *of Judah*, Ḳaushmelek of Edom, and Hanno of Gaza."

Tiglath-pileser was succeeded in 727 by Shalmaneser IV. who reigned till 722. Hardly any Assyrian records of this short reign have come down to us; and the Eponym-list, which usually notes briefly the expeditions of each year, is here provokingly mutilated, the word "to" under Shalmaneser's third, fourth, and fifth years being preserved, but the name of the country following being lost. From 2 Kings xvii. 3-5 we learn that Hoshea did not long remain loyal to the power which had given him his throne: relying upon the help of So, king of Egypt, he revolted: Shalmaneser came up against him, and besieged Samaria for three years (724-722 B.C.). So—or rather, as the Hebrew consonants might also be vocalized, *Sevè*—is, no doubt, Shabaka, the Sabako of Herodotus, an Ethiopian, the founder of the twenty-fifth (Ethiopian) dynasty. It is doubtful, however, whether he was at this time on the throne: in 720 a Sib'u (who seems to be the same person) is mentioned as being in alliance with Hanno of Gaza, and as being defeated by Sargon at Raphiaḥ on

---

[1] The approaching fall of Damascus is more than once foretold by Isaiah: see Isa. vii. 16, viii. 4, xvii. 1-3. Isa. ix. 1 alludes to the districts of Northern Israel which had been stripped of their inhabitants by Tiglath-pileser.

the border of Egypt; but he is called "turtan" (general) of Egypt, and is distinguished from the Pharaoh.[1] It is probable, therefore, that Sevè, though he held in 725-724 a position of some influence in Egypt, is called "king" incorrectly, by anticipation.

There follows a king, who, though mentioned but once in the Old Testament (Isa. xx. 1), had a long and eventful reign, and whom his numerous inscriptions shew to have been a brilliant and successful ruler. Sargon reigned for seventeen years (722-705). The Book of Kings speaks as though the "king of Assyria" who took Samaria was the same "king of Assyria" who had besieged it (2 Kings xvii. 6; cf. vv. 3, 4, 5); but that was not the case: the capture of the important stronghold which Omri had fortified was one of the first triumphs of Sargon's reign. He describes it himself:—

> The city of Samaria I besieged, I took; 27,290 of its inhabitants I carried into captivity; fifty of their chariots I seized: the rest of them I allowed to retain their possessions; my officers I appointed over them; the tribute of the former king I laid upon them.

And in a parallel text he adds:—

> I settled there the men of countries conquered [by my hand].

These statements agree with 2 Kings xvii. 6, 24, according to which Israel was carried away captive to Assyria, and people from Babylon, Cuthah, Avva, Hamath, and Sepharvaim were brought and settled in the cities of Samaria in place of the deported Israelites. The deportation of people to the "land of the House of Omri," or to Samaria, is mentioned also in two other passages of Sargon's inscriptions, though the places from which they are said

---

[1] This is the general view of the passage quoted; but Winckler has argued recently that "Muzuri" in the Assyrian text does not here mean Egypt, and that the reference is to Pir'u, the king of a country Muzuri in North-west Arabia.

to have been brought¹ are not those named in the Book of Kings. In *v.* 6 Ḥabor is the Khabour, a tributary flowing into the Euphrates, in the upper part of its course, from the north, and probably the river which formed the eastern boundary of "Mesopotamia" (above, p. 37): the Assyrian kings sometimes speak of crossing it on their expeditions from Nineveh to the West. Gozan is mentioned as the name of a city and land in the same neighbourhood. In *v.* 24 Cuthah is the ancient Kutu,— now, as bricks and tablets discovered on the spot shew, Tel Ibrahim, about twenty miles north-east of Babylon: in connexion with the notice in *v.* 30 that "the men of Cuthah made Nergal" to worship, it is interesting to find that Nergal, the lord of the under-world, was actually the patron-god of Kutu.² Sepharvaim (*v.* 24)—the termination is the Hebrew dual—are the two Sippars, Sippar of Shamash (the sun-god), and Sippar of Anunitum, situated on the opposite banks of a canal, flowing into the Euphrates, about twenty-five miles north of Babylon,—the former now called Abu-Habba. The celebrated temple of the Sun at the first-named Sippar was excavated by Hormuzd Rassam. Nabo-na'id, the last king of Babylon (555– 538 B.C.), describes how he restored "I-barra, the temple of Shamash of Sippar, and I-ulbar, the temple of Anunitum of Sippar."

Sargon's inscriptions enable us to form a vivid picture of the principal events of his reign, especially of his military achievements. In the neighbourhood of Judah his most troublesome enemies were the Philistines. Already, as we have seen, in 720, he had been obliged to quell a revolt in Gaza. Eight or nine years afterwards Ashdod rebelled·

---

[1] "Men of Tamud, Ibádid, Marsiman, Khayápá [above, p. 46], Arabian tribes inhabiting the desert," who, Sargon says, had never brought tribute to the kings, his fathers, but whom he had subdued.

[2] Cf. p. 36. On the other divinities mentioned in 2 Kings xvii. 30, 31 no certain light has at present been thrown by the inscriptions.

Azuri, its king, refused his accustomed tribute, and "sent to the princes of his neighbourhood invitations to revolt from Assyria." Another inscription tells us who his allies were:—

> The people of Philistia, *Judah*, Edom, and Moab, dwelling beside the sea, bringing tribute and presents to Asshur my lord, were speaking treason. The people and their evil chiefs, to fight against me, to Pharaoh, king of Egypt, *a prince who could not save them*, their presents carried, and besought his alliance.[1]

Egypt was at this time the evil genius of the peoples of Palestine; it encouraged them to revolt with promises of help, and then failed them when the hour of need arrived: Israel, the Philistines, and (as we shall see) Judah, all in turn paid the penalty of relying upon the same "broken reed." Sargon first removed Azuri, and appointed his brother Achimit as governor, hoping that he might succeed in securing Assyrian interests in Ashdod. But it was of no avail: the revolt broke out again, and Achimit was deposed. Sargon had consequently to resort to stronger measures; and the result was the siege of Ashdod alluded to in Isa. xx. 1. As Isaiah foresaw (*vv.* 4–6), the hopes of effectual assistance from Egypt were doomed to disappointment, the Philistine city capitulated, and the inhabitants were carried into captivity. Whether Judah suffered in any way for its complicity with Ashdod on this occasion we do not know: there is a passage at the beginning of one of his inscriptions[2] in which, amongst a number of other titles, Sargon styles himself "subjecter of the land of Judah, whose situation is remote": but this need not mean more than that he exacted tribute of it;[3] and Judah already paid tribute to Assyria, as the inscription just quoted shews, at the time of Ashdod's rebellion. No

---

[1] G. Smith, *Ass. Discoveries*, p. 291; Winckler, *Sargon-texte*, p. 189.
[2] *K. B.*, ii. 37; Winckler, *Sargon-texte*, p. 169.
[3] The expression "subjected to my yoke" is used in this sense in the inscription of Rammân-nirâri, cited above, p. 96.

invasion of Judah by Sargon is mentioned either in the Bible, or in any of the texts which describe continuously the events of Sargon's reign.[1]

Sargon was succeeded by Sennacherib (705–681 B.C.). The Biblical narrative of his invasion of Judah, and of the manner in which, against hope, Jerusalem escaped destruction, is well known (2 Kings xviii. 13—xix. = Isa. xxxvi., xxxvii.). The British Museum possesses in duplicate, on the Taylor Cylinder,—an hexagonal clay prism found by Colonel Taylor at Nineveh in 1830,—and in the inscription upon one of the colossal bulls brought by Mr. Layard from Kouyunjik, Sennacherib's own account of the stages of his campaign. The two important historical facts which are brought out clearly by the inscription, though they would not be suspected from the Biblical narrative, are that Hezekiah's revolt from Assyria was part of a preconcerted plan of rebellion, in which many of the cities of Phoenicia and Philistia took part, and that Sennacherib's invasion of Judah was but an episode in a campaign undertaken by him for the purpose of suppressing this general scheme of revolt. Nearly ten years had elapsed since (711 B.C.) the arms of Assyria had been seen in Western Asia; the young king, Sennacherib, was occupied with undertakings in Babylon and the East: the moment seemed thus to his disaffected subjects in Phoenicia and Palestine a favourable one for relieving themselves of the irksome duty of paying annual tribute, and for declaring their independence. In the north, the centre of revolt was Zidon; in the south, the Philistine cities of Ashkelon and Ekron. Egypt was ready with promises of aid; and the Egyptian party in Judah, which, as we learn from the pages of Isaiah, had been gradually gaining

---

[1] In his hypothesis that Jerusalem was besieged and taken by Sargon, Professor Sayce has not been followed by other Assyriologists.

strength there during recent years, at length succeeded in carrying the king with them, and in inducing him to raise the standard of revolt. But Sennacherib lost no time in taking measures to punish his rebellious subjects. He led his army first against the Phoenician cities, which were quickly reduced :—

11. [34] In my third campaign [701 B.C.] to the land Hatti (the Hittite land*) I went. [35] Lulii [Elulaeus], king of Zidon, the dread of the majesty [36] of my sovereignty overwhelmed him; and to a far-off spot [*in the parallel text:* from the midst of the West Country, to the land of Cyprus] [37] in the midst of the sea he fled; his land I reduced to obedience. [38] Great Zidon [Josh. xix. 28], Little Zidon, [39] Beth-Zitti, Zarephath [1 Kings xvii. 9], Machalib, [40] Ushu, Achzib [Judg. i. 31], Akko [*ibid.*], [41] his strong cities, the fortresses, the spots for pasture [42] and watering, the stations where his troops were quartered [43] (the terror of the arms of Asshur, my lord, had overwhelmed them) submitted themselves [44] to me. Tubalu [Ithobaal : cf. 1 Kings xvi. 31] I seated upon the royal throne [45] over them; and the payment of the tribute of my sovereignty, [46] every year without intermission, I laid upon him.

After this, Sennacherib received the homage of several neighbouring kings, of whom most, apparently, had not been implicated in the revolt :—

[47] Menahem of Samsimuruna, [48] Tubalu of Zidon, [49] Abdiliti or Arvad [Ezek. xxvii. 8], [50] Urumilki of Gebal [*ibid.*], [51] Mitinti of Ashdod, [52] Puduil of Ammon, [53] Chemoshnadab of Moab, [54] Malikram of Edom, [55] all the kings of Martu (the West Country), [56] rich presents and heavy tribute [57] brought before me, and kissed my feet.

Ten years before, in 711, Edom and Moab are described by Sargon as "speaking treason" in concert with Judah, and Ashdod was in Philistia the chief centre of revolt; now, their rulers come forward to court the favour of his successor. Sennacherib meanwhile had left Phoenicia, and arrived with his army in the country of the Philistines. In Ashkelon, he tells us, he deprived Zedek of his crown, which he bestowed upon Sarludâri, the son of a former king,—no doubt on the ground that he was friendly to Assyria: at the same time, he captured and plundered

* *I.e.* (see p. 84) Syria and Palestine in general.

four subject-cities belonging to Zedek, Beth-dagon (Josh. xv. 41), Joppa, Benê-barak (Josh. xix. 45), and Azuru. Next he proceeds to deal with Ekron. The Ekronites, in order to carry out their scheme of revolt, had deposed their king Padi, who remained loyal to Assyria, and sent him bound in chains to Jerusalem. Upon hearing of the approach of the Assyrians, they summoned the Egyptians to their aid, who arrived in large numbers, but were completely routed by Sennacherib at Altaku (probably the Eltekeh of Josh. xix. 44) :—

[69] The commanders, nobles, and people of Ekron, [70] who had thrown Padi their king, who had kept faith and oath [71] with Assyria, into fetters of iron, and delivered him with hostile intent to Hezekiah [72] of Judah, who imprisoned him in darkness,—[73] their heart trembled. The kings of Egypt, [74] the archers, the chariots, the horses of the kings of Miluḫḫi, [75] forces innumerable, they summoned together, and they came [76] to their aid. In front of Altaku [77] they drew up before me their battle array; they called forward [78] their troops. In reliance upon Asshur, my lord, [79] I fought with them, and accomplished their defeat . . . . . [82] . . . . . The cities of Altaku [53] and Tamna [Timnath, Josh. xv. 10] I besieged, I took, I carried off their spoil.

Sennacherib now soon reduces Ekron: he obtains, moreover, the surrender of Padi from Jerusalem, and restores him to his throne :—

III. [1] Then I drew near to the city of Ekron. The commanders, [2] the nobles, who had wrought rebellion, I slew : [3] on stakes round about the city I impaled their corpses. [4] Those inhabitants of the city who had practised misdoing and wrong [5] I counted as spoil; to the rest of them, [6] who had not been guilty of rebellion or of any other shameful thing, and had not practised the same crimes, [7] I proclaimed amnesty. Padi, [8] their king, from the midst of Jerusalem [9] I brought out; on the throne of his sovereignty over them, [10] I seated him; the tribute of my sovereignty [11] I laid upon him.

This is followed by the account of the measures taken by him against Judah and Jerusalem :—

And Hezekiah [12] of Judah, who had not submitted to my yoke, [13] forty-six of his strong cities, fortresses and smaller towns [14] of their border without number, [15] with assault of battering-rams, and approach of siege-engines, [16] with the attack of infantry, of mines . . . . [17] I besieged, I took. 200,150 people, small and great,

FIRST] SENNACHERIB'S INVASION OF JUDAH 107

male and female, [16] horses, mules, asses, camels, oxen, [19] and sheep without number, from the midst of them I brought out, and [20] I counted them as spoil. Himself, as a bird in a cage, in Jerusalem, [21] his royal city, I shut up. Siege-works against him I constructed, [22] and those coming out of the gate of his city [23] I turned back. His cities which I had plundered, from his domain [24] I cut off; and to Mitinti, king of Ashdod, [25] to Padi, king of Ekron, and to Zilbel, [26] king of Gaza, I gave them; I diminished his territory. [27] To the former payment of their yearly tribute, [28] the tribute of subjection to my sovereignty I added; [29] I laid it upon them. Himself, Hezekiah, [30] the terror of the splendour of my sovereignty overwhelmed: [31] the Arabians and his trusted soldiers, [32] whom, for the defence of Jerusalem, his royal city, [33] he had introduced, laid down their arms (?). [34] Together with 30 talents of gold, and 800 talents of silver, I caused precious stones, [35] brilliant . . . . -stones, great *uknu* stones, [36] couches of ivory, thrones of state, of elephant-skins and [37] ivory, *ushu* wood, *urkarinnu* wood, whatever there was, an abundant treasure, [38] also his daughters, the women of his palace, his male and [39] female . . . . . . (?), unto Nineveh, my royal city, [40] to be brought after me. For the payment of tribute, [41] and the rendering of homage, he sent his envoy.

Here the narrative of the inscription closes, the lines which follow relating to the campaign of the following year in Babylonia. The description, though there may be some exaggeration in detail, gives a sufficiently vivid picture of the desperate condition to which Judah and Jerusalem were reduced. Men must have needed all the encouragement which Isaiah, in anticipation,[1] or at the time,[2] could give. Sennacherib's narrative may be combined with that contained in the Book of Kings in more ways than one; but it is most probable that it corresponds with 2 Kings xviii. 13*b*–16 (which describes how Sennacherib took "all the fortified cities" of Judah, how Hezekiah sent to him at Lachish proposing terms of submission, and how he then imposed upon him a tribute of three hundred talents of silver and thirty talents of gold); and that the events recorded in 2 Kings xviii. 17—xix. 35 (the two missions of the Rabshakeh demanding of Hezekiah the surrender of Jerusalem, and the destruction which over-

---

[1] Isa. x. 16–34, xiv. 24–7, xvii. 12–14, xxix. 5–8, xxx. 30–3, xxxi. 8, 9.
[2] Isa. xxxiii., xxxvii. 6, 7, 22–32 (= 2 Kings xix. 6, 7, 21–31).

took Sennacherib's army) belong to a subsequent stage of the campaign, on which the Assyrian account is silent. Of Sennacherib's presence at Lachish, we have independent testimony in a bas-relief, now in the British Museum,[1] which represents the Assyrian king seated upon a throne, attended by his warriors in their chariots, and receiving the submission of a train of prostrate Jewish captives, with the inscription, "Sennacherib, king of multitudes, king of Assyria, seats himself upon a throne of state, and receives the spoil of the city of Lachish."[2]

In 2 Kings xx. 12 (= Isa. xxxix. 1) we read that Merodach-baladan,[3] king of Babylon, sent a congratulatory embassy to Hezekiah after his sickness. The inscriptions of Sargon and Sennacherib make frequent mention of this Merodach-baladan. He was a "Chaldaean": his home was a district called Bit-Yakin, at the head of the Persian Gulf: he is called accordingly "king of the sea," who "dwelt on the shore of the Bitter River" (the Assyrian name of what we call the Persian Gulf); and he was strenuous in his endeavours to make Babylonia independent of Assyria. He is first mentioned by Tiglath-pileser, as paying him homage in 731 B.C. Taking advantage, probably, of Shalmaneser's death (722 B.C.), he succeeded in establishing himself as king of Babylon, a position which, as we learn both from Sargon himself, and from one of the dynastic lists published by Mr. Pinches, he held for twelve years (721–710 B.C.). In his own inscription, now in the Berlin Museum, dating from this period, he is styled "king of Babylon,"

[1] See the illustration in Cheyne's *Isaiah* (in the "Polychrome Bible"), p. 48.

[2] For more detailed illustration of the light thrown by the Assyrian inscriptions upon Jewish history at this time, and especially upon the prophecies of Isaiah, the writer must refer to his volume on *Isaiah* in the "Men of the Bible" Series, esp. Part I., chaps. ii., iv., v., vi., vii.

[3] Properly Marduk-abal-iddin, *i.e.* "Marduk has given a son." Cf. Esarhaddon, *i.e.* Asshur-aḥ-iddin, "Asshur has given a brother."

exactly as in 2 Kings xx. 12.¹ During all these years, Sargon left him unmolested: but in the end he found himself obliged to organize two campaigns against him: in 710 he compelled him to evacuate Babylon, and entered it himself in triumph, in 709 he pursued him to Dur-Yakin, the stronghold of Bit-Yakin, whither he had retreated, and received there his submission. But he was not really conciliated; and Sennacherib had twice, in 703 and in 696, to expel him again from Babylon. It is probable that the embassy to Hezekiah, in spite of its being narrated after the invasion of Sennacherib, really took place about 712: its actual motive is generally considered to have been the political one of securing Hezekiah's friendship and alliance.

Sennacherib is said, in Isa. xxxviii. 12 (cf. 2 Kings xix. 37), to have been assassinated by Adrammelech and Sharezer his sons. For long, no parallel notice from Assyrian sources was known; but in the "Babylonian Chronicle" (above, p. 97), published by Mr. Pinches in 1884, we read as follows:—

> On the 20th day of Tebet [= December] Sennacherib, king of Assyria, was slain by his son in a revolt. For . . . . years Sennacherib had ruled the kingdom of Assyria. From the 20th day of Tebet to the 2nd day of Adar [= February] the revolt in Assyria continued. On the 18th day of Sivan [= May] his son, Esarhaddon, sat on the throne of Assyria, etc.

Only one son is mentioned here; but obviously another son might have assisted: so that there is no difficulty in harmonizing the two statements. There are indications that Esarhaddon, though he was not implicated in his father's murder, came to the throne amid domestic dissensions: in his inscriptions he speaks of himself as having been "selected" by Marduk (the patron god of Babylon) "out of the group of his elder brothers" to restore certain temples, and styles himself "the avenger

¹ *K. B.*, iii. 1, 185 ff.; cf. ii. 69, 277, 287.

of his father that begat him."¹ The names of the two parricides have not at present been found on the monuments. According to 2 Kings xx. 12, they took refuge in the land of Ararat (= Armenia). Esarhaddon, in an inscription describing the defeat of certain (unnamed) foes at the beginning of his reign, says that after Ishtar, the goddess of battle, had broken their ranks, the cry arose from their midst, "This is our king." The inference is not an unreasonable one that these foes were acting in concert with his parricide brothers.

Esarhaddon reigned from 681 to 668. One of the most important events of his reign was his conquest of Egypt (which both Sargon and Sennacherib had failed to accomplish), and his reduction of it to the state of an Assyrian province (670 B.C.). Esarhaddon's policy was to allow the native Egyptian princes to rule as vassals of Assyria. Here is the Assyrian ruler's own account of his conquest, from a triumphal stelè discovered in 1888 by the expedition organized by the German "Orient-Comité" at Zinjirli, about seventy miles north-north-west of Aleppo :—

Tarḳu ³⁹ king of Egypt and Kush (Ethiopia) from Isḥupri ⁴⁰ to Memphis, his royal city, a march of fifteen days,—I smote daily ⁴¹ in countless numbers his warriors. Himself I attacked five times with the point of the spear ⁴² in deadly combat. Memphis, his royal city, I besieged for half a day ; I took it, I laid it waste, ⁴³ I burnt it with fire. His children and possessions I carried away to Assyria. The roots of Kush ⁴⁴ I tore up out of Egypt. ⁴⁵ Over the whole of Egypt I placed afresh kings, governors, prefects, officers, overseers, ⁴⁶ regents. The tribute of my sovereignty, (to be paid) yearly without fail, ⁵⁰ I imposed upon them.²

This inscription is engraved upon a huge monolith, on which is also sculptured a colossal figure of Esarhaddon :

¹ In the inscription from Zinjirli, quoted below, line 25.
² Slightly abbreviated from the translation in the *Mittheilungen aus den Orientalischen Sammlungen* (Berlin, 1893), p. 41.

before him kneel the diminutive figures of two captive princes, each with a ring passed through his lip (cf. Isa. xxxvii. 29), from which passes a cord, the other end of which is coiled firmly round Esarhaddon's fingers.[1] One of these princes, it is clear from the dress and features, is intended to represent the Tarḳu of the inscription. This Tarḳu can be none but the Tirhaḳah of 2 Kings xix. 9, whose approach aroused the alarm of Sennacherib: he was the third ruler of the Ethiopian dynasty, which (above, p. 100) was founded by Shabaka (Sabako). It seems to follow, from Egyptian *data*, that he could not really have been on the throne as early as 701 B.C.: there is probably, therefore, an inaccuracy, similar to that which was noticed (p. 100) in the case of So, in his being described in 2 Kings xix. 9 as "king of Kush" (Ethiopia). Esarhaddon, in view of this conquest, styles himself elsewhere "king of the kings of Egypt, Paturis,[2] and Kush."

Another interesting fact from the same reign deserves mention. Esarhaddon tells us that, being about to build a new palace, he summoned before him "twenty-two kings of the land Ḥatti (the Hittite land), who dwelt by the sea and in the midst of the sea," and commanded them to furnish him with materials for the purpose. In a parallel inscription he gives us the names of these kings; *viz.*:—

1 Baal king of Tyre, 2 *Manasseh king of Judah*, 3 Ḳaushgabri king of Edom, 4 Muṣuri king of Moab, 5 Zilbel king of Gaza, 6 Mitinti king of Ashkelon, 7 Ikasamsu (?) king of Ekron, 8 Milkiasaph king of Gebal (Byblus), 9 Matanbaal king of Arvad, 10 Abibaal king of Samsimuruna, 11 Puduil king of the Ammonites, 12 Aḥimelech king of Ashdod— twelve kings of the sea-coast; 13 Ikishtura king of Idalion, 14 Pilâgura king of Kitrus, 15 Ki[su] king of Sillûa, 16 Itûandar king of Paphos, 17 Irisu king of Sillû (?), 18 Damasu king of Curium, 19 Rumisu king

---

[1] See Ball, *Light from the East*, p. 198.

[2] The Pathros of the Old Testament (Isa. xi. 11, Ezek. xxx. 14 *al.*: cf. the *Pathrusim*, or Pathrosites, of Gen. x. 14); Egypt. *pe-to-ris*, "the land of the South," *i.e.* Upper Egypt. See *K. B.*, ii. 151.

of Tamassus, 20 Damûsi king of Ḳartiḥadasht, 21 Unasagusu king of Lidir, 22 Puṣusu king of Nuri (?)—ten kings of Yatnana (Cyprus) in the midst of the sea.

The places mentioned are all, it will be noticed, in or near Palestine, or in Cyprus. That Manasseh was tributary to Assyria, we should not have gathered from the Book of Kings; but Asshurbanipal, Esarhaddon's successor, includes him in a very similar list; and it is possible that the subject condition of Judah under the last-named king is alluded to in a passage of the prophet Nahum (i. 13, 15), who wrote, probably, shortly after Asshurbanipal's death.

Esarhaddon was followed by Asshurbanipal (668–626), one of the most illustrious of the Assyrian kings, distinguished alike for his military achievements and for his love of letters. To the library which he founded, and for which he caused copies to be made of many older texts, modern scholarship is indebted for some of the most valuable monuments of old Babylonian literature which it possesses. Asshurbanipal is not mentioned in the Old Testament under this name; but it is very probable that he is the king referred to in Ezra iv. 10, where it is said that the "great and noble *Osnappar*" brought Babylonians, Susanians, Elamites, and men of other nationalities, and settled them in Samaria: Asshurbanipal is known from his inscriptions to have invaded Elam more than once, and taken its capital, Susa,[1] and also to have transported some of the inhabitants of Elam to different parts of the Assyrian empire.[2] An achievement of Asshurbanipal's, however, gives the point to a famous passage of Nahum's prophecies,

---

[1] *K. B.*, ii. 181-3, 195-9, 201-15,—all spirited descriptions, but too long to quote. He "coloured the waters of the Ulai (Dan. viii. 2, 16: the Eulaeus), like wool," with the blood of the inhabitants of Susa (p. 183).

[2] *K. B.*, ii. 209, 211. The names of the localities to which they were transferred are not, however, stated

in which the prophet ironically asks Nineveh whether she will fare better than " No of Amon, that was seated among the Nile-canals, that had the waters round about her, whose rampart was the sea, and her wall the waters," which had armed defenders innumerable, and which nevertheless encountered a cruel fate, and was led away into a dishonourable captivity. No, " the city," is a name of Thebes, the brilliant capital of the eighteenth, nineteenth, and twentieth dynasties, and Amon (or Amen) was its supreme god, in honour of whom the majestic temples which still remain were erected. The allusion is to the conquest of Thebes by Asshurbanipal, which took place probably in 663 B.C. Asshurbanipal's narrative is graphic :—

> Tarḳu, king of Egypt and Kush, whom Esarhaddon my father had defeated, forgot the might of Asshur, and Ishtar, and the great gods, my lords; and trusting in his own strength, advanced against the kings, the praefects whom my father had appointed, and took up his abode in Memphis, a city which my father had conquered. A messenger came to Nineveh, to report what had occurred. My heart was enraged, and my liver stirred up. I prayed to Asshur and Ishtar, set my troops in motion, and advanced towards Egypt. As my army was on its way, twenty-two kings [1] of the sea-coast, and of the midst of the sea, came to meet me, and kissed my feet. Afterwards, with their forces and their ships, they accompanied me on my way. Tarḳu heard in Memphis of my approach, and sent forth his troops to meet me. In the strength of Asshur, Bel, and Nebo, the great gods, I dispersed them far and wide. Tarḳu heard in Memphis of the defeat of his forces ; the terrible majesty of Asshur and Ishtar overwhelmed him : he fled by ship to Ni'i (No ; Thebes). This city I took, and marched my troops into it. The kings, governors, and praefects, whom my father had appointed (a list of twenty given), but who had been obliged to abandon their posts on account of Tarḳu, I reinstated in their places. Egypt and Kush, which my father had conquered, I again took possession of, and returned to Nineveh with much spoil.[2]

The kings, however, before long revolted, and made common cause with Tarḳu. But Tarḳu soon died, and was succeeded by Urd-amani (Rud-Amôn). Asshurbanipal again marched to Egypt to suppress the revolt. Urd-amani,

---

[1] See their names in *K. B.*, ii. 239, 241. With two exceptions they are identical with the twenty-two named by Esarhaddon (above, p. 111).
[2] Abridged from *K. B.*, ii. 159, 161, 163 ; 239 (a parallel text).

being obliged to evacuate Memphis, retreated to No, whither the Assyrian king pursued him:—

[36] He saw the approach of my mighty battle, abandoned Ni'i (No), [37] and fled to Kipkip. This city (No) in its entire compass, [38] in reliance upon Asshur and Ishtar, my hands conquered. [39] Silver, gold, precious stones, the treasure of his palace, the whole that was there, [40] richly woven garments, fine horses, men and women, [41] two lofty obelisks, weighing 2,500 talents, which stood before the gate of the temple, [42] I removed from their place, and brought them to Assyria. [44] Abundant spoil, without number, I carried away out of No. [45] Over Egypt and Kush [46] I let my weapons gleam, and I established my might. [47] With full hand I returned in safety [48] to Nineveh, the city of my sovereignty!

This, rather than what seems to have been Asshur-banipal's more peaceful entry on his first campaign, is the capture and sack of No, to which Nahum alludes.

In 2 Chron. xxxiii. 11–13, it is said that Jehovah "brought upon Judah the captains of the host of the king of Assyria, which took Manasseh with hooks, and bound him in fetters, and carried him to Babylon": in consequence, it is added, of his humiliation and penitence, he was released, and restored to his kingdom. It is remarkable that such a momentous event in the history of Manasseh, if it actually took place, should be unnoticed in the earlier and nearly contemporaneous narrative of the Kings: not only, however, is Manasseh's captivity not mentioned there, but his character is depicted, both by the compiler of the Book of Kings and by the prophet Jeremiah, as destitute of a single redeeming feature.[1] The Chronicles (speaking generally) consists partly of narratives excerpted, often with hardly any alteration, from the earlier books of the Old Testament, especially the books of Samuel and Kings, and partly of narratives written by the compiler himself, to which there is no parallel in the earlier books: and an independent study of the narratives of the latter class shews that they are strongly coloured by the religious feelings of the age (the third century B.C.) in which the

---

[1] 2 Kings xxi. 1–18; cf. xxiii. 26, xxiv. 3-4, Jer. xv. 4.

author lived, and that they are, to use a Jewish expression, examples of "Haggadah," or edifying religious narrative, rather than history proper, in our sense of the term.[1] The passage relating to Manasseh belongs to the last-named class: and his captivity and repentance have accordingly been held by many scholars to be unhistorical. The inscriptions do not decide the question. They shew that what is said to have happened to Manasseh is, in the abstract, possible: they do not shew that it actually occurred. We know from them, namely, (1) that, as was stated above, Manasseh paid tribute to both Esarhaddon and Asshurbanipal. We know (2) that in the reign of Asshurbanipal, about 648–647 B.C., his "false brother" Shamash-shum-ukin (whom, "in order that the strong might not harm the weak," he had made "king" of Babylon) organized an insurrection in Babylon, and the neighbouring cities of Sippar, Borsippa, and Kutha, and moreover persuaded the inhabitants of various countries, including "the kings of the West land" (*i.e.* Phoenicia, Palestine, Cyprus, etc.), to revolt from Assyria: the kings implicated are not mentioned by name, but it is reasonably probable that Manasseh was one of them. We do not, however, know what punishment, if any, Asshurbanipal inflicted upon the rebellious kings: all that he says in his inscription is that, the revolt in Babylon and its neighbourhood having been put down, the peoples which had been in league with Shamash-shum-ukin were again made subject to Assyria, governors being placed over them, and yearly tribute imposed.[2]

[1] See the writer's *Introduction to the Literature of the Old Testament*, ed. 6, pp. 526, 529, 532–4; also Sayce, *Monuments*, pp. 464 f., 467.
[2] *K. B.*, ii. 183 ff. (cf. 259–61), 195; *KAT.*³, pp. 369 f. Nothing, it is to be observed, is said in these passages respecting the treatment meted out to the *kings*. It is, of course, a *possibility* that they were brought to Asshurbanipal in Babylon; but the passage cited by Sayce, *Monuments*, pp. 459 f. (= *K. B.*, ii. 193, 195), is no proof of it; and the non-mention of the fact in a somewhat circumstantial narrative is rather ground for supposing that it did not take place.

There is, however, a curious parallel to what the Chronicler states to have happened to Manasseh. The subject kings of Egypt who, as mentioned above (p. 113), had revolted and joined Tarḳu, were bound "hand and foot in iron bonds and iron chains," and brought to Nineveh: one, Necho, king of Memphis and Sais, was, for some reason not stated, treated by Asshurbanipal with special clemency, and allowed to live: he was clothed in costly apparel, sent back to Egypt amid signal marks of the royal favour, and reinstated in his former position.[1] What happened to an Egyptian prince, *might*, of course, have happened to a prince of Judah. There is, however, no monumental evidence that it *did* happen; and the Chronicler remains still our sole positive authority for the captivity of Manasseh. The monuments shew that the statement is not, in the abstract, incredible: they do not neutralize the suspicions which arise from the non-mention of the fact in the Kings, and from its being associated in the Chronicles with the account of Manasseh's repentance, which, conflicting as it does directly with the testimony of both Jeremiah and the compiler of Kings, must certainly be exaggerated, even if it have any basis in fact at all.

No monumental notices of the events which led to the close of the kingdom of Judah have as yet been found. We possess many inscriptions of Nebuchadnezzar; but they relate almost entirely to his buildings (which were very extensive), and to the honours paid by him to his gods. There exist, however, inscriptions shewing (what had previously been doubted) that Nebuchadnezzar invaded Egypt, thereby fulfilling, at least in their general sense,—for we do not know whether the fulfilment extended to details,— the predictions of Jeremiah (xliii. 9-13, xliv. 30), uttered shortly after 586, and of Ezekiel (xxix. 19 f.; cf. *vv.* 8-12),

[1] *K. B.*, ii. 165, 167.

uttered in 570. In the Louvre there is a statue from Elephantine, representing Nes-Hor, governor of Southern Egypt under Pharaoh Hophra (Apries: 589-564 B.C.), the inscription on which seems to state that an army of Asiatics and Northern peoples, which had apparently invaded Egypt, intended to advance up the valley of the Nile into Ethiopia; but that this disaster to the district under his command had been averted by the favour of the gods. And a fragmentary (cuneiform) inscription of Nebuchadnezzar himself, now in the British Museum, states that he invaded Egypt in his thirty-seventh year (= 568 B.C.), defeated the king of Egypt, [Ama]-a(?)-su,—*i.e.* as can hardly be doubted, Amasis (570-526 B.C.),—and slaughtered, or carried away, soldiers and horses. It may be doubtful whether, as Wiedemann first thought, these inscriptions refer to two distinct occasions, or whether, as he afterwards thought, they refer to one and the same: it is at least clear that Nebuchadnezzar invaded Egypt.[1] Tell Defneh, on the north-eastern border of Egypt, is the ancient Taḥpanḥes: and it is highly probable that the large oblong platform of brickwork, close to the palace-fort built at this spot by Psammetichus I., c. 664 B.C., and now called *Kasr Bint el-Yehudi*, "the castle of the Jew's daughter," which was excavated by Professor Petrie in 1886, is identical with "the quadrangle which is at the entry of Pharaoh's house in Taḥpanḥes," in which Jeremiah was commanded to bury the stones, as a token that Nebuchadnezzar would spread his pavilion over them, when he led his army into Egypt.[2] It is further stated that there have been found in the same neighbourhood, though the exact spot is uncertain, three clay cylinders, bearing short inscriptions of Nebuchadnezzar, as though they had been dropped there at the time of his invasion.[3]

[1] Cf. Wiedemann, *Aeg. Zeitschr.*, 1878, pp. 2-6, 87-9, and *Gesch. Aegyptens von Psammetich I. bis auf Alexander* (1880), pp. 167-70.
[2] See Petrie's *Tanis*, Part II. (1888), pp. 47 ff., 50 f., 52 ff., 57 f., with Plate XLIV. [3] Sayce, *Academy*, xxv. (1884), p. 51; Petrie, *l.c.*, p. 51.

We must not leave the Books of Kings without pointing out the corrections in the chronology which have been necessitated by the Assyrian inscriptions. The methods of chronological computation adopted by the Assyrians were particularly exact: every year a special officer ("limu") was appointed, who held office for that year, and gave his name to the year (something in the manner of the "Eponymous Archon" at Athens); and "Canons," or lists, of these Eponymous officers have been discovered extending from 902 to 667 B.C. The accuracy of these canons can in many cases be checked by the information which we possess independently of the reigns of many of the kings, as of Tiglath-pileser, Sargon, and Sennacherib.[1] Thus, from 902 B.C., the Assyrian chronology is certain and precise. Reducing now the Assyrian dates to years B.C., and comparing them with the Biblical chronology, some serious discrepancies at once reveal themselves, the nature and extent of which will be most clearly perceived by a brief tabular synopsis:—

	Dates according to Ussher's chronology.	Dates according to Assyrian inscriptions.
Reign of Ahab	918–897	
Ahab named at battle of Karkar		854
Reign of Jehu	884–856	
Tribute of Jehu		842
Reign of Menahem	772–761	
Menahem mentioned by Tiglath-pileser		738
Reign of Pekah	759–730	
Pekah dethroned by Tiglath-pileser		734[2]
Reign of Ahaz	742–726	
Ahaz mentioned by Tiglath-pileser		734[2]
Hezekiah's accession	726	
Fall of Samaria in Hezekiah's sixth year (2 Kings xviii. 10)	721	722
Invasion of Sennacherib in Hezekiah's fourteenth year (ibid. v. 13)	713	701

---

[1] See G. Smith, *The Assyrian Eponym Canon*, pp. 26 ff., 72 ff.
[2] According to other authorities 733 or 732.

Manifestly, all the Biblical dates earlier than 734 B.C. are too high, and must be considerably reduced: the two events also in Hezekiah's reign, the fall of Samaria and the invasion of Sennacherib, which the Biblical writer treats as separated by an interval of *eight* years, were separated in reality by an interval of *twenty-one* years. It does not fall within the scope of the present essay to consider the different systems by which it has been proposed to rectify the Biblical chronology, so as to bring it into agreement with the Assyrian *data*: it must suffice to point out the differences. The fact itself agrees with what has long been perceived by critics, *viz.* that the chronological system of the Books of Kings does not form part of the original documents preserved in them, but is the work of the compiler, and shews signs of having been arrived at through computation from the regnal years of the successive kings, the errors which it displays being due to the fact that either the *data* at the compiler's disposal, or his calculations, were in some cases incorrect.[1]

After the fall of Nineveh[2] in 607, Babylon became a second time the seat of empire in the East, and under Nebuchadnezzar rose to a height of splendour and magnificence which had never before been surpassed. The following synopsis of dates at this period may be useful:—

    Nebuchadnezzar 604–561
    Destruction of Jerusalem 588

---

[1] See further the writer's *Isaiah*, pp. 12–14, with the references. The chronology of the Kings is in itself inconsistent; for the period from the division of the Kingdom to the fall of Samaria, if reckoned by the regnal years of the kings of the Northern Kingdom, amounts to 241 years, whereas, if reckoned by the regnal years of the kings of the Southern Kingdom, it amounts to 260 years.

[2] The fall of Nineveh is not mentioned directly in the Old Testament, though it is foretold in Nahum, and Zeph. ii. 13–15. For a notice of the allusion to it in a recently discovered inscription of Nabo-na'id (555–538 B.C.), see below, p. 197.

Amil-Marduk[1]	561–559
Neriglissar (Nergal-shar-uzur)	559–555
Labasʰi-Marduk	555 (nine months)
Nabo-na'id	555–538
Capture of Babylon by Cyrus	538
Return of Jews under Zerubbabel	536

We possess inscriptions dating from the reigns of all these kings, and long ones, descriptive especially of buildings and the restoration of temples, from those of Nebuchadnezzar, Neriglissar, and Nabo-na'id. The prophets of the Exile allude to Babylon in terms which can frequently be illustrated from these inscriptions. One prophet, for instance, speaks of Babylon as "the glory of kingdoms, the beauty of the Chaldaeans' pride" (Isa. xiii. 19); another calls her "a golden cup in Jehovah's hand," and "abundant in treasures," and alludes to her as "dwelling upon many waters," and having "broad walls" and "high gates" (Jer. li. 7, 13, 58); her land is said to be a "land of graven images, and they are mad after idols" (l. 38): in the ode of triumph which Israel is represented as singing on the day when the king of Babylon falls, the "fir-trees" and "cedars of Lebanon" are said poetically to rejoice, and to say, "Since thou art laid down, no feller is to come up against us" (Isa. xiv. 8). The "India House Inscription" of Nebuchadnezzar[2] contains an eloquent description of the temples, walls, outworks, and palaces with which the great king beautified or strengthened his capital. It is too long to quote *in extenso*; but a few extracts may be cited :—

ii. 30 Silver, gold, precious stones, copper, *musukanna*-wood, cedar-wood, all kinds of valuables, a large abundance, the produce of mountains, 35 the fulness of seas, rich presents, splendid gifts, to my city of Babylon, into his (Marduk's) presence I brought .... 43 E-kua, the sanctuary of the lord of the gods, Marduk—I made the walls thereof

---

[1] "Man of Marduk,"—the "Evil-merodach" of 2 Kings xxv. 27, who shewed favour to the exiled king Jehoiachin.
[2] *KP.*², iii. 104-23; *K. B.*, iii. 2, pp. 11 ff.

glisten like suns; with red gold . . . with *uknu* and *gish-shir-gal* stones I overlaid ⁵⁰ the hall (?) of the temple . . ; ⁵¹ the gate of E-zida and E-sagil* I made brilliant as the sun.

ⁱⁱⁱ. ³¹ The choicest cedars, which from *Lebanon*,ᵇ the noble forest, I had brought, for the roofing of E-kua, the sanctuary of his dominion, I looked out: the inner side of the huge cedar-beams for the roofing of E-kua with shining gold I overlaid. . . . . ⁴³ The cedar of the roofing of the sanctuaries of Nebo with gold I overlaid. The cedar of the roofing of the gate of . . . . I overlaid with shining silver.

After describing the two walls of the city, with the moat between them, and the huge rampart, "mountain-high," which he constructed outside them, on the east, as a further defence, Nebuchadnezzar proceeds :—

ᵛⁱ. ³⁹ That foes with evil purpose the bounds of Babylon might not approach, great waters, like the volume of the sea, I carried round the land; and the crossing of these was like the crossing of the great sea, of the briny flood.

In the palace of Nabopolassar, which he restored—

ᵛⁱⁱⁱ. ¹⁰ Silver, gold, precious stones, everything that is prized, and is magnificent, substance, wealth, the insignia of majesty, I stored up within it: splendid *kurdu*, royal treasure, I gathered together therein.

The "ziggurats" of E-sagil and E-zida are repeatedly alluded to in Nebuchadnezzar's other inscriptions;ᶜ and "carer for E-sagil and E-zida" is one of his standing titles. The numerous other temples, in different places, which in the same inscriptions he describes himself as building or restoring, are sufficient testimony to the multitude of "graven images," of which the land of Babylon was full.

The second Isaiah, foretelling the fall of Babylon, writes (xlvi. 1), "Bel boweth down, Nebo stoopeth." The inscriptions shew at once why these two gods are named in

---

* The temples, respectively, of Nebo in Borsippa and of Marduk in Babylon. The *ziggurat* mentioned above (p. 31) as restored by Nebuchadnezzar belonged to the temple of E-zida.

ᵇ The Assyrian kings also speak frequently of obtaining timber from Lebanon,—a fact which gives point to the figure used in Isa. xxxvii. 24.

ᶜ *K. B.*, iii. 2, pp. 32–71.

particular. Bel ("lord") was a title of Marduk (Merodach), the supreme god of Babylon, given the first place by Nebuchadnezzar and his successors in their inscriptions, and honoured with many august titles :[1] Nebo, in the same inscriptions, ranks next to Marduk. The India House Inscription begins with the words :—

Nebuchadrezzar, king of Babylon, the exalted prince, the favourite of *Marduk*, ... the beloved of *Nebo*.

And a few lines later in the same inscription Nebuchadnezzar says :—

Since *Marduk*, the great lord, exalted my royal head, and committed to me dominion over the hosts of men, and *Nebo*, who commands the hosts of heaven and earth, gave into my hand, for the rule of men, a sceptre of righteousness, I honour those deities, etc.

Nebo was also the principal god of Borsippa, the city almost adjoining Babylon on the south-west (above, p. 31). Bel and Nebo are thus rightly named by the prophet as the two chief deities of Babylon.

In 1879 or 1880 Mr. Pinches discovered, among the inscribed tablets in the British Museum, three which proved to be of particular interest, on account of the light thrown by them upon the closing years of the Chaldaean empire, and the conquest of Babylon by Cyrus. These inscriptions are commonly known as—(1) the Annalistic Tablet of Cyrus (or the Chronicle of Nabo-na'id and Cyrus), (2) the Cylinder-Inscription of Cyrus, (3) the Sippar Inscription of Nabo-na'id (found by Mr. Hormuzd Rassam at Abu-Habba, the ancient Sippar). Before, however, proceeding to consider these, it will be convenient to notice the inscriptions which mention Belshazzar, who, according to the Book of Daniel, was son of Nebuchadnezzar, and the last king of Babylon before its conquest by Cyrus. One of these inscriptions, found at Mugheir (the ancient

[1] As *bilu rabu*, "the great lord"; *bil iláni*, "lord of the gods"; *bil bili*, "lord of lords"; *rish ili*, "chief of the gods": and also *Bil*, "Lord," absolutely (*K. B.*, iii. 2, pp. 17, 47, 91).

Ur) has been long known: Nabo-na'id, after describing in it how he had restored the ancient "ziggurat" of Sin (the moon-god) at Ur (p. 38), proceeds:—

²⁴ And as to Bil-shar-uẓur,ᵃ ²⁵ the chief son, ²⁶ the offspring of my body, ²⁷ the fear of thy great divinity ²⁸ do thou [Sin] set in his heart; ²⁹ may he not give way ³⁰ to sin; ³¹ with life's abundance may he be satisfied.ᵇ

This inscription at once shews that Belshazzar was not son of Nebuchadnezzar, but of Nabo-na'id.ᶜ

Belshazzar is also mentioned in contract-tablets belonging to the same reign.ᵈ One, dated Nisan 21, in Nabo-na'id's fifth year (550 B.C.), speaks of a house "let for three years to Nabo-kin-akhi, the secretary of *Bil-shar-uẓur, the king's son*, for 1½ maneh of silver." In another, dated in Nabo-na'id's eleventh year (544 B.C.), we read:—

The sum of 20 manehs of silver for wool, the property of *Bil-shar-uẓur, the king's son*, which has been handed over to Iddin-Marduk, the son of Bâsa, the son of Nur-Sin, through the agency of Nebo-zabit, the steward of the house of *Bil-shar-uẓur, the king's son*, and the secretaries of *the king's son*.

In these inscriptions, it will be noticed, Belshazzar bears the standing title of "the king's son."

We may now pass on to the more important historical inscriptions mentioned above. The "Annalistic Tablet" describes, year by year, the events of Nabo-na'id's reign. The top of the tablet is broken off or mutilated: we merely gather from the parts which remain that the Babylonian forces had been one year in the land of Hamath, and in the following year had marched to the land "Martu" (Phoenicia, Palestine, etc.). In the sixth year of Nabo-na'id

---

ᵃ "O Bel, preserve the king" (*Belshazzar* is a corrupt form).

ᵇ *KAT.²*, p. 434; or *K. B.*, iii. 2, p. 97. Similarly in another inscription (*K. B.*, iii. 2, pp. 83, 89), after the description of the restoration of two other temples, the words occur twice: "Bil-shar-uẓur, the chief son, ... prolong his days, may he not give way to sin."

ᶜ Nor was even Nabo-na'id a son of Nebuchadnezzar: he was a usurper, son of one Nabû-balaṭsu-iḳbi (*K. B.*, iii. 2, pp. 97, 119, 120).

ᵈ Sayce, in *RP.²*, iii. 125–7; *K. B.*, iv. 223.

(549 B.C.), Kûrash (*i.e.* Cyrus), " king of Anshan " (a district in the south or south-west of Elam), is mentioned as warring against Ishtuvegu (Astyages); the troops of Ishtuvegu, however, revolted, and delivered their king into the hands of Cyrus, who then attacked and took his capital, Agamtânu (Ecbatana). In the seventh year (548 B.C.), we read, the king was in Tevâ [a]; he did not come to Babylon, and so the great annual procession of Bel and Nebo on New Year's Day could not take place : "*the king's son*, the nobles, and his soldiers were in the country of Akkad " (North Babylonia). The "king's son," in the light of the inscriptions just quoted, can hardly be any other than Belshazzar : it is a reasonable inference from this passage that he acted as his father's general. The eighth year is without incident. In the ninth year (546 B.C.), the statements respecting the king and the "king's son" are repeated : it is also added that in Nisan (March) Cyrus, "king of Persia," collected his troops, and crossed the Tigris below Arbela; and in Iyyar (April) attacked and conquered a country, the name of which is lost. In the tenth and eleventh years the statements respecting the king and the "king's son" are again repeated. We now come to the reverse side of the tablet. The parts relating to the twelfth to the sixteenth years are lost : under the seventeenth year (538 B.C.) we have the account of Cyrus' conquest of Babylon :—

¹² In [b] the month of Tammuz (June), when Cyrus, in the city of Upê (Opis),[c] on the banks of ¹³ the river Zalzallat, had delivered battle against the troops of Akkad, he subdued the inhabitants of Akkad. ¹⁴ Wherever they gathered themselves together, he smote them. On the

---

[a] Either a suburb of Babylon, or some favourite residence of the king in the country.

[b] The translations of this and the next-cited inscription are based upon those of Hagen in Delitzsch and Haupt's *Beiträge zur Assyriologie*, ii. (1891), pp. 205 ff. Those published in *RP.²*, vol. v., 158 ff., are in many respects antiquated.

[c] On the Tigris, about 110 miles north of Babylon.

14th day of the month, Sippar* was taken without fighting. ¹⁵ Nabo-na'id fled. On the 16th, Gubaru, governor of the country of Guti,ᵇ and the soldiers of Cyrus, without fighting ¹⁶ entered Babylon. In consequence of delaying, Nabo-na'id was taken prisoner in Babylon. To the end of the month, the shield-(bearers) ¹⁷ of the country of Guti guarded the gates of E-sagil: ᶜ no one's spear approached E-sagil, or came within the sanctuaries, ¹⁸ nor was any standard brought therein. On the 3rd day of Marcheshvan (October), Cyrus entered Babylon. ¹⁹ Dissensions (?) were allayed (?) before him. Peace for the city he established: peace to all Babylon ²⁰ did Cyrus proclaim. Gubaru, his governor, appointed governors in Babylon. ²¹ From the month of Kislev (November) to the month of Adar (February—*viz.* in the following year, 537), the gods of the country of Akkad, whom Nabo-na'id had brought down to Babylon, ²² returned to their own cities. On the 11th day of Marcheshvan, during the night, Gubaru made an assault (?), and slew ²³ the king's son (?).ᵈ From the 27th of Adar (February) to the 3rd of Nisan (March) there was lamentation in Akkad: all the people smote their heads, etc.

The stages in the conquests of Cyrus are here traced by a contemporary hand. First, in 549, he appears as king of Anshan (or Anzan)—evidently his native home—in Elam: in that capacity, the troops of Astyages desert to him, and he gains possession of Ecbatana. In 546 he is called "king of Persia": it is reasonable therefore to infer that in the interval since 549 he had effected the conquest of this country. In 538 his attack upon Babylon begins. First he secures Opis and the surrounding district of Northern Babylonia; then he advances to Sippar, which he takes "without fighting": two days afterwards, Gubaru, his general, enters Babylon, which also offers no resistance: Nabo-na'id is taken prisoner, but otherwise everything proceeds peaceably. Between three and four months afterwards,ᵉ Cyrus himself enters Babylon, and formally

---

* Near the Euphrates, about 70 miles north-west of Babylon.
ᵇ A land (and people) on the north of Babylonia (cf. p. 44).
ᶜ Above, p. 121.
ᵈ The tablet is injured at this point; but "the king's son" is the reading which those who have most carefully examined the tablet consider the most probable.
ᵉ Or, according to a probable correction, proposed recently by Ed. Meyer (*Tishri* [September] for *Tammuz* in line 12), 17 days afterwards.

proclaims peace to the country. A few days after Cyrus' entry (if the reading be correct), the "king's son," who it seems must in some way have shewn himself unwilling to submit to the new rule, was slain in a night affray by Gubaru.

In more respects than one, as Professor Sayce has pointed out,[1] the old ideas about Cyrus and the events of his time have been revolutionized by these inscriptions. In particular, Cyrus was not of *Persian* origin; he and his ancestors were kings of Anshan, a district of Elam; he only became "king of Persia" afterwards. There was no siege of Babylon by Cyrus; Gubaru and Cyrus both entered it without striking a blow: the well-known account given by Herodotus (i. 191) of the stratagem by which it was taken, the waters of the Euphrates having been diverted by Cyrus, and his troops then entering the unguarded gates of the city by the dry channel, while its inhabitants were engaged in festivities, is nothing but a romance; and the expressions in Isa. xiii. 15-8, xxi. 2, 5-7, xliv. 27, xlv. 1, 2, Jer. l. 14, 15, 38, li. 30, 31, 32, 36, etc., which have been supposed to fall in with this account, are merely the poetic imagery in which the prophets in question have clothed the general thought of the impending doom of Babylon. The same inscriptions shew further that the Book of Daniel is not the work of a contemporary hand, but springs from a later age, in which the past was viewed in a dim and confused perspective: Belshazzar was a real person, but he was neither "son of Nebuchadnezzar," nor "king of Babylon": it is possible that his military capacities caused him to eclipse his father in the memories of later generations, and that thus he came gradually to be pictured as the last king of Babylon; for the same reason his father Nabo-na'id was forgotten, and he was imagined to be the son of the well-known king Nebuchadnezzar.

[1] *Monuments*, chap. xi

Nor again was there any "king" who "received the kingdom" after Belshazzar's death, called Darius the Mede (Dan. v. 31, vi. 1, 28, ix. 1): the inscriptions leave no room for any king between Nabo-na'id and Cyrus[1]; and "Darius the Mede" is a figure which arose probably out of a confusion between Darius Hystaspis (the second successor of Cyrus, on the throne of Persia), and Gubaru, whom Cyrus, after his conquest of Babylon, made governor of the city.[2]

It appears further from the inscriptions,—and the fact serves also as at least a partial explanation of the ease with which Cyrus became master of Babylon,—that Nabona'id had made himself unpopular with his subjects: not only was he an unwarlike king, who left his son to take command of the troops, while he himself year after year remained in "Tevâ," but further, though keen on the restoration of ancient temples, he offended in other ways the religious prejudices of the nation: he did not bear his proper part in important religious festivals; and he made the mistake of removing the images of many local deities from their ancient shrines and transferring them to Babylon, thereby not only treating these deities with disrespect, but also detracting from the pre-eminence enjoyed by Marduk, and diminishing probably the perquisites of his priests.

[1] This fact is attested independently by the contract-tablets dating from this period, which are numerous, and which pass all but continuously from the 10th of Marcheshvan, in the 17th year of Nabo-na'id, to the 24th of the same month in the accession-year of Cyrus (Sayce, *Monuments*, pp. 522 f., 528; Strassmaier, *Bab. Texte*, i. 1887, p. 25, vii. 1890, p. 1).

[2] There are other archaeological indications which confirm this conclusion respecting the date of the Book of Daniel: for instance, the use in it of the term "Chaldaeans" (i. 4, ii. 3, etc.) to denote, not the ruling caste (above, p. 36 *note*) in Babylon, but a prominent class of *wise men*. This is a sense which is unknown to the language of Assyria or Babylon, and arose only after the close of the Babylonian empire (Schrader, *KAT*.², p. 429; Sayce, *Monuments*, pp. 534 f.): it dates, in fact, from the time when "Chaldaean" had come to be synonymous with "Babylonian" in general, and when practically the only "Chaldaeans" known were members of the priestly or learned class.

The priests and people being thus disaffected towards Nabo-na'id, after the defeat of the "king's son," with his troops, in Northern Babylonia, no serious resistance was offered to Cyrus' advance. And Cyrus also knew how to utilize the situation diplomatically. In the proclamation (the so-called "Cylinder-Inscription") issued by him to the Babylonians, soon after his entry into the city, he represents himself as the favoured servant of Marduk, specially chosen by him to undo the deeds of Nabo-na'id, and to restore to Babylon its ancient prestige :—

[7] The daily offerings he (Nabo-na'id) suspended. . . . . [9] On account of (the Babylonians') complaints, the lord of the gods (Marduk) was very wroth, and [forsook] their border; the gods dwelling among them left their abodes [10] in anger, because he had brought them to Babylon. Marduk . . . . [11] . . . . . took compassion. In all lands he looked around, [12] and sought a righteous prince, after his heart, to take him by his hand. Cyrus, king of Anshan, he called by name, proclaimed him for the sovereignty of the whole world. [13] Kutu (Gutium), the whole of the Umman-manda,[a] he subdued under his feet; the black-headed ones, whom he (Marduk) granted to his hands to conquer, [14] he cared for with judgment and right. Marduk, the great lord, beheld with joy the protection (?) of his peoples, his (Cyrus') beneficent deeds, and his righteous heart; [15] to his city Babylon he commanded his march, and made him take the way to Babylon; like a friend and a comrade he went at his side. . . . . . [17] Without fighting or battle, he made him enter Babylon. His city Babylon he spared distress. Nabo-na'id, the king, who did not fear him, he delivered into his hand. [18] All the men of Babylon, the whole of Sumer and Akkad, the nobles and governors, bowed themselves before him, and kissed his feet. . . . . [20] I am Cyrus, the king of multitudes, the great king, the mighty king, king of Babylon, king of Sumer and Akkad, king of the four quarters (of the earth) . . . . . . [22] . . . . whose rule Bel and Nebo love, whose dominion they desired for the gladness of their heart. . . . . . . [24] My vast army spread itself out peaceably in Babylon : the whole of [Sumer and] Akkad I freed from trouble (?) : [25] the needs of Babylon and ot all its cities I cared for justly . . . . [26] Their sighing I stilled, their vexations I ended. On account of my . . . . . deeds, Marduk, the great lord, rejoiced, and blessed me. . . . . [33] The gods of Sumer and Akkad, whom Nabo-na'id, to the displeasure of the lord of the gods, had brought to Babylon, by the command of Marduk, the great lord, [34] I caused to take up their abode safely in their shrines [b] in gladness of heart.

---

[a] Alluding to his conquest of Astyages; cf. below, p. 200.
[b] Cf. lines 21–22 of the Annalistic Tablet, quoted on p. 125.

And he ends with a prayer that all the gods whom he has thus "brought [back] into their cities" may daily intercede on his behalf before Bel and Nebo, and before Marduk, his "lord." The inscription thus shews that, although the general thought of the fall of Babylon before Cyrus, expressed by the Hebrew prophets of the Exile (Isa. xiii.—xiv. 23, xl.–xlviii., Jer. l.–li.), was fulfilled, yet the *details* by which they pictured it as accomplished did not, in many cases, correspond to the event: Babylon was not made a desolation by the Medes (Isa. xiii. 17–22; cf. xlvii.); and Bel, Nebo, and Merodach, instead of "going into exile" (xlvi. 1, 2), and being "put to shame" (Jer. l. 2), remained in their places, and were made by Cyrus the objects of special honour. It is also evident that the Hebrew prophet, in describing Cyrus as a worshipper of Jehovah (Isa. xli. 25), *idealizes* the character of his nation's deliverer; for in his inscriptions Cyrus speaks plainly as a polytheist, venerating the very gods, Bel and Nebo, who the same prophet (xlvi. 1, 2) declares should be sent into exile. The expressions in lines 12 and 22 are curiously parallel to those which the prophet represents Jehovah as using with reference to Cyrus (Isa. xlv. 1, "whose right hand I have holden," *v.* 4, "I have called thee by thy name," xlviii. 14, "whom Jehovah loveth").

The excavations carried on in 1884–6 by M. Dieulafoy on the site of the ancient Susa have thrown considerable light on the topography of "Susa, the palace"—or rather, as we should say, the acropolis—mentioned in Dan. viii. 2, and the books of Nehemiah and Esther, and have disclosed the magnificent character of the buildings which it contained;[1] but we have no space to describe these results in greater detail. Visitors to the Louvre may remember how several rooms in one of the galleries are devoted to the antiquities of some of the palaces of the ancient Persian kings.

[1] See his *L'Acropole de Suse*, and *L'Art antique de la Perse*.

It is during the period which has now been reviewed, beginning, *viz.*, with the reign of Rehoboam, and ending with the re-establishment of the Jews in Palestine under the Persian kings, that the inscriptions furnish the most direct and instructive illustrations of events mentioned or alluded to in the Old Testament. Again and again, a notice, or even a passing allusion, is elucidated by the inscriptions; and the event referred to is thrown by them into its proper perspective. In the larger light which the contemporary records cast upon them, both the history and prophecy of the Old Testament are removed from the isolation in which they previously seemed to stand: they are seen to be connected by innumerable links with the great movements taking place in the world without: and the prophecies, in particular, assume often in consequence a new meaning. The policy of Assyria in the age, for instance, of Hosea and Isaiah stands before us as a whole: we understand its drift and aim: we understand also the nature of its influence upon the movements of parties in Israel and Judah themselves; and we see how it determined, upon important occasions, the practical line adopted by the prophets. The prophets are not solely preachers of moral and religious truth: they are warmly interested in the secular welfare of their people; and their counsels, or warnings, on matters of national importance cannot be properly understood except in the light of the history which prompted them. The inscriptions complete the picture, which of course was familiar enough to those living at the time, but of which only a few touches here and there have been preserved to us in the pages of the Old Testament itself.

We conclude with some miscellaneous illustrations of the light thrown upon the Old Testament by Aramaic and Phoenician inscriptions.

Here is a portion of one of the Aramaic inscriptions from Zinjirli (above, p. 6), dating from the eighth century B.C. :—

¹ I am Panammu, son of Karal, king of Ya'di, who have erected this statue to Hadad. . . . .
² There stood up with (= helped) me Hadad, and El, and Resheph, and Rakûb'el, and Shemesh; and Hadad, and El, ³ and Rakûb'el, and Shemesh, and Resheph, put into my hand the sceptre of Hilbabah. And Resheph stood up with me. Whatever I take ⁴ into my hand [succeeds].

Then, after some mutilated lines :—

⁵ . . . . Also I sat upon the throne of my father: and Hadad gave into my hand ⁹ the sceptre of Hilbabah, [and kept off] the sword and tongue (of slander) from the house of my father.

There follow again some mutilated lines, in which Karal, Panammu's father, speaks, declaring how he had desired Panammu to succeed him, and how he had promised him success or the reverse, according as he honoured or not his god, Hadad; and the inscription ends (lines 24-34) with a curse, such as is very usual in Semitic votive or legal inscriptions, against any one who destroys or defaces the monument. In this inscription nearly every word illustrates something in the Old Testament. Hadad is the Syrian god, whose name appears in the proper names Benhadad and Hadad-ezer. Resheph is probably the fire-god : the same word occurs in Hebrew in the sense of a *fiery dart* (Deut. xxxii. 24, Hab. iii. 5, Ps. lxxviii. 48, and elsewhere). Shemesh (in Hebrew, "the sun") is the sun-god (so constantly in the Assyrian inscriptions : cf. Beth-shemesh). *Sceptre* is in the original the same word (rare in Hebrew), which is translated *rod* in Isa. xi. 1. For "tongue" in the sense of slanderous tongue, comp. the expression "man of tongue" in Ps. cxl. 11, and "betongueth" (*i.e.* slandereth) in Ps. ci. 5. Many similar illustrations might be quoted from other parts of the inscription.

Here is part of another inscription: the Panammu

mentioned is probably a grandson of the Panammu named in the former inscription:—

[1] This statue Bar-rekûb has set up to his father Panammu, son of Bar-ẓur, [in memory of the] year in which my father escaped [the destruction of the house of] [2] his father. The gods of Ya'di have rescued him from his destruction. There was a conspiracy in the house of his father; and there rose up [a conspirator ......, who brought] destruction [3] upon the house of his father, and slew his father Bar-ẓur, and slew seventy[a] brethren (*i.e.* kinsmen) of his father .....
[4] .... [And Hadad said, Because ye have brought] [5] the sword into my house, and have slain one of my sons (*i.e.* Bar-ẓur), I also have brought (?) the sword into the land of Ya'di, and Hilbabah .... And [6] corn, durra, wheat, and barley were destroyed; and a *peres* (of wheat) cost a shekel, and a *shatrab* [of barley] a shekel, and an *asnah* of drink a shekel. And my father carried [many presents] [7] to the king of Assyria; and he made him king over the house of his father, and removed (?) the stone of destruction from his father's house ......; [8] .... [and he rebuilt] [9] the house of his father, and made it more beautiful than it had been before. And wheat and barley and corn and durra were abundant in his days.

The result of Panammu's appeal to Tiglath-pileser was thus, that he was recognized as lawful king, and tranquillity was restored in his kingdom. It will be remembered how the same king assisted both Menahem of Israel and Ahaz of Judah in their difficulties. The inscription goes on to narrate how the Assyrian king bestowed further marks of favour upon his vassal, how Panammu accompanied "his lord, Tiglath-pileser," on his expeditions, until in one of them he died: Tiglath-pileser then organized a great funeral ceremony (a "weeping": cf. Gen. l. 4, 10) on the way, and had his body brought from Damascus to his home for interment. Bar-rekûb continues:—

[19] And as for me, Bar-rekûb, son of Panammu, through the righteousness of my father, and through my righteousness, my lord, the king of Assyria, has caused me to sit [upon the throne] of [20] my father Panammu, the son of Bar-ẓur. And I have set up this statue to my father Panammu, the son of Bar-ẓur ....
[21] ..... And may Hadad, and El, and Rakûb'el, the patron of the

---

[a] Cf. Judg. ix. 5, 2 Kings x. 7.

FIRST] INSCRIPTIONS FROM ZINJIRLI 133

house, and Shemesh, and all the gods of Yadi [cause any one who defaces this monument to be accursed] ²¹ before gods and before men.ᵃ

The name Tiglath-pileser—in Assyrian, *Tuklat-abal-i-shar-ra*—is written in this inscription precisely as it is spelt in 2 Kings xvi. 7. A second inscription of the same Bar-rekûb is also worth quoting:—

¹ I am Bar-rekûb, ² son of Panammu, king of Samal, ³ servant ᵇ of Tiglath-pileser, lord of ⁴ the four quarters of the earth.ᶜ For the righteousness of my father, and for my ⁵ righteousness, have my lord Rakûb'el ⁶ and my lord Tiglath-pileser made me to sit on ⁷ the throne of my father .... ⁸ ..... and I have run at the wheel of ⁹ my lord,ᵈ the king of Assyria, among ¹⁰ great kings, the possessors ᵉ of ¹¹ silver, and the possessors ᵉ of gold; and I have taken in possession ¹² the house of my father, and I have beautified it ¹³ more than the house of any of the great kings ; ¹⁴ and my brethren, the kings, have given liberally ¹⁵ to all the beauty of my house, and ¹⁶ through me has it been beautified .... for my fathers, the ¹⁷ kings of Sam'al. It is a house of .... ¹⁸ for them. Thus it is a winter-house ᶠ for ¹⁹ them, and it is a summer-house ; ᶠ and ²⁰ I have built this house.

The whole of that part of Syria in which Zinjirli lies abounds with similar mounds, concealing the remains of ancient castles and towers; and it is much to be hoped that the excavations there may be continued. Hittites and Aramaeans met in this neighbourhood: who knows how much a single bilingual inscription might contribute towards solving the problem of the Hittite language?

Here is part of an Aramaic inscription from Têma, about two hundred and fifty miles south-east of Edom (Isa. xxi. 14, Job vi. 19).ᵍ One Ṣalmshezeb ("Ṣalm has delivered": cf. Nch. iii. 4, Meshēzeb'ēl, "God delivereth")

ᵃ See further D. H. Müller, *Die Altsemitischen Inschriften von Sendschirli* (1893), and in the *Contemp. Rev.*, April, 1894, pp. 563 ff.
ᵇ Cf. 2 Kings xvi. 7, "I am thy *servant* and thy son."
ᶜ The form of this word is peculiar, and identical with that found in the Aramaic verse, Jer. x. 11. On the title, cf. above, p. 40.
ᵈ *I.e.* followed his chariot.
ᵉ *Ba'ălê,*—used similarly in Hebrew.
ᶠ Cf. Amos iii. 15. The "house" meant in these lines is seemingly a mausoleum: it is to be for the perpetual use of the kings of Sam'al.
ᵍ See the *Corp. Inscr. Sem*, II. i., pp. 108 ff.

had introduced a new deity, Ṣalm of Hagam, into the pantheon of Têma; and this inscription states that the native gods of Têma had made over certain annual dues to the new-comer, and had also conferred upon Ṣalmshezeb and his descendants a hereditary priesthood in the temple :—

⁸ This is the stelè ⁹ erected by Ṣalmshezeb, son of Petosiri, ¹⁰ in the temple of Ṣalm of Hagam. For the gods of ¹¹ Têma have granted d[ues] to Ṣalmshezeb, son of Petosiri, ¹² and to his seed, in the temple of Ṣalm of Hagam. And whoso ¹³ destroys this stelè, may the gods of Têma ¹⁴ pluck up ᵃ him and his seed ᵇ and his name ᵇ from the face of (the ground of) ¹⁵ Têma. And this is the due which ¹⁶ Ṣalm of Maḥram, and Shangala, and Ashira, ¹⁷ the gods of Têma, have given to Ṣalm of Hagam : *viz.* ¹⁸ from the (public) land 16 palms, and from the royal ¹⁹ treasure 5 palms, in all ²⁰ 21 palms, every year.ᶜ May neither gods nor men ²¹ remove Ṣalmshezeb, son of Petosiri, ²² from this temple, or his seed, or his name, as priests ᵈ in this temple [for ever].

Here is a Nabataean inscription from the façade in front of one of the rock-hewn tombs of el-'Öla, a little south of Têma ᵉ :—

¹ This is the tomb which 'Aïdu, son of Kuhailu, son of ² Alexi, has made for himself, and for his children, and their descendants, and for whoever produces in his hand ³ a writ of authorization from the hand of ⁴ 'Aïdu, as a sanction for him and for any one to whom 'Aïdu, during his lifetime, may grant the right of burial therein : in the month Nisan, in the ninth year of ⁵ Ḥârithat, king of the Nabataeans, lover of his people. And may Dusharā, and Manôtu, and Qaisâh ᶠ curse ⁶ whoever sells this tomb, or whoever buys it, or pledges or gives or ⁷ lets it, or whoever frames for it any (other) deed,ᵍ or buries in it any man ⁸ except such as are hereinbefore designated (lit. written). And the tomb and this its inscription ᵍ are inviolable,ʰ ⁹ after the manner of what is held inviolable ʰ by the Nabataeans and Salamians, in perpetuity.

ᵃ Deut. xxviii. 63 (the same word).   ᵇ Cf. 1 Sam. xxiv. 21.
ᶜ The idiom here used is one that is also common in Hebrew.
ᵈ The word is one found also in some other inscriptions, but in the Old Testament only three times, always of idolatrous priests: Hos. x. 5, Zeph. i. 4, 2 Kings xxiii. 5.
ᵉ Euting, *Nabat. Inschriften* (1885), pp. 25 f.
ᶠ Gods of the Nabataeans.
ᵍ Lit. *writing*. What is meant is the inscription itself, which is also, as it were, a legal deed, defining who are to have the right of burial in the tomb. Most of the Nabataean inscriptions are of similar import.
ʰ Or, sacred ; properly *shut off, prohibited*, and so *not to be infringed*.

Ḥârithat is the Aretas of 2 Cor. xi. 32; and his ninth year would be 1 B.C. "Lover of his people" (= Φιλόπατρις) is his standing title, both in these inscriptions and on coins. The month Nisan (March—April) is mentioned in Neh. ii. 1, Esther iii. 7: it is one of the names of the Assyrian months, which were borrowed by the Jews in post-exilic times.

The following Nabataean inscription is from one of the rock-hewn tombs in a Wády debouching into the Wady Mûsa, very near Petra, the capital of the ancient Edom [a]:—

¹ This tomb, and the great chamber within it, and the smaller chamber within [b] that, wherein the graves are, constructed in compartments, ² and the surrounding wall(?) in front of them, and the . . . ., and the houses therein, and the gardens, and the feast(?)-garden,[c] and the wells of water, and the dry places, and the rocks, ³ and the rest of all the ground(?) in these places, are (registered) as the sacred and inviolable possession of Dusharā, the god of our lord, and his . . . . . . council,[d] and of all the gods, ⁴ in the deeds relating to sacred spots, as is (stated) therein. It is the command of Dusharā, and of his council,[d] and of all the gods, that everything be done according as is (prescribed) in those deeds relating to the sacred spots, and that nothing whatever be altered ⁵ or taken away from what is (prescribed) therein, and that no man whatever be ever buried in this tomb, except those for whom the right of a grave is prescribed in those deeds relating to sacred spots.

The precise specification of everything appertaining to the tomb recalls the terms of Gen. xxiii. 17.

Here is an inscription from Palmyra, on an altar brought home by Wood in 1751, and now in the Ashmolean Museum in Oxford :—

¹ In the month of Elul, in the year 396, ² this sun-pillar and this altar ³ were made and dedicated by Lishmash and Zebeida, ⁴ sons of Malchu, son of Yaria'bel, son of Nesha, ⁵ who is surnamed the son of Abdibel, of the ⁶ clan of the children of Migdath, to Shemesh (the sun), ⁷ the god of the house of their father, for its life (*i.e.* safety), ⁸ and for their own life, and for the lives of their brethren ⁹ and their children.

---

[a] Nöldeke, *Zeitschr. für Assyriologie*, August, 1897, pp. 1 ff.
[b] The form of this word illustrates that which occurs in the Book of Daniel (iii. 6, 11, etc.).
[c] *I.e.*, probably, the garden in which funereal feasts were held.
[d] Lit. *session, assembly*: cf. Ps. cvii. 32 (Heb.).

The word for *sun-pillar* is the same which occurs in Isa. xvii. 8, xxvii. 9, Ezek. vi. 4, 6, Lev. xxvi. 30, 2 Chron. xiv. 5, xxxiv. 4, 7. The month Elul (August—September), as Neh. vi. 15. The year 396 (*viz.* of the era of the Seleucidae) is A.D. 85.

The following are four Phoenician inscriptions: a passage is occasionally mutilated, or uncertain, but the general sense is clear :—

¹ I am Yeḥawmelech, king of Gebal, son of Yaḥarba'al, grandson of Adommelech, king of ² Gebal, for whom the lady, the mistress of Gebal, made the kingdom over Gebal. And I call upon ³ my lady, the mistress of Gebal, [because she heard my voi]ce. And I have made for my lady, the mistress of ⁴ Gebal, this altar of bronze, which is in this [court], and this golden carving, which is on this . . . . , and the . . . . of gold, which is in the midst of the . . . . . . that is on this golden carving. ⁶ And this porch, and its pillars, and the [capitals] that are upon them, and its roof, I, ⁷ Yeḥawmelech, king of Gebal, have made for my lady, the mistress of Gebal, because, since I called upon my lady, ⁸ the mistress of Gebal, she heard my voice, and shewed grace unto me. May the mistress of Gebal bless Yeḥawmelech, ⁹ king of Gebal, and give him life, and prolong his days, and years, (as he rules) over Gebal, because he is a righteous king! And may the lady, the mistress of Gebal, give him favour in the eyes of the gods, and in the eyes of the people of this land; and may the favour of the people of the land ¹¹ [be with him continually?]. Every kingdom, and every man, who may make any addition to this ¹² al[tar, or to this car]ving of gold, or to this porch, I, Yeḥawmelech, [king of Gebal,] set [my face against] him who does such a work . . . . ¹⁴ . . . . . . And whoever . . . . . . upon this place, and whoever . . . . . , may the lady, the mistress of Gebal, [cut off, *or* curse] that man, and his seed.

Gebal was one of the cities on the coast of Phoenicia, mentioned in Ezek. xxvii. 9, called Byblus by the Greeks. Above the inscription there is a representation of the goddess seated, with the king standing before her, and offering her a libation. The inscription dates probably from the fifth century B.C. The resemblances which in several places its phraseology displays to that of the Old Testament will be noticed by the reader.

The funereal inscription of Eshmun'azar, king of Sidon,

from a sarcophagus, found in 1855 on the site of the ancient necropolis of Sidon:—

¹ In the month of Bul,[a] in the fourteenth year of his reign, *viz.* of Eshmun'azar, king of the Sidonians, ² son of King Tabnith, king of the Sidonians, spake King Eshmun'azar, king of the Sidonians, saying: I am snatched away ³ before my time [b] . . . . , and I lie in this coffin, and in this tomb, ⁴ in the place that I have built. I adjure (?) every royal person, and every man, that they open not this resting-place,[c] ⁵ nor seek treasures (?), for there are no treasures (?) there, nor take away the coffin of my resting-place, nor superimpose ⁶ upon this resting-place the chamber of a second resting-place. Yea, though men speak to thee (of treasures there), hearken not to their falsehoods (?). For every royal person, and ⁷ every man, who may open the chamber of this resting-place, or who may take away the coffin of my resting-place, or who may superimpose ⁸ anything upon this resting-place—may they have no resting-place with the Shades, and may they not be buried in a tomb, and may they have no son or seed ⁹ to succeed them; and may the holy gods deliver them up unto a mighty king (?) who may rule over them, ¹⁰ to cut off that royal person, or that man, who may open the chamber of this resting-place, or who may take away ¹¹ this coffin, and the seed of that royal person, or of those men; may they have no root beneath, or ¹² fruit above, neither any beauty[d] among the living under the sun, for I . . . . . am snatched away before my time . . . . ¹³ . . . . For it is I, Eshmun'azar, king of the Sidonians, son of ¹⁴ King Tabnith, king of the Sidonians, grandson of King Eshmun'azar, king of the Sidonians, and my mother Am'ashtart, ¹⁵ priestess of 'Ashtart our lady, the queen, daughter of King Eshmun'azar, King of the Sidonians, who have built the temples of ¹⁶ the gods, to wit, the temple of 'Ashtart in Sidon, the country by the sea, and have made 'Ashtart to dwell there . . . . , And we it is ¹⁷ who have built a temple for Eshmun, a sacred . . . . . in the mountains, and . . . . ; and we it is who have built temples ¹⁸ to the gods of the Sidonians in Sidon, the country by the sea, a temple for Baal of Sidon, and a temple for 'Ashtart, the name [e] of Baal. And moreover, the lord of kings has given to us ¹⁹ Dor [f] and Joppa,[g] noble lands of corn, which are in the field of Sharon,[h] for

---

[a] 1 Kings vi. 38.
[b] Job xxii. 16.
[c] Properly *place for lying in*,—used in Hebrew both of a bed (2 Sam. xvii. 28), and also, as here, of a couch, or resting-place, in the grave (2 Chron. xvi. 14, Isa. lvii. 2, Ezek. xxxii. 25).
[d] Fig. for posterity.
[e] *I.e.* (probably) manifestation (cf. Exod. xxiii. 21).
[f] Josh. xi. 2, xvii. 11.
[g] Josh. xix. 46, Jonah i. 3.
[h] Isa. lxv. 10, 1 Chron. xxvii. 29.

.... which I have done; and he has added (?) them ²⁰to the borders of the land that they might belong to the Sidonians for ever. I adjure every royal person, and every man, that he open not my chamber, ²¹ nor empty my chamber, not superimpose anything upon this my resting-place, nor take away the coffin of my resting-place, ²² lest these holy gods deliver them up, and cut off that royal person, or those men, and their seed, for ever.

This inscription dates probably from the fourth century B.C. The word for "Shades" in line 8 (which is also met with elsewhere in Phoenician) is the same ("Rephaim") that occurs repeatedly in the Old Testament in the same sense.[1] The similarity of expression between "root beneath, or fruit above" (lines 11, 12), and Amos ii. 9, Job xviii. 16, Isa. xxxvii. 31, is remarkable. 'Ashtart is, of course, the 'Ashtoreth of the Old Testament (1 Kings xi. 5, 33, and elsewhere).[2]

The following inscription is one found at Tamassus, in the centre of Cyprus, in 1885[3] :—

[1] This is the statue which [2] Menaḥem, son of Ben-ḥodesh, son [3] of Menaḥem, son of 'Araḳ, gave and set up to his lord, to Resheph of [4] Eleyith, in the month of Ethanim, in the [5] thirtieth year of King Malkiyathan, king of [6] Kiti and Idail, because he had heard his voice. May he bless (him)!

This inscription dates probably from about the middle of the fourth century B.C.: several, very similarly expressed, have been found at the neighbouring cities of Larnaca (the Greek Kition, here Kiti, whence the *Kittim* —*i.e.* the Kitians—of Gen. x. 4, Isa. xxiii. 1, 12), and Dali (the Greek Idalion, here Idail). For Resheph, see above,

[1] Isa. xiv. 9, xxvi. 14, 19, Ps. lxxxviii. 10, Prov. ii. 18, ix. 18, xxi. 16, Job xxvi. 5.
[2] The funereal inscription of the Tabnith, mentioned in line 2, shorter, but similar in its general import, was found at Sidon in 1887 (see the writer's *Notes on Samuel*, pp. xxvi-ix, with a facsimile). Here the desecration of a tomb is described as "'Ashtart's abomination": comp. the expression "Jehovah's abomination," Deut. vii. 25, xvii. 1, and elsewhere.
[3] Published by the late Professor W. Wright in the *Proc. of the Soc. of Bibl. Arch.*, ix. (1886), p. 47.

p. 131. The Phoenician month Ethanim ("ever-flowing streams"), as in 1 Kings viii. 2. The word for "statue," in line 1, is the rare Hebrew word found in Deut. iv. 16, Ezek. viii. 3, 5, 2 Chron. xxxiii. 7, 15.

Here, lastly, is the inscription on a small votive pillar from Carthage :—

¹ To the lady, Tanith, the face of Baal, and ² to the lord, Baal Hammân (or, the Solar Baal), which ³ 'Azrubaal, son of Hanno, son of ⁴ 'Azrubaal, son of Baalyathan, vowed, because she heard ⁵ his voice. May she bless him!

More than two thousand votive pillars or tablets, with inscriptions couched almost in the same words, the only difference being in the names of the offerers, have been found in North Africa. There are many allusions in the Old Testament to the practice of making vows. Tanith was the patron goddess of Carthage. The expression, "face of Baal," seems to indicate that she was in some way regarded as a representative of the supreme Phoenician god. "Hammân" is the same word which in the inscription from Palmyra (above, p. 135) was rendered *sun-pillar*: it implies that the Baal here spoken of was identified with the sun. Baal (like Zeus or Athene among the Greeks) received in different places different characteristic epithets : in the Old Testament, we have Baal of Peor (Numb. xxv. 3, Ps. cvi. 28), Baal of the Covenant (Judg. viii. 33), Baal of Flies (2 Kings i. 2); and similarly in Phoenician inscriptions we read of Baal of Sidon (above, p. 137), Baal of Lebanon, Baal of Tyre, Baal of Tarsus, Baal of Heaven, and, as here, of the Solar Baal.

Some examples may be added of scattered names and expressions which have been elucidated by the monuments. The names *Gad, Baal,* and *Ashtoreth* have been explained briefly already.¹ *Anath* (in the proper names, Anath,

---

¹ Pp. 47, 138, 139.

Judg. iii. 31, Beth-anath in Galilee, Judg. i. 33, Beth-anoth in Judah, Josh. xv. 59, Anathoth, a little north of Jerusalem, Isa. x. 30) is the name of a goddess, mentioned in Egyptian inscriptions of the nineteenth and twentieth dynasties, and in (later) Phoenician inscriptions. *Rimmon*, in whose temple Naaman craves pardon for bowing down (2 Kings v. 18), is the Babylonian and Assyrian air- and storm-god, *Rammân*: his name, it will be remembered, has already occurred in the Babylonian narrative of the Flood. *Siccuth* —or, better, *Saccuth*—in Amos v. 26 (R.V.) is a name of Adar, the Assyrian god of war and the chase. *Chiun*— or, better, *Kaiwan*—in the same verse, is an Assyrian name of the planet Saturn. Nahum (iii. 8) calls Thebes " No of Amon,"[1] and Amon (or Amen) is shewn by the inscriptions to have been the tutelary god of Thebes, who afterwards became the national god of Egypt. Tammuz (Ezek. viii. 14) is an old Babylonian (Sumerian) deity, *Du-mu-zi* (" the son of life "):[2] the fourth month of the Assyrian and Babylonian year was named after him.[3]

Some foreign official titles, occurring in the Old Testament, may next be explained. *Pharaoh* is the Egyptian *Per-âa*, " the Great House," a title (something like the " Sublime Porte ") constantly applied in the Egyptian inscriptions to the ruling sovereign. In 2 Kings xviii. 17 we read that Sennacherib "sent Tartan, and Rab-saris, and Rabshakeh from Lachish to Jerusalem." These terms, however, are not in reality proper names. "Tartan" (also Isa. xx. 1) is the Assyrian *turtanu*, or commander-in-chief of the army : Shalmaneser II., for instance, says, " In my twenty-seventh year, I summoned my forces, and sent Dâin-Asshur, the *turtan*, at the head of my army, to Urarṭu (Armenia)."[4] "Rab-saris" (also Jer. xxxix. 3), as Mr.

---

[1] The rendering, "populous No," of the Auth. Version, is incorrect.
[2] Cf. above, p. 20.   [3] Cf. p. 124.
[4] *K. B.*, i. 145; see also above, p. 101.

Pinches[1] discovered, is the Assyrian *rabu-sha-rêshu*, "chief of the heads," the title of a court-dignitary. "Rabshaḳeh" is the Assyrian *rab-shaḳ*, "chief of the high ones," the title of a high officer in the Assyrian army. Tiglath-pileser says, "My officer, the *rab-shaḳ*, I sent to Tyre," to receive tribute of gold,[2]—a curious parallel to what is here related of Sennacherib. *Peḥah*, 1 Kings x. 15 ("governor"), Isa. xxxvi. 9 ("captain"), Neh. ii. 7, 9, Hag. i. 1, and elsewhere ("governor"); and *sāgān*, Isa. xli. 25 (R.V. "rulers," marg. "deputies"); both words together in Jer. li. 23, 28, 57 (R.V. "governors and deputies"), Ezek. xxiii. 6, 12, 23 (R.V. "governors and rulers," marg. "and deputies"); are terms of exceedingly common occurrence in the Assyrian inscriptions: both (the latter in the form *shaknu*) are constantly used to denote the officer appointed over a conquered district or province : the former may be rendered for distinctness *governor*, the latter *deputy* or *prefect*. The viceroys, whom Asshurbanipal installed in Egypt, are called *piḥâti* :[3] Tiglath-pileser appointed *shaknus* over the conquered districts of Hamath and Northern Israel;[4] we read also of the *shaknu*, or prefect, of a city, as Babylon, Arbela, or Uruk.[5] In Jer. li. 27, Nah. iii. 17, there occurs the strange, and manifestly un-Hebrew word, *ṭiphsar*, the meaning of which was quite uncertain (A.V., guessing from the context, "captain"): it is now seen that it is the Sumerian, Babylonian, and Assyrian *dupsar*, "tablet-writer," *i.e.* scribe, registrar (hence R.V. "marshal"), used, for example, in the expression "the *dupsar*, who wrote this tablet,"[6] and found frequently in the contract-tablets, in the sense of *scribe*. The peculiar word (*appéden*) rendered "palace" in Dan. xi. 45 is found in the Persian inscriptions of Artaxerxes II. (405-359 B.C.), at Ecbatana[7] and Susa; it occurs, for

[1] *Academy*, June 25, 1892, p. 618.   [2] *K. B.*, ii. 23.
[3] *K. B.*, ii. 237, 239.   [4] *K. B.*, ii. 27, 33.
[5] *K. B.*, ii. 73, 115, 143.   [6] *K. B.*, iii. 1, p. 169.
[7] Evetts in the *Zeitschr. für Assyriologie*, 1890, p. 415.

instance, in the inscription on one of the columns of the great hypostyle hall, or throne-room, excavated by M. Dieulafoy at Susa.[1] Another Persian word, *dethābār*, "law-bearer, judge," Dan. iii. 2, 3 (A.V. "counsellor"), though the meaning was clear before from the Pehlevi, was found to occur frequently in the commercial inscriptions belonging to the reigns of Artaxerxes I. (465-425 B.C.) and Darius II. (424-405 B.C.), excavated recently by the Pennsylvanian expedition at Nippur.

Examples of the light thrown by inscriptions upon the lexicography of Hebrew and Biblical Aramaic might readily be quoted; but they would be of too technical a nature to interest the general reader. A few have been noticed above in passing. There are perhaps a dozen Egyptian words occurring in the Old Testament, but they are all such as were naturalized in Hebrew: they are not confined to the Pentateuch,[2] and they furnish no clue to the date at which the books in which they are found were written.

We have just room for two or three illustrations, in addition to those which have been already given, of the light thrown by the inscriptions upon tribes and places. The land of *Ararat* (Gen. viii. 4, Isa. xxxvii. 38, Jer. li. 27) is the *Uraṛṭu* of the Assyrian inscriptions, repeatedly mentioned in them, and occupying a place corresponding generally to what we now call Armenia. Tiglath-pileser III. tells us how he invaded the "land of Uraṛṭu," for the purpose of punishing the revolt of its king, Sardaurri.[3] *Minni*, in the same verse of Jeremiah (li. 27), are the

---

[1] "This hall (*apadāna*), Darius, my great-grandfather, built it; afterwards, in the time of Artaxerxes, my grandfather, it was burnt with fire. By the grace of Ormuzd, Anahita, and Mithra, I have restored this *apadāna*."

[2] For instance, *āḥū*, "reed-grass," Gen. xli. 2, 18, but also Job viii. 11 (not elsewhere): *yě'ōr*, the Egyptian name of the Nile, regularly throughout the Old Testament. The number of Egyptian words occurring in the Pentateuch has been greatly exaggerated by some writers.

[3] *K. B.*, ii. 7, 8.

Mannai of the inscriptions, whose home was south of Urarṭu : it is one of Sargon's boasts that he "reduced to order the rebellious Mannai"; and Asshurbanipal describes at some length a victorious invasion of their territory.[1] The "river Chebar," mentioned in Ezek. i. 1, 3, iii. 15, and elsewhere, as running through a spot where there was a colony of Jewish exiles, and which was the scene of Ezekiel's ministry, was for long searched for in vain in the inscriptions; but from two discovered at Nippur, and published only last year, Professor Hilprecht identifies it with great probability with the *Kabaru*, "a large navigable canal not far from Nippur."

In the preceding pages, the writer, as far as was possible, has allowed the facts to speak for themselves, merely, from time to time, pointing out the inferences which appeared to follow from them. But the reader will expect naturally some more definite reference to questions which are of present interest, and will desire to know what bearing the archaeological discoveries of recent years have on the so-called "Higher Criticism" of the Old Testament, and whether, on the whole, they support or not the conclusions generally accepted by modern critics respecting the authorship and historical value of the books of the Old Testament.

In considering these questions there is a distinction which it is important to bear in mind—the distinction, *viz.*, between the testimony of archaeology which is *direct*, and that which is *indirect*. Where the testimony of archaeology is direct, it is of the highest possible value, and, as a rule, determines a question decisively; even where it is indirect, if it is sufficiently circumstantial and precise, it may make a settlement highly probable: it often happens, however, that its testimony is indirect and at the same time not

[1] *K. B.*, ii. 37, 177, 179.

circumstantial, and then, especially if besides it should conflict with more direct evidence supplied from other sources, it possesses little or no cogency. Examples of the direct testimony of archaeology have been furnished by the Books of Kings, though, as it happens, these have related mostly to points on which there has been no controversy, and on which the Biblical statements have not been questioned. It would be an example of the second kind of archaeological testimony, if, to take an imaginary case, the Book of Genesis had described the patriarchs as visiting various places inhabited by tribes to which there were no references in later books of the Old Testament, but which the evidence of the monuments had now shewn to be correctly located: under such circumstances the agreement with the facts would be strong evidence that the narrator drew his information from trustworthy sources. In cases of the third kind of archaeological testimony, if its value is to be estimated aright, attention must be paid to the circumstances of the individual case. In the abstract, for instance, there is no difficulty in the statement that Manasseh was taken captive to Babylon, that he there repented, and was afterwards released: the difficulty (as has been explained above) arises solely from the circumstances under which the statement occurs in the Old Testament, and from its apparent conflict with statements made by earlier and nearly contemporary writers; and no amount of evidence respecting other kings taken captive to Babylon and afterwards released can neutralize the special difficulties attaching to the particular case of Manasseh. In the abstract, again, there is no reason why Hebrew names of a particular type should not have been formed at an early period: but if an induction from materials supplied by the Old Testament itself renders the fact doubtful, the circumstance that other Semitic nations framed names of this kind at an early period does not prove that the Hebrews did the same. Analogies drawn from what may have happened under different circumstances cannot neutralize the force of positive and particular reasons arising out of the circumstances of an individual case. Similarly, other indirect testimony, of the kind, for instance, frequently adduced by Professor Hommel, and consisting not in the actual statements found in the inscriptions, but in hypothetical and often precarious inferences drawn from them, is entirely destitute of logical cogency. The distinction between the direct and the indirect testimony of archaeology is one which must be carefully borne in mind, if false conclusions are to be avoided.

Now while, as need hardly be said, there are many points on which, as between what may be termed the traditional and the critical views of the Old Testament, the verdict of archaeology is neutral, on all other points the facts of archaeology, so far as they are at present known, harmonize entirely with the positions generally adopted by critics. The contrary is, indeed, often asserted: it is said, for example, that the discoveries of Oriental archaeology are daily refuting the chief conclusions reached by critics, and proving them one after another to be untenable: but if the grounds on which such statements rest are examined in detail, it will be found that they depend almost uniformly upon misapprehension: either the critics have not held the opinions imputed to them, or the opinions rightly imputed to them have not been overthrown by the discoveries of archaeology.[1] And in cases belonging to the latter category, the principal ground of the misapprehension lies in the neglect of the distinction between the direct and indirect testimony of archaeology which has been explained above. The conclusions reached by critics

[1] Examples of both these misapprehensions abound, unhappily, in Professor Sayce's writings.

have been opposed, not to statements made directly in the inscriptions, but to questionable and even illogical inferences deduced from them. A few examples will best illustrate the truth of what has been said.

The Tel el-Amarna tablets, it has repeatedly been alleged, by shewing that writing was practised in Palestine even before the age of Moses, have undermined the primary assumption of the criticism of the Pentateuch, so that the conclusions based upon it all collapse together. The statement implies a complete misconception of the real grounds upon which the criticism of the Pentateuch depends. The critical view of the structure of the Pentateuch, and of the dates to which its component parts are to be assigned, does not depend upon any assumption that Moses was unacquainted with the art of writing: it depends upon the internal evidence supplied by the Pentateuch itself respecting the elements of which it is composed, and upon the relation which these elements bear to one another, and to other parts of the Old Testament. The grounds on which the literary analysis of the Pentateuch depends may, of course, be debated upon their own merits; but archaeology has nothing to oppose to them. Indeed, according to Professor Sayce, the composite character of the Pentateuch, so far from being contrary to the "teachings of Oriental archaeology," is "fully in accordance with" them: other ancient writings are known to be of composite structure; "the composite character of the Pentateuch, therefore, is only what a study of similar contemporaneous literature brought to light by modern research would lead us to expect."[1]

Even in regard to the dates of the elements of which the Pentateuch consists nothing has hitherto been established by archaeology, that is inconsistent with those commonly assigned by them to critics. What has been alleged to the

---

[1] *Monuments*, pp. 31, 34. Similarly *Hist. of the Hebrews*, p. 129.

contrary is anything but conclusive. The argument, for instance, that Gen. x. 6—which speaks of Canaan as the youngest brother of Kush, Mizraim (*i.e.* Egypt), and Put— could have been written only under the eighteenth and nineteenth Egyptian dynasties, when Canaan was an Egyptian province, depends upon a most questionable exegesis: in no other instance in the table is political dependency indicated by a tribe (or people) being represented as a younger brother; equality, rather than dependency, is the relation that would naturally be understood as subsisting between brothers; and Mizraim does not even enjoy the pre-eminence which might be supposed to belong to the eldest brother in a family. Other parts of the same chapter, as Professor Sayce himself remarks, "tell a different tale," and must belong "to the seventh century B.C., or later."[1] It has been said, again, that Gen. xiv. is a translation from a cuneiform document, and the narrative of Joseph from a hieratic papyrus; but in both cases the grounds alleged are slender and inconclusive in the extreme. The sale of the field of Machpelah, as narrated in Gen. xxiii., it has been recently stated,[2] "belongs essentially to the early Babylonian and not to the Assyrian period." As a matter of fact, it does nothing of the kind. Of the expressions quoted in support of the statement, "before" occurs repeatedly, in exactly the same application, in the contract-tablets of the age of Sargon, Sennacherib, and Asshurbanipal;[3] and the others are of common occurrence in Hebrew writings of the period of the Kings and Jeremiah: even the term "current" occurs in 2 Kings xii. 4. The truth is that none of the earlier Biblical narratives have been shewn by archaeology to be contemporaneous with the events to which they relate. The inherent nature of the

---

[1] *History*, pp. 131 f.; *Monuments*, p. 9.
[2] Sayce, *History*, p. 61.
[3] *K. B.*, iv. 109, 111, 113, 115, 117, 119, 121, etc.

events recorded, for instance, in the narratives of Genesis respecting Joseph, and in the account of the Exodus, makes it exceedingly difficult to believe that they do not rest upon a foundation of fact : but no tangible archaeological evidence has yet been adduced shewing that any of these narratives were the work of a contemporary hand : the supposition that, at whatever date they were drawn up, they embody substantially true traditions is one that does abundant justice to the archaeological *data* which they contain. And of course there are many parts of these narratives in which even this supposition is not required by the facts of archaeology.

Nor does more follow from the topographical accuracy of the Old Testament. The Palestinian topography of the Book of Genesis is exact ; but, upon the view taken of it by critics, it was written by men familiar with Palestine ; so that topographical correctness is only what would be expected under the circumstances. As Professor G. A. Smith justly says, "that a story accurately reflects geography does not necessarily mean that it is a real transcript of history—else were the Book of Judith the truest man ever wrote, instead of being what it is, a pretty piece of fiction. Many legends are wonderful photographs of scenery, and, therefore, let us at once admit, that, while we may have other reasons for the historical truth of the patriarchal narratives, we cannot prove this on the ground that their itineraries and place-names are correct."[1] It is for this reason that exploration in Palestine, valuable and interesting as its results have been, has contributed but little towards solving the great historical problems which the Old Testament presents.

The verdict is similar when we pass to consider the bearing of archaeology, not on the narratives, as such, but on the histories which they recount. From this point of

[1] *Historical Geography of the Holy Land*, p. 108.

view, also, the results proved by archaeology have been greatly exaggerated. The question, be it observed, is not what archaeology has established with regard to *other* ancient nations, but what it has established with regard to Israel and its ancestors. Mr. Tomkins and Professor Sayce have, for example, produced works on *The Age of Abraham*, and *Patriarchal Palestine*, full of interesting particulars, collected from the monuments, respecting the condition, political, social, and religious, of Babylonia, Palestine, and Egypt, in the centuries before the age of Moses: but neither of these volumes contains the smallest evidence that either Abraham or the other patriarchs ever actually existed. *Patriarchal Palestine*, in fact, opens with a fallacy. Critics, it is said (pp. 1 f.), have taught "that there were no Patriarchs, and no Patriarchal age"; but, "the critics notwithstanding, the Patriarchal age has actually existed," and "it has been shewn by modern discovery to be a fact." Modern discovery has shewn no such thing. It has shewn, indeed, that Palestine had inhabitants before the Mosaic age, that Babylonians, Egyptians, and Canaanites, for instance, visited it, or made it their home; but that the Hebrew patriarchs lived in it, there is no tittle of monumental evidence whatever. They may have done so: but our knowledge of the fact depends, at present, entirely upon what is said in the Book of Genesis. Not one of the many facts adduced by Professor Sayce is independent evidence that the patriarchs visited Palestine,—or even that they existed at all. What Professor Sayce has done is firstly to draw from the monuments a picture of Palestine as it was in pre-Mosaic times, then to work the history of the patriarchs into it (chap. iv.), and having done this, to argue, or imply, that he had proved the historical character of the latter! It is, of course, perfectly legitimate for those who, on independent grounds, accept the historical character of the narratives of Genesis to combine them with *data* derived from the monuments into a single picture: but those who undertake to *prove* from the monuments the historical character of the narratives of Genesis must, at all costs, distinguish carefully between statements which rest exclusively upon the authority of these narratives, and those which depend upon the testimony of the monuments ; if they fail to do this, misunderstanding and confusion will inevitably result. Professor Sayce, unfortunately, often neglects this distinction ; and confuses the illustration of a narrative, known, or reasonably supposed, to be authentic, with the confirmation of a narrative, the historical character of which is in dispute. It is highly probable that the critics who doubt the presence of any historical basis for the narratives of the patriarchs are ultra-sceptical ; but their scepticism cannot, at least at present, be refuted by the testimony of the monuments.

The fact is, the antagonism which some writers have sought to establish between criticism and archaeology is wholly factitious and unreal. Criticism and archaeology deal with antiquity from different points of view, and mutually supplement one another. Each in turn supplies what the other lacks ; and it is only by an entire misunderstanding of the scope and limits of both that they can be brought into antagonism with one another. What is called the "witness of the monuments" is often strangely misunderstood. The monuments witness to nothing which any reasonable critic has ever doubted. No one, for instance, has ever doubted that there were kings of Israel (or Judah) named Ahab and Jehu and Pekah and Ahaz and Hezekiah, or that Tiglath-pileser and Sennacherib led expeditions into Palestine ; the mention of these (and suchlike) persons and events in the Assyrian annals has brought to light many additional facts about them which it is an extreme satisfaction to know : but it has only "confirmed" what no critic had questioned. On the other hand, the

Assyrian annals have shewn that the chronology of the Books of Kings is, in certain places, incorrect: they have thus confirmed the conclusion which critics had reached independently upon internal evidence, that the parts of these books to which the chronology belongs are of much later origin than the more strictly historical parts, and consequently do not possess equal value.

The inscriptions, especially those of Babylonia, Assyria, and Egypt, have revealed to us an immense amount of information respecting the antiquities and history of these nations, and also, in some cases, respecting the peoples with whom, whether by commerce or war, they came into contact: but (with the exception of the statement on the stelè of Merenptah that "Israel is desolated") the first event connected with Israel or its ancestors which they mention or attest is Shishak's invasion of Judah in the reign of Rehoboam; the first Israelites whom they specify by name are Omri and his son Ahab. There is also indirect illustration of statements in the Old Testament relating to the period earlier than this; but the monuments supply no "confirmation" of any single fact recorded in it, prior to Shishak's invasion. A great deal of the illustration afforded by the monuments relates to facts of language, to ideas, institutions, and localities: but these, as a rule, are of a permanent nature; and until they can be proved to be *limited* to a particular age, their occurrence, or mention, in a given narrative is not evidence that it possesses the value of contemporary testimony.

Of course, it is impossible to forecast the future; and what has been said in this essay rests solely upon the basis of facts at present known. The century which is now closing has seen many archaeological surprises; and the century which is approaching will, in all probability, see more. Many mounds in Babylonia and Assyria are still unexplored; there are others elsewhere in the East; there are many even in Palestine itself. The hopes of the future rest in systematic excavation. Experience has shewn that the more this can be carried on, the greater the probability of obtaining valuable results. Sites in Palestine, especially, ought not to be neglected. What the bearing of the results thus obtained upon present opinions may be cannot of course be foreseen: to the open-minded lover of truth, whether they correct or confirm them, they will be equally welcome.

PART SECOND
CLASSICAL AUTHORITY

CHAPTER I

EGYPT AND ASSYRIA

BY

FRANCIS LL. GRIFFITH, M.A.

EDITOR OF THE "ARCHAEOLOGICAL SURVEY" OF THE EGYPT EXPLORATION FUND

IN the annals of historical research the year 1802 is for ever notable. Then it was that the first solid foundations were laid for deciphering the writings of Egypt and the lands of the Tigris and the Euphrates. The sciences of Egyptology and Assyriology have both arisen within the present century. For many years their growth was slow; but after a certain stage had been passed, so rapid was the advance that now a time can hardly be far distant when the history and civilization of the whole of the Nearer East —including Babylonia, Assyria, Phoenicia, Syria, Asia Minor, Arabia, and Egypt—will be surveyed from a higher platform and read as in an open book taking back its readers by means of contemporary documents three or four thousand years beyond even the traditions of our forefathers. The perspective of time in the world's history that was commanded by our predecessors from classical and later standpoints is now more than doubled.

The early decipherers of EGYPTIAN found three forms of writing to be dealt with: the pictorial or "hieroglyphic" of the monuments, the cursive "hieratic" of the papyri, and the "demotic," which was derived from the hieratic in late times and employed for common purposes. The demotic preserves few traces of its pictorial origin, and the language itself when expressed in this writing is very different from the old language of the monuments. The script is complicated enough, but, like hieroglyphic, it includes a limited number of alphabetic characters with which many words and foreign proper names are completely spelled out; and here it was that the first success of the decipherer was gained.

In 1802 Akerblad, a Swedish Orientalist attached to the embassy in Paris, addressed to De Sacy a letter upon the demotic inscription on the trilingual Rosetta Stone, which had been discovered three years before. From the position of their equivalents in the Greek text he identified almost every one of the proper names in the demotic; he analyzed their component letters, and applied his newly won alphabet successfully to the identification of a few other words. This may be taken as the starting-point in the decipherment of Egyptian. The hieroglyphic text upon the Rosetta Stone was too fragmentary to furnish of itself the key to decipherment; however, in 1818, guided by it, Thomas Young, a brilliant but busy man of science and physician, identified the names of Ptolemy and Berenike in a very inaccurate drawing of a hieroglyphic inscription at Karnak. This was the first step towards the reading of monumental hieroglyphics. Young's analysis was by no means correct: the results of his Egyptological investigations given in the *Encyclopaedia Britannica* (1819) at first sight appear a mass of errors, but any competent judge can see that the attempt was full of the promise of ultimate success. Champollion, however, had in the meantime with single-minded devotion equipped himself with a knowledge of Coptic and with every attainable aid, including a wide study of original monuments, for the recovery of the Egyptian history and language. About this date he received a copy of the inscriptions on an obelisk at Philae. On the base was a Greek petition to Ptolemy IX. and Cleopatra, and in the hieroglyphic text on the monument itself was a Ptolemaic cartouche similar to that on the Rosetta Stone, and another cartouche terminating in signs which the French scholar and Young alike had elsewhere recognized as belonging to the names of female divinities. This cartouche therefore must represent the name of Cleopatra. The equations thus obtained worked out with almost mathematical accuracy: in a few weeks names of Macedonian and Ptolemaic kings and of Roman emperors were freely read on the monuments, and Champollion was able to construct an alphabet with numerous homophones shewing how these foreign names were spelled in hieroglyphics. Labouring incessantly and successfully in France, in Italy, and then in Egypt itself, before his early death in 1831 Champollion, and Champollion alone, founded the science of Egyptology. After his death it passed through an evil period of detraction, doubt, neglect, or misguided study ; but gradually in almost every civilized country it obtained serious recognition and progressed with rapid strides. At the beginning of the century Egyptian was an entirely unknown language buried in several most elaborate and entirely unknown scripts : in 1899 it is being taught by some twenty professorial exponents in the universities of Europe and America. It is a study which rewards its votaries, not only as philologists, but with a rich harvest of facts and ideas of antiquity, and the hieroglyphic writing is certainly in itself the most attractive in the world. It is not surprising that the number of its students annually increases, and that all liberal culture now takes cognizance of the results of their work. Yet to Egyptologists themselves it often seems as if they were only on the threshold of a satisfactory reading of the inscriptions, although progress in this respect has been very great during the last decade, chiefly owing to the carefulness of the German philological school of Erman. Now at length it is possible to produce a passable version of at least an ordinary text; yet great labour and caution are required for this. Formulae of which translations come glibly enough to the tongue too often cannot be analyzed, and the renderings of them are but conventions. The general meaning of most words has been well guessed, but their precise denotation and connotation are still obscure. Coptic, the nearest ally of Egyptian, is but a feeble aid to the student of the parent language of 4000 B.C.

The CUNEIFORM script has little of the attractiveness of Egyptian writing; the groups of wedges in their endless variety of combination seem, at first, intended only to puzzle and bewilder. In the Persian inscriptions, however, the spelling is simplified exceedingly, so that less than forty signs are required, and the words are separated from each other by a single slanting wedge: this was the form least impregnable to the attacks of would-be decipherers. In 1802, shortly after exact copies of several cuneiform inscriptions had been published by Niebuhr, Grotefend, with wonderful penetration, conjectured that two short texts from the rocks of Elwend, near Hamadan (Ecbatana), must read, " Darius the king, son of Hystaspes," and " Xerxes the king, son of Darius the king." So well reasoned was his argument that the results could not be gainsaid; yet for thirty years scarcely any progress was made, until at length in 1836 Lassen and Burnouf criticised and improved on Grotefend's work in detail. In the meantime in 1833 Henry Rawlinson, an officer in the Bombay army, had been called to Persia, and soon made his destiny apparent. After important researches into the classical and later geography of the country, he turned his attention to the early inscriptions. Knowing only vaguely that Grotefend had deciphered some royal names in cuneiform, Rawlinson quickly discovered the key that Grotefend had found; but his reading was of necessity less precise, since he had little or no knowledge of the early forms of Persian as found in the Zend-Avesta. This defect, however, was at once counterbalanced by the discovery of a treasury of new material in the great rock inscription of Darius at Behistun, and the copying of the long inscriptions at Elwend; at the same time Rawlinson obtained Grotefend's memoir, and studied Zend as best he could with the help of a native of some learning. In 1837 he was able to send home a tolerable translation of two paragraphs of the Behistun inscription, and in the following year he received from Europe the works of previous decipherers and Burnouf's commentary on the Yasna, which gave him a thorough insight into the language of the sacred books of Persia. His progress was now rapid, in spite of the attention required by his diplomatic duties, until in the winter of 1839 he was recalled to Afghanistan. Resuming the work in 1843, he copied and translated the whole of the Persian text at Behistun, and in 1845 was able to send it to England for publication. His work, truly an unparalleled triumph over every kind of difficulty, was received by European scholars with enthusiasm. In 1849 he returned home, bringing with him a complete copy also of the Babylonian version of Darius' great inscription, which he was able to publish with transcription and commentary in 1851. The large number of proper names (nearly a hundred) in the Persian text had furnished the necessary starting-point for decipherment of the parallel version. But previously to this, in 1849, Edward Hincks, labouring in an obscure parish in Ireland, had studied the closely allied Assyrian writing with the most brilliant results, his materials being the inscriptions discovered by the French in the palace of Sargon at Khorsabad. Hincks' treatise upon them was characterized by extraordinary insight and genius, and established the principles of that complex script. British scholarship may well be proud of the part it has taken in the decipherment of cuneiform. Since 1850 the progress of Assyriology has been rapid, chiefly in England, France, and Germany. In the last-named country it now flourishes exceedingly; and at length America is taking a very active share, not only in Babylonian exploration, but also in the work of decipherment.

It is from the native records and remains that scholars and archaeologists of the nineteenth century have begun to recover the histories of the Egyptian and Babylonian civilizations. But Greek and Roman writers did not neglect to describe notable places and things in the countries of the Barbarians with whom they came in contact, nor to place upon record what they might learn as to the history of such peoples. And here it is our first duty to examine how far their stories of Egypt, Babylon, and Nineveh agree with our newly won knowledge, and estimate, to the extent of this comparison, our historical gains from the decipherment of languages long dead, and buried in forgotten scripts. Afterwards we shall briefly review some of the wider results of Egyptology and Assyriology, both such as have flowed from decipherment and from material archaeology. Since the unravelling of the hieroglyphics began to yield its harvest soon after 1820, and cuneiform research to make rich returns some twenty years later, we can review the gains of three-quarters of a century in the one case and of half a century in the other, and from them forecast the future.

Biblical and classical writers are the first who present us with reasoned and connected history. Nowhere in the mass of ancient records to which Egyptology and Assyriology have given access has history of a higher order than the barest chronicles been found. In these, however, lies a mine of wealth for the seeker after hidden treasure of facts, and by means of them the historian is enabled to form his own estimates from original documents as to the march of events and the progress of civilization.

With the Biblical writers we are not here concerned. The earliest of the classical historians whose work has come down to our day is Herodotus. His professed aim in the nine books of his history was to expound the causes which led to the wars between Greece and Persia, at the same time putting on record the great and marvellous actions of both Hellenes and Barbarians. The Persian empire included the greater part of the known world; and as the thread of his narrative leads him from one country to another, Herodotus generally devotes some paragraphs to each, mentioning what he thinks noteworthy either in its natural phenomena or products, its cities, its institutions, or the deeds of its rulers. No country obtains so large a share of his attention as Egypt: for this land of marvels Herodotus reserves the whole of his second book, making his "account of Egypt so long, because it contains more wonders than any other land, and more works that defy description." Strange and foreign as it was, Egypt lay within easy reach; Greeks had long been in constant intercourse with it, the Athenians in particular having incessantly aided its efforts to retain or regain freedom as against the common enemy. A Greek traveller's description of the country was sure therefore to find an interested audience among his own people. Babylonia, which to us rivals Egypt in wonders, is treated by Herodotus with comparative brevity.

The only other ancient writer who covers the same ground as Herodotus is Diodorus. In his day the rise of the power of Rome and its successful conflicts with Carthage had widened the outlook. But Herodotus has always been the favourite: the Sicilian author of the "Historical Library" has not the exuberant freshness of the "Father of History."

The Nile Valley

Formerly, apart from Biblical records, the common knowledge of Ancient Egypt was derived from the narratives of Herodotus and Diodorus; Rhampsinitus and Sesostris were the typical Egyptian heroes, and their names were familiar to any man pretending to education. Some few scholars went further afield: not only would they examine the Manethonian fragments for the names and chronology of the kings, Plutarch's *De Iside et Osiride* for Egyptian religious beliefs, the works of Ptolemy and Strabo for geography, and those of Pliny for various lore connected with the country; but they would also collate scraps of information from a multitude of minor authors, Christian and pagan alike. Thus did the learned Jablonski in the middle of the last century when treating of the Egyptian deities, whose names he attempted to explain by the help of Coptic. But such laborious erudition could impart no additional animation to the tales of Herodotus, much less could it supplant them. It was founded, not on fact, but on authority, that being often of the most doubtful kind, and pressed into the service of unfitting theories. The everlasting conflict of testimony made drearier in proportion to their learning the efforts of *savants* to penetrate deeper into the secrets of the forgotten past; definite conclusions could only be reached by arbitrary methods and in harmony with the preconceived views of the theorist.

To-day our museums are filled with the gatherings of a century, amongst which figure largely the mummies, the monuments, the furniture, the ornaments, the implements, and the papyri of Ancient Egypt; even the East End Londoner finds a peculiar fascination in contemplating these speaking relics of so remote a past. Newspapers and popular magazines spread abroad stories fresh from the papyrus on which they were written three thousand years ago. The authority of Herodotus is no longer what it once was, and it is from very different sources that the schoolboy of to-day imbibes his first notion of Egypt. Yet Herodotus and Diodorus are still the links between the old-fashioned classical education founded on scholastic tradition and an altogether fresh interest in the progress of ancient history as revealed through the decipherment of dead languages and by the new science of archaeology.

In their works on Egypt those "ancient" writers have recorded the names of notable kings and private persons as connected with certain anecdotes and historical events; they have described the people, their customs and their laws, the geography of the country and its natural products, the names and myths of deities, and the rites with which they were worshipped. From the monuments, too, we have information quite as varied and far more abundant, though their *data* are as yet but half intelligible, and extend over so prodigious and bare an expanse of time that for no one period are they even approximately full. Hence it is often difficult for the Egyptologist to bring the classical writers to book in particular instances; and if in Herodotus personages, events, and customs are mentioned about which all the known monuments are silent, why not accept his statements, and place them to the credit of the historian, simply assuming that it is the monuments which are at fault? It will probably appear, however, on investigation that the chance of any such statement being correct is not large, and that the burden of proof must always fall on the apologist for the classical writers, not on the critic.

The history of Egypt as told by Herodotus may be divided roughly into what he would regard as Ancient and Modern, the former covering the time from the supposed formation of the land by the deposits of the Nile to the rule of the Dodecarchy; the latter extending from the accession of Psammetichus (670 B.C.) to his own day (*c.* 450 B.C.)

We are also told (Hdt., ii. 154) that, after the settlement of Ionian and Carian mercenaries in Egypt by Psammetichus, the Greeks through intercourse with them had a perfect understanding of events in that country. We will now consider first what Herodotus tells us of the Ancient History of Egypt, and ascertain to what extent he was able to gather exact information concerning it : afterwards we will test the accuracy of Greek recollection as shewn in Herodotus' Modern History ; in the third place we will test the writer's veracity and power of observation as a traveller by his notes on land and people, in each case comparing the records of Diodorus and of other writers.

For the Early period we find that Herodotus (ii. 99–153) professes to enumerate the names and deeds of the most noteworthy of the kings. Many of the names can be identified in the long list excerpted by Africanus from the lost work of Manetho, a native priest of Sebennytus, commissioned by Ptolemy Philadelphus (or Soter ?) to write the history of his predecessors on the Egyptian throne. This list of Manetho contains sundry mistakes, and the names in it are often strangely deformed ; yet on the whole it is confirmed by the monuments and by ancient lists drawn up in the time of the XIXth Dynasty. The kings, down to the conquest of Alexander, are arranged by Manetho in thirty dynasties, the XXVIth Dynasty being headed by Psammetichus ; and Egyptology has accepted his arrangement as a reasonable working basis.

Herodotus, who constantly quotes the priests as his authority for all matters concerning the Ancient History of Egypt, gives the succession of the early kings as follows: The first king was Menes, followed by 330 monarchs, of whom one was a queen, Nitocris, and the last was Moeris. Then, *in succession* be it observed, come Sesostris, Pheron, Proteus, Rhampsinitus, Cheops, Chephren, Mycerinus, Asychis, Anysis, Sabaco, Sethos, making a total of 341 kings after Menes. With regard to the name and place of the first king, Diodorus and Manetho are both in accord with Herodotus. Three out of four of the XIXth Dynasty lists place MNY (*i.e.* Menes) at the head; a fifth list begins with a later king. Menes is now thought to have been buried at Negadeh, opposite Coptos.[1] Soon we may learn more of his actual historical position; at present Egyptologists are content to style him the first king of the Ist Dynasty and the founder of the Egyptian monarchy. Moeris, last of the 330 kings, and excavator of the great lake that bore his name, can only be Amenemhat III., last king but one or two of the XIIth Dynasty. At the end of the VIth Dynasty in Manetho, and in the ancient Papyrus of Kings at Turin, is a queen Nitakert, evidently the Nitocris of Herodotus. 330 is apparently quite double the number of the kings who actually reigned from Menes to Moeris, and the statement[2] that none but those whom Herodotus mentions did anything worthy of note seems a hard judgment, at least on the brilliant IVth, Vth, VIth, and XIIth Dynasties. As we read on, however, we may be inclined to admit that down to this point, though decidedly meagre, Herodotus' Ancient History does contain some facts in correct order. But from Sesostris to Rhampsinitus it is all foggy in the extreme. Rhampsinitus is evidently to be connected with the Ramessides of the XIXth and XXth Dynasties. As being a mighty conqueror, Sesostris (ii. 102) should belong to the XVIIIth or XIXth Dynasty;[3] but Manetho places him in the XIIth, corresponding to Usertesen II., a not

---

[1] Borchardt's identification of the great royal tomb excavated at Negadeh in 1897 as that of Menes is disputed by several leading Egyptologists and awaits further proof.

[2] On the authority of the priests, as usual (ii. 101).

[3] There is evidence that Rameses II., perhaps the most likely of all the kings to become the greatest hero in story, bore the popular name Sesu, or Sesu Ra, with which may be compared Diodorus' Sesoosis for Sesostris.

very distinguished predecessor of Amenemhat III. (Moeris)- Pheron and Proteus (ii. 111–120) it is hopeless to identify, though the name of the former may well be compared with the Biblical title of the kings of Egypt, derived from a well-known royal designation—Per'o—which gave to Coptic the word *pero*, " the king." As Pheron is represented as the son of Sesostris, it may be that by this name is intended Merenptah, son of Rameses II., who is indeed supposed to be "Pharaoh" of the Exodus. Between Amenemhat III. and the XXth Dynasty the kings exceeded two hundred in number: according to Herodotus, whose Rhampsinitus must be of the XXth Dynasty, if of any, there were but three.

After Rhampsinitus, Herodotus places the group of great pyramid-building kings (ii. 124–136), Cheops, Chephren, Mycerinus, followed by Asychis, who is said to have built his pyramid of mud, and is probably the Sasychis of Diodorus. These can be none other than Khufu, Khafra, and Menkaura, and probably Shepseskaf of the IVth Dynasty. On comparing the monumental lists of the IVth Dynasty it will be seen that only Dadkara, a very unimportant king, is omitted. The first three built the great pyramids of Gizeh; but the tomb of Shepseskaf is still unknown. Except for the utter misplacement of the group in point of time, this is sound history.[1]

Diodorus follows up the name of Menes with a list in

---

[1] In an ingenious but erratic book, Dr. Apostolides has suggested that the sections of Herodotus referring to the pyramid builders have been put out of their place by a copyist, and should be read between ii. 99 and ii. 100. The "fit" is then in many respects admirable; the IVth Dynasty takes its proper place after Menes, and the three hundred less important kings appropriately follow. But the emendation produces a gap in the text, and it is doubtful whether Herodotus' general knowledge of the history is such as to justify our altering the text of the MSS. to make it tally with facts, especially as Diodorus agrees pretty well with Herodotus. At any rate our forefathers had to take the text as it stood.

greater disorder than that of Herodotus: Busiris, Uchoreus, Aegyptus, Moeris, Sesostris, Amasis, Actisanes, Mendes, Ketes (Proteus), Remphis (Rhampsinitus), and Nileus, most of these names being simply mythical. After them he inserts the builders of the Gizeh pyramids, as does Herodotus, calling them Chemmis, Chephren, and Mecerinus, but offering, as an alternative view, three other names that have nothing to do with these monuments.

From the kings of the IVth Dynasty to those of the XXVIth—really a period of from 2,000 to 2,500 years—it was but a little leap to the Greek historians. Herodotus allows for it scarcely more than two reigns: the reign of (1) Anysis (*i.e.* perhaps Bocchoris, XXIVth Dynasty) was interrupted by Sabaco the Ethiopian (XXVth Dynasty), who drove him into exile, but he was restored and eventually succeeded by (2) Sethon, priest of Hephaestos at Memphis.[1] Then, out of a brief combined rule of twelve

---

[1] The story of Sethon (ii. 141) is apparently one of a series of tales about the high priests of Ptah, two such stories having been discovered in late Egyptian papyri. "Sethon" is simply the high-priestly title, used as an appellative. Herodotus (who mistook the title for a proper name) states that his Sethon was king, as well as priest of Hephaestos —*i.e.* Ptah. "Sethon" systematically slighted the soldiery, and when threatened with an invasion under "Sanacherib" he was saved from disaster solely by the intervention of his god, who promised aid in a dream. An army of mice invaded the camp of the "Arabians" in the night, devoured their bowstrings, etc., and rendered them powerless to fight, whereupon they fled, not without losing multitudes of their host at the hands of the rabble troops of Sethon. In the troubled period of Ethiopian and Assyrian invasions the kings or princes had only local power, and whichever among them held Memphis would probably consider the high-priesthood of Ptah one of his chief titles to honour. This we know to have been the case with Tafnekht (730 B.C.). By "Sethon," therefore, we may understand a local king or prince of Memphis, officially devoted to the worship of the great god of the city, and with authority over at least the greater part of Lower Egypt. The story in Herodotus seems based on the same foundation as that in 2 Kings xix., and in the absence of more definite information it is not without historical value. (The Egyptian parallels indicate that Sethon rather that Sethos is the name intended in the ambiguous wording of the Greek.)

kings, rises Psammetichus (*c.* 670 B.C.), with which event the Modern History of Herodotus may be said to commence. Diodorus, too, gives only Bocchoris (XXIVth Dynasty), and "long after him" Sabaco, the latter being, in Manetho, the slayer and immediate successor of Bocchoris.

As Bunsen and others shewed long ago, Greek notions of the order of the earlier Egyptian kings were founded on a patchwork of different statements wrongly adjusted. Diodorus, more or less, follows Herodotus; and Herodotus would seem to have been the first to put the patchwork together, since he quotes the priests as his authorities for so many of its component parts. Probably the priests had recorded as legitimate three or four hundred rulers from Menes to Psammetichus; but while keeping to the number, Herodotus is hopelessly astray as regards the order. It has been shewn above that, beginning with Menes, he names three monarchs who reigned at long intervals from each other—from the Ist to the XIIth Dynasty—in correct order, only greatly exaggerating the intervals. As for the rest of the kings known to him by name, he imagined them to have reigned immediately afterwards, in succession. Among them is one solid group of the IVth Dynasty kings, before and after which he places the most incongruous names from Graeco-Egyptian legend.

That Herodotus, rather than the priests, was the author of the confusion is more than probable. The Manethonian and native lists testify that the Egyptians kept fairly clear records of the succession of their kings. The Turin Papyrus of Kings was the fullest of the native lists; but its terribly mangled condition prevents us from ascertaining even the plan of the compiler. Besides the names of the kings, it gave the length of each reign; and in the few instances in which these *data* can be tested, they are found to be probably accurate. Manetho also records the lengths of the reigns; but although Professor Petrie strongly upholds his statements, it seems impossible to credit him with a single date for the early period that tallies unmistakably with monumental evidence. The dynastic divisions and the epithets—"Theban," "Memphite," etc.—ascribed to the dynasties in Manetho generally stand the test of Egyptological research. Even the qualification of "Thinite," by which he designates the first two, has been shewn to be reasonable by some of the latest discoveries, although these kings reigned not less than three thousand years before his time. But why the Vth Dynasty should be of Elephantine still remains a mystery.

Obviously ignorant as to the succession of the kings, the classical authors can hardly be expected to exhibit much knowledge of events in Egyptian history of the early period. Herodotus has no knowledge even of the most important phases of the history, but entertains us profusely with frivolous stories of the treasury of Rhampsinitus and the clever thieves, or gravely relates how Sesostris went forth and subdued an empire greater than that of Darius, for not only did it include "all Asia" (as far as India, Bactria, etc.), but also Scythia and Thrace (ii. 103, 110). He was evidently not aware that the Egyptian empire never touched Asia Minor, nor crossed the Euphrates. Even Manetho, who must be classed apart from other writers in Greek on the same subject, affords no certain evidence of accurate acquaintance with the true history of his country. The few notes to the names in his lists of kings, as they have come down to us, are meagre in the extreme, and might be explained easily as additions of the excerptors. They refer, for example, to the legend of Sesostris, who stood four and a half cubits high, or state that Ammenemes (Amenemhat II.) was slain by his own eunuchs; it is rarely that they record anything of real historical interest. In many cases they seem to recall some leading feature of a popular legend by which the king could be identified in story.[1]

One long extract from Manetho is, however, preserved to us by Josephus; namely, the well-known account of the Hyksos. Josephus relates how, in the time of the Egyptian king Timaus, a strange ignoble people coming from the East subdued the country without a battle, ravaged the cities, and demolished the temples. At length they made themselves a king, who was called Salatis, and who dwelt in Memphis. In fear of the Assyrians he built and garrisoned on the eastern frontier a great stronghold called Avaris,[2] and here he made his summer capital. These foreigners, who called themselves Hyksos, *i.e.* "Shepherd Kings,"[3] retained possession of Egypt for 511 years. Several kings succeeded Salatis: Bnon, Apachnas, Apophis, Ianias, Assis. After this the kings of the Thebaid and the rest of Egypt made insurrection against the Shepherds,

---

[1] Even since the above was written a striking instance of the stuff history was made of has been furnished by Professor Krall. Africanus, the principal excerptor of Manetho, gives this note to the name of Bocchoris: ἐφ'οὗ ἀρνίον ἐφθέγξατο ἔτη ⳨ Ϛ, "in whose time a lamb spoke 990 years (!)" This has been a fine *crux interpretum*, who have changed the reading and theorized about the number. Krall has discovered the key to the meaning in some fragments of the last pages of a story, written on papyrus in demotic, about the "curses on Egypt after the sixth year of King Bocchoris." It is there related how in the reign of Bocchoris a *lamb* prophesied that the spoil of the temples of Egypt should be carried to Nineveh, and for 900 years the land should be in misery. Then God (?) would look upon the distress of His people, and lead them into Syria, the spoil would be won back, and Egypt again be in prosperity. This curious papyrus was written in the first years of our era; but there is no reason why Manetho himself should not have heard the story and noted it. In the time of Africanus (A.D. 221) the term of years from the reign of Bocchoris was already past; but by the change of 900 to 990 the hopes of the Egyptians were still kept up.

[2] The Egyptian Het-Wart (H.t-W'r.t, pronounced Ha-wari, in the Graeco-Roman Period), see p. 172. Its site is still doubtful.

[3] Such is the interpretation given by Josephus, not without reason. But the title belongs rather to the kings alone, and may mean "Ruler of foreign nations."

and a long and mighty war was waged between them. At length the Shepherds, being worsted by a king named Alisphragmuthosis or Misphragmuthosis, were driven out of all the rest of Egypt, and shut up in Avaris, where they fortified themselves strongly. The son of Alisphragmuthosis, named Thummosis, or Tethmosis, laid siege to Avaris with a vast army of nearly half a million men, but failed to capture it. At length the Shepherds capitulated on condition of being allowed to depart from Egypt unharmed whithersoever they pleased, and accordingly they left, in number not less than 240,000, and went towards Syria; but being afraid of the power of the Assyrians, they built a city in Judea large enough for their numbers, and called it Jerusalem. Still quoting from Manetho, Josephus gives the names of the successors of Tethmosis, and in a further extract he relates that the Egyptian king Amenophis consulted a wise priest of the same name, Amenophis, son of Papis, as to how he might behold the gods. The answer was that he might behold them if he would cleanse the country of all lepers and other unclean persons. This the king did: gathering together the defective inhabitants of Egypt to the number of 80,000 he sent them to the quarries. But among them were some learned priests; and Amenophis, the wise man, foreseeing the vengeance of the gods on their behalf, prophesied that the lepers would receive aid from another people, and hold Egypt for thirteen years. At length the city of Avaris, which had been left desolate by the Shepherds, was granted to the exiles to dwell in. They chose from among themselves a priest of Heliopolis, named Osarsiph, who enacted laws contrary to the customs of the Egyptians, and abolished the worship of the gods. He rebuilt the walls of Avaris, and sent ambassadors to Jerusalem, offering Avaris to the Shepherds if they would assist him against the Egyptians. Amenophis feared to do battle with the lepers and their allies, lest he should be fighting against the gods, and retreated into Ethiopia with all his army, taking with him the sacred animals, which would otherwise have been destroyed by the invading Osarsiph. The Shepherds again oppressed Egypt more barbarously than before, until Amenophis, returning with a great army from Ethiopia, expelled them.

We cannot be certain that the quotation in Josephus fairly represents the original Manetho; but if it does, it exhibits Egyptian notions of history in a very sorry light. The Hyksos period is still one of the most obscure to us. Two only of its kings are known by name from the monuments; both were called Apepa, and evidently Manetho's Apophis is one of them. To those who have seen the strange guise in which Egyptian names appear on the Greek lists, it is not surprising that the other is still unidentified. When the Egyptian names of the Hyksos kings have all been ascertained and placed in their proper order, then it may be possible to identify them in Manetho.

But from a tomb at El Kab we have definite information as to the expulsion of the Hyksos. Here the high admiral Aahmes, son of Abana, recounts how the city of Avaris was taken and the Hyksos were finally subdued by Aahmes I., the founder of the XVIIIth Dynasty :—

I came into existence in the city of Nekheb; my father was an officer of King Seqenen-ra; Baba, son of Reant, was his name. I acted as officer in his place on the ship of the Wild Bull in the reign of Nebpehti-ra (Aahmes I.), while I was still young and without wife, and slept in the *shenu* garment. Then, after I had made a household, I was taken to the Ship of the North for my valour. And I followed the king on my feet when he went forth on his chariot. They laid siege against the city of Het-Wart (Avaris), and I was valorous on my feet before his Majesty. Then I was promoted to the ship called Resplendent in Memphis. There was fighting by water on the Zedku (canal?) of Avaris; I made a capture and carried off a hand; it was announced to the royal reporter, and gold of valour was given unto me. Again there was fighting at this place, and again I made a capture there and took a hand, and I was given gold of valour a second time. They fought in the *Kemt* south of the city, and I took a live prisoner: I leapt into the water and he was taken, being captured on the road to the city, and I crossed over with him on the water. It was told to the royal reporter, and there was given to me gold of valour in double quantity (?). Then Het-Wart was captured, and I carried off thence one man and three women, in all four persons; and his Majesty gave them to me for slaves. Siege was laid to Sharhana[1] in the fifth year. His Majesty captured it; I took two women and a hand, and gold of valour was given unto me.

This siege of Sharhana indicates that Aahmes had absolutely subdued the Hyksos, or expelled them from Egypt, in his fifth year. In the Manethonian list Aahmes I. appears as Amosis; but in the fragment preserved by Josephus, Manetho represents the capture of Avaris as having been effected by Thummosis, son of Misphragmuthosis. Now these names occur *after* Amosis in Manetho's much-confused list of the XVIIIth Dynasty, where they represent kings of the time when Egypt was at the height of her power, long since delivered from the Hyksos, and now the envy and terror of the world. There are other details of great improbability in Manetho's account of these events, and we cannot treat the latter as more than legendary history with a basis of confused facts.[2] If, then, a native priest commissioned to write history by the king, having access to temple records and surrounded by inscriptions of historical importance the meaning of which he could readily gather,—if such a man, and so circumstanced, failed to collect materials better than those provided by tradition and popular legend, it is not to be wondered at that the priests and guides consulted by Herodotus should have led him far from the truth.

[1] On the border of Southern Palestine, in the country which afterwards was allotted to the tribe of Simeon.

[2] In agreement with facts are the importance attributed to Avaris in the Hyksos period, and the contemporaneity of Amenophis, son of Papis, with Amenophis, *i.e.* Amenhotep III. The memory of this great priest remained to a late time, and the honours paid to him reached their acme in the Ptolemaic period, when he was worshipped at Thebes as a god along with Aesculapius.

An almost incredible instance of utter lack of historical knowledge among the educated classes in Egypt can be quoted from a far earlier time than that of Herodotus. In the fine tomb of Khnemhetep at Beni Hasan, cut out of the rock in the XIIth Dynasty, the cartouche of Khufu appears several times conspicuously in the inscriptions, because it happens to form part of an ancient name current at that time for the provincial capital. At the end of the XVIIIth or beginning of the XIXth Dynasty a scribe visited this tomb and admired its splendid paintings. The cartouche of Khufu caught his eye, and he recorded his impressions in a graffito, of which the translation is as follows:—

> The scribe Amenmes came: "I have gone out to see the temple of Khufu, I find it like heaven when Ra rises therein; it (heaven) droppeth with fresh incense on the roof of the house of Khufu."

These remarks are confirmed by the graffito of another scribe, who uses almost the same words, and adds, "O that I may repeat the visit!" The full significance of this is better apprehended when we find that a scribe of the time of Thothmes III. commemorates his visit to the chapel attached to the pyramid of Senefru at Medum in identical terms in a graffito upon the walls of that building, substituting only the name of Senefru for that of Khufu. The whole style of the XIIth Dynasty tomb called out loudly against its being a temple of Khufu, and almost every line of its inscriptions proclaimed its real object. As to the preposterous notion of its being Khufu's place of sepulture, which is apparently implied by the graffito, was not his pyramid one of the wonders of the world at a later date, and the name of its builder well known even to Herodotus? Perhaps the attention of XVIIIth or XIXth Dynasty Egyptians was absorbed in the vigorous present life of the time, in the gathering of captives and spoil from every known quarter of the world, and in the erection of vast buildings and colossal monuments. They may have had little reverence or leisure for the study of the past, and the careful lists of kings which were compiled in the XIXth Dynasty may have been the result of a reactionary effort to preserve their memory to a more pious age. But later, when Lower Egypt again became the centre of government and Memphis outshone Thebes, then the pyramids were regarded with greater veneration, the Old Kingdom tombs about them became models for imitation, and unsuccessful combat with races more warlike than themselves drove back the Egyptians on memories of their mighty past. This late revival explains how Herodotus came to give so accurately the names and succession of the builders of the three Great Pyramids.

Deliberate priestly forgeries intended to bring honour to certain temples were not unknown in olden time. There is the story of the miraculous healing of a princess of the distant land of Bekhten by means of an image of the god Khons which was solemnly sent to her help from Thebes. The account of the successful performances of this image was inscribed and set up on a tablet in the temple of Khons. Professedly it was a contemporaneous narrative, dated in the reign of Rameses II.; but an analysis of the style and contents of the inscription proves it to be the production of a far later age. Another stela, apparently of the XXXth Dynasty, and placed in a temple near the Great Sphinx, records how that temple and various other buildings were the work of Khufu, thus taking advantage of the ready growth of legend to claim for them the reverence due to hoary antiquity. With equal piety and unveracity the planning and foundation of shrines were attributed to the gods themselves.

It will be seen from the foregoing that even the Egyptian materials must be handled with judgment and reasonable caution. The archaeological faculty is gradually developing among Egyptologists; sacerdotal monuments not long ago accepted as genuine records contemporary with Khufu or Rameses are now looked upon with interested amusement, presenting as they do every characteristic of the *basse époque*. Where modern scholarship has been so much at fault, we may well excuse the pious scribes who mistook the tomb of Khnemhetep for a work of the IVth Dynasty.

In this connexion it is important to note that an acute German archaeologist is now endeavouring to prove that the majestic statues of Khafra (the Chephren of Herodotus) are not the primeval masterpieces which they have hitherto been accounted, but are in fact the consummate productions of the XXVth Dynasty artists (c. 700 B.C.). He believes, too, that at the same late period a vast amount of anonymous rebuilding and reconstruction took place at the pyramids. One small fact is clear: the inscription on the coffin of Mycerinus, from the third pyramid, cannot possibly be earlier than the New Kingdom, and is probably later.

It is certain that in the XXVth Dynasty the archaistic tendency set in suddenly and strongly. Thereafter and in the XXVIth Dynasty the remains of the Old Kingdom were ransacked for models in subject and style for the sculptures of tombs and temples. As time went on the artists copied from these imitations, and the style gradually changed, though it never reverted to that of the New Kingdom. And here we may find another explanation for the New Kingdom names, such as Rhampsinitus, being placed before those of the Pyramid Kings by Herodotus, even as Diodorus put Thebes, the capital of the New Kingdom, to an earlier date than Memphis. The style of art under Psammetichus was to a not very exact observer the same as that under Khufu, while a world seemed to separate it from that of the New Kingdom. Hence to the

sojourner in Memphis it might seem correct to range the
builders of the pyramids just before the XXVth Dynasty,
and to throw the New Kingdom far back: there was,
however, no necessity to displace the whole of the Old
Kingdom along with the IVth Dynasty. Two sources of
information would influence the curious traveller: on the
one hand, the art connected the Pyramid Kings with the
XXVth and XXVIth Dynasties; on the other, the royal
lists in the temples, read over to him by the priests, shewed
that the New Kingdom intervened. It was probably this
conflict of evidence that led to new names of a later type,
Armaeus, Amasis, and Inaros (preserved by Diodorus),
being invented for the builders of the pyramids. Herodotus
noted on the one hand scraps from the temple lists, and
on the other bits of information from his guides at the
monuments; but any discrepancy between them he does
not seem to have observed.

We now come to the second and later part of the
Egyptian history of Herodotus. This refers to some
small extent to contemporary facts and events; for the
rest it covers a period stretching back scarcely more than
two hundred years before the historian's own day, and is
concerned with matters which according to his statements
were familiar to the Hellenes. Under the Saite (XXVIth)
and Persian (XXVIIth) dynasties numbers of Greek
mercenaries and traders had been settled in Egypt, and
had participated in its wars and in its commerce. In this
part of the history there is, then, as might be expected,
a decided improvement. The names and succession of the
kings of the XXVIth Dynasty are accurately given by
Herodotus, as well as those of the Persian invaders and
rulers—Cambyses, the false Smerdis, Darius, and Xerxes—
who appear in one part or another of the nine books.
Manetho's list confirms Herodotus. The chronology, too,

is fairly well ascertained; that of the Saite rulers given by Herodotus is closely accurate, and is confirmed by other authors and by the monuments, there being only one reign out of six the length of which he seems to have stated wrongly, and even that may perhaps be explained by a presumed co-regency. So far as they have any evidence to give concerning the chronology of Egypt during the Persian rule, the Canon of Ptolemy, the cuneiform records of Persia and Babylonia, and the Egyptian monuments are all in agreement.

None the less, the account of the Dodecarchy, immediately preceding the XXVIth Dynasty, and of how Psammetichus attained the throne and founded the Saite monarchy, is very inexact. It is certain, for instance, that Necho, the father of Psammetichus, was not slain by Sabaco, whom, in fact, he long survived. The Labyrinth (if, indeed, we know anything about it) was built ages before the Dodecarchy by "Moeris" of the XIIth Dynasty. The Dodecarchy of Herodotus and Diodorus is but a vague reminiscence of the divided state of Egypt during the times of the Ethiopian and Assyrian invasions. The omens of the brazen men from the sea and the helmet used by Psammetichus as a libation cup are suspicious items. It is only with the actual accession of Psammetichus that the work of Herodotus enters on its new phase of comparative accuracy; and here with our imperfect knowledge it is difficult for us to fix upon errors. Probably there are many of detail, and certainly the narrative is scanty enough. There is no sign in it of more than a general acquaintance with the history of the country. But the accounts of the Syrian campaigns of Psammetichus I., Necho, and Apries (Hophra), as well as the Ethiopian campaign of Psammetichus, are either probable enough in themselves or are confirmed by independent evidence from Biblical and monumental sources.

In regard to Cambyses' invasion and occupation of Egypt there are a few points in Herodotus to be refuted. The Greek historian connects the invasion with the marriage of an Egyptian princess to the Persian king. Of this story he gives three versions (iii. 1). One of these, that which makes Cambyses marry Nitetis, daughter of Apries, is chronologically improbable, for she would have been at least forty years old when sent to Cambyses. On the other hand, the Egyptian story that she was wife of Cyrus and mother of Cambyses seems rightly rejected by Herodotus as an invention designed to shew that the conqueror of Egypt was himself an Egyptian on the mother's side. Herodotus is quite right in assigning to Amasis a reign of forty-four years, and in making his son Psammenitus (Psammetichus III.) succeed him before the storm broke and the victorious invasion of Cambyses put a summary end to the dynasty (iii. 10). The story of the revenge taken by the Persian king on the mummy of Amasis (iii. 16) may find some confirmation in the fact that the name of Amasis has been erased on several monuments from Sais and in the north-east of the Delta. But Cambyses seems to have conformed to the practices of an Egyptian king. An Egyptian named Uza-hor-ent-res records on his inscribed statue, now in the Vatican, that he had been admiral under Amasis and Psammetichus III., that he was appointed to high office by Cambyses, and held an important commission under Darius. On his recommendation, Cambyses ordered the temple of Sais to be cleared of the profane, whose dwellings had accumulated in it; and on reaching the city the Persian king bowed down in the temple and sacrificed :—

> Now there came the great chief, the lord of every country, Kembath (Cambyses), to Egypt, the peoples of every land being with him; he ruled this whole land, and they established themselves therein. ... I petitioned in the presence of King Kembath concerning all the foreigners that were established in the temple of Neith to drive

them thence, to cause the temple of Neith to be in all its splendour as it was aforetime. Commanded his Majesty to drive out all the foreigners that were settled in the temple of Neith, to destroy all their dwellings and all their belongings which were in that temple. . . . The king of Upper and Lower Egypt, Kembath, came to Sais, and his Majesty himself proceeded unto the temple of Neith and bowed down before her Majesty very fervently, as is done by every king, and he made a great offering of all good things unto Neith the Great, the Mother of the God, and to all the great gods who are in Sais, as is done by every good king. His Majesty did these things because I caused his Majesty to know the greatness of her Maiesty, she being the mother of Ra himself.

But later, as the inscription tells us, there was a period of "great woe in all the land," which must have been the time of Cambyses' madness—described by Herodotus as following on the failure of his expeditions to the Oasis and against the Ethiopians—and that of the Magian usurpation:—

. . . I was a man good in his city. I rescued its people from the very great calamity that happened in the whole land, there never having been its like in this land. . . . (I provided for my whole family in Sais), for behold! a calamity happened in this nome in the very great calamity that happened in the whole land.[1]

In all the Greek accounts of Egypt Cambyses has a very evil name as a destroyer; hitherto modern discovery has enabled us to lay our finger on one only of his misdeeds. The Behistun inscription of Darius states that

[1] As illustrating the benevolent policy of Darius, a further passage is worth quoting: "The Majesty of the king Ndruth (Darius) commanded me that I should return to Egypt (not improbably he had left the country in attendance on Cambyses as physician), for his Majesty was in Arma (Aram or Elam)—behold, he was the supreme monarch of every land and the great ruler of Egypt—to establish the office of the Per Ankh (the College of Scribes) . . . after its decay. The peoples conveyed me from place to place, forwarding me on to Egypt, by the command of the Lord of the Two Lands. I did as his Majesty commanded me; I provided them with all their students, consisting of sons of men (of position), and there was not the son of a nobody therein. And I put them under the direction of every learned man [to instruct them] in all their work. His Majesty commanded that they should be supplied with all good things that they might do all their work. I provided them with all things advantageous to them, with all their appliances which were in writing, such as were among them aforetime."

Cambyses slew his brother Bardiya (Smerdis) before starting for Egypt. Doubtless this was a brutal but not unusual precaution for securing his own life and throne. It was clearly not what Herodotus represents it to be (iii. 30), one of the outrageous acts of madness of his last years. As regards Cambyses' stabbing of the Apis bull, it should be noted that in the eighth year of his reign one of these animals was certainly buried with all honour, though perhaps secretly by the priests without the king's knowledge.

Diodorus follows Herodotus' account of the XXVIth Dynasty pretty closely, but is very brief, and makes the mistake of attributing 55 years instead of 44 to the reign of Amasis. He counts Bocchoris, Darius, and Amasis, amongst the great legislators of Egypt, along with Mnevis, Sasychis, and Sesoosis; but here we cannot check his statement. After Amasis there is a gap in his history, which extends to Xerxes' invasion of Greece. Even in his laborious annals of the later times, Diodorus is in hopeless confusion as to the names of the Egyptian kings Achoris, Nectanebus, and Tachos during the struggles of Egypt with Persia. Whether his facts are in better order than his names may well be doubted; but Egyptology knows little of that time except the wonderful architectural activity displayed in the temples while the native kings were striving to hold their own against the Persians by the aid of Greek mercenaries.

In general regarding this period we are singularly ill-informed from contemporary monuments. Many of these exist, it is true; but few among them are of a historical character, or indeed calculated to throw light on the times. Throughout most of the earlier periods in Egyptian history the manners and customs of the country were depicted in lively fashion on the walls of the tombs, the wealth, services to king and country, and rewards of the deceased being often enumerated. In the New Kingdom especially, the bringing of tribute and gifts from the surrounding nations is represented. For the Saite period and onwards we are deprived of those precious illustrations because of the archaizing tendency which prevailed and ordained the slavish copying of subjects and designs borrowed from far earlier tombs. At this time touches of contemporary life were rarely added in tomb paintings or sculptures; the religious taste of the period suppressed biographical inscriptions, while covering the walls with ritual scenes and texts in astonishing variety and abundance. These texts were mostly copied from very ancient originals, and had they been more intelligently reproduced might throw a flood of light on early beliefs; perhaps much may still be done with them. Taken as a whole, the inscriptions of the Saite time, a period of really great historical interest, impress one as a wilderness full of dead bones laboriously collected and laid together, which cannot be made to live.

There is, however, little doubt that historical stelae were set up in some numbers under the later Pharaohs. Fragments of such are occasionally found; but the facts that Sais, in the Delta, was now the capital, and that the activity of the country centred in Lower Egypt, are sufficient to explain why so little of importance has come down to us. The temples of Lower Egypt are utterly destroyed. Their materials were of first-rate value in a stoneless country, and from age to age they have served as quarries. Granite, basalt, quartzite, and other hard stones are now used for millstones and mortars; in times of greater luxury they were in request for the embellishment of buildings in Cairo, Rosetta, or Alexandria. Limestone, however, of which the great temple walls were usually built, is and always has been the greatest prize. Mosques and villas can be built and rebuilt of it, the stone being easily fashioned. Now that the supply from the ruins is almost exhausted, stray pieces can at least be burnt for lime and whitewash. The temple area in the midst of the rubbish mounds of a city has become a mere hollow filled with chips and dust. The walls are gone, the pavement has disappeared, the foundations to the water level are removed. On the sand or mud at the base lie shattered remains of statues, columns and architraves in hard stone where they have been levered backwards and forwards in the effort to get at and extract the underlying blocks. Huge fragments have been wedged out for millstones, heads and limbs are broken off and gone from the statues, often the solid square block of the throne is all that has survived, oftener still nothing but a few chips. Thus have the pious or egotistical records and monuments of whole dynasties of kings, the polished labours of whole generations of artists and skilled and toiling slaves, been reduced by their successors without a pang of remorse to the original raw material, and this again re-worked and reduced to chips and dust. From the temple of Sais, the capital of the Psammetichi, of Necho, Apries, and Amasis, not a single monument has been recovered beyond what had been transported elsewhere in ancient times. An obelisk of Apries is at Rome, whither many other choice pieces of sculpture were carried, and where they have been disinterred anew. Fragments from Sais can be identified at Alexandria; others are in several of our museums. But the mounds of the city are a mass of clay walls filled with dust, chips, and potsherds, from which probably no substantial monument will ever emerge. A broken sarcophagus lid of fine workmanship alone marks the site of the necropolis in which the nobles of the Saite court were interred.

It is impossible therefore to test the statements of Herodotus concerning the monuments erected by the Saite kings. Great monolithic shrines of granite such as the one he describes at Buto are certainly characteristic of the time: here at any rate is a true touch. Again, the Greek colony of Naucratis which the historian described has been identified, and its ruins and remains—a heap of crude brick and dust, in the midst of which shards of Greek painted pottery "crackle under the feet of the traveller" —testify to the general truth of his statements which connect its foundation and importance with the XXVIth Dynasty (ii. 178). The ancient temples of the Milesian Apollo and of Hera were clearly traced by vases with inscribed dedications, which had been broken and cast away. A late inscription naming the temple of Zeus was recovered, and a large enclosure was provisionally identified with the great Hellenium. The last two sites may be settled by further excavation. Two other temples of Naucratis which must have existed in his day are not recorded by Herodotus; namely, those of Aphrodite and of the Dioscuri. The former at least was important and much frequented.[1] The ruins of Daphnae likewise have yielded ample evidence of occupation by Greek soldiers in the same age. Fragments of stelae of Darius have been found on the canal to the Red Sea, and confirm Herodotus' statement that it was excavated by that enlightened ruler (ii. 158).[2]

Darius the king saith: "I am a Persian; a Persian I govern Egypt. I commanded to cut this canal from the Nile, which is the name of the river that runs in Egypt down to the sea that is connected with Persia. Then the canal was cut here. I commanded this canal to be made, and said, 'Go from . . . this canal down to the shore of the sea. . . . Such is my will.'" (Some read, "Destroy half the canal from the city of Bira to the sea.")

---

[1] [To these the most recent excavation (March, 1899) has added shrines of Herakles, Poseidon, Demeter, and Artemis. It has also shewn that the Hellenium was probably not in or near the large enclosure at the south of the site, but was at the north, and it has thrown some doubt on the situations previously assigned to the temples of Hera and the Dioscuri.—Ed.]

[2] Of the previous attempt in the same direction by Necho we have at present no monumental evidence.

Strabo (xvii. 804) says that before the time of the Trojan war Sesostris began the canal, but left it unfinished. The portion that passes along the Wady Tumîlat is certainly very ancient, and the name of Rameses is common on the monuments of Pithom, which is on its banks.

With regard to the foundation of cities, Herodotus says that Menes was the founder of Memphis, perhaps only on the strength of the name. The shrine of Ptah must be of extreme antiquity, probably established long before Menes. As early as the IIIrd Dynasty the centre of power gravitated to the Memphite region; but Memphis itself was not the settled capital of the country before the VIth Dynasty, and its "profane" name, Men-nefer, *i.e.* Memphis, is taken from the name of the pyramid of Pepy, the second king of that dynasty.

Diodorus represents Thebes as founded before Memphis, and eventually overshadowed by it. This idea, though absolutely contrary to history, might well be suggested by the grandeur of ruined Thebes and the fact that Memphis was still great in the writer's own day. Egyptian Babylon (Old Cairo) was founded, he says—offering the choice of two myths—either by the rebellious Babylonian captives of Sesoosis, as Egyptian Troy (Turrah) was by Trojans, or by the Assyrian queen Semiramis when she invaded Egypt! But what of Thothmes, Amenhetep, and Rameses?

Later still the Arab historians and geographers entertain us with a new type of eponymous heroes as founders of the cities of Egypt, intervening Christianity having cut them off from the Pharaonic tradition which was still strong in the time of Herodotus and even of Diodorus.

The power of monumental record to preserve the memory of events in the minds of men is feeble: the works of one generation are forgotten by the next, no matter how carefully the one engraves its memorials on stone or brass and the other is taught to read. Rarely has the historian like Maqrizi arisen, to put in books the dedications of gateway, tomb, and mosque, and so give them a longer lease of life. The ordinary Muhammedan of culture takes no note of the antiquities even of his own faith and language. It is only Western inquisitiveness and modern culture combined that will interrogate the monuments of a dead language and a dead civilization.

A person who has travelled in a little-known country is nowadays expected to describe localities, scenery, and buildings with considerable accuracy, and to have carried away with him definite pictures photographed upon his memory of the more remarkable sights and scenes that he has witnessed. Even if the turn of his discourse does not lead him into description, his casual references to places and things that he has seen will be in general correct. In Herodotus such picturesque touches are exceedingly few. Although the art of travel, as now practised, was then utterly unknown, one would expect a person with any natural faculty of observation to have dealt very differently with the physical conditions of things and the mighty works that everywhere met his eye in Egypt. The few keen or critical observations made by Herodotus may very well have been suggested to him by his guides or companions. Take, for instance, his note as to the difference of thickness between the skulls of Persians and Egyptians on the battlefields of Papremis and Pelusium (iii. 12). In the temple of Sais he saw a number of handless wooden statues, which he was informed represented the tiring maids of a princess, whose hands were cut off for treachery to their mistress. This statement was too much even for the credulity of Herodotus; yet he records it for its relish, only adding that from his own observation he knew it to be untrue : the hands lay at the feet of the statues, and had evidently dropped off from decay. But if now and again mildly critical, Herodotus generally preferred to acquiesce in what was told him. When one considers the folklore that clusters round castles and churches in England of to-day, and the inconsequent stories reeled off by uninstructed guides, there is no need to suppose that Herodotus on his Egyptian travels had more than an ordinary share of absurdity poured into his ears.

The Greek mind was artistic and speculative, and in the literary man was not trained or disposed to matter-of-fact in the smallest degree. Thus Herodotus was very ready to take up any strange stories—sometimes not of the most seemly—that were told to him, especially such as appeared to have a philosophical bearing, to listen to other versions, and to report them all with the merest superficialities of criticism. He appears, indeed, to have been entirely dependent on his cicerones, not only for explanations, but also for noting the existence of the wonders he describes, except when he borrowed from the writings of his predecessors. If occasionally his descriptions are truthful, they present so marked a contrast to the general standard of his history that one is disposed to credit them to other vision than his. Regarding Egypt, at any rate, he is simply reporter to the Greek world of the current gossip of the traders, guides, and priests whom he met there, so far as it accorded with the plan of his history. Let us not revile him for this. What other sources had he to draw upon? To investigate matters for himself in a foreign land was not within the compass of a Greek traveller's notions. The sacrifice of ease and comfort and the throwing of oneself out of one's own nationality in order to penetrate the history and thoughts of another race was an ideal undreamt of. The traveller in those days can have had little energy left for observation. To have accomplished a journey to Egypt at all was a considerable feat. Again, trading was understood, and would meet with a ready response from the Egyptians; but a foreigner hunting relentlessly for information, and to this end intruding into every sacred enclosure, would receive scant courtesy at their hands.

It is, however, the frequent absence of even superficial knowledge that tries our belief in the veracity of Herodotus. When once the Delta is passed, Egypt is the easiest of all countries to comprehend in its main features and landmarks, without the aid of a map. If the traveller and his boat be not buried deep in the trough of Low Nile, as he passes up and down the river he can look over the whole valley to the hills which bound it on either side of him. Yet Herodotus has practically nothing to tell us of the Upper country; his few geographical remarks upon it (ii. 8 *et seqq.*) seem only to shew his complete ignorance of Egypt above Memphis. He appears to think that the eastern range of hills did not run parallel to the Nile, but turned off a little above Memphis in a long trend to the Red Sea or the Indian Ocean, where incense trees grew on its terminal slopes. In all Egypt, he says, there was no sandy hill except the range over Memphis, on which the pyramids stood (i. 8, 12). His estimate of the width of the valley is far too high, and the notion of a great widening comparable to that of the Delta four days south from Heliopolis is absurd. His visit to Chemmis (Ekhmim), "in the Theban nome," was productive only of a most fantastic tale of its temple being dedicated to Perseus, a story one would think more easy to credit or invent when gossiping at home than when traversing the streets of Chemmis itself. How could Herodotus, of all people, have failed to tell us, when mentioning Elephantine, that it was built on a little island in the midst of the river? and how could he leave without a word all the real wonders of the upper country? Yet Herodotus states that he not only visited Thebes (ii. 3, 143, cf. 54), but even went as far as Elephantine (ii. 29). Beyond the First Cataract his geography is of course extremely faulty. The mention, however, of Meroe (ii. 29) as the capital of the Ethiopians who worshipped Zeus (Ammon) and Dionysus (Osiris) is good, and some enthusiasts may find references even to the Bahr el Ghazâl and the dwarfs of the Congo (ii. 31, 32). The story about the springs of the Nile at Elephantine (ii. 28) Herodotus justly doubts, but rather it would seem because it was contrary to other information that he had received than from his own observation. There was, in fact, a mystic idea that the springs, or perhaps some secondary sources of the Nile, were in the Cataract, and the spot was reverenced accordingly. This view was imparted to Herodotus by a priest of some standing in the temple of Neith at Sais, and Herodotus is careful to specify the rank of his informant. The idea that the Nile flowed from the Cataract southward into Ethiopia, as well as northward, was possibly a logical development of the priestly account, due only to the Greek historian. Professor Sayce holds the view that Herodotus never went south of the Faiyûm, and it is hard to avoid adopting the same conclusion.

Egyptologists are, nevertheless, grateful to the Father of History for an interest in Egypt which to many constitutes almost the only claim of the subject on their regard. It is, of course, as a *raconteur* about Egypt, not as a guide or authority for its history or monuments, that he wins our affection. Yet the industrious seeker after facts will constantly meet with statements on the pages of the second book which he knows to be unquestionably true. Often they have served as useful hints to the investigator; and when circumstances point to a particular conclusion without proving it, the statement of Herodotus in support of that conclusion is not without weight.

In contrast to his scanty information regarding the Upper Country, the references of Herodotus are numerous to localities in the Delta, and even throughout Lower Egypt and as far south as the Faiyûm—to the mouths of the Nile, to Naucratis, Daphnae, Bubastis, Heliopolis, Memphis, and to the Labyrinth, pyramid and statues in the Faiyûm; and if not correct, these references are at least intelligible. His account of the coastline is very fairly accurate. Of Naucratis he knows a good deal; but the cities which he names as having been passed in journeying thither are mostly unknown to us. He seldom gives clues to the relative positions of places. Several names, such as Myekphoris and Papremis, that figure in his pages more than once, are still undetermined, though some of them, according to him, represent nomes or nome capitals. His distances, even in the Delta, are all wrong, and the statement that at a day's sail from the coast of the Delta the sea was only eleven fathoms deep (ii. 5) is very far from the truth: probably the depth would be sixty fathoms. The Greeks ought certainly to have known this.

None of the geographical or local information vouchsafed to us by the classical writers is without value. The Greek and Roman place-names are in themselves part of the later history of the country, and have left their mark in the modern nomenclature. The main lines of Egyptian ancient geography are now well known, yet in the Delta especially the situation even of some of the nomes is still uncertain. Strabo's list of the nomes is very accurate. His summary treatment of those above the Hermopolite nome in Upper Egypt, under the term "Thebais," is shewn to be in accordance with later usage by the famous Greek Revenue Papyrus of Ptolemy Philadelphus. The same writer is also very correct in indicating the positions of cities. Ptolemy is here, as usual, fairly trustworthy; yet considering that he lived at Alexandria, his geography of Egypt might have been far more complete as well as more accurate than it is. The distances between cities and stations given in the Roman itineraries are often quite wrong, yet the order of the names is right.

It follows, from what has been said above in reference to the sculptures and inscriptions of the later period, that the pictures drawn by Herodotus of Egypt and Egyptian life are not easily tested by contemporary native documents. The manners and customs of the XIIth and XVIIIth Dynasties are better known to us than those of the fifth century B.C. Nevertheless, while we can point out some instances in which his observation is correct, there are others in which it cannot be. In fact, where we are able to check his individual statements, they generally seem unfounded, or a distortion of the facts, or applicable to the exception rather than the rule. To take a favourable instance, the Indian or rose lotus (*Nelumbium*) has only been found among remains of Roman date; the evidence of Herodotus (ii. 92) for its cultivation as a vegetable as early as the fifth century B.C. is valuable, and is not likely to be controverted. Probably this lotus had been introduced by the Persians. Again, in saying that the *arura*, the standard field measure, was a hundred cubits square he is right, and has aided in the solution of a fundamental problem of metrology. But, in spite of Herodotus, no one doubts that beans were eaten as freely in ancient as in modern Egypt (ii. 37), nor will the texts allow us for a moment to believe that Egyptians despised barley and wheat as food (ii. 36). "They use barley wine, for they have not vines in their country" (ii. 77).[1] Barley beer was, indeed, the universal beverage, and a

[1] In the first edition there here followed an instance of apparent error in Herodotus, the proof of which was founded on the silence of the monuments—always a dangerous argument in Egyptology.

portion of it was allowed to every labourer; but wine was largely drunk at banquets and much used also at sacrifices, as in most countries, and in gardens the vine was greatly cultivated. Athenaeus judged the Mareotic wine good, and in inscriptions from the earliest times onwards four kinds of wine are very commonly mentioned. There is no doubt that *kiki* oil was much used by the inhabitants of the marshes; but that they spread their fishing-nets over their bodies at night to keep off the gnats is beyond belief (ii. 94, 95). The division of the Egyptian soldiers into the Calasiries and the Hermotybies (ii. 165) and their apportionment amongst the nomes is a mystery to Egyptologists.

Herodotus cites a number of Egyptian customs reversing, as he says, the practice of other nations. Few of these can be traced as prevailing either in ancient or in modern Egypt; hence we may fairly argue that they were not really much in vogue in his day. Wiedemann, in an excellent commentary on the second book of Herodotus, is time after time driven to desperate expedients to suggest even the shadow of basis for such statements of his author. For instance, according to Herodotus, women in Egypt carried burdens on their shoulders, while the men carried them on their heads, this being exactly contrary to the usage of the rest of the world. Wiedemann suggests, as the origin of this wondrous assertion, that Herodotus may perhaps have seen women carrying their babies on their shoulders, as is commonly done in modern Egypt, though never represented in the ancient paintings. Now and again, too, men would be seen carrying baskets and trays on their heads, as occasionally they have done at all times and, one would think, in all countries.

Egyptian religion knows nothing of the three orders of deities of which so much has been made, nor can we find in it the famous doctrine of metempsychosis, at any rate in the full form in which it is stated by Herodotus. The soul was not supposed to pass through the whole gamut of creation and then to re-embody itself in human form, though certainly the pious Egyptian hoped to be able to take upon himself after death any form he pleased, and to return from time to time to the sunlight as a sacred hawk, a heron, an egret, a scarabaeus, a lotus, or, in fact, as any living thing he chose. The Pythagorean doctrine may, however, have entered Egypt as a systematizing of this idea, and have found some acceptance without affecting the religious formulae. Herodotus seems generally to designate the Egyptian deities by the same Greek names as later writers; but his mythological allusions much need confirmation, and his air of mystery over the name of Osiris is amusing. Perhaps it is pardonable that he should have thought the Greeks borrowed their twelve great gods from Egypt (ii. 4), though he thereby displays an utter absence of the critical spirit. In excluding from the Egyptian religion Poseidon and the Dioscuri, or any equivalent for them, he is right (ii. 43).

The goat of Pan at Mendes should be a ram (ii. 46). The little horned snake, or *cerastes*, he speaks of as harmless, whereas it is the most deadly of all the Egyptian serpents (ii. 74). Occasionally a piece of description is true to the life; such is the excellent portrait of the sacred ibis (ii. 76). "The head and all the throat are naked: it is white in the feathers, except the head and neck, and the tips of the wings and the tip of the tail, these parts that I have mentioned being exceedingly black. The legs and the face are like the other sort" (*i.e.* legs cranelike and bill somewhat hooked). Here Herodotus is truer to fact than many a richly illustrated modern book, in which a figure of the Indian variety does duty for the sacred bird of Egypt. But how isolated is this gem of veracity! "Hardly Herodotus," one would say, on reading its wondrous context. After all, even the most unobservant of theorists and the most irresponsible of writers may sometimes stumble into accuracy.

Diodorus, who travelled in Egypt before he wrote his historical work, relates in his first book, on the ancient or "mythological" history of Egypt, page after page of absurdity, such as the travels of Osiris and the wars and other achievements of Sesoosis (Sesostris), the greatest of all kings that ever reigned in the world. Even here, however, we not only have genuine Egyptian names constantly occurring, but out-of-the-way facts characteristic of Egypt are curiously interwoven with ideas utterly alien. He mentions, for instance, that five deities—Osiris, Isis, Typhon (Set), Apollo (Horus), and Aphrodite (Nephthys)—were born on the five intercalary days, and Egyptian inscriptions affirm that these were the birthdays of Osiris, Horus, Set, Isis, and Nephthys respectively, only Isis and Horus have been transposed by the Greek writer. The designation of Isis as the goddess of healing is a true touch; but how absurd and exaggerated is the description of the boundaries of Egypt and of the dangers of the harmless salt marsh known as Lake Serbonis! The tomb of Osymandyas has strong reminiscences of the Ramesseum, the funerary temple of Rameses II., though not his tomb. The law—attributed to an Ethiopian conqueror, Actisanes—for cutting off the noses of malefactors and banishing them to Rhinocorura in the desert can be paralleled in the decree of Horemheb (XVIIIth Dynasty), where oppressive and cheating government officers are condemned to lose their noses and to be banished to a place in that very neighbourhood, on the north-eastern frontier of Egypt. The other laws recorded by Diodorus we altogether fail to trace.

The origin of his idea that burial was refused until the deceased had been judged worthy of it may easily be found in the Book of the Dead. Here the dead man is not admitted to the presence of Osiris until his heart has been weighed and found free of evil, and he has replied to each of the forty-two assessors that he is guiltless of the different sins of which they respectively take cognizance. Also, if the literature of the Egyptians were more fully known to us, possibly we might find a papyrus of precepts for kings, conceived more or less in the vein of the laws which Diodorus says regulated every act of the royal life in every hour of its day : at present, however, it is safer to regard them as the outcome of Greek imagination.

In Plutarch's *De Iside et Osiride* the main lines of the ancient myth can be seen through the clouds of comment, expansion, and transformation in a more connected and fuller form than elsewhere. The *Hieroglyphics* of Horapollo are apparently a composition of the Middle Ages ; at any rate they are more misleading than any of the casual statements of the early Greeks with regard to the hieroglyphic writing. It is seldom that the fancies of this author can be supported by more than shreds of fact, and his representation of the nature of the writing must have been a terrible stumbling-block to the early decipherers.

Valleys of Tigris and Euphrates[1]

On the remote history of the Euphratean peoples Herodotus is almost silent: from the little he says about it his ideas seem to have been very far from correct. In the Assyrian history which he promised (i. 184; cf. 106), but perhaps never wrote, we should doubtless have had as plentiful and entertaining a store of myths as in the book on Egypt. He never distinguishes clearly between the Assyrians and the Babylonians, calling them both Assyrians.

[1] The writer has to express his obligation to Mr. T. G. Pinches, of the British Museum, who has read the proofs of the sections referring to Assyriology, and suggested important improvements.

The name, of course, properly belongs only to the Ninevite kingdom, which may be considered almost as an offshoot of Babylonia. But for a century before the fall of Nineveh the latter had been subject to the power of Assyria, though occasionally in rebellion; and it was probably for this reason that after Nineveh and Assyria had been blotted out the inhabitants of Babylonia were still known to the Greeks as Assyrians. Assyriology has come to be the universally accepted name for the study of the Euphratean civilization in all its branches and developments.

Diodorus, in his second book, has much more to say on the subject. His chief authority, Ctesias, a Greek physician at the court of Artaxerxes Mnemon, drew his information—so he tells us—from the royal records of Persia. But if this is true, the Persian records must have been almost incredibly bad as history, and have consisted merely of popular tales; yet we know that the Babylonians were active in compiling and copying lists of their former kings in the time of Darius. Berosus, a priest of the time of Antiochus Soter, wrote a history of Babylon in Greek; of this unfortunately little survives beyond the title of the dynasty, its duration, and the number of its kings, the names of the individual sovereigns being lost. Ptolemy, in his canon of the later kings of Babylonia, recorded for astronomical purposes their succession down to Alexander, and the lengths of the reigns, which covered in all 424 years. When compared with the monuments, this record is correct, except that the names of the kings are curiously deformed, and reigns of less than a year are not noted.

The only mention of an Assyrian king by Herodotus occurs in the Egyptian section, where he tells how "Sanacherib" (704–681 B.C.), called, strangely enough, king of *the Arabians and* Assyrians, was miraculously overthrown on the Egyptian frontier.[1] Herodotus can hardly

---

[1] See above, p. 167 note.

have understood what an Assyrian king meant. Though the detailed annals of Sennacherib's reign afford no hint of a defeat, the Biblical narrative of the destruction of his army (2 Kings xix. 35) suggests that the story was not without some basis of fact; and chronologically it is sound.

A reference to Assyrian domination occurs in Herodotus in connexion with the origin of the power of the Medes. He refers to the fall of Nineveh as a great event, but perhaps without understanding its full significance: he regards it, not as ending the Assyrian empire, but as depriving the Assyrians of their northern capital and causing the transfer of the seat of power to Babylon. This view has been partially justified by recent discoveries. Even when Assyria was hastening to her ruin only a few years before the fall of Nineveh, Babylon was not wholly independent: it still acknowledged at least the nominal sovereignty of the weak descendants of Assurbanipal, and contract-tablets dated in their reigns are found in Babylonia. An inscription of Nabonidus, however, shews that a king of Babylon, apparently Nabopolassar, joined in the attack of the *umman-manda*—"the hordes of the Manda" or "of the nations"—which overran Assyria and wasted its cities.[1]

The Assyrian stories quoted by Diodorus from Ctesias are more wildly imaginative than the Egyptian stories of Herodotus. Ninus, the alleged founder of Nineveh, who is said to have conquered an empire as extensive as that of Persia in its most flourishing days, is quite unknown to cuneiform writings; his name is simply that of Nineveh—in Assyrian Ninua, in Greek Ninus. Semiramis, his queen and successor, whose exploits rivalled his own, has the name of Sammuramat, wife or mother of Rammānu-nirari III., king of Assyria (about

---

[1] Professor Driver has kindly given me information about this inscription, as well as valuable comments and suggestions, which have been utilized throughout the chapter.

812–783 B.C.). Warlike expeditions, principally to the north and west, are recorded of this king. It is possible that some faint recollection of the rise of the second Assyrian empire in the ninth century B.C. is preserved in the stories of Ninus and Semiramis. Many pages of the second book of Diodorus are occupied with the marvellous deeds of Semiramis, and she is even mentioned by Herodotus, who, however, regards her as Babylonian. What are we to think of her twenty-eight luxurious successors, down to Sardanapalus, each more orientally effeminate than the last? To Diodorus one of them only appears worth naming on account of his connexion with the Trojan war. Tithonus was governor of Persia when his son Memnon was sent by Teutamus, king of Assyria, to the help of his vassal Priam of Troy! When at length we are vouchsafed a gleam of history in the attack on Nineveh, Diodorus expressly states that no impression could be made on the walls of the city by the Medes and their allies, because battering-rams and suchlike engines had not yet been invented. But both in Egypt and in Assyria the battering-ram was regularly used at least some centuries before this time. By Diodorus the king of the Medes is called Arbakes (Cyaxares in Herodotus): the cuneiform documents do not name him. Belysis, who brought the Babylonian contingent, is no doubt Nabopolassar. Sardanapalus has long been thought a fancy portrait of Assurbanipal (667–626 B.C.), under whom learning and the arts flourished, and the Assyrian empire reached the zenith of its magnificence while hastening to its ruin. But (as Mr. Pinches remarks) this idea can hardly be maintained, for it is now known that Nineveh was not destroyed until twenty years after his death, probably in 607 B.C.: Sin-sharra-ishkun (Saracos) was the last king of Nineveh, and of him we practically know nothing. Clinton, arguing from the Greek sources, placed the fall of the Assyrian empire at 876 B.C., a date which happens in reality to be marked by the beginning of its great development.

Among the rulers of Babylonia, Herodotus tells us of two queens. One was Semiramis; she threw up embankments to prevent the river from flooding the plain round the city. The other was a Nitocris, who, after the capture of Nineveh by the Medes, improved the fortifications of Babylon along the river, and added greatly to their strength. He says that she was mother of Labynetus, who was deprived of his kingdom by Cyrus. This Labynetus, son of Labynetus, is evidently Nabonidus, whose father, however, was an officer named Nabo-balatsu-ikbi.[1] His mother's name is unknown: that she was a queen in her own right seems improbable, though she may have belonged to the royal family of Nebuchadnezzar. Her death in the Babylonian camp is prominently mentioned in a record by Cyrus of the events of the reign of Nabonidus, and from this we may gather that she was a personage of real importance, and that, unlike the king himself, she was active in the defence of his realm. "Nitocris" is an Egyptian name of the same period, and it is quite possible that the mother of Nabonidus was of Egyptian descent. The works ascribed to her by Herodotus belong, however, rather to the reign of Nebuchadnezzar. Semiramis, who reigned five generations before Nitocris, we cannot at all identify; but for this the monuments may be at fault, seeing that they scarcely ever record the name of a queen. Of queens reigning in their own right there is only one recorded in the lists of Babylonia and Assyria; she was named Azaga-Bau in Akkadian, Bau-ellit in Semitic Babylonian, and belongs apparently to

---

[1] All those kings whose names begin with the name of the god Nebo seem to be called Labynetus by Herodotus. Thus (i. 74) Labynetus, who mediated between the Lydians and the Medes (Alyattes and Cyaxares), must stand for Nebuchadnezzar.

the earliest period, some twenty-five or thirty centuries B.C., when Babylon was still an obscure city.

The rise of the power of the Medes is recounted by Herodotus at considerable length. He says (i. 96) that after the Assyrians had ruled Asia 520 years, the Medes were the first to revolt from them. From this it would seem that the Medes, after being long subject to the Assyrians, finally contrived to throw off their yoke; but this does not agree with the evidence of the cuneiform texts. There is, indeed, doubt as to who the Medes were. In the texts from the eighth century onwards we read of the "Madai" inhabiting Media as being from time to time attacked by the Assyrian kings, and that the western border of their country was overrun. But there are also the *umman-manda*, who are supposed to be Scythian nomad invaders, in or about Cappadocia in the time of Assurbanipal, about 670 B.C.; and Astyages, the king of the Medes overthrown by Cyrus, is Ishtuwegu, the king of the *umman-manda*. The Medes should be Aryan; but this, of course, the Scythians are not.

However that may be, Herodotus says that the Medes, who had previously lived in separate communities, united themselves under a king Deioces into one body and built Acbatana; during the reign of Deioces they prospered exceedingly. Media was anciently inhabited in all probability partly by the true Aryan Medes, partly by non-Aryans. In the north of this very region Sargon (715 B.C.) captured a chief named Diakku, and transported him to Hamath. Deioces' son, Phraortes, who was killed in battle, bears at least a Median name; for the inscription of Darius at Behistun tells of a Mede named Phravartish, who rebelled during that king's reign. The name of Cyaxares, successor of Phraortes, is thought by some to occur in an Assyrian inscription. Finally, Cyrus states that the soldiers of Astyages, "king of the *umman-manda*,"—an expression which has been rendered "the hordes of the nations,"—revolted and gave up their king to him. This to some extent confirms Herodotus, who in his long account of the relations of Astyages with Cyrus represents the former as unpopular with the Medes, who were almost as ready to desert him in the battle as the Persians themselves (i. 127 and 124). The capital of the Medes at this time was Acbatana, and Cyrus carried the spoil of Acbatana (Agamtana) to his kingdom of Anshan. Herodotus says that it was built by Deioces, which is improbable, and in seven circles, each circle of a different colour. This idea, mythical as it is, is derived from the Babylonian towers: in the Birs Nimrud at Borsippa each stage was coloured differently to symbolize the colours of sun, moon, and planets, one perhaps being even plated with silver, another with gold.

It may be conceded readily that Greek accounts of early Mesopotamian conquerors were mythical, and yet it may be contended that the conquests of Cyrus mark an epoch after which history was clearer and the classical versions of it trustworthy. The fall of Nineveh, Lydia, and Babylon left the Persians in possession of a vast empire, and with their power Asia Minor and the Greeks early became only too well acquainted. But even as regards this period the old confidence in Greek historians meets with rude shocks, and that notwithstanding the scarcity of historical *data* for the time amongst the cuneiform inscriptions. One of the most surprising discoveries made from those inscriptions is that Cyrus was not a Persian who rose from a subordinate position, as Herodotus had led us to believe, but that he was king by inheritance of a part of Elam called Anshan, as were his father Cambyses, his grandfather, and other ancestors before him.[1] Xenophon, in his unhistorical *Cyropaedia*, represents the father of Cyrus as king of Persia, and so is nearer

[1] See pp. 124, 126, in Part First.

the truth than Herodotus. It was not until after the overthrow of Astyages that the Elamite king called himself king of Persia. After this readjustment of our ideas as to the origin of Cyrus, we are less surprised to find that he acted as a polytheist, and professed himself a devout worshipper of Bel Merodach at the capture of Babylon, restoring the worship of the gods whom Nabonidus (Labynetus) had neglected.

The untrustworthiness of the accounts in Herodotus is evident as soon as they can be definitely compared with monumental records. The famous siege and capture of Babylon by Cyrus is contradicted by his inscription, which relates that, after a battle at Opis and another at Sippara, his general, Gobryas, entered the city without a struggle. Babylon had stood many sieges before the time of Cyrus, and stood many more afterwards: it is thought that one of the two captures by Darius, whose general was also named Gobryas, may have been confused with the entry of Cyrus. The inscription of Wady Brissa seems to shew that Nebuchadnezzar had built a great wall,[1] stretching from the Tigris at Opis to the Euphrates at Sippara, and intended to ward off attacks from the north by flooding the country above it. He continued this defence on the east of the Euphrates, behind Babylon, by a great wall and artificial marshes. The area enclosed included enough cornland to support the country during the most prolonged wars. Cyrus' trick of diverting the stream and entering along its bed may have been practised in reality for overcoming this outer defence at Opis and at Sippara, instead of at Babylon, as Herodotus represents. The story of how Cyrus avenged the drowning of a sacred horse in the river Gyndes at Opis is perhaps another version of the same occurrence. It is quite intelligible that after such a disaster to the country the capital should

---

[1] The "Median Wall" of Xenophon.

have opened its gates to Gobryas. It is instructive to note that Herodotus counts this as the first capture of Babylon; yet it had been besieged by one Assyrian king after another, and Sennacherib had taken it with cruel slaughter 689 B.C., and Assurbanipal as late as 648. No one, however, had before contended with the great Babylon of Nebuchadnezzar.

Of Cambyses there is little to say apart from his connexion with Egypt; but his long absence in that country prepared the way for the subsequent troubles in Assyria. The monuments of Darius are numerous, and the great inscription of Behistun tells how, belonging to the old royal family, he first wrested the empire from the hand of the usurper and afterwards quelled eight rebellions during the early part of his reign:—

Saith Darius the King: "This was what was done by me before I became king. One named Cambyses, son of Cyrus, of our race, he exercised the dominion before me, and this Cambyses had a brother named Bardiya, of the same mother and the same father with Cambyses. Then Cambyses slew that Bardiya. When Cambyses slew Bardiya, the people knew not that Bardiya was killed. Then Cambyses proceeded to Egypt. When Cambyses had proceeded to Egypt, then the people became wicked, and the lie was great in the land, both in Persia and in Media and in the other lands. And there was a man, a Magian, named Gaumata: he revolted in Pishiauvada, on a mountain named Arakadrish. On the 14th day of the month Viyakhna he revolted. He lied to the people: 'I am Bardiya, the son of Cyrus, the brother of Cambyses.' Thereupon all the people fell away from Cambyses and went over to him, both Persia and Media and the other lands. He seized the dominion. On the ninth day of the month Garmapada they fell away from Cambyses, and thereon Cambyses died by suicide."

And King Darius saith: "That dominion of which Gaumata the Magian deprived Cambyses, the same (?) dominion our family exercised from ancient days. Thereupon Gaumata the Magian deprived Cambyses both of Persia and of Media and of the other countries, and he seized the sovereignty over them according to his will."

And King Darius saith: "Of the men there were none, whether Persian or Mede, or one of our family, that would have deprived the Magian Gaumata of the sovereignty. The people feared him; he slew much people who had known the former Bardiya. On this account he slew much people—'that they may not recognize me that I am not Bardiya, the son of Cyrus'; and no one ventured anything in regard to the Magian Gaumata, till I came. Then I prayed Ahuramazda. Ahuramazda brought me aid. By the grace of Ahuramazda I slew, with a few men on the 10th day of the month Bagayadish, Gaumata the Magian and the men who were his chiefest adherents. In a city named Sikayauvatish, in a country named Nisaya, in Media, there I slew him, I deprived him of the dominion. By the grace of Ahuramazda I exercised the dominion: Ahuramazda gave me the dominion."

Herodotus makes two Magi, brothers, seize the throne while Cambyses was in Egypt, the one called Smerdis pretending to be Smerdis, the younger brother of Cambyses, whom that king had privily put to death. Darius confirms this, but mentions only one Magus, and says that his real name was Gaumata, not Smerdis. From the same inscription it appears also that Cambyses committed suicide, and did not kill himself accidentally (as Hdt., iii. 64). Herodotus gives with great accuracy (iii. 70) the names of the six conspirators who with Darius slew the Magians; only one among them is incorrect. The account is also quite right in representing that none but these seven conspirators were concerned in the plot. The scene of the assassination is, however, wrongly given as the palace of Susa, whereas the Behistun inscription states that the Magus was slain in the fort of Sikayauvatish, in the district of Nisaya in Media. The fall of Intaphernes (iii. 118) had not taken place at the time of engraving the inscription. The Babylonian revolt told of in Herodotus (iii. 150) must have occurred at the beginning of the reign of Darius, preparations for it having been made during the reign of the false Smerdis. This would coincide in time with the revolt of Nadintu Bel, which was, as the contract-tablets shew, put down after ten months; but the incidents related by Herodotus do not agree with the record left by Darius.

Herodotus also tells us something of the land and its geography, of the city of Babylon, and of the religion of the Persians. His description of "Assyria" really applies to Babylonia only. According to him the land, though intersected by irrigation canals, is unlike Egypt in that the river does not rise sufficiently to inundate it ; this, however, is hardly the case. Its richness and fertility are rightly insisted on, and it is fairly true that fig, olive, and vine do not grow there. Besides Babylon, he mentions only three places by name. Is, where the bitumen wells were, at eight days' journey from Babylon, is evidently the modern Hit, about one hundred and eighty miles up the Euphrates. Of Ardericca nothing is known, and Opis seems rather misplaced. The description of Babylon is somewhat fantastic, and would at once condemn a modern traveller ; but perhaps we must accept the statement that Herodotus really saw the place, even if he carried away no true idea of it except that it was big, that the Euphrates ran through it, and that it was marked by great tower-temples. The site, he tells us, was a square of one hundred and twenty stadia (*i.e.* fifteen miles), which, judging by the extent of the ruins, seems an enormous exaggeration. The stupendous height attributed to the walls—two hundred cubits—is absurd.[1] Such figures may well be the product of a story-teller's imagination in dealing with a city which was no doubt the great typical city of the world and far enough off from Greece to be described freely. Something of Nineveh also may be included in the description. The lofty walls of that city on the top of its gigantic mound must have been hugely imposing ; the total height of the Assyrian capital combined with the area of the Babylonian capital—each considerably multiplied—furnish remarkable figures, and Herodotus was not the man to question the actuality of the result. Little is known of the topography of Babylon ; but so far as it is known it is difficult to bring any part of the description of Herodotus into agreement with it.

The most famous and picturesque of the Babylonian customs related by Herodotus is that of the marriage

---

[1] It is curious, however, that Nebuchadnezzar speaks of walls that he built as being " mountain high."

market in the villages. Unfortunately his pretty story has received as yet no confirmation. Neither have any of the other customs mentioned received fresh warrant from Assyriology, though it would be foolish therefore to deny that they existed. Nuptial documents are very numerous among the cuneiform remains, but they are chiefly concerned with marriages of wealthy men in the great towns with women who were either equals or slaves.

Of the Babylonian religion Herodotus says nothing except in a passing reference while describing the temple of Zeus Belus (Bel Merodach?) at Babylon. The Persian religion is set forth with some fulness; but it is difficult to reconcile the description with the facts as known to us. Probably religion in Persia was at that time very various: some sects would be strict monotheists (Zoroastrians); others, worshippers of the elements (Magians); others, again, would combine elements of both Zoroastrianism and Magism, adding also gods from the cults of the provincial nations. Cyrus and his Elamite ancestors had probably long worshipped gods borrowed from Babylonia, and he certainly acted as the faithful servant of Bel Merodach. It is clear from his inscriptions that Darius was a Zoroastrian, and restored the Zoroastrian temples, though Herodotus represents the Persians as worshipping the elements and being without either temples or altars.

One cannot expect that a Greek like Herodotus would know the Persian language, even if he was born at Halicarnassus and had travelled long in the Persian dominions. It is not surprising, therefore, that he thought all Persian proper names terminated with s; this is true enough of all of them in their Greek dress, but in Persian only a moderate proportion end in s, or rather in sh, even in the nominative singular. Herodotus says that Persian boys were taught only three things—to ride, to shoot, and to speak the truth. This may or may not be correct; but it is interesting to find that in the Behistun inscription Darius particularly condemns liars, and frequently uses the word "lie." It must be admitted, though, that a king who suffered from provinces revolting under pretenders on no less than nine occasions had unusual cause to be impressed with the evil of lying.

The genealogy of Xerxes is given by Herodotus (vii. 11) as follows: 1 Achaemenes, 2 Teispes, 3 Cambyses, 4 Cyrus, 5 Teispes, 6 Ariaramnes, 7 Arsames, 8 Hystaspes, 9 Darius, 10 Xerxes. The authenticity of the mere names is shewn by the Behistun inscription, in which Darius gives his ancestry as 1 Achaemenes, 2 Teispes, 3 Ariaramnes, 4 Arsames, 5 Hystaspes, 6 Darius, and says that he was the ninth of the kings in his family. Thus it seems at first sight as if Herodotus gave the full and correct genealogy; but according to him (iii. 70), Hystaspes was not a king, and cannot therefore count among the eight kings of the family of Darius. Cyrus, however, did belong to the family of the Achaemenids, though to a different branch. He himself gives his genealogy as follows: 1 Shispish, king of Anshan; 2 Kurash, king of Anshan; 3 Cambuzia, king of Anshan. The family branched at Teispes (Shishpish). Probably, therefore, Darius reckoned his royal relatives according to the following tree, especially as in a later passage of the same inscription he includes Cambyses in his family; in this case Herodotus is not quite accurate:—

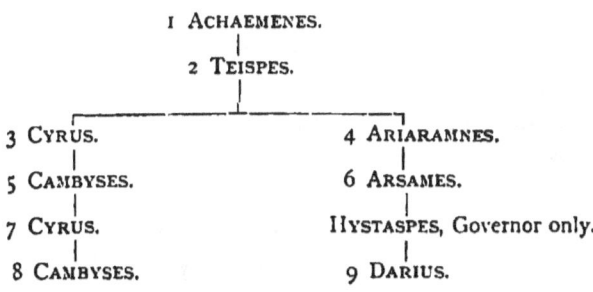

The Reconstruction of Ancient History

How different is the standpoint of the modern student from that of the Greek or Roman writers, and how radically opposed to that of the mediaeval schoolman! We may praise Herodotus for his excellent perception, at that early date, of what is required of the historian of a country, even though we may notice that arts, science, and literature figure little in his narrative of Egypt, for at any rate the land, its history, chronology, traditions, religion, manners, and customs, its domestic animals, its zoology, are all touched upon. Here was a broad sketch for his successors to correct, extend, and fill in, if only the Baconian philosophy had been known and practised by the sages of Alexandria. But a world seems to separate us of the passing nineteenth century from their methods, and even from those of a hundred years ago; and it has been reserved for us to draw forth the true history of Egypt and Babylonia straight from their soil and ruins. The classical writings on the Ancient East are now studied more as records of the views of the time and of the personalities of the authors than of facts, and only those rare scraps of the old lore that bear rigorous testing are fitted into the new structure. No Greek or Roman ever dreamed of such a study, even of his own country, as we are attempting for Egypt in illustration of the history of man.

In briefly reviewing some of the salient points of this reconstruction we cannot omit to note the triumphs that have been won by the spade of the scientific excavator in Egypt. Scientific excavation is among the latest developments of Egyptology, and is mainly the personal achievement of a single Englishman. Northern archaeologists long since divided the early history of man—or rather the pre-history—into periods which resemble in name at least those imagined by the classic poets: the stone age, the bronze age, and the iron age, with their subdivisions into palaeolithic and neolithic, early bronze and late bronze, early iron and the rest. Before the nineteenth century, history began for us in the iron age, and only traditions or μῦθοι remained of earlier stages of civilization. Since then the decipherer has reconstructed the succession of the Egyptian kings, and carried the history of their recorded deeds thirty centuries beyond 600 B.C. The excavator has followed, late, but still not too late, and he has pushed back historic archaeology some twelve centuries, to the beginning of the late bronze age, in the dark period between the Middle Kingdom and the New. He finds that then, and not till then, must stone have been practically driven out of the field by bronze as a material for weapons and implements. Through the Middle Kingdom and the Old Kingdom he is further tracking back the use of stone in ever-increasing proportion, side by side with copper and bronze, until twenty centuries have been added to the twelve, and Menes, the traditional founder of the Egyptian monarchy, is reached. Beyond this still he tracks it, but with no rule for the measurement of time, until metal becomes rare indeed, and the perfection of the flintwork testifies to the enormous labour which had been spent on it. In the subtle curving, symmetry of flaking, ripple-marking, and serration of its flint knives, Egypt has come into competition with the whole of the primitive world, and has carried off the prize unchallenged. The excavator perseveres: inscriptions have long since ceased, the art of making pottery on the wheel disappears, but copper or bronze, though rare, seems ever to be present. The beginning of the early bronze age still lies hid, and the work of neolithic man in Egypt has not yet been disentangled from that of his successor who ran metal from the furnace into the mould and invented coloured glazes and glass itself. Far behind the later stone age again is palaeolithic man, who may have lived before the Nile valley was grooved out by the river, and whose rude implements strew the desert plateaus of Egypt and Somaliland.

Thus we gain from Egypt some insight into the chronology of the ages of man in the world. At least we learn that the antiquity of even the later stages of civilization is respectable, and that probably each period was immensely longer than its successor and shorter than its predecessor. When Babylonian archaeology has been followed out on the same lines and the early chronology of the two countries fixed, we shall have the means of estimating the course and speed of the different waves of civilization that carried the metals or the knowledge of their uses from one country to another and spread them over the globe. In Egypt iron, though perhaps long known, had not begun to be in common use much before the seventh century B.C.; in Britain, probably not before the third century.

The leading aim of Flinders Petrie throughout his years of excavations in Egypt has been to establish dated series of common objects, especially pottery, by means of which the age of any remains associated with similar types can be approximately fixed, even when unaccompanied by inscriptions. Brickwork, stonework, objects in flint, in metal, and in wood, all bear the impress of the period to which they belong, all can be made to tell their tale and to furnish a basis for wide-reaching conclusions. To Hellenic archaeology in particular the Egyptian excavator has already contributed a *datum* of first-rate value in the synchronism of the XVIIIth Dynasty with the early Mycenaean Age.

The source, or perhaps rather the *nidus* of development, of the Nilotic and of the Euphratean civilization must have been a fertile river valley. A certain degree of Semitic influence or relationship is observable in each at a very early period. Egyptian, like most of the other languages of North Africa, is of a sub-Semitic type, though no Semitic traits are to be discerned in the features of the ancient people. In Babylonia the Semites were numerous and powerful at the earliest known period; but the language of the earliest texts is neither Semitic nor Aryan, and the sculptured type indicates, some say, a dark Australasian race of which relics still exist in the neighbourhood of Susa, in Beluchistan, and in India. The power of Egypt was hemmed in by deserts on three sides, and not until the XVIIIth Dynasty did she burst her eastern barriers and overrun Syria to the Euphrates. The frontiers of Babylonia were not so delimited, and struggles with tribes of almost equal power in surrounding plains and mountains rendered her sons hardy and warlike. It seems that thirty or forty centuries B.C. Sargon of Agadè led a host up the Euphrates and across Northern Syria to the Mediterranean —a feat imitated by few but the most powerful of the Assyrian kings. It was at that time, too, that art apparently reached its culmination in Babylonia, judging by the delicate and impressive relief representing Naram-Sin, the son of Sargon. But there is nothing from the Euphrates or Tigris to compare with the noble and exquisite sculptures of the IVth Dynasty in Egypt. In warlike and cruel Assyria, which borrowed all its culture from Babylonia, the finest work known is the latest, the reliefs in the palace of Assurbanipal being both spirited and delicate. Babylonia was the birthplace of astronomy, and arithmetic and geometry were more highly developed there than in Egypt; the latter was especially the home of art. In neither country was there any profound science or philosophy, nor any literature of signal merit.

To chronology, the results of modern researches are most precise and important in Babylonia and Assyria. Here the clay-tablets have preserved to us several "canons" by which dates were intended to be identified. The Ptolemaic canon of Babylonian kings, which agrees absolutely in its chronology with the cuneiform evidence, gives a fixed starting-point B.C. In Assyria the dating of documents was by means of annual eponymous magistrates, canon-lists of whom exist that cover nearly 250 years, one ending 667 B.C. in the reign of Assurbanipal, and stretching back to 902 B.C. The date of accession of each king is noted in them. This is all positive chronology, so that the precise dates of a vast number of events in Assyrian history are now exactly known. For Babylonia we have several long lists of kings with the lengths of their reigns, the years of which were summed up at the end of each dynasty. One of these lists was compiled or copied for the library of Assurbanipal at Nineveh, others date from the Persian period. They reached back regularly to about the twenty-fourth century B.C., shortly before the unification of the country under Khammurabi, to the time when Babylon first became a royal city; those at present known are too fragmentary to yield of themselves a positive chronology, but the date of their starting-point seems ascertained within a century. Apparently these lists were compiled from shorter canons of one or two dynasties each, which had been constructed from time to time in order to interpret the dating of legal and other documents. In the earlier periods such documents were dated only by the name of the king or viceroy, and the principal military expedition or other event of the year. An almost contemporary canon of the years of the first seven kings in the first dynasty of Babylon has been published recently by the British Museum, and proves that authentic materials go back to a very distant age. It was written in the reign of the tenth king, the fourth in succession from Khammurabi. A much later tablet from Babylon gives the lengths of the reigns of this dynasty apparently in a rather careless copy. A total reduction of 19 years in about 202 is observable in the earlier document.

Not unfrequently, when some previous ruler is prominently referred to by the Babylonian and Assyrian kings in the records of their own exploits, a statement is added as to the length of time which separated him from them. The most famous example of such a document is that in which Nabonidus (555-538 B.C.) assigns to Naram-Sin, the son of Sargon, king of Agadè, the remote date of 3200 years before himself. Opinion is much divided as to the trustworthiness of this date. Until the recent excavations of the Americans at Nippur laid bare the handiwork of Sargon, a considerable school in Germany considered him mythical. So little is as yet known about the early chronology that, while many affirm that there is no reason to doubt the correctness of the date of Naram-Sin in this inscription, one Assyriologist, Lehmann, after devoting a book to careful examination of the chronological *data* and probabilities, concludes that the scribe employed to reproduce a hastily written original must have read one stroke too many in the numerals, and so made an excess of a thousand years. Others consider it impossible that Nabonidus should have known the real date of Naram-Sin. The chronological statements concerning even a far later time are not perfect. The different copies of one and the same canon have their slight discrepancies, and in the evidence of different documents there are greater apparent inconsistencies. Lehmann has succeeded in removing some of these as being due to misreadings by modern decipherers of originals that are injured or not very clearly engraved. But plenty of others remain to accuse the ancient scribes of carelessness or uncertainty, if not of wilful perversion. Vast numbers of dated tablets exist for almost all the flourishing periods of

Babylonia. The local record offices were involved in the periodical overthrow of cities by foreign conquerors; and when a city prospered again, rebuilt upon its own ruins, it was not convenient for a later king to restore the uncertain chronology by excavating the buried documents. This work is reserved for our own day. Thirty thousand record-tablets have already been found at Nippur by the American expedition, and every great museum is adding annually to its own stores of them.

In any case the Assyriologist may hope in course of time to complete the canons and control their statements by dated documents to such an extent that he will be able to trace his way back almost year by year to the beginning of the importance of Babylon, an epoch generally considered to fall about 2300 B.C. A clear chronological table for any one of the Euphratean countries after the unification of Babylonia will serve in great measure for them all, owing to their constant intercourse in peace and war. Whether the chronology before that time can ever be more than very roughly estimated is still extremely doubtful.

In Egypt we have not much that is positive in chronology to set against the precise canons of Mesopotamia. Doubtless the need of such documents was sometimes felt; but the Egyptians were probably not so exact in their business arrangements as the Semitic Babylonians, and, even if they were equally precise, the early papyrus records have perished almost utterly, important and unimportant alike. The Turin Papyrus of Kings was only written about the time of Rameses II. (XIXth Dynasty), and its tattered fragments are still unique of the kind. Persian and Assyrian documents carry back the chronology of Egypt by occasional synchronisms to the end of the XXVth Dynasty, 674 B.C., the date of Esarhaddon's first invasion. Again, about

1450 B.C., in the XVIIIth Dynasty, a correspondence was carried on between certain Pharaohs and Babylonian and Assyrian kings, for which the Euphratean records as yet afford no precise date. This synchronism is, in fact, quite as valuable for Babylonian as for Egyptian chronology. A calendrical notice at the beginning of the XVIIIth Dynasty is interpreted by astronomers with great probability as giving a date close upon 1550 B.C.

The first twenty dynasties of Egypt are divided for convenience into those of the Old Kingdom (*flor.* Dyn. IV.-VI.), those of the Middle Kingdom (*flor.* Dyn. XI.-XIII.), and those of the New Kingdom (*flor.* Dyn. XVII.-XX.). Of these groups the first two begin and end in the utmost obscurity. On the other hand, as far back as the beginning of the New Kingdom (*c.* 1650 B.C.) there is a certain solidity about our information; our lists of the kings belonging to this time are very full, and dated monuments are numerous throughout, so that the error in any assigned date probably does not exceed a century. Behind the New Kingdom, unfortunately, we have no synchronisms, and the great gaps in the dynasties, which fill but slowly, make even a rough estimate of the lapse of time difficult. A low estimate (Meyer's) places the XIIth Dynasty about 2100 B.C.; a high one (Petrie's) places it about 2800; while for the Ist Dynasty we have 4777 B.C. (Petrie), as against 3180 (Meyer), shewing a difference of over 1,500 years. And these are not extreme estimates. The attempt has often been made to cut down the figures by making Manetho's less important dynasties contemporaneous; but the progress of discovery is constantly reducing the field available for this treatment, and one hesitates to apply it even to such shadows as the VIIth, VIIIth, IXth, XIVth, and XVth Dynasties, of which we know practically nothing. The method of dating in Egypt from the earliest times was by regnal years, so that for some brilliant periods where there is an abundance of documents we know the length of almost every reign in a dynasty. Even then comes the question, often difficult to decide, how many of these years must be discounted as belonging to times when father and son were associated together on the throne. But generally the documents are scanty indeed, and a laborious guess at the probabilities from the number of known kings and the apparent peacefulness or turbulence of the time has to serve. Perhaps our best chance for a true reconstruction of the chronology will be in the recovery of another Graeco-Egyptian Manetho with names and figures ungarbled, or another Ramesside Papyrus of Kings; some clear astronomical *data* may also be looked for, and would be of great value.

Suppose now for a moment that the classical writings on Egypt and Assyria had been wholly blotted out of existence, what would have been our loss? Less for the history of Mesopotamia than for that of Egypt. Egypt is nearer to the West historically as well as geographically; by commerce and by politics her life became organically connected with that of Greeks and Romans; and of old, as to-day, cultivated European travellers, notebook in hand, were attracted to the pleasant and accessible banks of the Nile. Yet for the history of the country the loss of their works would be little felt until the Saite and Persian periods are reached. From that point onward we are greatly dependent for filling the canvas upon the statements of Greek authors, in which, however, we can have but little confidence. The later history, from the conquest of Alexander, would of course have been a miserable remnant if gathered only from Egyptian sources. Even for the earlier times the loss of Manetho, Berosus, and the Canon of Ptolemy would be very appreciable; the loss of the geographers too would be felt. It would be difficult also to compile from the monuments alone a good outline of the important myth of Osiris such as may be obtained from the immensely garbled and overlaid version in Plutarch.

Nevertheless, and apart from the innumerable statements in the classical authors that have proved at least usefully suggestive, the loss of their works to Oriental learning would have been immense. The literary value and interest of their writings on the East led to a deep study of the subject-matter by highly trained minds. No doubt at first this prejudiced many against receiving evidence that tended to overthrow classical authority; but in many other cases it originated a desire to learn more from any warranted source. The existence of imperfect yet interesting work calling for improvement is one of the most powerful incentives to the exercise of originality and observation. The loss of the classical writings on Oriental subjects would have diminished the prestige of research into Oriental antiquity, by which so much illumination may be reflected back on to Hellenic studies. For in Egypt and Mesopotamia the attitude of Greek and Roman writers to the world around can be better understood than in their own native countries, and their perception of fact in remote antiquity can be more definitely tested than where inscribed monuments earlier than the fifth century B.C. are rare.

But suppose, again, that the monumental records of Egypt and Mesopotamia were non-existent, and that the classical accounts of their history and civilization alone remained. The critical faculty of endless Grotes and Niebuhrs could not decide finally whether to prefer Manetho and Berosus on the one hand, or Herodotus and Ctesias on the other. The history and archaeology of these unfortunate lands would, in fact, be a mass of more or less contradictory legend, the supposed bases of which would be discovered and re-discovered periodically in different forms until the happy day might dawn when scholars should cease at length from the hopeless and unprofitable quest.

Egyptology and Assyriology are now alive at every point, and their sober yet quickening influence on study is felt in every direction. Those who cultivate these sciences see them growing under their hands in every branch and twig, and thus are constantly incited to further effort. In the course of a few months a carefully formulated theory may be definitely swept out of the field by new evidence, or modified and crystallized into ascertained facts. Three successive years have just added to the realm of Egyptian archaeology, not only the period of the first two dynasties, hitherto absolutely unrecognized from contemporary remains, but also a long prehistoric period. Assyriology likewise has lately been pushed back into antiquity with almost equal rapidity. Though the subjects will probably always have their limitations, yet the insight of scholars and explorers is opening up new vistas on all sides. Picturesque and sustained narrative may be entirely wanting to the records except in tales and myths. The connexion of events in history has generally to be supplied as best it may by the modern writer. Yet Egypt and Assyria have left us a rich legacy of glimpses and pictures of human life, arts and manners and modes of thought in far-off times; and upon this legacy we are abundantly entering. For its due appreciation we must recognize that the interest is essentially anthropological and in no wise literary.

Our prospect for the future is bright. Egypt itself seems inexhaustible. Few of the cities of Babylonia and Assyria have yet been excavated, and each of them had its library and record office of clay-tablets as well as monuments in stone and bronze. In Northern Mesopotamia are countless sites still untouched; in Elam and in Armenia monuments are only less plentiful. In Arabia inscriptions are now being read which may perhaps date from 1000 B.C. The so-called Hittite hieroglyphs still baffle the decipherer; but as more of the documents become known these will in all likelihood prove a fruitful source for the history of North Syria, of Cappadocia, and of Asia Minor throughout. Occasionally, too, though it is but rarely, an inscription in the Phoenician type of alphabet yields up important historical facts.

When all is done, there is but scant hope that we shall be able to construct a consecutive history of persons and events in the ancient world. All that we can be confident of securing, at any rate in Egypt, is the broad outline of development and change, chronologically graduated and varied by occasional pictures of extraordinary minuteness and brilliancy.

1908 Nov. 2.

CHAPTER II.
PREHISTORIC GREECE

BY

D. G. HOGARTH, M.A.

DIRECTOR OF THE BRITISH SCHOOL OF ARCHAEOLOGY AT ATHENS

THAT there were great men in Greece before Agamemnon has been a familiar saying these two thousand years; but it has been left to the present generation to recognize actual work of their hands. Hardly twenty-five years ago the first significant documents of that prehistoric age were happened upon by the enterprise and the fortune of Henry Schliemann, but some years had still to pass before the true character and significance of what first he found was brought home to scholars at large. Signs that a revelation was at hand had indeed appeared a few years earlier, but they had been little regarded because little understood. Certain representations of Aegean races bringing tribute or booty to the Pharaohs of the Middle Empire, which had been remarked on Egyptian monuments, were discredited by the acknowledged possibility of serious error in the identification of race-names and lands. Indeed, it is only since we have had actual remains of those races themselves that their counterfeit presentments have had much meaning for us. Now that we can recognize the true nature of their garments by comparison with "Mycenaean" engraved jewellery and idols, and identify the objects they bear with the products of "Mycenaean" graves, we can assign to the Egyptian tributaries their racial family and habitat, without recourse to the still not too certain names of tribes and regions inscribed in hieroglyphic above or beside them. Furthermore, certain implements of an Aegean stone age had been collected; but these were felt to be evidence of no more singular a fact than that "man everywhere has the same humble beginnings." Early dwellings, containing painted stucco and vase fragments, had been found in the Santorin group of islands under secular lava deposits; and tombs had been opened at Ialysus in Rhodes full of pottery, implements, and ornaments of highly developed, but not Hellenic, type and technique. But in the absence of parallel objects elsewhere, and the prevailing state of ignorance concerning west Asiatic products, these stray Rhodian finds conveyed no intelligence to the world of scholars, and lay, little noticed, in the British Museum. The Homeric poems remained still the objective and farthest limit of archaeological criticism. By help of material documents, scholars had not been able to approach within centuries even of the Epic world; nor did their most sanguine hopes aspire higher than some day to attain so distant a goal.

Neither hoping nor expecting more than they, Henry Schliemann in 1868 brought his hard-won wealth and childlike belief in the literal accuracy of the Homeric Epics to the area of Homer's world. Money, an intimate and uncritical knowledge of the Epic text, boundless enthusiasm and equal persistence, a simple faith impervious to ridicule, and a humility always ready to be taught and to share credit with others—these were his stock-in-trade. Of archaeological experience he had next to nothing, nor up to the day of his death much sense of archaeological propriety or method. But in Schliemann's case, as in that of Mariette, the immensity of his discoveries makes it[1] impossible to compare what he failed to see and what he destroyed with what he found.

All the world now knows how Schliemann believed that the palace of Odysseus, the gates and towers of Ilios, and the bones of King Agamemnon were waiting only for his spade. His earliest essay in Ithaca ended in disappointment; but, undeterred, he went on to the Troad in 1870, and cut into the mound of Hissarlik, long marked by one school of topographical critics for the site of Troy, and actually opened first by Mr. Calvert, the American consul at the Dardanelles. In the next two years Schliemann succeeded in arousing only sufficient interest to be accounted a spy by the Porte and a harmless enthusiast by Europe. But the year 1873 was to bring promise of greater things; for, above one or perhaps two very primitive settlements on the bed-rock, Schliemann revealed a burned city with strong ramparts, something like a palace, a gate to serve for the Scaean, and, for crowning mercy, a regal hoard of goldsmith's work hidden in a crumbling coffer between interstices of masonry. Who could doubt this was Priam's own treasure, hastily concealed while the Achaeans fired and looted Ilios? The world was startled out of its habitual apathy in regard to its own past, and England especially, led by Mr. Gladstone, was disposed to believe, despite a few protests that, Ilios or no, this "Burnt City," besides being but insignificant in size, took archaeology in virtue of its products back at a bound, not merely to Homer, but far behind him.

The Porte, aggrieved by the division of the treasure, kept Schliemann away from Hissarlik awhile, and diverted his restless energy to Greek soil. Pausanias had recorded that in his day the burial-place of the house of Atreus was pointed out at Mycenae. Why should it not be there still in Schliemann's day? It was then 1876. Schliemann concentrated his efforts, in August of that year, on the site of the Achaean capital, notorious since the revival of interest in Greece for its walls, its sculptured gate, and its great domed tombs. While searching afresh one of these, the already rifled "Treasury of Atreus," (which yielded little or nothing), and clearing the Lion Gate, the German had also been having a great hole, a hundred feet this way and that, dug just within the citadel, somewhat at random, but also, apparently, after reasoning out in his own way the topography of Pausanias' narrative. His diggers came presently on a high double ring of slabs, fallen or standing. The Homeric analogy suggested itself at once to Schliemann. Here was such a "well-polished circle of stones" as that on which the divine artificer of Achilles' shield seated his elders by the city gate. Why then, it was asked at the time, dig deeper, for what in reason was to be found in the artificial filling in of a place of assembly? But one of this particular searcher's secrets of success was a rigid rule not to stop short of virgin rock, and down to virgin rock, despite protests, he would now go. Encouragement was speedily granted. Certain slabs of soft stone came into view bearing reliefs. If these were, as they seemed, funerary, Schliemann could not doubt whose tombs should lie below; for who but a city's greatest heroes could be, and in historic Hellas ever were, laid in its *Agora*?

For some reason, however, he paused on the brink of discovery to wind up other work, and not till late in November persevered in the Circle. The remaining earth was soon dug out, and one after another, at different levels, appeared five rock-hewn graves, once roofed, but now in a state of ruin and filled with detritus. This was scraped away from the graves as each was found, and piece by piece was revealed one of the most wonderful hoards that have ever met a treasure-seeker's eye. Gold appeared in abundance never before seen in Greek tombs, or indeed in any but Scythian, beaten into face-masks, head-bands, breast-pieces, and innumerable stamped plaques, into bracelets, necklaces, rings, baldrics, trinkets, dagger- and sword-hilts. Ivory, silver, bronze, alabaster were there as well and in profusion, the whole treasure in mere money value being worth thousands sterling. Some loose lying objects and a sixth grave were found later, the latter not by Schliemann.

To the discoverer, and to many others (who have representatives yet), the supreme interest of this marvellous treasure-trove consisted in the relation it was conceived to bear to the great " Achaeans " of Homer's story. The discoverer proclaimed far and wide that he had found Agamemnon and all his house; and Mr. Gladstone, writing a preface to the narrative of discovery, quoted approvingly Schliemann's inferences drawn from the "hasty character" of the burials and the "half-shut eye" of one male corpse —*videlicet*, the murdered king's, denied by Clytaemnestra the last sad rites of piety! Less sanguine scholars, however, demurred. The grave-furniture was not all of one period ; the condition of the corpses and the half-shut eye were due to the collapse of the grave-roofs; the number of persons and their apparent sexes did not fit either with the legend or with Pausanias, nor was it held conceivable that that traveller could have seen the actual graves in the second century A.D. Wonder turned to laughter, laughter which Schliemann's fanaticism, issuing in headlong joyous discovery of trivial realities in the Homeric story, was always in danger of arousing. But there is less laughter to-day. Twenty years have brought opinion almost round to him again. The majority of critics now admit the extreme probability that what Schliemann found was at least what Pausanias intended to denote. If the Greek traveller in his account followed any geographical order, and if he meant by the wall, within which was pointed out to him the burial-place of Atreus and his house, not the mean *enceinte* of the lower town, but the great conspicuous rampart of the Acropolis, then the traditional cemetery of the city's Heroes in the second century after Christ was that which Schliemann was destined to unearth in the nineteenth. Whether these graves contained the real Atreus and Agamemnon and their house we are not, and shall probably never be, able to say; but little doubt remains that what were believed to be their remains as long as seventeen centuries ago have now been brought to light. And it must be added that the pre-eminence of splendour which these Circle-graves still retain at this day, after Mycenae and its vicinity have been ransacked from end to end by the Greek Archaeological Society, creates a strong presumption that they were indeed those of the Heroes *par excellence* of heroic Mycenae. The tombstones may have been visible to Pausanias; or those, as well as the graves, may have been covered in his time by the earth-slides from the Acropolis (as was the case when Schliemann first went to Mycenae), and only their situation may have been pointed out by the awed tradition of the surrounding shepherds. This, however, may be asserted with confidence, that, either by sight or by faith, Pausanias became aware of the Circle-tombs, and handed down a tradition concerning them which probably contained more truth than falsehood.

But the gain accruing to science from the Mycenae hoard does not consist in this academic question. As soon as the Treasure was cleaned and arranged, the student of early civilization found himself confronted by a wholly new element of first-rate importance, whose place had to be found and fixed—products of an art which, as Charles Newton was the first to proclaim, could not be identified with any other art known at that time. Hellenists of the old school were forced to take account of the momentous fact that a civilization, capable of higher achievement, had preceded the primitive Hellenic in Hellas. What must have been their mutual relation, and to whom to ascribe this art before history? The world revealed by it recalled in some respects that depicted by the first articulate utterance of the Hellenes, the Homeric Epics; but also it diverged in vital points.

The glitter of the Mycenae gold drew many eyes, and by its light earlier discoveries were seen more clearly and fresh discoveries were made possible. While it was discerned that the Ialysus vases, now rescued from their obscurity, and certain intaglios known as "island gems," bespoke a wide area for this "Mycenaean" civilization, the products of the "Burnt City" at Hissarlik fell back into a place long antecedent. The world had gained cognizance already of an earlier and a later stage in a long process of prehistoric civilization in the Greek lands.

Thenceforward the eyes of archaeologists were open to a new sort of documents in the Aegean lands, whether walls or tombs, pottery or work in metals, gems, ivory, sculptured stone, or modelled clay; and it was not long before the revelation, first made by Schliemann at Hissarlik and Mycenae, came to be extended far beyond the point contemplated by him or any one else in 1876. Twenty years have brought an uninterrupted series of discoveries, of which the succession and particular nature up to 1896 have been set forth too lately in short and clear form to call for enumeration now; many of them will be referred to in the sequel.[1] The two years that

[1] Up to 1890 the prehistoric discoveries in Greece have been gathered together in Dr. Schuchhardt's *Schliemann's Excavations* (Eng. tr.); up to 1896, in the *Mycenaean Age* of Messrs. Tsountas and Manatt, and the third volume of Mr. J. G. Frazer's *Pausanias*, pp. 98 ff. The same ground is also covered by the sixth volume of Perrot and Chipiez, *History of Art*. More special attention is devoted to the

have elapsed since 1896, in spite of war and rumours of war in the Levant, have proved little less productive. The troubles, in which Crete has been involved, did not prevent Mr. Arthur Evans from acquiring new evidence from that island in the shape of engraved seals and other objects belonging to both the earlier and later bronze-age civilization. The general result is to differentiate further the two prehistoric systems of Cretan writing whose discovery was announced in 1894 and to refer them to separate origins. The pictographic system, now believed to be the later, shews strong Egyptian influence, and perhaps like the returning spiral ornament is owed to the Nile valley in the time of the twelfth dynasty. The linear system, on the other hand, whether syllabic or alphabetic or neither, seems to go back to more primeval times—possible relations with the Nile valley and Libya have been mooted—and to have been in the more general use. Latterly over fifty of its symbols, similar to those already known in Crete and the Fayûm, and shewing close parallels to the Cypriote characters, have been found scratched on Melian sherds. Dr. Tsountas has opened graves of a most early sort in Naxos and Paros, ante-dating, apparently, the well-known Amorgan cemeteries; and the Greek *savant* has continued the exploration of both the citadel-houses and the rock-tombs of Mycenae, finding, among other things, a head which finally establishes the prevalence of tattooing in the later bronze age. A Mycenaean cemetery has been explored at Thebes, and the existence of a civilization of the same period at Delphi

earliest and island remains in the Danish summary of Dr. Blinkenberg, translated into French by E. Beauvois (*Mem. des Antiq. du Nord*, 1896), *Antiquités Premycéniennes*. A good rapid summary of the whole "Aegean" question from first to last has appeared in *Science Progress* (1896-8), from the pen of Mr. J. L. Myres; and a survey of the evidence from Sicily and Italy has been published by Professor Petersen in the Bulletin of the German Arch. Inst. in Rome, xiii. 2 (1898).

has been proved by sherds found in tombs and the substructures of the Temple of Apollo. Throughout the Cyclades it has been shewn by the explorations of Messrs. Tsountas and Mackenzie that the sites and cemeteries of the most primitive civilization, on the edge of the neolithic age, far exceed in number those recorded hitherto for that region; and especially in the island of Melos, the site of Phylákopi, long known for its tombs, rifled about 1830, and its obsidian "razor" blades and very early potsherds noticed by Dummler in 1885, has been taken in hand by the British School at Athens, and shewn to contain remains of three distinct early settlements, one built on the ruins of the other, the latest being "Mycenaean," while the earliest is a typical unwalled village of the late Mediterranean neolithic period, called into existence by the local working and export of obsidian; between earliest and latest lie the remains of a strongly fortified town of the early and middle period of bronze, inhabited through many centuries. Influences of Asia, Crete, and the European mainland meet on this site, whose further exploration ought to contribute notably towards the solution of the problems which concern the origin and development of civilization in the Aegean.

The whole face of the Aegean prehistoric problem has been changed by these discoveries. Summarizing them geographically we find that remains, attaching to a more or less homogeneous prehistoric civilization in various stages of development, have been yielded sporadically by all Hellas, but chiefly by the south-eastern mainland and the Cyclad isles. The west Asian coast, as yet very imperfectly explored, has produced similar, though more scanty, evidence, chiefly at Hissarlik, in a regular stratification culminating in the sixth and greatest city, which

Schliemann, failing, by a strange irony, to recognize the only "Troy" that could possibly be contemporary with his Mycenaean graves, had called Lydian. Crete, not much better known, is evidently a focus of the earlier and later culture of the prehistoric period, and probably of much "sub-Mycenaean" survival. Cyprus has given abundant evidence of this civilization and of its later derivatives. Egypt, under Mr. Petrie's hands, has yielded deposits of prehistoric "Aegean" pottery—to use a term invented by the discoverer for momentary convenience— in the Delta, the Fayûm, and even on the Middle Nile. Finally, in the western Mediterranean, Sicily in chief, Italy less plentifully, Sardinia, and Spain sporadically supply parallels to the same class of products, whether of native or imported fabric. In Greece itself, the principal find-spots have been in the Argolid and in Attica. In the former region most has been learned from the palace-fortress at Tiryns, so complete in ground plan, and from the further exploration of Mycenae itself, where not only have most important architectural remains been exhumed, but, bit by bit, from the remains of the palace and the numerous smaller houses on the Acropolis, and from unrifled rock-tombs west of the city, a treasure of almost equal interest with that of the Circle-graves has been collected by M. Tsoúntas into the Athenian Museum. In Attica have been found the most remarkable "Mycenaean" dome-tombs outside Mycenae, one alone excepted, that of Vaphio in Laconia; remains of early houses have been unearthed at Thoricus and in Egina; while every-where in and about Athens the early sherds underlie later varieties. Indeed, such has been found to be the stratification on every prehistoric site that has been dug thoroughly in southern Greece; while Thessaly, Delphi, and most recently Thebes, Eleusis, and Corinth, have given earnests of what may be expected when the rest of Greece comes to be searched systematically for early remains.

Historically, if the interrelation only of all this discovery be considered, the result, rounded in a paragraph, is this : that before the epoch at which we are used to place the beginnings of Greek civilization, that is, the opening centuries of the last millennial period B.C., we must allow for an immensely long record of human artistic productivity, going back into the neolithic age, and culminating towards the close of the age of bronze in a culture more fecund and more refined than any we are to find again in the same lands till the age of iron was far advanced. Man in Hellas was more highly civilized before history than when history begins to record his state ; and there existed human society in the Hellenic area, organized and productive, to a period so remote, that its origins were more distant from the age of Pericles than that age is from our own. We have probably to deal with a total period of civilization in the Aegean not much shorter than in the Nile valley.

The remains of this vast age before history, so far as we may yet interrelate them, may be distinguished, for clearness' sake, as representing three periods. The first, stated broadly, is a primitive age of stone implements, vases, and idols, and of a brittle hand-made pottery, not painted or varnished, but often highly polished by hand, with piercings for suspension by cords, and, when not plain, bearing incised rectilinear or spiral ornament. Metal is only just beginning to be worked, and gold is not found. The dead are buried in cist-graves. To the settlements of this type, as yet best known in the Cyclad islands, are related the lowest strata of remains at Hissarlik (into which, however, enters a strange element, probably owed to inland Asia), and, apparently, Dr. Orsi's "pre-Sikel" remains in Sicily.

The second period in this artificial classification seems to cover an immense space in time. It is characterized by a great advance in building both with squared and unsquared stone, by the erection in its later ages of great fortifications and of many-chambered residences with ornament in stucco, by the introduction and full development of paint on ware, and by the passage from stone to bronze implements and work in many metals but not in iron, and by the first appearance of written symbols. The dead are buried in chamber-tombs. Of this period was Schliemann's first " Troy," the " Burnt City " of the second (or third ?) layer of Hissarlik ; of the earliest part of this period are the village settlements found five years ago at Thoricus in Attica and on the island of Egina ; and of two stages in this period are the first and second settlements at Phylákopi in Melos. To the latter part of the same period belong the oldest parts of Mycenae and Tiryns themselves, the earlier prehistoric remains found in Crete, the buried houses in Therasia, that class of Egyptian remains which Mr. Petrie was the first to separate from the " Mycenaean " by the light of discovery in the Fayûm and to call " Aegean," and the foreign influence noted in Sicily in products of the early Sikel period.

Finally, the third period, an immediate consequent of the second, is that " full flower of the European bronze age," the distinctively " Mycenaean," revealed in the Circle-graves, but there already on the verge of decline. Its apogee seems to fall in the middle of the second millennial period B.C. Its later products, ere the tribes of the north scattered it and in part destroyed it, seem to be represented by the contents of the Vaphio tumulus and of the Spata tomb in Attica, and to belong perhaps to the thirteenth and twelfth centuries. Later still we find its style surviving in Egina. In this period we meet fully developed colour, glaze, and varnish on the baked ware; the ornament has become mostly marine in motive, but human, animal, and vegetable forms also appear rarely. Processes of gold and silver work have been brought to great perfection, and the smiths have learned to make and use various alloys; bronze is still the useful metal, but iron is just beginning to be wrought. The horizon of intercourse has grown very wide, and materials, models of form, and motives of decoration, which are derived from the neighbouring civilizations outside Europe, appear in profusion. Men live in walled citadels of elaborate plan, constructed on methods approaching to the later Hellenic, and are buried in beehive-tombs; and all their remains seem to speak to a widely extended baronial system, possessed of great wealth and power, and having connexions in commerce and politics, which transcended Greece and the isles, and reached far into neighbouring continents.

Neither the precise dates nor the precise relation which these periods bear each to the other can be determined as yet. They are consequent, not coincident,—so much has been established by the stratification of more than one site in the Aegean; and that, starting to ascend from about 900 B.C., we cannot halt till at least the opening of the third millennial period is rendered certain by the depth of overlying deposits, by the many stages of the development in style, and by the comparison of parallel Egyptian objects. The derivation of various decorative motives, and probably of the returning spiral, from twelfth-dynasty scarabs (which seems established), takes Cretan art back at least to 2500 B.C.; and in all probability there is yet another millennium to be reckoned with. But what ethnic or political changes divided the Aegean periods, if indeed any such changes did divide them, is matter as yet for argument, not statement. The available evidence seems to point to a more or less unbroken continuity in Aegean production, but to that production having been focussed successively in different localities, now the eastern islands, now Crete, now the south-eastern extensions of the European mainland. The productive race was probably more or less identical everywhere and all the time; but its political condition varied, perhaps according as influences from outside were active or the reverse, and the race lived under its own lords or under intruders. That the eastern Mediterranean was the scene in early times of the passage and temporary settlement of intrusive warrior clans, mostly moving from east to west, is hardly doubtful. Such in all probability were the "Phoenician" dynasty of Minos in Crete and the Etruscans in Italy; and such too perhaps were the "Pelopid" kings of the Argolid. But the whole matter is still so new, that, while some consensus has been arrived at in regard both to the origin and to the ultimate fate of this prehistoric civilization in the Greek lands as a whole, few views have yet been propounded on the vicissitudes of its internal and intermediate history, and those few as various as the persons that propound them.

The better supported of these, however, will come up incidentally in the statement of those more momentous matters that regard the beginning and the end of the whole. Whence originated this great early civilization of the Greek lands? and what in the end became of it?—these are the questions that concern the world at large; for they bear in general on the mysterious origins of our civilization in Europe, and in particular on that seeming miracle of spontaneous growth, the art and culture of the Hellenes. And in all discussion of the latter problem must be involved also some discussion of a universal heritage of civilized man, the Homeric Epic.

Before Mycenae had been excavated by Schliemann

archaeologists had become familiar with an extensive bronze-age civilization of central and western Europe. Still earlier had they become familiar with bronze-age products of western Asia and the Nile valley; and a prejudice due in about equal parts to philology and to the Hebrew story of the dispersion of mankind caused it to be generally assumed that the culture of the bronze period in Europe was in some way the child of Asia. This, however, was no more than a presumption: no sound links were known, and there was on the whole more positive evidence for independent development from independent neolithic ages in each continent, than for the affiliation of the bronze age of one to the bronze age of the other.

In the geographical interval between these two areas rose to view in 1876 a bronze-age civilization of the Aegean. Since the minds of the classical scholars, in whose special province it was assumed to fall, were disposed, by all Greek literary tradition and the trend of a century of discovery in Egypt and Mesopotamia, to relate south-eastern Europe only to itself or at most to the East, the opening controversy already mentioned, upon the relation of Mycenae to Homer, led at first only to this further question, To which of the peoples, known to the Epic, and influenced by what civilization, also known to the Epic, should the newly found objects be ascribed? So strong at that time was the belief that Hellas derived the finer arts from the Orient—belief for which the Hellenes themselves are responsible—that an immigration or at least an importation from beyond sea was inevitably presupposed; and both the examination of the Circle Treasure and the evidence of later discoveries seemed for a time to confirm this *a priori* view. For many of the Mycenaean objects, early found at Mycenae itself and in Rhodes, have beyond all question come from the East, most obvious among these being fragments of Egyptian porcelain glass and paste, an ostrich egg with clay dolphins moulded on its surface, scarabs and porcelain plaques bearing hieroglyphic inscriptions and a *cartouche* of the eighteenth dynasty. The cleaning of the oxidized matter from dagger-blades, found in the Circle-graves, revealed inlaid scenes of most Oriental character, where figure the palm and lotus, lion and cat; the human figures seem to wear the scanty raiment of a sub-tropic clime; and the scenery is that of the Nile valley. The technique of these blades recalls nothing so much as the *intarsia* of the Ramesside epoch, of which superb examples are exhibited at Cairo. Two splendid goblets found later at Vaphio in Laconia were held to reflect in some degree an Assyrian style; and the ivories, which the tombs of Attica, as well as the graves found after Schliemann's time at Mycenae, have yielded, are even more suggestive of decorative motives and methods of fabric peculiar to the Semitic East.

It was not, however, conceived to be possible that either actual Egyptians or actual Assyrians imported the Mycenaean culture to Hellas, much less that they settled there. But an intermediary was looked for, and found at once in the Semites of Phoenicia. Homeric tradition made strongly in their favour. Their seafaring fame accorded well with the distinctly marine character of much Mycenaean decoration in metal or ceramic, which derives its motives from polyps and *algae*; and Greek legend, reinforced by the philological analysis of place-names on the Greek coast-line, of cult-epithets, and the like, and by the discovery of unmistakable remains of purple fisheries at Cythera and Gythium, created a positive presumption that the finer Mycenaean work had been created by Sidonians, of whose products, as it chances, we know otherwise very little; for the mass of the Phoenician objects, as yet surely ascribed, issue from the later stylized and eclectic art of Tyre.

It was soon remarked, however, that a large proportion of the art-work at Mycenae and other prehistoric sites could not have been produced otherwise than on the spot. This was obviously the case with all the architectural ornament, even such as a fresco at Tiryns and a similar ceiling of Orchomenus, whose motives seemed most certainly derived from the East, the counterpart having been found in a tomb of Egyptian Thebes. It was the case also with the stone reliefs, widely divergent as they are in style and period, set up on the citadel gate at Mycenae and above the Circle-graves; with the gold death-masks, which Mr. Frazer suggests were designed to keep a ghostly "evil eye" from the royal dead; with much even of the smaller gold ornamentation, for the moulds have been found in which that was fashioned; and, of course, with the architectural fabrics, one type of which, that of the dome-tomb, presupposes a very long process of development in constructive methods.

Mere importation by Phoenician traders, therefore, would not meet the necessities of the case. It had to be assumed that either Phoenician artizans had come repeatedly to inland Greece, or Phoenicians had been settled there for a long period. The difficulty felt about either of these assumptions in the face of Homer, Greek tradition, and philology, led presently to the appearance of counter schools of belief, which, having searched Greek literary authorities for an early race settled in Hellas and reputed productive, pitched now upon the "Carians," to whom Herodotus and Thucydides, if not Homer, attached importance before history; now on the "Pelasgi" of many legends and many genuine survivals; now, in defiance of the chronologists, even on the Dorians of the brilliant early Tyrant period. Each claimant-race had its supporting arguments: in one case, the supposed presence of analogous art-motives in Asia Minor, where "Carians" were also established in historic times, and their supposed historic connexion with the islands of the Aegean; in another, the wide area of "Mycenaean" remains, more or less coincident with that extensive range which vague Hellenic tradition ascribed to the "Pelasgi"; in the third, the evidence of continuity between "Mycenaean" and Hellenic products, and the late date at which Mycenaean decorative motives and fabrics have certainly been found in both south-eastern Greece and the isles. In the face, however, of these and all other views has persisted the Phoenician claim, put forward again and again by Dr. Helbig; and it still finds furtive and half-hearted support among certain archaeologists.

The longer, however, the investigation is continued and the deeper and farther afield it is carried, the more hopeless becomes the case of these particular Semites, whom, on all other shewing, we know to be the least original of their great family.[1] Out of all the positive evidence of documents, now collected from Syria and the Lebanon, there is nothing to shew that a culture identical or even kindred with that of the Aegean bronze age ever existed at all on the east coast of the Levant. On the other hand, the forms most characteristic of Phoenician art as we know it—for example, the cylinder and the scarab—are conspicuous by their absence among the products of the bronze-age culture of the Aegean.

For many years now we have had before our eyes two standing protests against the traditional claim of Phoenicia to originate European civilization, and those protests come from two regions which Phoenician influence, travelling west, ought first to have affected, namely, Cyprus and Asia Minor. In both these regions exist remains of early systems of writing which are clearly not of Phoenician descent. Both the Cypriote syllabic script and the

[1] A. J. Evans' Address at Liverpool Brit. Ass., 1896.

"Hittite" symbols must have been firmly rooted in their homes before ever the convenient alphabet of Sidon and Tyre was known there. And now, since Mr. Evans has demonstrated the existence of two non-Phoenician systems of writing in Crete also, the use of one of which has been proved to extend to the Cyclades and the mainland of Greece, it has become evident that we have to deal in south-eastern Europe, as well as in Cyprus or Asia Minor, with a non-Phoenician influence of civilization which, since it could originate that greatest of achievements, a local script, was quite powerful enough to account also for the local art.

Those who continue to advocate the Phoenician claim do not seem sufficiently to realize that nowadays they have to take account neither only of the Homeric age nor only of even half a millennium before Homer, but of an almost geologic antiquity. Far into the third millennium B.C. at the very least, and more probably much earlier still, there was a civilization in the Aegean and on the Greek mainland which, while it contracted many debts to the East and to Egypt, was able to assimilate all that it borrowed, and to reissue it in an individual form, expressed in products which are not of the same character with those of any Eastern civilization that we know. This intense individuality of artistic style displayed in the prehistoric Aegean products is the one point in all the "Aegean Question" that has commanded the general assent of archaeologists since Newton proclaimed it in 1878. And this character belongs not only to the later products, but to the earlier. The development of those from these is certain. If the Sidonians were the authors of "Mycenaean" art, they were the authors equally of the earlier "Aegean" art.

Without adventuring into too remote a period, we can now be fairly sure that, at the opening of the bronze age in the Aegean, the islands and perhaps the indented coasts of much of the mainland were peopled by a folk which had attained to commerce with their Eastern neighbours and to an independent development of civilization; and the probability is that the Aegean peoples, rather than the inhabitants of the harbourless Syrian coastline, were the pioneers of Levantine navigation.

To a vigour and enterprise, such as were later to characterize the historic inhabitants of the same area, these pre-Hellenic folk added a like originality. In the course of their traffic with the productive and prolific populations of the early bronze age in the Nile valley and inland Asia, they acquired, among many other things, from one the decorative motive of the returning spiral, which had come into being even before the use of metal was known, from the other the Ishtar types of cult-image and cult-symbols; but in each case they grafted the borrowed thing on to their own indigenous products, and gave, as it were, to the alien art a wholly new expression in new and native materials. The later we descend in time, the more frequent grows this sort of borrowing; till in the later period of bronze, the "Mycenaean," when there were possibly colonies of actual Aegean folk established in northern Africa, some of whose remains Mr. Petrie found in the Fayûm, there was so much intercourse with Egypt that on the one side half the finer art-motives and many of the fabrics of Mycenae were derived from the Nile, and on the other Mycenaean art in its turn came to influence that of the later Pharaohs; and the Aegean folk, bearing their characteristic products, become familiar objects in Egyptian paintings and reliefs.

That the Phoenicians also had intercourse with the Aegean people in the later bronze period no one proposes to deny. Homer can be amply justified, if not made to ascribe more to the Sidonians than actually he does. For a close analysis of the Epics will reveal the fact that the most art-production is there ascribed, not to Phoenicians, but to the Gods; and the most seafaring is done by Greek not Sidonian ships. And perhaps in their historical character of carriers of other men's goods these Semites did indeed constitute no small part of the medium by which a measure of Semitic symbolism and cult-ritual came to permeate the native Aegean religion in the later prehistoric age. But they carried away from Mycenae as much as they brought, and in the words of Mr. Evans[1] "the Tyrian civilization of historic times, so far as we know its actual remains, is little more than a depository of decadent Mycenaean art."

Schliemann's find at Mycenae, then, represented a late stage of an Aegean, or rather Levantine, civilization, which, like other high civilizations that the world has contained, borrowed all that it could, and as soon as it could, whether from Egypt of the twelfth dynasty by way of Crete, or by way of Phoenicia from immemorial Babylonia, whose city mounds seem to be almost as old as the river deposits on which they stand, or through the mediation of that "Hittite" kinfolk of northern Syria and Asia Minor, whose probable part in the history of transitional civilization, at first unduly trumpeted, and now unduly depreciated, must be estimated by their two unquestioned achievements, the development of a particular system of writing and a peculiar art. But not for all these debts was the culture of the Aegean bronze age one whit less individual and original than the civilizations from which it borrowed.

Thus, when we come to the ethnological question, we know at any rate what Aegean civilization was not. It was not the disguised product of any of the eastern peoples with which we have long been acquainted, least of all of the Phoenician Semites. But we can assert less

---

[1] Brit. Ass. Address, *cit. supra*.

positively than we can deny; and no name more distinctive than "Aegean" can yet be applied to the folk that produced the Aegean products. There were probably at different times different racial elements in its composition, that had come or came to share a common civilization. Some of these had been fused during the countless ages that Man had existed on the earth, even before the prehistoric Aegean productive period: some were fused wholly or partially only during that period. The small collection that has been made of skulls from the earliest graves of the region shews wide varieties of type in such neighbouring islands as Syros and Paros. If the later Hellenic and hellenized immigrants from the north detected in the early populations that they conquered or assimilated traits akin to their own, and called these "Pelasgian" or what not, there was also in that early people much that was non-hellenic, and always escaped Greek notice. We know now much more of the prehistoric ethnology of Greece than was known to the Greeks, and how should it serve us, therefore, to insist on the vague ethnics of their tradition? As we may not be sure even in the historic period how much of the Hellene there was in the Greek race, and how much of the hellenized alien, we may resign ourselves to silence at the present time concerning the precise ethnology of the prehistoric Aegean civilization.

And if we do not know the great racial family of the prehistoric Aegean folk, still more do the individual proveniences and vicissitudes of their sub-families and tribes escape us. The bechive tombs have been said to shew that the men, who originated that type of sepulchre, copied it from subterranean dwellings in a northern country such as central Europe. But the need for such dwellings is a matter, not of latitude, but of altitude above sea-level, and they might exist as well on the

Lebanon as the plains of Germany. Also this type is not a primitive one, but succeeds the rock-chamber with pitched roof, and is itself the product of more highly developed powers of construction. Again certain stone boxes in hut form, and the statement that Mycenaean houses had often a lower story not used for human inhabitation, have been held to indicate a tradition of pile-dwellings surviving from a lake region such as Switzerland. But the hut-boxes (far from certainly "huts" at all) are found in Melos and Amorgos—pile-dwellings in the arid Cyclades!—and this "lower story" has been shewn to be no story at all, but the foundation walls only, carried down underground to the rock. We shall probably learn something some day of the origins of these several peoples, but not by such subtleties as these.

The history of Aegean culture, could it ever be recovered entire, would almost certainly prove to be a history like the Egyptian, of intermittent renascences. After a period of decay or a tribal catastrophe, the old root revived under fresh influences from within and without, and put forth blossom again; but each renascence owed much to survivals from the one before it.

In proportion as "Mycenaean" art declined by stages, of which we have positive evidence in the series of finds from Mycenae itself and in the late dome-tombs, we fortunately approach the beginning of reliable literary tradition. The passage from decadent Mycenae to renascent Corinth and Athens is illumined for us by the Dorian and Ionian legends, which many Greek authors have preserved, and by the poems which go under the names of Homer and Hesiod.

Greek legend, which, as a living authority has declared, is not in the light of archaeological discovery "lightly to be set aside," is strongly reminiscent of some great southward movement of men of the north not long before the opening of the Hellenic period. The result was represented in Greek literature as a conquest of the Peloponnesus and the establishment there of the typical Hellene, the Dorian, in succession to dynasties of god-descended kings. These, however, and their subjects were not imagined to be other than in some sense Hellenic, were they Achaeans, Danai, Pelasgians, or what not. Moreover, not only does literary tradition not countenance the belief that these elder inhabitants were wholly swept out of existence or out of their homes by the Dorian immigration, but there are many well-known anomalies in the later institutions and social state of both the Peloponnesus and continental Greece which seem to attest positively the survival of a civilization older than that of the Hellenes of history—for instance, those non-Spartan inhabitants of Laconia, where three great burial-places at least attest the presence of "Mycenaeans": the similar subject population of the Argolid where stood Tiryns and Mycenae; the "Pelasgian" origin claimed by inhabitants of Attica, Arcadia, and many other regions of the mainland and isles, even to Asia, Italy, and Crete; the Pelasgian worships, the cults of some particular families, the survivals of very rude and materialistic native creeds, the discrepancy between the Mysteries and the ideas and the ritual of typically Hellenic religion, the barbarian tongues spoken in Hellas. These instances are a few only out of many which strongly predispose a historian to believe that many elements from a prehistoric civilization continued long to exist in Hellas beside the historic; and that these were, like the Mysteries, neither unimportant in the social life of Greece nor without their bearing on the heritage which the races of that country have bequeathed to Europe.

To turn to archaeological discovery—while that supports strongly the tradition that at about the opening of the first millennial period B.C. some incursion of half-civilized but not wholly alien peoples, eclipsed for a time a high precedent culture in the Peloponnesus, almost blotting its centre, Mycenae, out of the list of cities,—it has at the same time, as we have indicated above, been shewing of late more and more clearly that that culture survived or reappeared in neighbouring quarters. Now Attica, for example, was a traditional refuge of the "Pelasgi" and the scene of the historic coexistence of a primitive race with immigrant Ionians; and here we find an early cemetery near the Dipylon Gate of Athens covering the transition from the practice of inhumation to that of burning the dead. The later pre-eminence of the inhabitants of the Attic area in the domain of art may well have been due to the numerous survival there of an elder race, preserving older artistic traditions. In this connexion it is interesting to note that archaeologists are tending more and more to see in the earliest historical style of Attic art, the geometric or Dipylon ornament, not a new creation, but an importation or a revival of a much earlier geometric style, found in the earlier strata of prehistoric Aegean sites; and perhaps this style was never lost by the makers of cheap ware for the common folk, even in the Mycenaean period. Be that as it may, it is possible, even probable, that in Attica either a less rude spirit than the Dorian or a conquest less complete than that of the Peloponnese caused the immigrants to profit by cohabitation with an artistic subject people, to share their blood, and to adopt and assimilate their art. In short, the "Ionian" of Attica in the historic period was a blend of old and new, a sub-Mycenaean hellenized. And if that is true of the Ionians in Attica, it may hold equally for the Ionians in Asia. Indeed, there is much to be said for the opinion that the ancient "Mycenaean" civilization on the east of the Aegean, of which the "sixth city" at Hissarlik—the real Ilios, if Ilios there were—is a surviving memorial, was largely reinforced by fugitives driven from the cities of the west by the Dorians; and that to this fact the world owes the splendid but mushroom civilization of the coast cities in the early Hellenic period, and, probably, the sending by way of the Black Sea and the Danube of sub-Mycenaean art fabrics and decoration to stimulate that culture of central Europe, of which the Hallstatt graves have given up admirable products.

As a memorial of the passing away of the greatness of Mycenae—possibly as an early product of this Ionian "after-glow"—we have the Homeric Epics. It would not be easy nowadays to find any one seriously to deny that as a whole the lays, which go to form these two great Epics, were inspired to some extent by the culture which Schliemann was the first to reveal. They are not contemporary with the great days of Mycenae—indeed, they do not profess to deal with contemporary or even recent events—but they are strongly reminiscent of the "Mycenaean" world, as of a heroic age still in all men's mouths. A striking series of coincidences between the Homeric and the late bronze-age civilization may be found set forth in all the latest handbooks:—that general identity between the Achaean Hegemony and the geographical area over which purely "Mycenaean" remains are spread, and between the cities and districts glorious in Homer and glorious in the annals of "Mycenaean" discovery, the greatest in both being no other than "golden Mycenae"; that well-known similarity between the Epic and "Mycenaean" society and the later Hellenic consisting in the fact that both are monarchical, and not exclusive of a "barbarian" world; that similar condition in which the two civilizations seem to have been in respect of literary expression, both possessing a writing system, but using it little (for both the sets of prehistoric Aegean symbols continue to be found only either in such short combinations on gems as suggest that they spell names or charms, or singly as marks of fabric on pottery and stone, there being as yet only one longer text, the half-dozen characters on the sacrificial table found in the Dictaean cave of Crete); that coincidence in the choice of ethical subjects for treatment in art, instead of the mythological, that were the rule in later Greece; that close correspondence between the scenes, the treatment, and the technique on the one hand of Homeric metallurgy, the shield of Achilles, the corselet of Agamemnon, the brooch that Odysseus says he saw in Crete, or the cup of Nestor with its stays on either hand, and of the other part such "Mycenaean" treasures as the fragment of a silver cup chased with a siege-scene such as both Homer and Hesiod describe, the *intarsia* work of the famous dagger-blades of Mycenae, Sparta, and Therasia, the Vaphio goblets with a series of intaglios bearing parallel motives, and certain of the gold cups found in the Achaean capital; that close parallelism of weapons, shields, armament, and war-chariots, established by Dr. Reichel, with one apparent exception, which, if true, goes far to prove the rule; that architectural agreement between the palaces of Alcinous or Odysseus and the ground plans of the royal dwellings on the hills of Tiryns, Mycenae, and Hissarlik;—all these and other minor coincidences would outweigh even weightier discrepancies than those that actually exist. For the latter, of which so much has been made in the past twenty years, have lost much of their force with the progress of discovery, and, all taken together, need imply nothing more serious than that difference in date between the Epics and the Mycenaean age which must be assumed in any case. Homer sings of the beginning of the age of iron; but the word "bronze" is still in use as the conventional term for lethal metal. At Mycenae, on the other hand, bronze is the material for implements and arms, but iron is already known and fashioned into rings; and weapons of both metals were found lying beside the dead in the tombs recently opened on the slope of the Areopagus at Athens. The women of Homer wore unsewn garments, and pinned them with the *fibula*, or safety-pin; the women of Mycenae, if we may judge from gems and other representations, affected for the most part garments pieced and sewn;[1] but still, since a few *fibulae* have been found there, the fashion of the Homeric and later dress was not altogether unknown.

And now for a more serious divergence. The dead in the Epics, with one or two special exceptions are burned, though sometimes after temporary embalmment; the "Mycenaean" corpses in the flourishing period of the Circle-graves and the later age of the chamber-tombs were never incinerated, but always inhumed, and laid swathed and embalmed at full length, or more often simply clad as in life, and placed in a sitting posture. Now the two practices of incineration and of inhumation presuppose two very different creeds concerning the other world— the one holding that all that will still exist of the man departs to a distant nether region of the dematerialized, the other that something of him will continue to live in the tomb as once it lived in a dwelling-house. Those who hold the one creed usually resolve arms, treasures, and necessaries of life with fire, that they may be admitted together with the corporal spirit into a dematerialized world; those who hold the other creed shut up these things, or *simulacra* of them, entire in the tomb. It must be gravely doubted whether the same people have ever resorted now to one treatment of a corpse, now to the other; and the argument that the discrepancy between

---

[1] It has been suggested that the peculiar tight bodice and flounce skirt, noted on certain bezels and gems, is Babylonian, and belongs to the imported Ishtar worship, of which we shall presently speak.

Homer and Mycenae may be overcome by supposing that those who inhumed their dead in the time of peace were prompted by the stress of war to burn leaves out of sight both all the teaching of anthropology and also the fact that the Homeric burning was no hasty process, but was carried out with all pomp, the ceremony being often postponed for many days till the survivors had due leisure to perform it worthily. Nevertheless, although the burial and burning of a corpse were regarded in antiquity (and still are regarded by thousands of educated Christians) as not less vitally opposed than right and wrong, resurrection and future bliss being held compatible with one and not with the other, we have actual evidence in more than one region of the possibility of a change even on this point taking place gradually in local opinion, a change due no doubt to the admixture of some new element with the old population. All the stages of such a transition can be seen in the Hallstatt burials at the dawn of the iron age in central Europe; the Dipylon cemetery of the ninth century or thereabouts at Athens shews inhumation in its older graves, incineration in its later. There are many instances of a corpse being inhumed, but its furniture and food supply burnt, and of the two practices long coexisting, though not being interchangeable, in one community. The discrepancy, therefore, between the Epics and the remains of the great Mycenaean period in this respect also need be due to nothing more than a slight difference in their respective periods.

The bards of Ionia or Thessaly, or wherever the Epic arose, while they aimed at true "local colour," were, like all early romancers, often unconsciously anachronistic; and especially in matters affecting religion or semi-religious usages they could not but shed an incongruous atmosphere, contemporary with themselves, about past men and things. So in the great Alexander Cycle the romance-writers of various faiths, while preserving a skeleton of historic truth, see in the Macedonian a Jew or a Christian or a Prophet of Islâm.

No more recondite explanation is required to explain also the divergence—if divergence there really be—between the cult ideas and ritual of the Homeric world and those inferred from Mycenaean remains. And the less weight attaches to this discrepancy since this one fact emerges from the fog, still enveloping the question of the "Mycenaean" religion, that it was catholic and eclectic in its ritual, its symbolism, and even its divinities. If there was beast or totem worship, which is not proved, or a *theriomorphic* ritual, the wearing of beast-heads and the taking by the priest of the shape of the god, which is hardly more certain, there was also something like the Babylonian Shamas with his sun-rays, and something like Ishtar of the Semites with her doves and shrines, and something like prototypes of more than one of the deities of later Hellas. Probably a loose polytheism characterized prehistoric as much as it characterized historic Greece. There was room within that aggregate of kindred races for the giant human deities of Homer and for much else ; and differences in geographical position or period bring before us different denizens of the Pantheon.

Finally, there is a possible, but not important, divergence between the position of women in Homer's family and the family of the Mycenaean age—*harem* at Tiryns, no *harem* in Homer. But was there a *harem* at Tiryns, and is there no trace of a *harem* in Homer? It is pure assumption that the secondary block of chambers to the north-east of the main house on the Tirynthian hillock represents women's apartments. These may equally well have been another house altogether—offices, storerooms, what you will. They contained, when first opened, nothing to indicate their character. On the other hand, there are many degrees in the *harem* system. The freedom of women in Homer is not more than that allowed to the women of many Eastern races, who yet would consider themselves, and be considered, to be inmates of a *harem*. In this and other respects the essentially Oriental character of Homeric life, as of later Hellenic life, has been unduly minimized.

So we find that there is no sudden and violent breach between Mycenaean and Homeric civilization, just as the later Hellenes felt there was no sudden and violent breach between the Homeric world and their own. The spade gives corroborative evidence. The earliest form of fluted Doric column ; the ground plan of the propylaeum, portico, and cella ; the pitched roofs of the temples,—these characteristics of Hellenic architecture exist in embryo in Mycenaean architecture. Gems, especially a class found in Crete and Melos, link the Mycenaean to the Hellenic art-motives ; the graves of the Dipylon and the Areopagus at Athens shew the Mycenaean types of pottery and metal-work passing into those of early Hellas. The "Mycenaean" Egina treasure in the British Museum is of the ninth century, an epoch when Corinth and Athens, lying in sight a few miles away, were already inaugurating the Hellenic styles. In Cyprus, and also in Rhodes, potters reproduced sub-Mycenaean forms far into the historic age.

Vague generalizations about Aryan blood and favourable conditions of climate and soil are, as M. Perrot has well said, altogether inadequate to account for the shortness of the apprenticeship served by the races of classical Greece to art. Archaeology and Homer, read in the light of archaeology, supply a better reason of the seeming miracle. Hellenic civilization developed in the direction of art with such marvellous celerity simply because the tradition of an earlier and high culture was still existent among a considerable element of the population in both European and Asiatic Greece. The ground was prepared from of old, the plant was alive but dormant; models existed already; methods of fabric and principles of decoration were there to be learned from others, and had not to be evolved anew by long and painful experiment. After a century or so of restlessness and struggle came a time of peace in the Greek lands, and inevitably with it another and the greatest renascence of the endemic spirit of art. By so much archaeology may claim to have explained away the miracle; it can shew whence came the vehicles of Hellenic self-expression, and why the Hellenes employed the vehicles they did. But, like all archaeology, it does not explain the existence of the Hellenic spirit, or tell us whence the Greek derived the political, the social, or the religious ideals which lifted him above his fellow-men. And so in this microcosm, as in the universe, we come back to miracle. We trace back the circumstance and the house of life, but not life itself.

The part thus played by "Mycenaean" civilization in prompting the rise of Hellenic culture gives it a place in universal history. The fact that it inspired the Homeric Epics puts all art in its debt. And the further fact that it supplied the real setting (so far as there was any real setting) for the events of the Homeric story gives it a more than merely antiquarian interest, especially for ourselves, who, like other northern nations—perhaps owing to some instinctive sympathy with a primeval age, some sort of deep-lying survival of the barbarian from which we spring—appreciate the greatest of Greek Epics not so much for their supreme poetic quality as for the character of their subject-matter.

But these are not the only obligations under which the bronze age of the Aegean lands has placed civilization. In the last few years the attention of archaeologists has been

called more and more generally, chiefly by the researches
and synthetic instinct of Dr. Montelius and Mr. Arthur
Evans, to the very considerable coincidences that exist
between patterns of fabric and decorative motives, characteristic of Mycenaean products in their latest period, and
certain patterns and fabrics which mark the renascence of
prehistoric art in central Europe at the opening of the age
of iron, which was soon to give rise to the early efforts of
Keltic productivity.[1] This was probably not the first time
that Aegean art had communicated a motive to northern
Europe, for far back in the bronze age the typical returning
spiral seems to have found its way, perhaps through inter-
tribal barter, along the amber-trade route of the Moldau
and Elbe valleys, to Denmark and Sweden, and even to
primitive Ireland. But at a much later epoch, the eighth
century B.C., we come on renewed and more remarkable
evidence of an Aegean influence. The great cemetery of a
prehistoric salt-mining community found at Hallstatt, in
the Salzkammergut, has given up abundant remains of a
civilization in many respects parallel to that of Greece in
the "geometric period." It has similar derivatives from
Mycenaean forms, following paths of degeneration similar
to those of the pendant disc jewels and open work in
gold which distinguish the Aeginetan Treasure of the
British Museum, a sub-Mycenaean product of the ninth
century. But Mr. Evans[2] distinguishes another contemporary civilization, that represented by the many cemeteries
lately explored in the lands, Illyrian and Venetic, about
the head of the Adriatic. This was in part a southern

[1] *I.e.* probably about the eighth century, a century later than the
beginning of the iron age in the Aegean. These "ages" are of course
not contemporary all the world over. Metal found in one country, *e.g.*
copper in Cyprus, causes the stone age there to give way earlier than
elsewhere. Iron seems to have travelled northwards from Africa *viâ*
Cyprus to Mycenae, and thence, or from Asia Minor, to the Danube.

[2] Rhind Lectures at Edinburgh in 1895, not yet published. Cf.
also Brit. Ass. Liverpool Address *cit. supra.*

extension of the Hallstatt culture, and in many respects moved parallel with it; but its remains shew more distinct "Mycenaean" survivals. Both civilizations owed their acquaintance with the Aegean art to the double route opened for the amber trade, on the one side overland through the Balkans, on the other by sea up the Adriatic, the two converging near the site of the later Carnuntum on the Danube. But of the two centres of early iron-age culture it is the "Venetic" or "Illyrian" that has most affected north-western Europe; for with it an important branch of the Keltic stock came in contact about the fifth century. This it was which, coming south of the Alps, has left such striking evidence of the degree to which it was influenced by the art of north Italy, both near Bologna, and in the graves of its race dug after the return to Switzerland, notably at La Tène. Through these Kelts the returning spiral, the *triquetra*, and other originally Mycenaean motives passed to the Belgae, and by their mediation ultimately to our islands, to reappear in native imitations on early British sword-hilts and caskets and trinkets, and, ere all recollection of it was finally banished to Ireland, to suggest a scheme of decoration to the sculptor of the Deerhurst font.

CHAPTER III.
HISTORIC GREECE

BY

ERNEST A. GARDNER, M.A.

YATES PROFESSOR OF ARCHAEOLOGY, UNIVERSITY COLLEGE, LONDON

IN the great revival of Greek influence, which we call the Renaissance, appreciation of Greek literature was intimately associated with appreciation of Greek art and antiquities; in the second Renaissance, as it may almost be called, at the end of the eighteenth and the beginning of the nineteenth century, the two studies were less closely combined. This was more particularly the case in England, and the unfortunate consequences survive to a great extent even to the present day. The growth of specialization, and the restriction of the field within which detailed and accurate knowledge is possible to the individual scholar, have affected the scope and methods of classical studies. The disadvantages resulting from too narrow a pursuit of the linguistic and literary side are as obvious as those that attend too exclusive a study of art and antiquities. If the one tends to degenerate into pedantry, the other, if separated from its relation to history and literature, may well sink into mere antiquarian dilettantism. It is only to a scientific and appreciative combination of the two that we can look for the continuance and progress of classical studies. There is no doubt that in recent years a great change has come over the methods and the position of classical archaeology, especially in England. This change is in some respects only a part of the advance that has taken place in all scientific investigation; for archaeology, when it deals with the material remains of ancient life, has much in common with the physical sciences, and pursues similar methods, whether in the acquisition of new *data* by excavation and exploration, or in classification and comparison of what is already found in the laboratory or the museum.

It is not, however, the improved scientific status of archaeology that now concerns us, so much as its relation to classical study and to modern education in general. And for the classical scholar, as well as for all educated people, the chief gain from excavation, in particular, does not lie in the discovery of works of art or of other things that can be carried away, much as these may teach us about the surroundings and even the thought of the Greeks. It is, above all, the revelation of the sites themselves, as they appeared in ancient times, that aids us in realizing Greek life and history. The narratives of Herodotus and Thucydides gain a new meaning for us as we trace the foundations and the architecture of the temple destroyed by the barbarian invader, the old Pelasgic walls of the Acropolis, and the cleft through which the Persians climbed to attack from the rear the defenders of the wooden wall; and the Plutus of Aristophanes becomes far more real when we see, at Athens and Epidaurus, the actual porticoes in which the patients slept to await the healing visitations of Asclepius. Travelling in classical lands is a very different thing now from what it was even twenty years ago. For the impressions of an earlier traveller, admirably adapted by reading and sympathy to appreciate all he saw, one can turn to a book like Wordsworth's *Greece*. In the earlier years of this century, it was the position and natural surroundings of the various places, the outlines and colouring of the landscape, that combined with classical associations to make the peculiar charm of Greek travel; but upon most ancient sites there was little to be seen to indicate the topography, still less to shew the character of the buildings; the few scanty remains that were not hidden beneath the soil were often, as even on the Acropolis itself, surrounded by the mean hovels of modern inhabitants. But travelling in Greece has now acquired a new character and interest. It may, indeed, have lost something of the fascination of uncertainty and the constant chance of new discovery that used to reward the traveller : such things must now be sought farther afield —in Asia Minor, for example. But, in compensation for the loss, the modern traveller can tread the very pavement of the ancient buildings, can trace their plans, and study the works of art with which they were once decorated, and can restore in his imagination the temples and shrines, sometimes even the public buildings and private houses, as they stood two thousand years ago.

It is true that the earlier traveller might derive aesthetic pleasure from the quaint confusion with which ancient and mediaeval and modern were mingled together. At Athens, for example, it is a doubtful gain, from the picturesque point of view, that the little town of Turkish times, with its walls and minarets, should have been replaced by the modern city, though the fact is a pleasing testimony to the renewed prosperity of Greece. But at least the Acropolis has been purified from modern and mediaeval occupation, and restored to an undisturbed enjoyment of its classic glory ; and if an excess of zeal has led to the abolition of some later features that had their own historical associations, such as the Frankish tower or the bastion of Odysseus Androutsos, these few mistakes cannot be set in the balance against the incalculable gain that has resulted. The scientific study of the Acropolis has culminated in the systematic excavations that have searched the whole site down to the living rock, and restored to light the records of early Attic religion and art. For it has been found that the whole area was covered, from a level a few feet above the rock up to nearly the present surface of the ground, with a mixture of fragments of architecture, sculpture, bronzes, vases, and other antiquities that could only have been placed there when the hill was being surrounded with its massive walls and terraced up to its present height and shape. It follows that the great mass of *débris* which fills in the terracing must be the remains of the buildings and works of art destroyed by the Persians when they sacked the city in 480 B.C. The returning Athenians, instead of trying to mend or restore these fragments, simply used them as rubble to support a terrace on which the splendid monuments of the fifth century were to stand; and the result is that they have presented to our age a magnificent and representative collection of all their attainments in the various arts at the time immediately preceding the Persian wars—a record as valuable as if a museum, formed by them for this very purpose, had been preserved intact to the present day. A somewhat similar state of things has been found elsewhere also. Thus at the Greek colony of Naucratis in Egypt the contents of the temple of Aphrodite had all been broken up and thrown out in the precinct, probably when the Persians captured the town in 520 B.C.; and afterwards a new temple was built over the fragments.

The value of the accurately dated examples from the Acropolis as representing an epoch in the history of art is peculiarly clear in the case of sculpture, architecture, and vase-painting. But the foundations of the various buildings themselves have also their own tale to tell. With their help we can follow all the stages by which the Acropolis was transformed from the fortress of a primitive settlement into that glorious centre of religion and art, itself a dedication to Athena, that has become a familiar conception to us. First we can trace the circuit of the enormous "Pelasgic" wall of fortification, like those of Mycenae and Tiryns; this wall follows the natural contours of the rock, and is provided with a postern approached by a long flight of steps. On the summit are the scanty but characteristic remains of an early hall, such as we may also see at Tiryns and Mycenae—doubtless the "well-built house of Erechtheus," that was a favourite resort of Athena, and probably identical with her earliest temple. However this may be, we can see upon the same site all the foundation-walls of what was evidently the chief temple of Athena down to the time of the Persian wars. From these we learn that the core of the building, which consists of stones quarried from the Acropolis rock, goes back to very early times, and that it was later surrounded by a colonnade, dating in all probability from the time of Pisistratus. We may also see the entablature of this colonnade and portions of its columns built into the northern wall of the Acropolis, and, in the museum, considerable remains of the great marble group that filled one of its pediments—Athena in the midst of the great battle of Gods and Giants. Numerous other architectural sculptures have been found also, most of them of earlier date and of ruder material, which decorated smaller shrines on the Acropolis.

By the help of all this evidence we can reconstruct in our mind a picture of the Acropolis as it was in the days before the Persian wars—a fortress on a hill, of irregular contour, and surrounded by colossal walls. Near the highest point of the natural rock, between the sites on which the Parthenon and the Erechtheum now stand, was a great temple, its coarse limestone columns and entablature covered with stucco and enriched with painted ornaments, and its pediments already shewing promise of the excellence in sculpture that another century was to bring. Around it were smaller shrines, each with its quaint decoration in architecture and pedimental groups, while innumerable dedications of statues and vases filled both the buildings and the space that surrounded them.

We can now appreciate the extraordinary nature of the transformation that came over the Acropolis in the fifth century, and can trace the phases through which it first had to pass. When the Athenians came back, victors of Salamis and Plataea, to their ruined walls and blackened temples, we have no historical record of their first measures to restore the Acropolis; for the walls built with haste at the suggestion of Themistocles were the walls of the town, not of the citadel. There seems to have been no attempt to give back to the Acropolis its character as a defensible stronghold; as a fortress it had been dismantled since the expulsion of the Tyrants, though its natural strength always made it easy to defend by barricades. The intention was to terrace up the interior so as to gain a more imposing and more level space for the great precinct of Athena, the centre of Athenian art and religion; the northern wall was constructed in part of the *débris* of the buildings destroyed by the Persians; but the splendid sweep of the eastern and southern walls, which gives a unique character to the whole plan, was due to the design of Cimon, and was fittingly provided for by the spoils of his victory over the Persians on the Eurymedon. We can now see how far these walls were set outside the old Pelasgian fortification, and appreciate the boldness of the design which not only added a large space to the Acropolis, but gave a new symmetry to its outline. We can see also the traces of the old gateway, contemporary with these walls, that was superseded later by the Periclean Propylaea, and the huge basis constructed so as to place the new temple of Athena in that commanding position that the Parthenon now occupies—a basis used, with some modification, for the Parthenon itself.

Thus we have a picture also of the Acropolis in the period between the Persian wars and the middle of the fifth century; and if we can find in it only traces of temples that were never completed, we can also see the promise that was to meet with such rich fulfilment in the buildings of the Periclean age. On these buildings themselves there is no need to dwell. Though we have learnt many details as to their plan and construction from recent study, the Parthenon and the Erechtheum must remain for us what they were for earlier travellers. But excavation has given us new evidence as to the works of later periods also; for example, the temple of Rome and Augustus that stood in the midst of the open space before the east front of the Parthenon—a typical monument of a degenerate age. Outside the Acropolis, too, excavation and topographical study have extended our knowledge of ancient Athens. Only within this last year the caves of Apollo and Pan have been found beneath the northern rocks of the Acropolis—not so near the west entrance as was formerly supposed; and close to them is the deep natural cleft in the rock through which the Persians doubtless ascended when they captured the Acropolis, and down which the Arrhephoric maidens descended every year with their mysterious burden. Even for those whose interests are mainly or even exclusively on the literary side, it is evident how much is gained by a more exact knowledge of the Acropolis, and of its appearance at various stages of its history. Homer's mention of the well-built house of Erechtheus, Athena's favourite resort, and of the rich temple of the goddess in which she set the hero to be honoured by the sons of the Athenians, as the years went by, with sacrifices of bulls and rams, seemed to have little to do with the perfect gem of Ionic architecture that we know as the Erechtheum. But now that we can trace the history of the early shrines upon the same site back to a prehistoric palace in which the kings of Athens must have lived, both the literary reference and the extant building acquire a new significance and interest; and we can advance many steps towards the origin of the tradition from which the literary version is derived. Other instances such as this will readily occur to those who think about the matter. The results, at least, of archaeological investigations are already indispensable to all classical students.

The Acropolis of Athens must serve as a typical example to shew how much new and unexpected material can be gained by excavation, even upon a site that was already familiar, and that seemed to bear upon its surface all its most distinctive monuments. It would be impossible here to give even an equally summary sketch of the numerous other excavations that have taken place in Greece, some of them on a larger scale, some on a smaller, some more varied in their results, others throwing light only on a comparatively limited question, but all alike contributing their quota to the rapid accumulation of archaeological evidence as to the art, the history, and the social life, in some cases even the literature, of the Greeks. A few more instances must suffice to indicate the nature and the variety of what has been found.

The most valuable results gained by excavation on the Acropolis at Athens are due, as we have seen, to the sack of the city by the Persians. The accumulation of *débris* on a classical site is, however, only in exceptional instances to be traced to a single historical event. Thus at Olympia and at Delphi, the two most extensive sites in Greece that have ever been thoroughly cleared, a vast number of objects of all kinds, dating from the earliest to the latest times, have been recovered; and it has often been possible, by an accurate and minute observation of the exact position where these were found, and their relation not only to the larger buildings but also to smaller constructions such as the bases of statues or the watercourses of various periods, to establish either their absolute or their relative date, and so to introduce certainty and rigidity into the chronology of Greek art and antiquities.

The excavation of Olympia, the first of these great sites, an excavation still unsurpassed in its scale, its thoroughness, and the richness of its yield, is already familiar to English readers. Where before there were visible but a few broken columns emerging from a cultivated plain, we can now trace the sacred Altis with its temples and altars, its treasure-houses and innumerable bases of statues, the council-chamber and the sacred hearth, the gymnasium where the athletes were trained and the stadium where they ran, even the very grooves cut in the stone sill for their toes to grip as they started, the halls for the reception of official envoys, and the porticoes that served to house less distinguished pilgrims. Amid these surroundings, the Olympian worship of Zeus and the great athletic festivals of Hellas seem to take new life before our eyes, and the odes of Pindar gather fresh meaning as we stand amidst the surroundings where many of them first were sung.

From Olympia we naturally turn to Delphi, which the French have excavated with a brilliance that emulates the performance of the Germans at Olympia. It would be difficult to imagine two sites more different in their natural features than these. While Olympia is all on a level, covered over before excavation by several feet of alluvial earth, and situated in the smiling valley through which the Alpheus wanders over its broad and stony bed, Delphi clings in a succession of terraces to the side of the mountainous gorge of the Pleistus. Below it is a precipitous descent to the river; above it overhanging cliffs border the great plateau from which rises the summit of Parnassus. Each site presents peculiar engineering difficulties of its own; at Delphi these have been overcome by an admirably planned series of tramway lines, that carry the earth about half a mile and shoot it into the ravine below. Now one can enter the sacred enclosure, and follow the route of the old processions up the still extant paving of the sacred way, that zigzags from terrace to terrace up to the temple itself. On either side are the treasuries of the various Greek cities, and the bases of statues or groups set up to commemorate the most stirring events of Greek history. It has, indeed, been necessary to remove the sculpture that once adorned these treasuries, and was found lying around their walls, to the temporary museum; but this sculpture still remains at Delphi, and will remain there when a new museum has been built to hold it. Thus it will always be possible, here as at Olympia, to study the sculpture in the place where it was set up, and to realize its effect in the surroundings for which it was originally designed. If we mount the steep slope above the sacred enclosure, we reach what is perhaps the greatest surprise that Delphi has to offer: high on the mountain-spur is the levelled space of the Pythian stadium, still shewing the starting-place and goal of the runners, and the tiers of seats for spectators. Here more than anywhere else it is possible to realize what a Greek stadium looked like when it was perfect, and to appreciate the graceful curves and unbroken lines of the seats.

Perhaps no centre of Greek religion has excited more curiosity in all ages than Eleusis, chiefly because of the mysterious secrecy of its rites. The excavations made early in this century by the Society of Dilettanti had only served to enhance this curiosity by the discovery of subterranean passages and chambers that were supposed to have some connexion with the celebration of the Mysteries. A systematic excavation of the site, undertaken by the Greek Archaeological Society, has indeed dispelled this illusion as completely as Lobeck's *Aglaophamus* discredited the older speculations about the mystic doctrines of Eleusis: the subterranean passages were but drains and cisterns. But on the other hand, we now have a complete plan of the sacred precinct of Demeter and of the great Hall of the Mysteries, surrounded by tiers of steps on which the initiated were to sit; and as we look at this great square hall filled with columns, we at least appreciate the setting of the sacred drama, though we have still to be content with the scanty evidence of literature as to its action and dialogue.

At Epidaurus a side of Greek religion hitherto but little known has now been made familiar to us in many of its details. We can see the plan of the sacred precinct of Asclepius, the theatre and stadium provided for those who visited his shrine and sought his aid, and the numerous inscriptions that record the cures of the god and the dedication of grateful patients. From these inscriptions we learn many interesting details as to the methods of cure. Allowing for pious exaggeration, we still have many records of cases which seem to shew a kind of faith-healing, such as even to-day is efficacious at places like Lourdes and Tenos, especially in various forms of hysteria. Besides these cases we find others in which surgical aid seems to have been given by the priests, with the help of narcotics or anaesthetics. But in early cases we find that all cures are almost, if not quite, immediate, the regular formula being that the patient slept in the *abaton*, saw a vision, and went out whole the next morning; in the visions, the snakes and dogs that accompanied the god frequently appeared as healing agents. In later times, whether faith had decayed or therapeutic skill had increased, we find instances of patients who stayed for a long time at Epidaurus, and underwent a regular diet and regimen of baths and exercise; but there is no trace of such a custom in the best days of Greece. And the Hieron of Epidaurus can add to these interests the remains of its unique Thymele or Tholus, which rivals the Erechtheum in delicacy of execution, and its theatre once famous as the most beautiful in Greece, and still, fortunately, in an extraordinarily perfect state of preservation, both buildings designed by Polyclitus the Younger.

A site of very different character is offered by Megalopolis. Founded to form the capital of federated Arcadia in 370 B.C., it can pretend to no monuments of remote antiquity; but it is an example of a town laid out on a consistent plan, and furnished with civic buildings to match its new institutions. On one side of the broad bed of the Helisson excavation has shewn the Agora, still surrounded with its porticoes and temples; on the other is the theatre, the largest in Greece; and forming part of the same design is the Thersilion, or parliament house of the ten thousand Arcadian deputies. This building is unique in its purpose and in its plan. It resembles both the Persian Halls of Audience at Susa and Persepolis and the Hall of the Mysteries at Eleusis, but with a difference; for its floor slopes up from the centre to the sides, and it also has a very curious radiating arrangement of its numerous columns, so that they would fall into rows, one behind another, when viewed from a central point in the hall, and obstruct the view of a speaker as little as possible.

These excavations, and many others which it would

require much space to enumerate, have not only laid bare to our eyes most of the sites that are richest in classical associations, but they have also yielded, in the objects found and the circumstances of their finding, a knowledge of the development of Greek art such as was hitherto unattainable. The use of topographical knowledge to the historian is too obvious to need illustration; and we have already seen examples of the advantages it offers to the student of Greek literature. Perhaps at first sight a knowledge of the history and attainments of Greek art may seem less indispensable, and therefore may call for more consideration. The light thrown by vases and by coins upon the religion, the mythology, the daily life, and the history of the Greeks is indeed evident, and we shall later notice some examples of its revelations; but the history of art itself, and especially of sculpture, the most characteristic art of Greece, perhaps may be thought by some to belong to the archaeological specialist rather than to the scholar or the general reader. So far as details, and especially controversial details, are concerned, this is doubtless true; but the more general results of archaeological study in this department cannot be safely ignored by any one who wishes to obtain a wide and comprehensive view of Greek life and thought. Phidias and Praxiteles and the Pergamene sculptors are just as characteristic of the ages to which they respectively belong as Aeschylus or Euripides or Theocritus, and had hardly less influence on their contemporaries and successors. The development of literature and art does not indeed always proceed on the same lines or at the same pace. But it is impossible for those who are not familiar with the sculpture of the Greeks to realize the manner in which they created their gods after their own image; the higher ideal embodied in such works as the Zeus and Athena of Phidias—themselves indeed lost, but yet reflected in numerous imitations and repetitions—is expressly stated to have had a strong influence upon the religious conceptions of the whole people; and the subtle distinctions of personality, the expression of mood and of passion as well as of character, that we can trace in the sculpture of Praxiteles and Scopas, are a product of the same spirit that inspired the poems of Euripides and Menander. Or again, the subtle study of symmetry and proportion built up from numbers a perfection of form that culminated in the Canon of Polyclitus; and this fact is the most apposite and the most explicable commentary upon the arithmetical speculations of Pythagoras and of Plato. And, even apart from literary parallels, if art is to have any place in modern life, can we afford to neglect the work of those who created the types and images to which all later thought and imagination have conformed, and embodied in their statues a degree of physical perfection that has never before or since been equalled or even approached?

The revelation of the prehistoric age of Greece is perhaps the most remarkable of all the recent results of archaeology; but the exact relation of the prehistoric to the historic, of Mycenae to Corinth and Athens, offers a problem which still awaits its final solution. It is easy to trace survivals from the art and handicraft of Mycenae into the historic age; it is easy also to trace foreign influences that were unknown to the earlier civilization, but had considerable influence in moulding the beginnings of what was ultimately to develop into the art of Phidias and Praxiteles: but there is yet need of more discoveries and further research before the indigenous and the exotic can be clearly distinguished. The Homeric poems stand in the gap; it cannot be doubted that they preserve, on the one hand, many traditions of the glory of Mycenae, nor that they shew, on the other hand, many indications of a new order of things. Chief among these is the prominence of the Phoenicians, both as the makers of the finest works of decorative handicraft and as the chief traders and seafarers. The Phoenicians, in fact, took advantage of the decay of the great naval power which the kings of the Mycenaean age had inherited from the thalassocracy typified in the legend of the Cretan Minos, to establish trading and mining posts in the Aegean; and they did not give way until they were expelled by the growing power of the Greek colonies, reinforced by those last remnants of the Mycenaean power that were driven out by the Dorian invasion. It is to these eastern Greeks, rather than to the Phoenicians, that we have to look as the channel of the Oriental influences that have so great an effect on the rise of historic Greek art; Rhodes and Cyprus, Naucratis and Daphnae in Egypt, have yielded evidence of their artistic activity, and it is probable that systematic excavation of sites in Asia Minor itself will add even more valuable results to the scattered finds that have already come from that district—among them the magnificent sarcophagus from Clazomenae now in the British Museum, the finest of all examples of early Ionic painting. We find the eastern Greeks imitating in their pottery—that pottery which they had inherited from their predecessors of the Mycenaean age—the woven stuffs of Mesopotamia with their quaint friezes of wild beasts and winged monsters, and adopting from their Phoenician rivals the alphabet which was to be the vehicle in which the literature not only of Greece but of Europe should find its means of expression and preservation. It was through these eastern colonies, too, that sculpture, when at a later date it began its independent career, acquired the types and technique of its earliest attempts.

But in the meantime the Greeks of the mainland had

not been stagnating. The Dorian conquerors from the north were, indeed, of ruder and sterner character than those whom they supplanted; but they were of kindred race, with the same possibilities of social, intellectual, and artistic development; nor is it to be supposed that they expelled all the earlier inhabitants, many of whom remained as a subject people. Although the arts and civilization of Mycenae were already decadent even before the Dorian invasion, they had left behind them an artistic tradition and a skill in the minor handicrafts which preserved the germs from which a new growth was to spring. In some cases this new growth seems to be almost a spontaneous and direct continuation of the old; in others, racial differences have given it a new character, or foreign influences have modified its development. Thus the American excavations at the Heracum,[1] overlooking the Argive plain, and less than five miles from Mycenae itself, have produced an immense series of small and delicate vases, of the type commonly called by the unsatisfactory name proto-Corinthian. There is little doubt that these vases represent a local revival of Mycenaean technique; though new elements, some of them of foreign origin, are introduced, the fabric and the colouring closely resemble those of Mycenaean pottery; and while the series attaches itself to Mycenae at one end, at the other it passes by imperceptible stages into the Greek pottery with Oriental motives that is associated with the names of Corinth and Rhodes.

The connecting link supplied in this instance is the more valuable because elsewhere there is a more distinct break between the Mycenaean pottery and that which succeeds it. This next style is commonly known as

[1] The Heraeum pottery is still unpublished. Without making any one else responsible for the opinions here expressed, I wish to acknowledge my obligation to Dr. J. C. Hoppin, who is to publish the pottery found in Professor Waldstein's excavations.

geometrical, or, in its commonest and most characteristic form, as Dipylon ware, from the fact that great quantities of it have been found in the cemetery outside the Dipylon Gate at Athens. The style of decoration is by no means restricted to pottery, but occurs also on carvings in bone and wood, on tripods and other vessels of bronze; but pottery naturally offers the best means of classification, owing to the quantity in which it has been preserved and its almost universal distribution. The chief characteristics of the geometrical style are a rigid and structural division of the field to be ornamented, and a prevalence of such decorative forms as lend themselves to geometrical rather than to freehand drawing. Thus the spiral of Mycenaean art, which can only be drawn freehand, gives way to the rows of concentric circles connected by tangents, which can be drawn with a rule and a compass or a circular punch. The pattern familiar as the Greek fret, maeander, or key pattern, which is but a rectilinear simplification of the spiral, is also a favourite motive on Dipylon vases. It has been proved by excavation that this geometrical system of decoration overlaps, in its earlier phases, the later developments of Mycenaean pottery. In its later examples it is contemporary with decorative work, both in pottery, bronze, and other materials, in which Oriental motives become predominant. We have already noticed the Greek settlements to the east of the Aegean from which these Oriental motives came to be imported into Greek art; in Greece itself the chief centre of what is briefly called the Oriental style was at Corinth, the great emporium for the traffic from East to West across the Isthmus; Chalcis also and Eretria, from their close association and rivalry with the eastern Greeks of Miletus and elsewhere, are affected by the same influences, which penetrated from Euboea into Boeotia; while the Attic geometric or Dipylon style shews the same tendencies in its later examples, commonly known as Phaleric ware, from the specimens of it found at Phalerum. Later again the fabrics of Corinth and of Athens act and react upon one another, until there springs from their union that great series of Attic vases which is generally known as the typical Greek pottery, and is contemporary with the earlier stages of Greek sculpture.

It will be seen from this brief sketch that the Greek art and handicraft of the intermediate period, between the fall of Mycenae and the rapid rise of Greek art in the sixth century B.C., is now no longer known to us by a few isolated examples, but by whole series in connected development, which have been recovered by the excavation and by the study of the last few years. There are, it is true, many problems still awaiting solution. If we regard the Argive pottery from the Heraeum— the so-called proto-Corinthian—as a survival from Mycenae, and mainly the work of the earlier race, subjugated by the invading Dorians, what are we to say of the geometric style? The vigour and conciseness of its ornament, and the structural feeling of its composition, may well suggest, and indeed have suggested to some authorities, that it is to be assigned to the Dorians themselves, or at least to their influence. But if so, we are faced by the astounding fact that such a Dorian influence finds its fullest expression in the Dipylon vases of Attica. This may seem incredible; but in any case we have to face the problem of an entirely new system appearing, fully developed, in Attica, whose inhabitants claimed to be indigenous and to have suffered from none of those immigrations that had changed the face of the rest of Greece. For we cannot at present trace any direct development from the Mycenaean art, early prevalent in Attica, to the Dipylon style. This is one of the great gaps that still remain to be bridged;

and when so much has been done in this direction during the last few years, we need not despair that the discoveries of the immediate future may solve this as well as other riddles.

In one of Brunn's most suggestive papers, written before the discoveries of recent years had thrown so much light on this intermediate period—which we might almost call the dark ages of early Greece—he had discussed the curious phenomenon that, while the Homeric poems are full of descriptions of works of art, we know practically no names of historical Greek artists earlier than the sixth century. It is no small testimony to his insight and to the correctness of his methods that the solution he found to this problem is essentially the same as that which we must still accept, though we are now able to add a wealth of illustration and detail which was formerly inaccessible. The objects described by Homer are products of decorative art, whether armour or dresses or cups, not statues or other independent works. Of such decorative designs we have a continuous series recorded; Brunn suggested that while their general conception and arrangement was essentially Greek, their technique, and even the groups and individual figures of which they were composed, were of foreign, perhaps Phoenician, origin. We may now, in the light of recent discoveries, correct and supplement this suggestion. While foreign influence is not to be rigidly excluded, there was also in Greece, during this period, an extensive survival of Mycenaean traditions, partly preserved in heirlooms and other actual objects that had belonged to the earlier chiefs, partly in the skill and handicraft of artisans who still carved gems and made metal reliefs in a manner that they had inherited from their ancestors or predecessors in the land. These traditional survivals were the common inheritance of the Greek race; and they, together with the artistic skill they imply, make it easier for us to understand the wonderfully sudden rise to perfection of Greek art of the classical period. This appeared almost inexplicable formerly, when the Greeks used to be regarded as a new and uncultivated race, with no artistic tradition behind them; it seems much more natural now that we can regard the great advance of the sixth century rather as a renaissance, dependent only in part on foreign influence, and mainly due to the rich and rapid expansion of the germs that had already produced the earlier bloom of Mycenaean art.

When we come to the sixth century, the age of rapid development and progress in Greece, we are no longer exclusively dependent on archaeological evidence; but the great accession of this evidence that we have gained in recent years has both supplemented the literary traditions and enabled us to test their accuracy. The difference between the study of Greek art at the present day and in the last generation is due in the main to two causes—the more systematic arrangement and study of what was even then already known, and the great and continuous acquisition of new material. In many cases also the new material, either from its nature or from the circumstances under which it has been found, has enabled us to group around it, and so to date and classify, much of what was known before, but could not be identified. The chronology, both absolute and relative, of Greek vase-painting affords perhaps the clearest example of this. Though recent excavations have produced a certain number of fine vases, and a great many fragments of the most exquisite workmanship, these discoveries, mostly made on Greek soil, cannot compare either in quantity or in preservation with the vases found in the cemeteries of Italy. Most of these had already found their way into museums or private collections, and were commonly known, from their provenance, as Etruscan vases—a name which, although it has long been restricted to its proper sense in scientific nomenclature, is still sometimes to be heard in conversation. Even those who recognized the finest vases as the work of Attic artists found it very difficult to draw the line between genuine products of Greek art and their Italian imitations, or to decide the exact age of the various phases of Greek vase-painting. There was, in particular, a tendency to assume that the finest vases must have been made about the same time as the finest sculpture, and so to make the painter Euphronius a contemporary of Phidias. It is strange and also instructive to see how a preconceived notion like this could hold its ground, and be repeated as an ascertained fact in all handbooks; not only was there no evidence in its favour, but all indications were against it, as is clearly enough seen now that definite facts have been found to prove that it is wrong. Here, as in other cases, the new information has come from the Acropolis at Athens; for in the strata of *débris* which were buried just after the Persian wars there were found fragments of vases of the finest style, including some that are signed by Euphronius and other known artists. Thus the finest period of Greek vase-painting of the severer style has been exactly dated, and the progress of the art has been found to be far more rapid than was hitherto supposed. The whole early history of Greek art is thus put in a clearer light. The vigorous but refined and delicate work that marks the vase-painters of the beginning of the fifth century finds its exact counterpart in the sculpture of the same age, and we can trace the relation of these two sister arts and their action and reaction upon one another in a way that was impossible when we were misled by a false notion as to their relative chronology. Moreover, the discovery of such quantities of pottery in Athens itself has settled once for all the question as to when and where certain styles of work were produced, and has shewn, for example, that a great deal of the pottery of coarse and careless execution that was hitherto supposed to be of late or imitative work was really made in the same place and at the same time as the finest vases. It would be easy to multiply examples like this, both in the department of vase-painting and in other branches of antiquities; but it is clear enough already how much has been gained in this matter by thorough excavation and careful observation of its results.

It is obvious how great and direct an influence these results must have on the study of what is already known and preserved in museums and elsewhere. To continue our illustration from vases, it has been found possible to date and to classify, with the aid of the new evidence, whole series of vases that were before either wrongly placed or isolated. And careful and systematic study has had yet another result. In the case of sculpture, the work of the modern artist who had completed or worked over a fragmentary statue was only too obtrusive, and could not be ignored as soon as any critical history of art was thought of; the first necessity was obviously to get rid of the additions of the modern restorer before proceeding to the study of such part of a statue as was ancient. But in the case of vases, though the principle is precisely similar, it has only come to be realized and acted upon within recent years. Old illustrations and catalogues simply give pictures or descriptions of vases as they were—that is to say, in most cases, as they had come out of the hands of the antiquity-dealer, pieced together and restored and repainted until often nothing of the original surface was visible. The presence of a few vases fresh from excavation and untouched by this abominable process sufficed to shew the necessity of careful testing, and, if possible, of cleaning away the restorer's additions. The result has been that in most of the great collections it is now possible to see vases as they were painted by Greek artists, not by Italian antiquity-mongers of this century or last; and thus to find in them a trustworthy source of information, instead of a confused and misleading medley of old and new. This improvement was the more necessary, since we are dependent upon vases for so much evidence as to the religion and mythology of the Greeks, as well as their manners and social life. The poets and mythologists have preserved for us but a small proportion of the myths and legends of Greece; and these often in a form far removed from their primitive significance. Hence we must look to vases not only for the illustration of passages familiar to us in ancient literature, but also for the preservation of much that would otherwise be lost. For example, we can, by their help, realize many of the most tragic or picturesque scenes of the Epic Cycle—the death of Troilus or Neoptolemus, or the meeting of Menelaus and Helen after the capture of Troy—as vividly as if we could read the poems of Lesches or Arctinus. The beautiful episode of the visit of Theseus to Amphitrite, now restored to us in Bacchylides, was already recorded on vases, especially on the cup painted by Euphronius, itself a poem worthy to set beside the exquisite description of the ode. On vases, too, as in the works of Aristophanes, we seem to be admitted to the company of the Greeks in all their business and recreations. But while the poet must usually leave all details of dress or surroundings to inference or to the imagination of the reader, the vase-painter places the actual scene before our eyes, idealized perhaps into a beauty of line and pose which cannot have been universal even in Greece, but which does not obscure the reality from which it is derived any more than the jest or ridicule of comedy. We can see the market-place and the palaestra, the women at their toilet or their household employment, the boys at school and at play, the banquet and the symposium, while the white lecythi painted for the tomb shew us how the Greeks thought of death, and symbolize the affection and tribute offered by the mourners to their departed friend. And, moreover, now that all the pictures painted by the great artists of antiquity are irretrievably lost, it is the vases that reflect, however inadequately, the development of their character and technique, and can give us some notion of the work of Polygnotus and of Zeuxis.

The first stimulus to a connected and historical study of Greek sculpture probably came from the transference to accessible museums of great series of architectural groups and figures, which could be dated and assigned to certain schools or masters. Foremost among these come the Elgin marbles, which have since been joined in the British Museum by the sculptures of Phigalia, of Miletus, of Ephesus, and of the Mausoleum ; to the same category belong the Aegina pediments at Munich, and, of more recent discoveries, the series found at Athens, Olympia, Delphi, Pergamum, and Sidon. These, together with isolated statues of original Greek workmanship like the Venus and Asclepius of Melos and the Demeter of Cnidus, not to speak of later acquisitions, were a revelation to those who had before to be content with the faint reflexion of Greek genius in the Laocoon, the Apollo Belvedere, or the Venus dei Medici.

The history of sculpture, though it has not undergone in recent years any transformation so revolutionary as that which has come about in the history of vase-painting, has been supplemented by a greater accession of new material ; indeed, for the earlier period, what has been found within the last few years exceeds both in quantity and in quality all that was known before. This is mainly due to systematic excavations such as those that have already been mentioned, but partly also to isolated discoveries on Greek soil. It is no small testimony to the correctness of the methods by which the history of Greek art was reconstructed out of scanty records, that the new evidence has, on the whole, supplemented rather than altered our notions as to the periods and development of sculpture. Perhaps the greatest change has been in our knowledge of early Attic art. The literary authorities on this subject are very meagre, partly because the writers on whose works the extant compilations are based were more interested in other local schools, partly because the records and inscriptions had been hidden from sight with the statues to which they referred in the Persian sack of Athens. Hence it is that the very event that led to our knowing so little formerly about early Attic art is also the cause of the abundant discovery of its monuments in recent excavation. We can now see in the Acropolis Museum at Athens the sculpture that once decorated the temples that the Persians destroyed, as well as the statues that surrounded them, and consequently we are able to form a very clear notion of the art of Athens before the Persian wars. The earlier of these Attic sculptures is a series of architectural groups in the soft limestone of the Piraeus, that must once have decorated the smaller temples or shrines that stood on the Acropolis. What these shrines were we cannot say; the fragments of their architecture have also been found in the same layers of *débris*: but it is a curious and hitherto unexplained fact that most of them represent exploits of Heracles, his fight with the Hydra, his wrestling with Triton, the "old man of the sea," or his combat with the monstrous snake Echidna, this last contest forming one group with another in which the father and husband of the two combatants, Zeus and the three-headed Typhon, are also opposed. The sculptors seem to revel in the quaint monstrosity of these composite forms; their art has neither the conventional beauty usually associated with Greek art, nor the grotesque horror which a northern artist might have given to such subjects. But it has a quality of its own which is essentially Greek in character—an admirable adaptation of the design to the space to be filled, and an originality and boldness of conception that promise well for the succeeding age.

These primitive architectural sculptures date from the earlier or middle part of the sixth century, a time when, under Pisistratus, Athens was peculiarly open to foreign influences; and we can find the nearest analogy both to their vigour and their quaintness in works of Ionian origin. Perhaps the most striking thing about them is the remarkable preservation of their colouring, on which they depended to a great extent for their effect. Such coarse material as they are made of was never meant to be seen, whether in architecture or sculpture, but was always covered by an opaque coat of paint. The series that succeeds them consists of statues in marble—not yet in the Pentelic marble that was constantly used in Athens in later times, but in the even more beautiful marble of Paros. In these statues also the colour is excellently preserved, since many of them must have been thrown down and broken, and subsequently buried soon after their completion; and they have enabled us for the first time to realize what is meant by the application of colour to sculpture among the Greeks. When this material, the most beautiful in texture and in colour that exists, was substituted for the coarse limestone that had previously been used, the practice of colouring was by no means given up, but rather it changed its nature. It was no longer desirable to hide the texture of the material with an opaque coat of pigment; and perhaps it was more or less of a coincidence at first that led to the greater part of the surface being left plain. For the white of a woman's skin or of her drapery no pigment could be so fitting or so beautiful as the transparent creamy tint of the marble itself; and its texture was not obscured, but brought out more clearly by the contrast when details were added by painting—the eyes, lips, and hair, and the rich borders and scattered ornaments that varied the surface of the dress.

Both the statues of the Acropolis and the metopes of the Athenian treasury at Delphi shew us the Attic art of the early fifth century as refined and delicate, with considerable power of composition and expression, but lacking in the dignity and severity that belong to the greatest age of sculpture in Greece. There are, however, examples which already shew the influence of the severer and more exact though less versatile art of the Peloponnesus, and foreshadow the new tendency that was to lead up to the sculptures of the Parthenon. We can now realize, as we never could before, that the new epoch of Greek art and history which begins with the Persian wars was marked by a panhellenic feeling, and that Athens became the representative city of Hellas, gathering to herself and giving expression to the national art of Greece, of which her own art had hitherto been but one among many branches. And the history of vase-painting, in the light of its new chronology, illustrates and confirms this impression; for in it, as in sculpture, we see the extreme refinement and delicacy of Attic work suddenly reinforced at the beginning of the fifth century by a new strength and vigour that was partly Attic and partly national. And to the masterpieces of this transitional Attic art we must also assign, if we agree with M. Homolle's most recent view, the magnificent bronze charioteer that is the finest individual product of the great excavations of Delphi.

In our new knowledge of early Greek art, Athens takes the most prominent place; but it is not only Attic art of which we have learnt so much from recent excavations. Whether from scattered discoveries or from the great accumulation of works of art on such panhellenic sites as Olympia, Delphi, Delos, and even the Acropolis of Athens itself, we now possess examples of the work of artists who were but names to us before, and of schools that previously only offered an open field for conjecture as to their artistic tendencies. The early sculptors of Chios, of Naxos, of Melos, of Argos, of Megara, of Sicyon, and of many other cities are now represented by extant works, while individual discoveries would require much space even for a barren enumeration.

For the succeeding period the new acquisitions are certainly not inferior either in number or interest, though their proportion to what was previously known is not so great. Foremost come the pediments of the temple of Zeus at Olympia—works of such importance in the history of art that before they were discovered many theories were propounded as to what they must have been like. These theories have all been discredited by the results of excavation, their fundamental error having lain in the assumption that the pediments were to be assigned to pupils of Phidias, since Pausanius records that they were made by Paeonius and Alcamenes. Whether Pausanius is in error, or another explanation must be sought, is a problem that has exercised archaeologists ever since the pediments were found; but whatever view we may finally accept upon this question, the Olympian pediments have now taken their rank among the cardinal monuments of Greek sculpture, occupying a position intermediate between the pediments of Aegina and of the Parthenon. And, whether Paeonius had anything to do with these sculptures or not, he is at any rate represented by the beautiful figure of a floating Victory that was also found at Olympia. The Greek excavations at Rhamnus have recovered the reliefs on the pedestal of the great statue made by Agoracritus, or, according to some authorities, by Phidias himself; and the American exploration of the Heraeum has shewn, as was already to be suspected from the fragments previously discovered there, that the influence of Athens, at least in architectural sculpture, prevailed even in the domain of Argos, her great artistic rival; and so we find Athens at the end of the fifth century repaying the influence that she had borrowed at its beginning. And the monument of Gyolbashi, now transported to Vienna, shews something of the same influence, though it bears stronger traces of pictorial design and of the Ionic style that had been earlier prevalent in Lycia.

The fourth century, if, with the exception of the discoveries at Epidaurus, it has recently yielded no series of sculptures so great as those just mentioned, is admirably represented by the individual masterpieces that have been recovered within the last few years. In the Hermes of Praxiteles at Olympia we now possess a work which comes directly from the hand of one of the greatest masters of antiquity, and which affords a standard to which we can refer for comparison all the attested copies or unknown statues with which our museums are filled; and the heads by Scopas from Tegea, mutilated as they are, have proved almost as valuable for comparative criticism. Another very interesting master who was previously known only by name is Damophon of Messene; of his colossal group at Lycosura three heads and many other portions have now been recovered, and offer yet another problem for our study; for their style has led some authorities to infer, perhaps needlessly, that he did not belong to the fourth century, as had previously been supposed, but to a later age. But the greatest surprise of all comes from Sidon, the last place where one would have looked for genuine Greek work of good period. The magnificent series of sarcophagi now transferred to the museum at Constantinople shews that a succession of Sidonian princes must have employed Greek artists for several generations to carve their tombs, and the fortunate recovery of these sarcophagi, in an unrivalled state of preservation, even their colour being in some cases almost unspoiled, has given us a series of examples of the finest Greek sculpture at various stages of its development, from the early fifth century down to the end of the fourth ; and these do not merely reflect the various stages of Greek, and especially of Attic, sculpture, but are worthy to be placed on a level with its finest products both in design and execution. By their help we are enabled to realize what many of the most beautiful but now most fragmentary monuments must have looked like when they were fresh from the sculptor's chisel and the painter's brush. This is most of all the case with the latest of the sculptured sarcophagi, in which Alexander himself figures amidst battle and hunting scenes. No one who has not seen these reliefs can realize the amount of expression that can be added to sculpture by judicious colouring, and how far the white and lifeless statuary that we now see in our sculpture galleries is removed from the reality and vigour of a Greek work as it was meant to be seen. Another great series of sculptures that has afforded us a revelation of the character of Hellenistic art is the frieze of the Great Altar at Pergamum, now transferred to Berlin. In this we can see all the dramatic vigour of the Pergamene school ; and if it lacks the repose and sculptural dignity of an earlier age, it is perhaps more imposing and overwhelming in its restless profusion and dramatic force than any other monument that has survived to our day. It would be easy to go on and enumerate other sets of sculptures or isolated statues that have been recently added to our store. But even if these were all, they would suffice to have revolutionized our knowledge of Greek art, filling many of the gaps that had hitherto existed, and throwing a new light on the history and relations of what was previously known.

Another branch of archaeological work is not always directly connected with excavation, though it has owed much to the stimulus of new discoveries and to the acquisition of new *data* for its investigations. This is the work of reconstruction and comparison which must be carried on in museums and libraries. The most notable examples of such work have been concerned with the study and publication of the results of excavation. But it is not only new discoveries that have provided it with its subjects. Of the statues preserved in our museums only a small minority has practically been available for the reconstruction of the history of art, so long as that history was content to deal almost exclusively with statues that could be associated, on external or on circumstantial evidence, with sculptors or works of art known to us from the literary authorities. Such statues must always form the basis of any historical study of Greek art; but their number is limited, nor can we expect that it will be greatly increased by future identifications as brilliant and as certain as those by which Brunn recovered the Marsyas of Myron and Friederichs the Tyrannicides made by Critius and Nesiotes. It is therefore a most fascinating pursuit to try to group around them, from a comparative study of style, such other works as shew an affinity to them, and so to build up by degrees a continuous series that shall ultimately come to include most of the extant sculptures that have any distinctive artistic character.

This process has now been begun, the first systematic attempt having been made in Professor Furtwängler's *Masterpieces of Greek Sculpture*; and although, in so problematic a study, it is not to be expected that all his results will meet with acceptance, there is no doubt that he has opened up a method of inquiry that cannot be ignored by any future archaeologists. At the same time the conditions are so complicated that the method is an extremely dangerous one, and can only be applied with safety by those whose knowledge of monuments and keenness and accuracy of observation qualify them for the task. This is especially the case with copies, where it is often difficult, if not impossible, to distinguish the manner or additions of the copyist from the characteristics of the original he has imitated. A too rash and indiscriminate application of what is, in its right use, a valuable aid to study may well bring the whole method into discredit.

Our knowledge of Greek architecture, much as it must always owe to the earlier travellers like Stuart and Cockerell, has been greatly increased and modified by more recent research and excavation. The accurate measurement of the Parthenon by Mr. Penrose was a revelation of the exquisite refinement of Greek architectural forms; and with his discovery of the subtle curves of stylobate and architrave, as well as of the mathematical precision of parabolic and hyperbolic sections in column and moulding, a new era may be said to have begun in the appreciation of architectural design. The results of more recent discoveries are, to a great extent, so intimately bound up with the study of topography that it is impossible to consider them separately. Some excavations, especially those at Olympia, have yielded much evidence as to the early development of Greek architectural forms; and this evidence, interpreted as it has been by Professor Dörpfeld, necessitates the rewriting of the history of architecture—a task that still awaits performance. The Heraeum at Olympia, above all, shews in the various stages of its construction, stone columns being substituted for the original tree-trunks as they decayed, the gradual growth of Doric architecture as we know it from the primitive wooden structure of the peristyle and entablature; the rich terra-cotta ornamentation of early temples has been carefully studied; and the custom of building walls of mud-brick on a stone foundation, strengthened at all corners and openings by wooden jambs—a system that can be traced in structures of the Mycenaean age, and that also finds its counterpart in the houses of a modern Greek village—shews us the explanation of many features that survive even in the Propylaea and the Parthenon.

Some classes of buildings, both public and private, have been so frequently the subjects of recent investigation that our knowledge of them has acquired a new character. Foremost among these stands the Greek theatre. At Athens and Epidaurus and Megalopolis, and on many other sites, such as Oropus, Sicyon, Eretria, and Delos, and Tralles and Magnesia in Asia Minor, theatres have been excavated. The auditorium of Epidaurus, with its perfect curves of white limestone seats, set like a great shell in the hillside, shews a beauty of design that must be seen to be appreciated; and with this beauty it combines the most perfect acoustic properties. But it is on the stage buildings, here and elsewhere, that the interest of scholars and of explorers has mainly been concentrated. Unfortunately it must be admitted that excavation has very little to tell us of the stage in the period when all the masterpieces of the Attic drama were produced; but for later times, from the third or possibly the fourth century downward, the evidence is plentiful and consistent. In later Greek theatres we invariably find, in front of the higher mass of the stage buildings, the remains of a long low structure, faced with a colonnade, and about ten or twelve feet high and from seven to ten feet broad. This corresponds almost exactly to what is described by Vitruvius as the stage in the Greek theatre; and as he expressly says that the actors appeared upon the top of it, while an inscription found at Delphi describes it as the λογεῖον, or speaking-place, its use is extremely well attested. Dr. Dörpfeld, indeed, maintains that it was not a stage at all, but only a background before which the actors performed; his arguments, however, do not rest on direct architectural evidence, but rather upon considerations of taste and convenience such as it is very hard for us to apply correctly to so conventional a performance as the ancient drama; and the evidence of ancient writers and of vases tells very strongly against his theory. With the stage of the fifth century the case is different; we are left entirely to the internal evidence of the plays themselves and the probabilities of the case, so that differences of opinion are likely to continue on the matter. If we accept the suggestion that there was probably at this time a low stage, easily accessible from the orchestra, and intermediate between the table of Thespis and the higher platform of later times, we must at the same time acknowledge that this is a matter of inference rather than of direct evidence.

We have also learnt something of the private houses of the Greeks from recent excavations. In Athens a whole street has been unearthed; and although the buildings that border it are but scantily preserved, some of them are of early date, and they materially assist the imagination in reconstructing the appearance of an ancient town; perhaps the most striking feature is that, although the road was in all probability a main thoroughfare from the market-place to the Acropolis, it is only about sixteen feet wide. At Priene it is reported that so great a number of Greek private houses have been found that it will rank as another Pompei ; and although in this case there was no eruption of a Vesuvius to preserve the houses and their contents intact, what there is belongs to a better period, and to Greek, not Graeco-Roman, civilization. At Delos also many private houses have been found, and from them one can gain a very fair notion of the plan of an ordinary Greek middle-class house. As the result of these discoveries the old notion of the Greek house derived partly from Pompei, partly from a misinterpretation of Vitruvius' description of a Hellenistic palace, must be given up as neither in accordance with literary evidence nor with extant remains. In the Delian houses the usual features are a single courtyard, almost always provided, at one side or in one corner, with a recess catching the low winter sun and sheltered from the prevailing winds, and a large room, probably for feasts and entertainments, beside the usual smaller rooms and offices. It is such a house, probably, that we must look on as the normal habitation of the Greek citizen, not the extensive mansion, with two courts and abundance of space, which could never have found room within the crowded area of an ancient town.

The systematic study of Greek coins, as monuments both of history and of artistic development, is another branch of archaeology that has made great advance in recent years. In former days a numismatist was satisfied if he could assign the various types to the city that made them and explain the allusions in their legend and subjects. Several most valuable numismatic studies have been recently made, in which the whole series of coinage of an ancient city has been placed in order, and dated at intervals by correlation with recorded political events, so that every type and variation falls into its place, and thus confirms, corrects, or supplements historical records. Thus the coinage of Syracuse, as arranged by Mr. Head, expresses the many vicissitudes of Sicilian history, the victories over the Carthaginian foe, the no less famous victories over Greek competitors at Olympia, the succession of splendid tyrants, and the advent from Corinth of the liberator Timoleon, reflected in the types that came with him from the mother city; and a remarkable episode in the rivalry of Pisa with its too powerful rival Elis finds its sole record in a series of coins that can only have been struck at the time when the supremacy of Thebes enabled the oppressed nationalities of the Peloponnese to assert their rights. The present state of numismatic science may be seen in Mr. Head's *Historia Numorum*, in which all the known coinages of Greek cities are not only arranged in chronological order, but divided into periods of which the limits can be approximately dated. It is evident that coins, when thus systematically arranged, afford a sort of index to the variation and development of art in different places and periods.

The kindred study of gem-engraving has also made progress, especially in the difficult distinction of the true from the false. In this case it is not, as in sculpture and vases, a mere question of restoration; but the high prices offered by collectors had tempted forgers of extraordinary skill to imitate antique styles and subjects. Here, as in the case of vases, a study of the examples that bear the artist's signature affords a basis for classification and historical treatment; and the criteria for deciding both as to genuineness and period are being accumulated.

The value of inscriptions for the study of Greek history, religion, social life, and art has long been appreciated. If the fulness of material has allowed some modern epigraphists to advance beyond Boeckh, it has only been by following his methods; and the Essays of Sir Charles Newton on Greek inscriptions, published more than twenty years ago, are still recognized as the standard introduction to the study of the subject. But the accession of material is as great here as in any department of Greek antiquities: excavations have been most fruitful; more than fifteen hundred inscriptions were found at Delos alone, over 2,500 at Delphi, and other sites have been almost as prolific; while numerous journeys in Asia Minor and elsewhere have added their contributions to the tale.

It is true that the salient events of history are not likely to be recorded except indirectly by inscriptions: but on all those details that form the framework and background of history, treaties with foreign states, and matters of organization and administration at home, inscriptions give us the fullest and most trustworthy information; while the lists of the archons of Athens or of the provincial governors of Asia Minor, now recovered almost completely by the laborious study and comparison of inscriptions, are an immense gain to chronology. On legal antiquities also epigraphy has much to tell us; the most striking example is offered by the early code of laws found at Gortyna in Crete, which throws much light upon primitive institutions. But it is above all in adding to our knowledge of the social and religious conditions of Greek life that inscriptions have proved invaluable. From them is derived practically all we know of the ephebic system at Athens, the ancient equivalent of the university life of our own day, but more universal in its scope and more influential on social and physical training. And to inscriptions again we owe an intimate knowledge of the organization of those associations for religious purposes that find only a few scattered references in literature, but that undoubtedly met the needs of many who had lost faith in the established religion of the state, and that gave practical expression in pre-Christian days to the doctrine of the equality of mankind, whether Greek or barbarian, slave or free. From inscriptions, too, we learn much of the administration of temples, the estates they owned, and the wealth of offerings they contained; of their ritual, and the intimate way in which they were bound up with the state and with the daily life of the people; and of the appointment, functions, and privileges of the priests. There is hardly a department of religious, social, or private life on which epigraphy has not taught us more than we could learn from literary authorities, simply because classical authors naturally took for granted a knowledge of the customs that inscriptions frequently record. For this reason inscriptions are invaluable as a supplement to literature; but they can also sometimes restore to us actual literary documents. Thus the poems of Isyllus were found inscribed upon slabs set up at Epidaurus; and Delphi has yielded not only the text of several hymns to Apollo—a form of Greek poetry hitherto almost unknown—but also the notes to which they were to be sung, recorded in musical notation,—a discovery of incalculable value to the history of music, and one that has appealed in an unusual degree to popular enthusiasm. We may almost place in the same category the wonderful discoveries of papyri that have been made in Egypt, and that have not only enabled us to compare our texts of Homer and Plato with versions earlier than had hitherto been preserved, but actually have restored such valuable works as the poems of Bacchylides and Herondas, and Aristotle's *Constitution of Athens*. We may congratulate ourselves that in this department at least the chief prizes have fallen to England; while in the application of the *data* acquired from inscriptions, from historical and topographical research, and from the many kindred studies that form the equipment of the geographical traveller, English scholars, from Leake to Ramsay, have held a foremost position.

So far we have been mainly concerned with archaeology as dealing with the actual remains left behind them by the Greeks; and even its contribution to our knowledge of their social and religious institutions is based to a great extent upon the evidence of excavation and epigraphy. In another branch of its activity, the study of mythology, the evidence offered by monuments, especially vases and reliefs, is also considerable. But mythology deals also with less tangible materials, such as the customs and beliefs both of earlier times and of the present day; and it is in the methods and the point of view adopted by the mythologist as regards this evidence that the greatest change has taken place within recent years. In old days it is hardly too much to say that when the facts recorded by classical authorities had been collected, the mythologist set himself to supplement and explain them by an unfettered exercise of his own imagination. In a few cases, perhaps, when he possessed an intuitive sympathy with the forms of primitive thought or fancy, the results were valuable; but there were no means of distinguishing the true from the false, and it was frequently the most improbable suggestions that met with the widest acceptance, because they happened to suit the notions, not of the early Greeks, but of the writer's own contemporaries. The next stage in the development of mythological study was indeed more systematic, but probably even more misleading. It consisted in taking some one theory, which perhaps did explain the origin of certain myths, and applying it as a universal key to the interpretation of mythology. The abuse that has been made of the theory of the solar myth, for example, has been so often ridiculed that there is no need now to dwell upon its absurdity; but probably many of us do not realize exactly where the weakness of the theory lay. Certain myths no doubt do shew a connexion with the sun and moon, with clouds and storms and other phenomena of nature; but we cannot find out what the connexion is by comparing figurative and often sentimental conceptions of our own day, or even of classical poets, who were often just as far removed in thought from the origin of the myth. To understand the working of the minds of those among whom the myths grew up, we must compare the customs and beliefs of people in a similar stage of mental development, whether European peasants or savages in the remoter regions of the world; for the myths we find in the Greek poets were not invented by them or by their contemporaries, but were survivals from a more primitive stage than any of which we have literary record. Of such primitive customs and beliefs we have learnt much from the researches of McLennan and Tylor. Mannhardt was the pioneer in the systematic application of the principle to the explanation of classical myth and ritual; he has found followers among the most competent mythologists in England, though in Germany the importance of his methods seems hardly yet to be recognized. The result of these methods is sometimes not far removed from what can be reached by less scientific means; but the difference, though apparently slight, is essential. One example will suffice to shew this. The Centaurs who tore up trees and hurled rocks upon Mount Pelion had been conjectured by some earlier mythologists to be personifications of storm-winds or torrents; Mannhardt compared the legends about such destructive agencies in Northern Europe, and found that the havoc wrought was actually attributed by the people to the combats of supernatural beings. Accordingly, while others had regarded the Centaurs as "impersonations of natural phenomena," he explained them as "spirits of the forest or the mountain, to whose action these phenomena were assigned." Now impersonation or figurative speech belongs to a highly developed and artificial stage of thought, while the belief in such spirits as actually existing is primitive and universal. Another result of the comparative method in mythology is to shew the intimate connexion between myth and ritual. The primitive rites practised everywhere by peasants, especially at critical periods of the natural year, often bear a striking resemblance to the tales that they tell, and also to the myths which we find in a more artificial and poetical form in Greek mythology. It is an obvious inference that the story has grown up to explain the custom of which the real purpose was forgotten even by those that practised it, and that myth has thus been the offshoot of ritual. Of course it is possible to abuse this principle of explanation, just as other theories have been abused; but with the help of the scientific and systematic method that is being established in this, as in other branches of archaeology, there should be less danger than before, though caution must always be required in its more speculative applications.

It would be easy to continue almost indefinitely this sketch of the methods and results of archaeology in relation to historic Greece; but enough has been said to give some notion of the scope and variety of the subjects that come within its domain, and the scientific manner in which it is now equipped to treat them. In the case of the Greeks, indeed, we are not, as in the case of other ancient peoples, dependent on archaeological evidence for almost all we know of the country and its inhabitants. But in the case of a people whose history, life, and thought are so fully displayed by their literature, archaeology occupies a different position. It possesses, in the first place, an immense advantage in the possession of this literary evidence, which not only supplies a framework within which each new fact ascertained by archaeological evidence falls easily into its own place, but also affords a test by which theories may be judged. Partly for this reason, and partly because of the unique influence of Greek history, language, and literature upon our own times, the archaeology of Greece has been developed in a more thorough and systematic way than has in other cases been possible. The result is that, wherever archaeology is pursued as a serious study, classical archaeology is regarded as supplying a basis and a training in method, much as the classical languages are recognized as offering the indispensable foundation for the literary and linguistic education of our schools and universities. Hence the very prominent position which it has come to occupy in the curriculum of many foreign universities, while the same principle is already recognized to a less degree in Oxford, Cambridge, and Edinburgh, doubtless soon to be followed by the other universities of the United Kingdom. The intimate relation of the life and thought of ancient Greece to so much of what is most characteristic in the literature and progress of the present age has given a peculiar stimulus to a study of which the aim is to realize the social, religious, and artistic surroundings apart from which Greek poets, philosophers, and historians can be but imperfectly understood.

CHAPTER IV.

THE ROMAN WORLD

BY
F. HAVERFIELD, M.A., F.S.A.
STUDENT AND TUTOR OF CHRIST CHURCH

FROM Greece we pass to Rome, from Eastern to Western Europe and to the Latin civilization.

The differences between Greek and Roman history are many. Till lately, they have been somewhat obscured to modern minds by the educational system which has dominated Europe since the Renaissance, for that system has treated Greece and Rome not merely as the two representatives of classical antiquity, but as twin representatives, allied and similar as twin children. Hence the languages, literatures, and histories of these two halves of the older European world have been regarded as closely akin, so that one might judge them by the same canons, study them by the same methods, and in general look at them with the same eyes. It has been thought till lately, and it is still thought by many, that a man who can teach or write Greek history is for that very reason qualified to teach or write Roman history. We have had, that is, an exaggerated idea of the resemblances between Greece and Rome. We are now advancing beyond that. Knowledge, it has been often said, begins by seeing similarities and progresses to discern differences, and so it is now recognized that the kinship of Greek and Latin means far less than was once asserted.

But the difference between Greek and Roman history which is most marked and noteworthy at the present time is a difference of another kind. It is not so much a real difference between these two subjects; it arises largely from the state of our knowledge at the present day. Through a variety of causes it has resulted that at this moment Greek and Roman history diverge in nothing so much as in the extent to which they depend on archaeological evidence and on the authority of written records. They agree so far that both depend on both sources of knowledge: they agree also in this, that in both cases the archaeological evidence has only recently become known to us: until the beginning of the nineteenth century Greek and Roman history alike were based wholly, or almost wholly, on the written records of literature. But the written authorities for the two, as we now see, are by no means similar, and the archaeological evidence gathered slowly during the last eighty or ninety years has not added any element of similarity. The Greek historian is well provided with both aids, and in a large portion of his subject he can lean on both at once. His first or prehistoric chapter necessarily lacks the support of written authorities, but archaeology supplies the deficiency. The student can reconstruct in some not wholly unsatisfactory fashion the Aegean culture of Troy and Crete, Mycenae and Tiryns, and discern, though dimly, the empire of a great and long-forgotten people. For the rest of his subject, throughout the historic period, a fairly continuous series of narratives and literary records, most of them good, most of them nearly contemporary, describes the fortunes of the chief Greek cities in the chief periods of their existence. Archaeological evidence, less complete, but very valuable, confirms or occasionally conflicts with these literary authorities, and in either case refers principally to topics or persons mentioned in them.

The Roman historian has a different and a more difficult task. In the long roll of centuries which form his subject, the written record and the archaeological evidence are often defective and rarely united. For the prehistoric period, the patient and skilful labours of Italian archaeologists have led to the accumulation of abundant evidence, so that the student of prehistoric Italy is perhaps at this moment in an even more favourable position than his colleague who studies prehistoric Greece. The historic period may be divided, as indeed it naturally divides itself, into two periods—that of the Roman Republic and that of the Roman Empire. The Republic has been described for us by a series of ancient writers, some few of them adequate and contemporary, many of them the complete reverse. Good or bad, these writers stand alone: we possess at present little archaeological evidence to check or supplement their narratives. This missing archaeological evidence may perhaps be supplied to some extent as research progresses, but it is likely that we shall never possess any great abundance of it to illuminate the history of the Roman Republic. For that Republic was one of those states which mark the world but not individual sites with their achievements. Such in Greece was Sparta; and, as Thucydides saw long ago, the student of such states must be content to work without demanding abundant archaeological testimonies. The Roman Empire is different. Its literary records are few, and their historical value is not very great. It is not the fault of the Empire, though the Empire has been freely blamed for it. Histories enough, we know, were compiled under Imperial rule; real research was carried on, as research was then defined; and Renan's epigram was justified that learning best flourishes under the security of a despotism.

But the extant remains of this intellectual activity are meagre and unintelligent; and, so far as we can tell, the books which have not survived were no better than those which we actually have. The truth is, that, like most great political organizations, the Roman Empire was only half understood by the men who lived in and under it. Some few wrote brilliantly; but not even Tacitus appreciated the state to which he belonged: he gives his readers little better than a backstair view of court intrigues, palace politics, social scandals. The machinery of government, the ideals of statesmen, the fluctuations of commerce, the advance of civilization,—all the real history of five centuries was ignored by almost every one of those Greeks or Romans who essayed to describe the Roman Empire. On the other hand, the archaeological evidence is extensive and indeed extraordinary. No state has ever left behind it such abundant and instructive remains as the Roman Empire. Inscriptions by hundreds of thousands, coins of all dates and places, ruins of fortresses, towns, villas, roads, supply the great gaps left by ancient writers. Most of this evidence has been uncovered in the last fifty years: the Empire, misdescribed by its own Romans, has risen from the earth to vindicate itself before us.

The historian of Rome, then, depends at the present time very largely on archaeological evidence for two out of his three periods. For the third period, the Republic, he has little such evidence, and perhaps he never will obtain it; but for the other two the spade has witnessed. The following paragraphs are an attempt to illustrate shortly the nature of this evidence and its value, first for our knowledge of prehistoric Italy, and secondly for our knowledge of the Empire.

The archaeological discoveries which illuminate prehistoric Italy are principally the results of the last thirty years. Since the definite constitution of the Italian kingdom in 1870, the Italians have conducted a systematic exploration of their national antiquities, establishing for the purpose a definite machinery and organizing local inspectors and excavators under a central director. They have not succeeded even thus in coping with the vast and almost infinite mass of ancient remains in their country, but they have made real progress to that far-off goal, and their skilful and patient labours have brought marked additions to our knowledge. They have not neglected the prehistoric period. Cemeteries and villages have been examined, especially in the Po valley, in Etruria, and in the extreme south, and the beginnings of Italy are becoming clear to our eyes. The results may not seem so striking as those which the explorers of prehistoric Greece have attained on the shores of the Aegean Sea. But this is no fault of the Italian excavators. The Aegean coasts were the home of an extensive, coherent, and elaborate civilization in prehistoric ages. The plains and mountains of Italy were occupied by various races, and the forms of civilization which prevailed were (with certain exceptions) neither rich nor widespread. The study of prehistoric Italy cannot in itself compete with the study of the greater civilization which once dominated the eastern half of the Mediterranean. It claims our notice, for it tells us how Rome became Rome.

The picture of early Italy revealed by recent research has two distinct features. On the one hand, it shews a steady drift of immigrant tribes moving down from the north through the passes of the Alps, and bringing with them their whole civilization, their fashions of dress, of artistic workmanship, of house- and town-building, of burial. We do not know the racial character or blood or language of these immigrants, but our evidence is sufficient to prove that we are dealing with a migration of men, and not merely an influx of foreign fashions. On the other hand, our picture shews an influx of fashions from the south—that is, from the Eastern Mediterranean. The art and ideas of the east, Aegean, Greek, or Oriental, each in turn reached the coasts of Southern Italy and influenced its inhabitants. To some extent the men of the east came too, but in fewer numbers than the tribes of the north. Italy has been throughout history a land where the men and manners of Central Europe met those of the Eastern Mediterranean. It was just such a meeting-place before recorded history began.

First the immigrants from the north. Besides several tribes whose origins and fortunes are still obscure, Illyrians, Euganeans, and what not, two immigrant peoples stand out prominently, the tribes which we may call Italians and the Gauls. The Italians are the tribes which later on formed the predominant and characteristic elements in Central Italy, in Latium, and in Rome itself. They came through the Alps some twelve or fourteen centuries before the Christian era, not as one people, but as a succession of tribes. They drove the Ligurian population out of the Po valley into the steep and tangled hills which look down on Genoa, where alone the name and the stock of this older people survived. Presently they learnt the use of iron, and crossed the Apennines to spread themselves over Etruria and all Central Italy, and one tribe of Latins occupied Latium and founded Rome.

Three instances will shew what excavation has done to illuminate the history of these tribes, and in particular the growth of their towns. Virgil long ago noticed the towns of Italy as its striking feature:

> tot egregias urbes operumque labores
> Tot congesta manu praeruptis oppida saxis
> Fluminaque antiquos praeterlabentia muros.

And in truth towns are the distinguishing element of that genuinely Latin civilization which Rome inherited. It is no accident, perhaps, that we can trace these towns in prehistoric centuries. When the Italians first occupied the Po valley, they dwelt in marsh villages built on piles: as they moved up from the low ground, they built villages, which retain obvious resemblances to their earlier homes. These villages are the so-called *terramare*, excavated during the last twenty-five years by Chierici, Pigorini, and other skilful archaeologists. The best known is that of Castellazzo di Fontanellato, near to Parma. It is a little village of some thirty acres, in outer shape quadrilateral and nearly rectangular: round is a solid rampart of earth and a moat one hundred feet wide. As in a lake village, there seems to be only one entrance to this artificial island. Within, two main streets cross at right angles, and divide the area into four nearly equal parts. Lanes run parallel to the main streets, and near the central crossing stands a small citadel, with ditch and rampart of its own. Without is a little burning *ghat*—for these men burnt their dead—and, for a cemetery, a platform of urns, set curiously like the village of the living. It is a strange place. If the discoverers' enthusiasm has not led them too far, we may accept their opinion that here we have the prototype of the later Italian town. The principles on which the *terramare* seem to be laid out are just those which underlie the later Italian city-plan and land-measurement. Here we stand at the beginning of the Italian towns.

We can trace their development further. We can shew what the earliest Rome was, the Rome of Romulus on the Palatine, and how it grew to be the City of the Seven Hills. The City itself, crowded with the wrecks of twenty-five centuries, preserves to-day few memorials of its earliest age; but excavations made on two sites, one close to Rome, one a little further north in Etruria, explain the process very clearly. The traveller who approaches Rome by the Via Salaria sees, just where Tiber and Anio join, a modern fort on an isolated rock. Here was Antemnae, destroyed (according to legend) by Roman jealousy very soon after Rome itself was founded. The legend seems to be true, at least in substance. On this hilltop excavations have shewn a little village within a wall of stone: it had its temple and senate-house, its water-cistern, and square huts, thatched or timbered, for dwelling-houses. The relics found there shew that the site was abandoned, never to be again inhabited, about the time at which the legend fixes the fall of Antemnae. Here we have Rome's earliest rival. From the rival we may guess what the earliest Rome was like on the Palatine rock, and what all the little Italian towns were in their infancy.

Their growth and expansion can be illustrated from another site. Rome grew, as its legends assert, by annexing hill to hill: one after another the heights around the Palatine became part of the town, and the Agger of Servius yet remains to prove the legend. It was no unique process. Thirty miles north of Rome, in the Faliscan territory close under Mount Soracte, was one of the many Italian settlements in Etruria. The Italians, it seems, first camped on the hillsides: thence descending into the valleys, they built first Narce, and afterwards Falerii. The results of the excavations there are not wholly satisfactory, but it seems that Narce grew like Rome. In its origin a single height, bearing a little fortified cluster of huts like Antemnae, it soon put forth an arm and embraced the next height, fortifying it by a wall of stone. Later on it took three more hills within its circuit, and by the beginning of the sixth or seventh century before Christ it had become a town on five hills. Then it met its end: the Etruscans captured it, and an alien civilization came to reign where hitherto all had been Italian. This civilization came from the East: now, as at other times, Italy was the meeting-place of persons and things from opposite quarters of Europe. We may turn here to consider what these Eastern influences meant for the Peninsula.

The Etruscan was not the first of these influences. All through the periods of the Mycenean or Aegean civilization, there had been trade and intercourse between Southern Italy and the Aegean. Objects brought from prehistoric Greece, or copies of such objects, have been found in the cemeteries of the Sicels, who may claim to be perhaps the primitive population of Southern Italy. The current continued even up the Adriatic coast. Far in the north, at Bologna, the spade has disinterred something strangely like the sculpture which gives its name to the Lion Gate of Mycenae. Aegean influence is visible in many remains of the Italians: it even spread across the Alps, there to enjoy a splendid future which does not now concern us. But the Aegean influence was, in a sense, superficial: it is otherwise with the influence which comes next in time, the Etruscan. The mystery surrounding this strange race is familiar. Their origin is unknown; their language is undecipherable. From somewhere they entered Italy; they conquered the district which still bears their name and much else besides; finally, as Roman writers tell us, they were overcome by the Romans about 300 B.C., and the Etruscan race vanished. Such at least is the impression given us by the ordinary narratives. If we look closer at their remains, we can discern a little more. We seem to see an alien people, few, dominant, intrusive. Their language, their art, their physical features pourtrayed in their magnificent tombs, shew them to be un-Italian. Their position as a dominant minority shews them to be no mere survival of an older age. But even these results are small.

At last, during the decade which is now ending, archaeology has thrown some light on this strange people. Researches in North Italy prove that it never entered the Peninsula from the north. Researches in Etruria itself prove that the earliest Etruscan civilization resembled that which prevailed in the Eastern Mediterranean in the last days of the Aegean period. After all, the old legends were right. The ancients told how the Etruscans came from the east: archaeological evidence is now accumulating to confirm the legends. Precisely when they came or why is still obscure, nor can we identify them yet with any special tribe in prehistoric Greece, Pelasgian or other. Probably they were driven from their old homes, like the Phoenicians who built Carthage and the Phocaeans who built Marseilles. First they settled in Northern Etruria, conquering but not expelling the Italians whom they found there: thence they spread northwards over the Apennines and southwards to Rome. Their remains abound in both directions, cemeteries, rock-hewn and painted tombs, huge city walls, at Marzabotto (near Bologna) even the streets and houses of a town built about 600 B.C. Everywhere these remains bear the same character: they are the remains of an upper class which has subdued but not displaced the population over which it rules. Italian civilization did not disappear from Etruria when the Etruscans came: it survived in a subordinate, depressed condition; and when finally the Etruscan power was overthrown, the Italian renewed its interrupted supremacy. This was apparently the case at Rome, which was for a while under Etruscan rulers, though little archaeological evidence survives to confirm the assertions of historians. It was equally the case in Etruria itself. The causes of the Etruscan downfall are well known. A new invasion came from the north, that of the Gauls: in the south the Latins grew stronger; and between these upper and nether millstones the Etrurians were crushed. The archaeologist can trace Gaulish remains abruptly displacing Etrurian, for instance at Marzabotto, and marking thereby the abrupt succession of victorious Gaul to routed Etruscan. He can equally trace Roman things succeeding Etruscan, as at Falerii, which thus came again under the power of the race that founded it. With these events we enter the region of written history. But archaeology attests one more result. When the Etruscan power fell, the Etruscan civilization vanished. The Italian culture which had survived beneath the Etruscans came once more into full vigour: Etruria became again an Italian district. Here and there Etruscan nobles retained their wealth and prestige: there were one or two of them left even in the days of the Emperor Augustus. But these were to all intents Romans: the old alien civilization, as a coherent force, vanished more than three centuries before. It left an heir. It had taught the Romans much in the days of its supremacy, and the Roman profited by the inheritance. But, except for this, the historical importance of the Etruscans vanished at their fall.

In these and other results which archaeological research has gained in its inquiries into early Italy, one feature perhaps deserves notice. The results confirm strongly certain of the legends which the ancients themselves told about Italian origins, and in particular about the origins of peoples. Legends said that Antenor of Troy reached the very north of the Adriatic and founded Padua, and that Arcadian Evander and Trojan Aeneas came to Latium. These legends are not all invention. Beneath the names lies the fact that the culture, if not the men, of the Aegean really penetrated into Italy, and even into North Italy. Legends said, again, that the Etruscans came from Lydia: we have seen that they almost certainly came from the Eastern Mediterranean. Or again, the "authorized legends" (as it were) of Rome's infancy described the city's growth from hill to hill, its brief conquest by Etruscans, and its final triumph over them: again the results of archaeology confirm the legends. There comes into view a new method of testing legends, a new touchstone to try them. The old method of probing the legend itself is useless. It is easy to shew of most legends that they are either impossible, or highly improbable, or self-contradictory, or absurd, or otherwise seriously defective. But that after all is implied when the legend is called a legend. Some external touchstone is wanted which will in each case help to sift false from true. We must not, however, exaggerate the significance of such confirmations. If one or two or three stories rest on a basis of fact, it does not follow that all do; and though it is interesting to know that such and such legends are based on fact, we have to learn the fact first before we can say anything about the legend. Such coincidences between fact and legend are, after all, little more than encouragements to the explorer. They do not advance knowledge, but they cheer the historian on what is often an obscure and lonely road.

We have now reached the point where the written history of the Roman Republic commences to be full and continuous, and here, as was said above, archaeological evidence commences to be thin and fragmentary. Hardly one building erected during the days of the Republic can now be traced in Rome. The gloomy mass of the Tabularium at the top of the Forum may be the work of Sulla, though dedicated by another, and may perhaps be connected with the reforms of that statesman. The great wall, called of Servius, is held by some good judges to belong not to the prehistoric period of the kings, but to the years succeeding the Gaulish invasion. Otherwise we have nothing but dimly discernible foundations, buried deep below the accumulations of centuries, and so faint and broken that we cannot piece them into any kind of unity. Outside Rome it is the same. Here and there are town walls of Republican date, as at Falerii, rebuilt and refortified after the Etruscans were expelled. Here and there are bits of bronze preserving the texts of laws proposed by the Gracchi or Julius Caesar. Such details have individual value : they are interesting illustrations to our ancient literary authorities. But they are few and unconnected ; they provide us with no view of the Republic. We can reconstruct, to some real extent, the tale of prehistoric Italy from archaeological evidence. We could do nothing of the kind for the Republic.

With the establishment of the Principate by Augustus, the relation between our authorities is at once reversed. The birth year of the Empire is conventionally fixed to 27 B.C. For four and almost for five centuries after this date our ancient written authorities provide a meagre narrative, sometimes no better than a chronological table. The bulk of what we know about the Roman Empire is supplied by archaeological evidence. That tells us of emperors, of political institutions, of wide-reaching tendencies, of social, religious, commercial phenomena, which ancient historians never mention. It transfigures the whole conception. As pictured by ancient writers, the Empire is mainly (though not wholly) a vast space of earth ruled from one city of Rome by one ruler and his favourites, like some Oriental despotism. As presented to us by archaeology, it is a highly organized and coherent state, a complex machine of wheels within wheels, in which the Emperor is often less important than the statesmen round him, and the central city less noteworthy than the populations of the provinces. The following paragraphs are intended, first, to describe the researches to which we owe our archaeological evidence for this period, and, secondly, to give some instances of the new knowledge which results from it.

The existence of this evidence is, of course, no new discovery of the last half-century. Ever since the Renaissance it has been an object of increasing attention to scholars. Ruins have been drawn and described: inscriptions have been collected and discussed. But during the nineteenth century the study has advanced prodigiously. Much is due to one man, Theodor Mommsen. The great historian was an undergraduate at Kiel (1838-43) just at the time when the value of inscriptions was beginning to be properly understood; and through the genius of Boeckh Borghesi, and others—mere names to-day, but pioneers of knowledge then—epigraphy was winning its place in the circle of scientific studies. Mommsen felt their influence. Early in his career he gave his attention to Roman inscriptions, and in his long life he has achieved results of which his ablest predecessors had scarcely ventured to dream. To him we owe, in the first place, the greatest work of learning executed during the nineteenth century, the stately row of folios entitled the *Corpus Inscriptionum Latinarum*, in which almost all known Roman inscriptions have been accurately and scientifically edited and indexed. Between 1824 and 1853 Boeckh issued in three volumes a Corpus of Greek inscriptions. Borghesi had cherished dreams of a Roman Corpus: Mommsen realized the vision on a splendid scale. With the singular organizing faculty which distinguishes him even among Germans, he laid his plan so broad and deep that subsequent experience has demanded no serious alterations; he secured collaborators, directed their exertions, and surmounted even that hardest task of getting volume after volume duly completed. Now, after forty years, the labour is almost done.

Meanwhile, men's conceptions of archaeological research were fast widening. They no longer remained content with recording, in the old style, only such ruins or inscriptions or other remains as chance had brought to light. They commenced to prosecute definite and systematic search for new remains and inscriptions, and the last twenty-five years have witnessed frequent efforts and much success. Neglected or little-known districts have been traversed, explored, and even surveyed—parts of Asia Minor by Professor W. M. Ramsay and his colleagues, parts of Bosnia by Mr. Arthur Evans, the Balkan peninsula and much of Asiatic Turkey by distinguished Germans and Austrians, Tunis and Algiers by no less distinguished Frenchmen. These explorations have been principally effected under circumstances which forbid the use of the spade, and, although systematic and scientific, have necessarily been limited almost entirely to things above the surface of the ground. But the generation which recognized their value was naturally quick to see the still greater value of excavations; and though it needs more money and organization to excavate than to explore, the cost has not been grudged. Rome, as is fitting, has been the principal scene both of digging and of discovery. Quite early in the nineteenth century attempts were made to excavate at Rome. The French during the Napoleonic occupation (1810-13) did good work in the Forum Romanum and the Forum of Trajan; Italian archaeologists like Nibby and Canina were admirably active in succession to them; and Rosa explored part of the Palatine for Napoleon III. But the great period of excavation came later. It began in 1870, when Rome became the capital of the Italian kingdom. The Government took up the task of excavating, especially in the Forum and on the Palatine: at the same time, the new position of Rome as head of united Italy caused rapid expansion, and the building operations which extensively followed greatly facilitated research. A high authority, Professor Lanciani, has calculated that ancient Rome spread over nine square miles, and that nearly half this area was explored in one way or another between 1870 and 1885. Since 1885 financial troubles have impeded though they have not put a stop to progress. The multitude of objects discovered has led to the construction of three new museums. The number of buildings identified has made possible Lanciani's great "Forma urbis," perhaps the most splendid plan of an ancient city which has ever been attempted.

Outside Rome the uncovering of Pompei, commenced a century and a half ago, proceeds slowly and steadily to completion; but connected and systematic excavation of other Roman sites has been rarer than is always realized. Italian archaeologists have been busy with prehistoric remains—not without reason—and the great Archaeological Societies of England and France and Germany and America have sought Greek and Egyptian in preference to Roman antiquities. Incidentally their labours illustrate Roman history. Excavations at Delos have thrown a flood of light on the part played by that island, once Apollo's shrine, as a commercial free port in the second century before our era, and we have thus learnt more about Roman mercantile enterprize in the Eastern Mediterranean at that date. Excavations in Egypt have yielded precious documents in stone or papyrus, and have thus revealed, even in its minutest features, the nature of the peculiar administration which the Roman Emperors applied to the Nile valley. But these are fortunate accidents, hardly contemplated when the excavations were first designed. If we turn to excavations which are definitely intended to increase our knowledge of Roman antiquities, we shall find only one undertaking which can compare in magnitude with the Greek and Egyptian enterprizes just mentioned. This, as one might expect, was planned by Germans, and indeed to some extent by Mommsen himself: its scene is also laid in Germany. Its object is the excavation of the forts, walls, and earthworks which once defended the long Imperial frontier between Bonn on the Rhine and Regensburg on the Danube, and its extent is more than three hundred miles. Subsidized by Government, directed by a central committee, carried out by qualified local workers, each responsible for one section of the "Limes," it may fairly claim to be considered a serious and important enterprize. But it stands alone. No such scheme of connected excavation has ever been instituted by Englishmen for the proper examination of the two Walls which once guarded Northern Britain against Caledonian invasions, nor can the Continent shew any parallel.

On the other hand, excavations of single sites, sometimes complete, sometimes limited to special buildings, a theatre or a temple, have frequently been carried out. Thus French archaeologists have been active at Lambaesis and Thamugadi, and other odd-named towns or fortresses of Roman Africa. Thus a Viennese Society has for some years tried patiently to uncover the ruins of Carnuntum, once a Roman frontier-fortress and a prosperous town, twenty-five miles down the Danube from Vienna. Thus too, six summers ago, a party of Oxford archaeologists dug out the chief public edifices of Doclea, in Montenegro, Diocletian's reputed birthplace. Such isolated excavations have been carried out in every European land that once formed part of the Empire, from Roumania and Hungary to Belgium and France. In our own island the London Society of Antiquaries has essayed the complete unearthing of the little Romano-British town of Calleva, now Silchester near Reading, and has more than half achieved its object. Villas of Romano-British landowners have been cleared, and planned in several of our southern counties. Fortresses like Chester, smaller forts like those at Birrens and Ardoch in Scotland, at Chesters and Housesteads on Hadrian's Wall, have been the scenes of serious work. In comparison with the size of Britain, the amount completed is not wholly inconsiderable, nor is the knowledge acquired by any means valueless.

The mass of material yielded by these and many similar researches is both large and varied, and the historian who tries to use it has a special and difficult task. Inscriptions, which provide a considerable part of this material, provide also the clearest instances of the conditions attending its use. Thanks to Mommsen—for the organizer of the Corpus was also its interpreter— we know how to study the inscriptions of the Empire. Many of them are striking, but the most striking are rarely the most important. The importance of any one of these inscriptions does not, as a rule, depend on its individual merits or interests, but on its place among other inscriptions. Epigraphy is a democratic science. If an inscription can be combined with others like it to prove some fact, it possesses importance; if not, it is unimportant. Among the tens of thousands of Imperial inscriptions known to us, perhaps a hundred may claim an individual value: such an one is the Ancyran Monument, which is the brief, imperial, passionless auto- biography of Augustus. A few more may claim notice as found in far-off corners of the Empire, whither one would not have expected Roman habits to have penetrated: they gain a value from their place. But the vast majority of these documents are valueless and uninstructive until they are combined.

Consider, for instance, the military inscriptions. They are numerous and of all sorts—tombstones of every degree, lists of soldiers' burial-clubs, certificates of discharge from service, schedules of time-expired men, dedications of altars, records of building or of engineering works accomplished. The facts directly commemorated are rarely important. It is no great gain to historians to learn that at a certain date water was laid on to one frontier fort, and ten years later a granary repaired in another fort. At Chester you may see the tombstone, or the cenotaph, of an under-officer *qui naufragio periit*, who died by the chance of the sea, on the eve of his promotion. At Bonn on the Rhine you may see the monument of a centurion named Caelius who fell *bello Variano*, in the great fight when Arminius destroyed three Roman legions amidst the mosses of North-western Germany. One of these inscriptions possesses a peculiar pathos; the other mentions a world-famous event: yet neither the one nor the other is any more valuable to the historian than hundreds of other soldiers' tombstones which are absolutely devoid of striking features. But when these hundreds are considered together, they become important, for they reveal secrets. They are mostly brief enough—at most, the soldier's name, birthplace, regiment, age—and these brief notices are singly worthless. But if you tabulate some hundreds or thousands of birthplaces, you can trace the whole policy of the Imperial Government in the matter of recruiting. You can ascertain the answers to numerous important questions,—to what extent and till what date legionaries were raised in Italy; what contingents for various branches of the service were drawn from the provinces, and which provinces provided most; how far provincials garrisoned their own countries, and which of them, like the British recruits, were sent as a measure of precaution to serve elsewhere; or, finally, at what epoch the Empire grew weak enough to require the enlistment of barbarians from beyond its frontiers.

So, too, with any other military inscriptions. Each certificate of discharge mentions incidentally the whole number of regiments in the province from which men were discharged at the same time as the recipient of the individual certificate. The dedications and building-records equally mention the regiments of the dedicators or builders. Put them together : add the indications which can obviously be derived from soldiers' tombstones and similar sources, and it will be easy to arrive at the strength of each provincial army, the troops which composed it at various dates, the stations which it occupied, the system of frontier defence which it maintained—if in a frontier province—and in fact the whole organization of the army. Comparisons have often been drawn between the Roman Empire and that which we hold in India. Should any one wish to compare the armies of the two colossal administrations, the inscriptions would tell him as much about many aspects of the Roman army as he would ever learn from books about the existing garrison of India.

This is an instance, roughly outlined, of how inscriptions can be made to reveal the unrecorded history of the Roman Empire. All other archaeological evidence can be utilized in the same manner. The pottery and smaller artistic remains of provinces can be combined and contrasted, and they will tell us how far the Roman civilization, on its material side, spread over non-Italian lands. The ground-plans of houses in Greece, in Italy, in Africa, in Gaul, can be put side by side ; the public buildings, town-halls, and the like can be similarly compared ; and again the spread of Roman material civilization can be estimated with tolerable accuracy. Research has not, it is true, progressed very far in this direction. Not only is the material still somewhat inadequate in amount, but its value is sadly diminished by the difficulty of assigning dates to it. Inscriptions are not always easy to date, but pottery bowls or architectural fragments or mosaic pavements are far more puzzling. Yet such objects must be dated if we are to learn all that we ought from the uncovering of country houses or municipal edifices which happen not to contain inscriptions. Quite recently archaeologists have begun to study the chronology of these things. Their progress has hitherto been slow, but their sooner or later success is not doubtful. We shall never gain so much from these objects as we gain from inscriptions; but we have already learnt a little, and we may confidently hope to learn more of problems about which even the inscriptions are dumb.

It remains briefly to illustrate by examples the additions which archaeological evidence has made to our knowledge of the Empire. Such examples are not altogether easy to select. The Empire has fared very differently from prehistoric Italy. The change introduced into our conception of the latter by recent archaeological research may be compared to the completion and correction of a picture of which only part had been previously painted, and that part imperfectly. The change introduced into our conception of the Empire resembles rather the substitution of a new picture for an old one. The old chronological framework survives nearly intact, but the picture is very different from the old one, though both treat the same subject. A full account of the difference would describe the whole Empire, and far exceed the limits of an essay or a volume. But some leading features of the Empire may be found which specially illustrate the influence of archaeological discoveries, and may provide examples.

The Empire was constitutionally a double-headed state, ruled by both Emperor and Senate. The division dates from the foundation of the Empire, and is characteristic of its founder. Augustus was faced by two facts: on the one side the naked need of a despotism; on the other, the existence of the senatorial oligarchy, the only administrative body in the dead Republic. With his unique capacity for adapting old things to a new order, he accepted both facts. The administration was nominally divided between the Senate and an untitled Emperor, veiled under a courtesy appellation of Princeps. The senatorial magistracies, the consulship, and the rest continued; but a new body of Imperial officials rose beside them, slowly and to contemporaries perhaps imperceptibly. From the first the division was nominal: power rested with the uncrowned king. Very soon the facts followed openly the hidden truth. As we read the names of Emperors on inscriptions, we can trace the growth of a title. Caesar was at first a family name: just a hundred years after Actium it became an Imperial title, and was used as such. A century later a new and harsher title was introduced: the Emperor was henceforward *dominus* not only in the mouths of court poets, but of lawyers and official draughtsmen.

Similarly with the Imperial officials. Augustus had commenced their activity. He had taken into his own hands, and administered by officials whom he appointed, the management of the City of Rome, its supplies of corn and water, its police and firemen, its river-banks and public buildings. He had instituted, or perhaps copied from Julius Caesar, his own Treasury beside the State *Aerarium*. The system grew rapidly. Claudius developed it extensively; he gave the Imperial Treasury its name of *Fiscus*, and created a series of procurators for financial or even administrative work in Rome and the provinces. A third stage came with Hadrian early in the second century—the organization of the existing elements into a definite Civil Service, with regular order of promotion, separate bureaux with staffs of secretaries, and a great increase in the number of offices. A man began as financial procurator in a small post at home or abroad, rose to larger posts, perhaps governed a small province, held the control of the corn supply or the chief financial secretaryship in Rome, and ended as one of the two prefects of the Praetorian Guard, or as governor of the specially regulated province of Egypt. The total list of possible offices is long. There were Treasury officials in the *Fiscus*, and officials who controlled the collection of those taxes which formed the income thereof. Others superintended the Imperial mines in various provinces—in Spain or in Dacia or in Britain—the Imperial coinage, the despatch-service, the roads in Italy, the fleets which policed the Mediterranean, the harbour at Ostia and the corn which was imported there, the games given by the Emperors, the public libraries which they maintained in Rome, and the expenses of their private households. Most of these posts are known to us only from inscriptions: their development, their seniority, their pay, are learnt from the same source.

While this Service grew, the Senate sank. Two violent conflicts, first with Nero, secondly with Domitian, ended in the destruction of those who most loved the Republic and hated the Empire, and fulfilled somewhat the purpose served in English history by the Wars of the Roses. By the end of the first century the Senate had ceased to be republican and hostile to the despot. In the inscriptions of senatorial personages we can trace the gradual extinction of the old blood, and its replacement with new men, passed into the Senate by the Emperors, especially by Vespasian and his successors. For an instance of the latter take the family of the Quintilii, known from both inscriptions and literature. They were

Roman citizens resident originally in the Roman *colonia* founded by Augustus near the site of ancient Ilium. The first to be famous was one Sextus Quintilius Valerius Maximus, some time chief magistrate in his municipality. He was granted senatorial rank by Nerva in A.D. 98, held the praetorship and other posts, and was sent by Trajan as special commissioner to examine the disordered affairs of certain towns in Greece. His two sons were consuls in the same year, A.D. 151, and governed provinces: their sons were also consuls. Finally the Emperor Commodus swept the whole family away in A.D. 182. Possibly he needed their wealth, which is shewn to have been considerable by the leaden pipes and other objects stamped with their names at Rome. Possibly also he hated them as senators; for though the old republicans were gone, the antithesis of Senate and Emperor lasted visibly in numerous details.

We can trace in other ways the growth of the Emperor's power and its advance towards absolutism. Let the reader recall the great buildings of Roman date which are visible to-day in Rome, and especially the multitudinous ruins on the Palatine hill. There numerous archaeological discoveries combine with a few literary allusions to illumine the rise of the Principate. In the last years of the Republic the Palatine was the fashionable quarter of the city: it was covered by the residences of those who were distinguished for long ancestry or great talents or enormous wealth. The patrician Catiline had a house there—inherited, we may suppose, from his forefathers. The banker Crassus bought one there, just above the Forum, and sold it subsequently to the successful barrister Cicero. A small house near it belonged to Cicero's rival, Hortensius, and Augustus himself was born on the hill. The first Princeps therefore did no more than any rich noble might have done when he acquired the residences of

Hortensius, Catiline, and others, and finally built his own house on the western cliff of the hill, looking out across the Circus to the Aventine. The "Domus Augustana" was a magnificent structure: still more magnificent was the Temple of Apollo which Augustus built near it, and the court poets were quick to call it an emperor's habitation, and to turn the name of the hill into the word for palace. Nevertheless, it is not incorrect to say that Augustus lived there like any citizen of high rank, and Tiberius followed his example. He did not enlarge the "Domus Augustana," and his own "domus Tiberiana" was at first probably no more than a private residence, inherited from his father, T. Claudius Nero. Prominent citizens still dwelt on other parts of the hill, like Statilius Sisenna, who occupied the house of Cicero. Caligula and Nero built extensively, but their edifices were pulled down after their deaths, and the details are matters of controversy. Probably their extravagance set a new fashion in Imperial luxury; probably, too, they largely increased the Imperial property on the hill by purchase or by the easier mode of confiscation.

A new period opened with the Flavian dynasty in A.D. 69. Just as at their accession the name "Caesar" ceased to be a family *cognomen* and became an official title, so the Imperial residence on the Palatine ceased to be a great private house and became a State palace. The *aedes publicae* which Vespasian and Domitian built declares this plainly. The new palace, as the visitor can see to-day, was not a dwelling-house at all. It contained what no previous Imperial house had contained—rooms for State ceremonies, councils, trials—and its character illustrates the new position of the Princeps. Frequent changes followed in the great complex of buildings. Domitian laid out a new park, and provided a new water supply, brought by a siphon of solid leaden pipes from the

Aqua Claudia. By the use of huge arches, the platform of the hilltop was enlarged : in the reigns of Trajan and Hadrian the face towards the Nova Via and the Forum was thus extended. Finally, in the opening years of the third century, Septimius Severus built his palace and baths, and his son Caracalla built the Septizonium, towering out to the south. They are characteristic enough of that able, vigorous, and brutal African dynasty which by the grace of the army ruled the Empire for a little period, and ruled it well. They are also the latest Imperial edifices on the Palatine, and in this context too they are remarkable. Rome had begun even in the early part of the second century to lose its importance as the centre of the Empire, and the change can be seen in the buildings. Hadrian, greatest of Imperial builders, touched the Palatine only in details : indeed, he added few features to Rome itself. His Mausoleum and the bridge leading to it, his Temple of Venus and Roma in the Forum, and his restoration of the Pantheon—the last named by no means yet fully understood—complete the brief list, and his own residence was away under the hills near Tivoli. The precedent which he set became in the third and fourth centuries the rule. As we can trace on the Palatine the rise of the central Imperial Government, so we can watch its transference from the hill above the Tiber to many towns by other waters—to Augusta on the Mosel, to Sirmium on the Save, to Ravenna on the Adriatic coast, to Constantinople on the Golden Horn.

From the central authorities we turn to the local government. No State in ancient or in modern times has allowed so much local autonomy to its citizens and subjects as the Roman Empire. The first Emperors inherited the policy from the statesmen of the Republic, who were perhaps actuated by nothing higher than *laissez-faire*: they continued the policy with wiser aims. Every Greek town, every Gaulish canton, which could rule itself was allowed to do so, and the result was a contentment in the provinces which is remarkable in the history of empires. The Roman Government interfered only if the local administration failed. When corruption and extravagance dragged Greek cities into debt and distress, special commissioners visited them. Quintilius was sent to Greece, Pliny to Bithynia, much as an official might be despatched from England to examine the affairs of some Crown colony or Indian municipality. In the second century permanent *correctores* were found necessary for this control. But in general the Roman policy was that of Gallio at Corinth: it cared little for the inner life of the provinces.

To this, however, there is one marked exception—the extension of the Italian town-system through the western provinces. That system meant an organized municipality, town-council, elected magistrates, citizens who were also citizens of Rome, with a dependent territory round which was often as large as an average English county, though much less populous. The title of the municipality was *colonia* or *municipium* (the two do not widely differ): it could be established only by the authority of the Central Government. At the end of the Republic, Italy was covered with such towns, and laws, still partly extant among our inscriptions, had been passed to introduce uniformity and abolish local peculiarities of constitution. These towns formed the basis of all local government. In Imperial times, there was no part of Italy, except a few Imperial and private estates, which was not "attributed" to some town. The Republic had made a feeble beginning of extending this system into the provinces: the Empire carried it further. The early Emperors of the Julio-Claudian house moved cautiously in the matter. Augustus, like Caesar before him, established many "colonies" in which to settle the legionaries disbanded after the Civil Wars, and the same method was subsequently used to provide for the regular discharges of time-expired men from the ordinary Imperial army. The "colonies" thus founded formed, like the colonies of the older Republic, strongholds of Roman power. Thus Claudius founded Colonia Victricensis, as it is called on an inscription, at Camulodūnum (Colchester), and the Roman tombstones found there prove that in part at least it was inhabited by men who had served in the Roman legions. But neither Claudius nor his house cared to confer the cherished privileges of the Roman franchise and municipal government freely on native towns in the provinces. Gradually, however, this narrowness faded, as the provinces grew more and more like Rome in speech and manners. Vespasian, free by birth and training from traditional prejudices of many kinds, was here, as in other matters, an innovator. Under his rule and that of his successors numerous provincial towns acquired the title and privileges of a Roman municipality. Their inhabitants, we may suppose, had become Romanized, or Romans had settled among them for trade or other purposes, or the place had in some other way become fitted to receive the distinction. Henceforward the system spread through the western provinces, Africa (that is, Tunis and Algiers), Spain, Southern Gaul, and the Danubian lands: it failed to take root only in Northern Gaul and Britain. In the East less is heard of it. There the countless Greek cities, founded long before the Roman conquest, left little room, and indeed little necessity, for the introduction of a new type. No such ancient civilization dominated the West. The native town life of Gaul and Spain, and even of Carthaginian Africa, was a lower type than the Italian, and the introduction of the latter, wherever it was suitable, must have marked an advance in the local administration. We need not feel surprised that, as the provinces grew more Roman, the Emperors were glad to supersede the old native systems by the stronger and better Italian town organization.

Particular notice is due, perhaps, to a particular way in which the establishment of *coloniae* and *municipia* was accelerated. It is not mentioned in literature: it was important enough in reality. Roman custom forbade civilians to dwell within the ramparts of their forts or fortresses. In consequence there grew up outside the gates of each stronghold a little settlement of traders, women, and others, to which the name *canabae* (huts) was given. These *canabae* often grew to a considerable size. Not only had the needs of the garrison to be satisfied: traders found the protection of the fortress convenient, and discharged soldiers often chose to settle in familiar places rather than wander to new homes. Little towns arose round the fortresses, as they did round mediaeval castles; and as the inhabitants of these towns were mostly Romans or natives living in close contact with Romans, the *canabae* often became quickly fit to receive the rank of a municipality. For an instance take the fortress and town of Carnuntum on the Danube. The place was a Roman military post as early as the reign of Augustus, and a legion was stationed there not very long afterwards. Vespasian, whose activity along the middle course of the Danube has left few traces in books and many in stone, rebuilt the fortress in A.D. 73, and organized a river-flotilla, the *Classis Flavia Pannonica*, called Flavia because Vespasian was himself a Flavius. A military centre of such importance attracted numerous settlers to its *canabae*, all the more that Carnuntum was the head of a trade-route into the Baltic lands, whence amber came to Rome. We have the brief epitaph of one such trader, C. Aemilius of Patavium, who died at Carnuntum, aged twenty-five: he is called Lixa, "camp-follower," whether by way of cognomen or as a description. Hadrian gave the *canabae* municipal existence: it took his name Aelius, and became *Municipium Aelium Carnuntum*, and henceforward ruled itself through its own civic senate and magistrates. It had also guilds—one a volunteer fire-brigade, formed by discharged soldiers who had settled near their old cantonments. Finally, about A.D. 195 the Emperor Septimius Severus created it a *colonia*; for though *colonia* and *municipium* did not seriously differ, the former was the more honourable and coveted title. The rise of Carnuntum is in no way unique. Two neighbouring fortresses, Brigetio and Aquincum—the latter the ancestor of Buda Pest—rose in precisely the same way; and a third, Vindobona (now Vienna), certainly became a *municipium*, though its fortunes are otherwise unknown.

The general establishment of municipalities on the Italian model meant much more than the improvement of local administration. It meant also the introduction of uniformity into the inner life of the provinces. It was a result, and doubtless in turn a cause, of what we call the Romanization of the provincials. This uniformity can be detected in other points. Not only do *coloniae* and *municipia* throughout the Empire possess the same kinds of civic magistrates and senates. They possess too—and not they only, but other towns which have not their rank possess—the same forms of municipal buildings which we find in Italy. The forum of an ordinary Italian town, whether in North or in South Italy, may be described as a large colonnaded "Piazza," oblong or square, surrounded by the chief public buildings—the Curia of the town council, the local law-courts, the public hall known as the Basilica, a temple or two, and usually some banks or other shops. Not many *fora* have been excavated in the provinces, but the half-dozen known to us agree remarkably in following very closely this Italian type. The forum at Martigny, in the Rhone valley, has been excavated with some care. It is a nearly square block, rather less than two acres in extent, the buildings facing on to the central court. Three sides of this court are fronted apparently by a corridor, into which the buildings open: on the fourth side is the Basilica, a hall 200 feet long by 100 wide. It is just like any of the other *fora*, a little plainer, may be, for Roman Martigny was a small town, and a little more roofed in too, for Roman Switzerland was rainy. But apart from minor variations, it well illustrates the prevalent uniformity: we should not be surprised to find it in Africa, or Raetia, or Britain, or Italy.

This uniformity goes deeper than official arrangements, or the edifices constructed to accommodate them. It pervades the arts, and can be traced in the objects of daily life. In the Western Empire, except perhaps in Africa, the lesser material civilization was all copied from Rome. Before the Roman conquest there flourished in Gaul and the British islands a vigorous native art, of which the chief characteristics, as a fine art, are its fantastic employment of plant and animal forms, and its free use of the spiral ornament. It was an ancient art; it could trace its descent on one side to the Aegean civilization of prehistoric Greece. But this art and the culture which went with it vanished before the Romans. The organized coherent civilization of Italy was too strong for it, as indeed such a civilization must always prove when face to face with ruder though more picturesque arts. Thus the finer pottery used in the western provinces was not a native style. It was the so-called Samian, a red glazed ware, not without merit, were it not that it is a direct copy of an Italian. The original ware was made at Arezzo in Etruria: the Gauls imitated this freely, and the imitations which they made in large quantities were used all over Britain, Spain, and Gaul. The ornamentation of this ware betrays no sign of native influence, and it reigns supreme and universal. Here and there one finds traces of the older art; but they are rude, inferior wares, and their manufacture is confined to isolated sites: they are survivals. The real future of the native art was outside the bounds of the Empire. Far away in Ireland and in Scotland its tradition survived, shewing itself especially in fantastically graceful metal work; and when the Empire had fallen and the prestige of its civilization abated, the native Celtic ornament, enshrined in Irish illuminated manuscripts, became a living influence in European art.

Still, this provincial uniformity itself was never wholly complete. The funeral monuments of the Western world were almost entirely based on Roman originals; but those originals were modified in slightly different methods in different places. The student who wanders across Europe, from museum to museum, meets these variations everywhere—one fashion of gravestone at Dijon and another south of the mountains at Arles, one fashion in Dacia and another in Pannonia. A familiar instance of a local manner is afforded by the basreliefs made for funeral monuments in North-eastern Gaul. At Neumagen on the Mosel chance revealed in 1877 a striking set of such sculptures. They had once adorned sepulchral structures: then torn from their first use, they were built into the foundations of a fortress which some ascribe to Constantine and some to mediaeval architects. Their subjects are the scenes of daily life: boatmen rowing wine-casks down the Mosel and tapping the casks meanwhile, tenants bringing rent or gifts in kind to their lords, ladies at toilette, children at school. The designers of these genre-sketches in stone were plainly acquainted with Roman and with Greek art: they may owe some of their inspiration ultimately to that Graeco-Egyptian art which produced the genre-pictures still surviving in the museums of Rome and largely influenced the whole Roman art of the Empire. But this Gaulish art is not, like the Gaulish pottery, a mere copy: it possesses some originality, and it is, above all, a definite individual manner. It was, in fact, with Roman provincial art as it was with Roman provincial speech. The speech was originally one: it became the Romance languages. The art did not develop identically with the speech, but it too became several kinds of the one art.

We have glanced at the internal arrangements of the Empire. We may turn from the centre to the circumference, from the pacific interior to the frontiers, and the armies which were posted along them to defend the peace within. These frontiers form a separate part of the Empire; they must be carefully distinguished from the districts behind them. As a general rule, the Roman armies were stationed only in these frontier districts, along the edge of the Sahara, in North Britain, along Rhine and Danube and Euphrates. The interior was empty of troops: the garrisons on the Rhine were very powerful, but Gaul itself was controlled by a nominal force; the garrison of Hadrian's Wall in Britain was strong, but there was scarcely a soldier in Southern Britain. The history of these frontier defences has been carefully studied during the last few years, but as yet we know too little to speak positively about them. The defences of Britain, the Rhine, and the Danube have been examined, and some parts of them have been scientifically excavated; but those of the Euphrates, the Arabian desert, and the Sahara have only been explored by flying English, French, or German archaeologists, whose work—most valuable in itself—needs to be supplemented by more systematic examination whenever that is made possible by obvious circumstances. In general, one fact emerges from all that we know. The earlier Empire owned no scientific frontier. Its rule was to defend its frontiers by its armies, not by its fortifications. Ἄνδρες, οὐ τείχη, πόλις might have been its motto. But as the years went by, the glad confidence of the first century faded, and in the reigns of Domitian and Hadrian we meet definite efforts to organize the defences. It was Hadrian who built the great Wall and forts which stretch like a Wall of China across Northern England for some eighty miles from Tyne to Solway. That was meant to be an everlasting barrier between the province of Britain and the unconquerable Caledonians.

Of all these frontiers, the best known to us, and the only one which has been properly excavated, is that which stretches across Germany from Bonn to Regensburg. Augustus had cherished dreams of conquering all the land which lies between the Rhine and the Elbe: the defeat of Varus had stopped those dreams. After that fatal day in A.D. 9 the Roman frontier towards the German tribes coincided roughly with the Rhine. The defeat of Varus was a severe loss in men, and it also indicated that additions to the army were needed if Germany was to be conquered and made a Roman province. Augustus and Tiberius had not the necessary funds: the weakness of the Roman Treasury rather than of its legions saved the independence of the Germans. But an advance was made under Claudius and Nero: Vespasian and Domitian were masters of all the fertile plain of Baden and of the hills to the east of it. Before Trajan mounted the throne in A.D. 98, a palisade of wood, with towers of the same material, had been carried along the frontier wherever it was not river, and forts had been built at suitable spots. Soon the line moved eastwards: Hadrian probably, and certainly Pius, saw to its fortification, and in the third century a rampart of earth or stone, known still as Pfahlgraben or Teufelsmauer, was carried along the outer edge of the frontier. Several points in the history are still obscure, but the general direction of it is unmistakable. Here we see plain—at the teaching of archaeology—that the Roman Empire did not stand still for ever after the triumph of Arminius over Varus. Successive rulers pushed slowly forward across the middle Rhine, that is, the river between Mainz and Strassburg, and, though they never attempted to realize the dreams of Augustus, and Germany remained free, a considerable area was gradually added to the Empire in what is now Baden and Württemberg.

Such are some general features of the Empire as revealed to us by archaeological research. They are not the only prominent features, and some might say that they are not altogether the most prominent, nor are the discoveries which support them the most striking or sensational. Forts and frontiers, sepulchral ornament and Samian ware are not promising subjects. But that is not the whole account of the matter. Interesting and sensational discoveries are not always helpful to the historian. We may unearth the Basilica of Caesar and the cloister of the Vestals in the Roman Forum. We may trace the Sacred Way, and on the Palatine above we may think to identify the very corridor where Caligula was murdered. We may find an inscription cut by order of Augustus, and in it the words, "Carmen fecit Q. Horatius Flaccus"—Horace wrote the Carmen Saeculare for the Epochal Games of Augustus. We may decipher on Pompeian stucco, or on a tile found, as it seems, at Silchester, Virgilian or Ovidian fragments. At the end we shall but make reflections like those of Addison in Westminster Abbey. These things provide pleasures to the imagination which are forbidden to the student of history. Nor, again, do the completest remains always tell the most. The streets and storehouses of Ostia and the endless mansions of Pompei, the Court of the Praetorium at Lambaesis, the amphitheatres at Thysdrus and Pola, the huge theatre wall of Orange or the massive arches of the Pont du Gard, cannot fail to impress. But their special value is educational, not historical. The amphitheatres of Thysdrus or Pola are not more instructive to the historian than a dozen less perfect—Varhely, Buda Pest, Carnuntum, and so forth. Their proper function is to convince the beholder of the reality of ancient life, quite as much as to increase his knowledge of it. An ancient model of an ancient building is better than a modern model, for it is more accurately vivid; but the material question is the vividness, and not the accuracy. A well-preserved Mithraeum, like that discovered in 1870 under San Clementi in Rome—now unhappily full of water—or that still visible at Ostia, may help the visitor to realize that Mithraism was once a real religion, rival and formidable rival to Christianity for nearly two centuries. But in the end it is not the edifice at Ostia, but countless inscriptions and sculptures, whole or imperfect, scattered over the whole Empire wherever soldiers were quartered or trade was active, that tell us what Mithraism actually meant. Perhaps it may not be amiss, even in a survey like the present, to look away from the more interesting and popular remains, and to contemplate those insignificant objects which are yet so significant for the history of a vast and complex Empire.

PART THIRD
CHRISTIAN AUTHORITY

BY

THE REV. A. C. HEADLAM, B.D.

FELLOW OF ALL SOULS COLLEGE, OXFORD

PART THIRD
CHRISTIAN AUTHORITY

I. The Early Church

THE purpose of this and the two following chapters is to estimate the gain accruing to our knowledge and conception of early Christianity from archaeological discovery. With Christian life in its later developments, archaeology has always had an intimate connexion. From the first basilicas of the time of Constantine onward, the ideas and thoughts of Christians have been expressed in a permanent form by architecture and painting. Our knowledge of these periods is so ample that we do not require to use monumental evidence to provide ourselves with historical information in studying doctrine or custom; we are able to use literary sources to interpret the remains. But if we were to eliminate St. Sophia or the churches of Salonika from our study of Byzantine history, if we were to try to realize the Church of the Middle Ages apart from the great cathedrals and monasteries of the twelfth and thirteenth centuries, our conceptions would be very inadequate. Modern historians may correct a too idealized mediaevalism from the *chronique scandaleuse* of an episcopal registry, but all realism is untrue which leaves out man's most ideal thoughts and creations. In the earlier periods the function of archaeology is different. The circumstances of Christianity and the Church precluded the production of anything great or magnificent, and the evidence on many points is so scanty, that what we ask for is new information. Does archaeology give us real sources of information about the earliest days of Christianity?

The answer to this question will be given so far as is possible in the following pages; but it may be convenient to sum up at once the classes of evidence that we possess and the extent to which they are available.

In the first place, archaeology has helped us by the discovery of literary sources, rescued from the sands of the Egyptian desert. This class of evidence will be discussed first, as being rather apart from the rest. Broadly speaking, it is not different in kind from the writings that we already possess; it supplements them, and must be treated in the same way. Yet this statement requires some modification, for there are two not altogether insignificant differences. The larger number of papyrus documents which have been discovered are fragmentary, and there is very great danger, in consequence, of incorrect deductions. An illustration of this will be given later. A second point of difference lies in the fact that the majority of the relics of early Christianity which have survived in manuscripts have done so because they were thought to be worth keeping and transcribing, while those which are discovered in the rubbish heaps of Oxyrhynchus may have found their way there just because they were thought to be worthless. This does not in the least take away from their value; in a historical sense it may increase it. Often two sets of opinions have been in conflict; that which ultimately prevails will generally be exceedingly unfair to that which is suppressed, and all tokens of the party in opposition will disappear. The judgment may very likely be right, but the historian will treasure every fragment that survives, enabling us to understand what has disappeared. He wishes to be fair to both sides. Nevertheless there is therefore a certain amount of caution necessary in making use of new literary discoveries. Their importance runs a danger of being exaggerated at first. The sense of proportion may be lost. The crude speculations of some half-educated Christian may be thought to be genuine tradition. A writer who merely blunders because he is ignorant may be supposed to give us new information. The argument from silence may be used when silence arises from the document being fragmentary. There is danger in new discoveries; but if rightly used, the information they give may be all the more valuable from being unofficial and unrecognized.

If we pass to archaeology proper, to the information, that is, which is acquired from inscriptions and other monumental remains, by far the most important gain to early Christianity is that which is indirect. The immense mass of Latin and Greek inscriptions which date from the period of the early empire have enabled its history, organization, and provincial life to be reconstructed, often down to the most minute details. It is this background to Christianity from which we learn most. When we see an effigy of Tiberius or Nero, with the insignia of an Egyptian king, on the walls of a temple in Egypt, we have the opportunity of learning a great deal about the genius of the empire. Almost the whole of the history of the elaborate provincial organization for imperial worship has to be reconstructed from inscriptions. A knowledge of Greek organization for religious purposes, of the various religious guilds and mysteries, is clearly necessary in order to understand the way in which Christianity would have been likely to spread; and that knowledge is given us by inscriptions. It would be wandering too far from our special purpose to describe these general results of archaeology in the domain of secular history, even though they have an indirect influence on Christian history, and we must refer to the writings of others—for example, to Sir Charles Newton's fourth essay on Art and Archaeology; but some examples can be given by studying the actual illustrations of the text of the New Testament. Wherever there is any direct reference to the imperial or provincial organization,—and that we find especially in the Acts of the Apostles,—we are enabled to check and illustrate the statements given. The value of this is double. It has an illustrative value, and, to a certain extent, it has a critical value. It is an almost infallible sign of a later or a forged document, that it blunders in the minor points of local government and geography. An antiquarian knowledge was impossible in early days, and a writer almost inevitably gives us the arrangements, not of the times he is describing, but of his own day. Illustrations of this might be given from later Lives of the Saints and spurious Acts of Martyrs. If, then, we find that the accuracy of a work in geographical and administrative details is largely corroborated by inscriptions, it is strong presumptive evidence of its historical value as a document. This argument may be pressed too far; it will not cover all points; a document may be contemporary and correct in geographical details, but untruthful. Yet the fact that it is trustworthy, where we can test it, is presumptive evidence in favour of its general credibility. It will therefore be necessary to give some space to the historical illustrations of the Acts of the Apostles.

We now turn to the monumental remains of early Christianity. It is interesting to notice that early Christian writers give two instances of the use of monumental evidence. The first instance is one adduced by Justin

Martyr, and copied from him by Eusebius. He tells us that Simon Magus had performed miracles in Rome by the aid of magic, that he was considered as a god, and that a statue of him was erected on the island of the river Tiber, between the two bridges, with the inscription, *Simoni Deo Sancto—To Simon, the Holy God.* In 1574 a statue was found in the place indicated, with the inscription on it, *Semoni Sanco deo fidio,* i.e. to *Semo Sancus,* a Sabine deity. It is almost universally agreed that this was the cause of Justin's mistake, and probably also of the origin of the legend which brought Simon Magus to Rome.

A second instance is given by Eusebius. He tells us that at Paneas, otherwise called Caesarea Philippi, it was said that the woman whom the Saviour cured of an issue of blood came from that city, that her home was shewn there, and also a statue. By the gates of the city there was the brazen image of a woman kneeling, with her hands stretched out as if she was praying. Opposite, there was another upright image of a man, made of the same material, clothed decently in a double cloak and extending his hand towards the woman. This was said to be a statue of Jesus, and Eusebius had seen it himself. There is not the same evidence to enable us to explain the origin of Eusebius' error; but it is generally supposed that this was a statue of an emperor, as sun-god, addressed as *Saviour,* and that some such word as this caused the mistake.

These two instances have been mentioned as professing to give us archaeological evidence of the earliest period of Christianity, and as enabling us to point out in contrast the comparatively late date of all archaeological Christian remains. There is nothing at all as yet known which touches in any way the earliest history, or really affects the credibility of the Gospel narrative, nor is it in any way likely that anything should be found. Christianity was not likely to leave any memorials of itself during its earliest and most obscure period. It had neither the freedom nor the wealth, nor, we may add, the motive. The earliest memorials are contained in the Catacombs, and they possibly represent the end of the first century. They might give some evidence about Apostolic history; they can give none about the Gospel period. The Christian monuments, then, that we have to describe do not give us information about the beginnings of Christianity, and they do not therefore touch any of the essential truths of belief, except possibly as overthrowing certain extreme critical theories. They represent the beliefs and practices of the second and following centuries, and they presuppose the Biblical writings. Nor will they ever be of any great value for controversial purposes in ecclesiastical history. Their evidence is to a certain extent unsubstantial, it is often symbolical, often slightly enigmatic: it requires literature to supplement and interpret it. There is a great deal in the Catacombs, for example, that can be interpreted according to the point of view of the writer. The evidence in any direction is rarely clear enough to admit of being used as proof. At the same time, it will become apparent (and instances will be given later) that writers from certain points of view have, in order to support their belief, allowed themselves to indulge in a good many theories, both archaeological and historical, which will not for a moment hold good.

The real value of these archaeological remains is purely historical; that is, they illustrate phases in Christian history. They allow us to look at the Christian community from a side which no literature—or hardly any literature—exhibits to us. A Christian sermon and the religious conceptions of the less educated members of a congregation are very wide apart. The former may be more valuable, but the latter will often be more interesting. It is the latter that the inscriptions very largely give us. They

HISTORICAL VALUE OF THE EVIDENCE

represent the popular cults, conceptions, and ideas, especially concerning the departed. They represent the gradual and almost unconscious transformation of ideas. They shew us the life and organization of a Christian community from another and different point of view to that which theological literature gives. This is the real gain of archaeology. Incidentally there may be other gains; some corroboration of historical documents, or lives of the saints. Incidentally, again, there may be evidence, at any rate worth quoting, on points of controversy. The present writer may express his belief that a good many modern Christians, who hold rather extreme views in certain directions, would have been singularly uncomfortable—morally as well as physically—if they had attended any religious service in the Catacombs. But we must learn to be historians first; and when we have become historians, a good many controversial questions will assume rather different proportions to those they assume at present.

Speaking generally, our monumental remains of early Christianity come from two districts—from Phrygia, and from the Catacombs of Rome. The remains elsewhere of an early date are isolated, and can only serve to illustrate what we get from these two districts. After therefore saying something about the literary remains recovered from Greek papyri, and about the archaeological illustrations of the New Testament, and especially the Acts of the Apostles, two chapters will be devoted to the Christian remains in Phrygia and to the Roman Catacombs. These essays do not aim at being exhaustive; but probably in this way enough will be said to enable the reader to estimate the value of archaeological research in its bearings on Christian history.

We begin with the discoveries of papyri in Egypt. For a long time papyrus fragments containing Greek documents have been preserved in our museums; but within a comparatively short period the numbers have increased enormously The first great find was that of the Archduke Rainer's papyri brought from the Fayoum: amongst these (which unfortunately are for the most part very fragmentary) was discovered and published in 1882 by the well-known Roman Catholic theologian Professor Bickell a short Gospel fragment containing six lines (incomplete) of about seventeen letters each. He claimed it as containing a fragment of one of the earlier sources of our Gospels.[1] The following is a translation of this fragment, the parts conjecturally supplied being put between square brackets. As the fragment contains, obviously, words of our Lord preserved in the Synoptic Gospels, and as the length of the lines can be fixed, the restorations are for the most part certain; but towards the end they are only probable:—

. . . to eat according to custom. All of you shall be offended [in this] night [according] to the Scripture: I will smite the [shepherd and the flock] shall be scattered. When Peter [said], and if all, yet n[ot I]. [Before] the cock twice cr[ow thou shalt to-day three times] deny me.

It is pointed out that this passage is much shorter than the narrative in St. Matthew or St. Mark; that the words (Matt. xxvi. 32, Mark xiv. 28), " And after I am risen I will go before you into Galilee "—which seem to be an interruption in the narrative—are omitted; and that the words of our Lord are given without any historical setting. It is therefore claimed that this represents a fragment of an earlier Gospel. A moment's reflection will shew how very unsubstantial this argument is. An author making extracts might often abridge; any one quoting in a sermon will often put words shortly, because they are well known; the omitted verse might easily be omitted because not

---

[1] The fullest account is by Harnack in *Texte und Untersuchungen*, v. 4, p. 283, which gives the literature.

required for the purpose in hand; while the complete absence of the introductory expression, "Jesus saith to him," etc., makes the passage almost unintelligible to any one who is not acquainted with the Synoptic Gospels. It may be added also that Dr. Hort has shewn that generally in the Fathers where this passage is quoted, the verse omitted in the fragment is omitted in the quotations, although it is undoubted that these quotations come from the Gospels. The reference to the passing to Galilee had of course no immediate connexion with the denial of Peter; and although that may suggest that it is an interpolation, it also gives a reason for omission. It is not our business to suggest any explanation. It was necessary to refer to this discovery, for it created some stir at the time in the newspapers, and the fragment is often quoted as undoubtedly belonging to an original Gospel. It must be obvious how very slight a foundation for any theory can be given by so small a fragment. Several hypotheses can be suggested to account for the variations. One may be more probable than the other; but what is probable to a scholar is published as a certainty by a newspaper. This instance illustrates the great danger which attends so many papyrus documents. They are so often so fragmentary as to raise problems instead of solving them.

One recent discovery, luckily, does not suffer to the same extent from being incomplete. In 1892 there were published by M. Bouriant, in the Memoirs of the French Archaeological Mission at Cairo, three documents which had been found some years previously at Ekhmim, in Upper Egypt, in a tomb. They were, a considerable portion of a narrative of the Crucifixion, an Apocalyptic fragment, and a portion of the Greek text of the Book of Enoch. All these discoveries are of very great interest. With regard to the first two, there is a general concurrence of opinion that they are portions of the Gospel of Peter and the Apocalypse of Peter, which are referred to by various Church authorities as existing in the second century. There can, in fact, be no reasonable doubt that we have here considerable fragments of these two early Christian documents; and, as is well known, any Christian remains of the second century are of first rate importance. To go further than this would be to enter into a long discussion in the arena of Christian literary history, which would be decidedly foreign to the purpose of this essay. It may be permitted, however, to express a personal opinion that the Gospel is considerably later in style and character than any of our four Gospels, that it makes use of all of them, that it contains no independent tradition, and that the passages where it differs from our Gospels are of the character called *tendenz* by German critics; that it, in fact, represents a rewriting of the narrative in a manner which suited a certain section of the Christian public in the second century, just as Dr. Farrar has rewritten the Gospel narrative for the benefit of the nineteenth century.

The third and most recent discovery is curiously enough a document similar to the above. In the winter of 1896-7, on the site of the ancient Oxyrhynchus, the capital of a nome of Middle Egypt, Messrs. Grenfell and Hunt had the good fortune to discover by far the largest collection of papyri yet known.[1] It will take some years to decipher them all; but so far there have been published, among Christian remains, an early fragment of St. Matthew's Gospel, two curious Christian documents —unfortunately very imperfect—and, what immediately concerns us, a short collection of "Sayings of our Lord." It may be interesting to give a translation of these. It is based mainly on the revised text of Professors Lock and

---

[1] *Oxyrhynchus Papyri*, I., Grenfell and Hunt, p. 1; Lock and Sanday, *Two Lectures on the "Sayings of Jesus."*

Sanday, which, if occasionally too conjectural, gives us the document in the most readable form :—

1. [Jesus saith, Cast out first the beam out of thine own eye], and then shalt thou see to cast out the mote in thy brother's eye.

2. Jesus saith, Except ye fast to the world, ye shall not find the kingdom of God ; and unless ye keep the true Sabbath, ye shall not see the Father.

3, 4. Jesus saith, I stood in the midst of the world, and in my flesh I was seen of them, and I found all men drunken, and not one found I thirsty among them; and my soul is weary for the souls of men, for they are blind in their heart and see [not, poor and know not] their poverty.

5. Jesus saith, Wherever there be [two, they are not without] God, and if anywhere there be one I am with him: raise the stone and there thou shalt find me, cleave the wood and there am I.

6. Jesus saith, A prophet is not received in his own country, nor doth a physician heal his neighbours.

7. Jesus saith, A city built on the summit of a lofty mountain and firmly established cannot fall nor be hidden.

8. Jesus saith, Thou hearest with [one ear], but the other [hast thou closed].

It would be beside our purpose to enter into a detailed discussion of the meaning and history of these Sayings. Although more interesting than the Fayoum fragment, like it they provide ample opportunity for conjecture without giving us the material for a solution. Do they come from any lost Gospel? Do they contain any independent and correct tradition of our Lord's words, or are they apocryphal embellishments of the second century? These are questions easier to ask than to answer. The discoverers sum up their own conclusions about them as follows : "(1) that we have here a collection of sayings, not extracts from a narrative Gospel ; (2) that they are not heretical ; (3) that they were independent of the Four Gospels in their present shape ; (4) that they were earlier than A.D. 140, and might go back to the first century."

We have grouped together thus these discoveries because they all refer directly or indirectly to the life and sayings of our Lord, and they suggest the question,

Have we obtained any authentic and independent evidence about the first beginnings of Christianity, or are we likely to do so? In answer to these questions, it will be obvious at once that the Fayoum papyrus gives us nothing certain; a perusal of the Gospel of Peter will make it quite clear that the narrative in it is not more credible nor more authentic than that in the other Gospels, and our only chance lies with the last discovery. Here we have Sayings which are at any rate remarkable; whether they are really genuine (where giving new teaching) seems to the present writer very doubtful. They rather represent a later contemplative literary aspect than the genuine tone of the Gospels. We cannot, we believe, as yet claim to have any fresh information about our Lord's life and words. Nor, it may be hazarded, are we likely to acquire any. We know fairly well what information Christian writers at the end of the second century possessed, and it is clear that they knew little or nothing about our Lord which we do not. Such traditions as are preserved are rarely of any real value. They are all more or less apocryphal in their character. Of the history of the text of our Gospels we may get very full information; of the various works known to the Fathers —the Gospel according to the Egyptians, the Gospel according to the Hebrews, and others—we may hope for more complete texts; the traditions concerning the Church of the Apostolic age we may get in a more authentic form; the discovery of the works of Papias and Hegesippus, two early writers who preserved traditions of previous generations, is of course quite within the limits of possibility. We may, in fact, gain a large amount of material for reconstructing the history, the traditions, and the knowledge of the second century, and thus for solving many questions which have been raised. But if, as we have suggested, the second century had no more authentic knowledge of the origin of Christianity than we possess, our general position will not be changed. We could undoubtedly use the information that Eusebius possessed better than he could; it will mean to us much more than it meant to him: but Eusebius had no sources of information at all authentic concerning the first century which we do not possess, nor can we hope to find anything that he had not.

As illustrating a later period of Church history, an interesting document may be quoted. It is well known that the great mass of papyri discovered have been not literary remains, but official or private documents—tax-gatherers' receipts, bills, leases, letters, horoscopes, and so on. Amongst these, two have been found of very great interest. They are both *libelli*, that is, certificates of having sacrificed, given by commissioners during a persecution of Christians. The more complete reads as follows:—

> To the Commissioners of sacrifices of the village of Alexander-Island from Aurelius Diogenes Satabus of the village of Alexander-Island, a man of eighty-two years of age, with a scar on his right eyebrow.
>
> I have both always continued sacrificing to the gods and now in your presence I have sacrificed according to the decrees, and have poured libations and eaten of the sacrifices, and I ask you to sign this petition.
>
> Fare you well.
>
> I, Aurelius Diogenes, have presented this petition.

Then followed the signatures of the commissioners, so badly written (as was natural) as to be quite illegible, and then the date:—

> In the first year of Imperator Caesar Gaius Messius Quintus Traianus Decius Pius Felix Augustus, on the second of the month Epiphi (*i.e.* June 26, 250).

In the Decian persecution, five commissioners were appointed whose business it was to visit every town and village, and compel every one to appear before them and offer sacrifice. Those who sacrificed received a certificate, of which this is a specimen; and many who did not sacrifice themselves obtained from the magistrates, by giving a small bribe, certificates that they had done so. Archaeology has given us two instances of such documents. We cannot exactly say that they add to our information; but the actual possession of such a relic of times of persecution enables us to realize the situation in a way which no ordinary history would render possible. It is not a copy; it is the original document.

The examination of papyrus discoveries due to archaeology happened to concentrate our attention mainly on the Gospel narrative. The next stage will take us to the history of the early Church and the Acts of the Apostles. It is well known that concerning the latter writing there has been, and continues to be, a large amount of controversy both as to its authorship and as to its historical credibility. With many of these questions it would be naturally beside our purpose to deal. But in one direction, and that an important one, archaeology does give us very interesting evidence; for the writer of the book has preserved a large amount of local colour, and the discovery of inscriptions has enabled us, in a considerable number of cases, to test his information. The evidence applies necessarily to the latter portion of the book, and its exact contribution to the larger questions involved must depend on a number of various considerations.

In the diversified life of the Eastern empire in the first and second centuries an interesting feature—at any rate to the antiquary—was the infinite variety of city organization. It had ceased to mean very much, for it was now only municipal; but it was a relic of the time when towns, which still preserved the proud name of free, or confederate, cities, had been free in reality as well as in name,—sovereign communities, with full and real self-government. All this variety existed when St. Paul travelled, and it is reflected in the Acts of the Apostles.

When St. Paul crossed over into what we now call Europe, the first important city that he came to was Philippi. The narrative here is for a time in the first person plural, and evidently, for some reason, the city is described with some fulness: "Setting sail therefore from Troas, we made a straight course to Samothrace, and the day following to Neapolis; and from thence to Philippi, which is a city of Macedonia, the first of the district, a *Roman* colony."

Coins and inscriptions combine to tell us that this city was a Roman colony bearing the name of "*Colonia Augusta Iulia Philippensis.*" The further description is, however, a little more difficult. In the first place, a very unusual word is used to describe the "district"; so unusual is it that Dr. Hort writes: "None of these readings gives an undeniable sense. *Meris* never denotes simply a region, province, or any geographical division: when used of land, as of anything else, it means a portion or share."[1] He suggests a primitive error and a conjectural emendation. When that was written, Dr. Hort's statement was—as far as our knowledge went—absolutely correct. Now it has been proved to be untrue. Among the documents found in the Fayoum, a considerable number use just this word *Meris* to describe the divisions of the district. Nor is this unconnected with Macedonia. We know that the Fayoum was colonized by veterans from the army of Alexander—that is, by Macedonians—so that, just as the name *Pella* tells us of the presence of Macedonians in the country beyond the Jordan, so the word *Meris*, used of a division of the

[1] See Westcott and Hort, *Greek Testament*, vol. ii., Appendix, p. 96.

Fayoum, is a sign of Macedonian colonists in Egypt. This word, then, which even a cautious scholar like Dr. Hort condemned and considered to be a sign of a primitive corruption, is now proved to be used in a legitimate sense, and one particularly associated with Macedonia. The author of the Acts has thus probably provided us with the ordinary local name for the four divisions into which, from other sources, we know that Macedonia was divided.

But there is still another difficulty. The city is called "first of the district"; but Amphipolis, we are told, was really capital of this division. Has the author made a mistake? Or are we, like Blass, to suppose another primitive error, and adopt the somewhat meaningless conjecture "of the first division," or will our previous experience make us a little chary about finding primitive errors? Surely the following commentary of Professor Ramsay, based on the assumption that the author of the Acts was a native of Philippi, is infinitely more probable:—

"The description of the dignity and rank of Philippi is unique in *Acts*: nor can it be explained as strictly requisite for the historian's proper purpose. Here again the explanation lies in the character of the author, who was specially interested in Philippi, and had the true Greek pride in his own city. Perhaps he even exaggerates a little the dignity of Philippi, which was still only in process of growth, to become at a later date the great city of its division. Of old, Amphipolis had been the chief city of the division, to which both belonged. Afterwards, Philippi quite outstripped its rival; but it was at that time in such a position, that Amphipolis was ranked first by general consent, Philippi first by its own consent. These cases of rivalry between two or even three cities for the dignity and title of 'first' are familiar to every student of the history of the Greek cities; and though no other evidence is known to shew that Philippi had as yet begun to claim the title, yet this single passage is conclusive. The descriptive phrase is like a lightning flash amid the darkness of local history, recording in startling clearness the whole situation to those whose eyes are trained to catch the character of Greek city history and city jealousies."[1]

Now there is an element of conjecture in this, as there is in a conjectural emendation, and as there must be in much constructive history; but it is conjecture based upon knowledge. This illustrates the service of archaeology even more than an inscription which described Philippi as " first of the district " would, for archaeology does not mean making accidentally a brilliant discovery of something striking,—there must be an element of luck in that; but it means studying every fragment of antiquity, every inscription or building, comparing them with the literary remains that are extant, and thus imbuing the whole mind with the spirit and thought and sentiment and ideas of antiquity. Any one who has had the patience and industry to do this becomes capable of interpreting an ancient document. He will appreciate it from its historical side, and not from that of the *a priori* theorist. He may make mistakes, as every one must, which may be corrected by others working on the same lines; but his method is the only one which will ultimately lead to real historical knowledge.

Philippi was a Roman colony, and therefore had a constitution analogous to that of Rome. It would be governed by two *duumviri iuri dicundo*, corresponding to the consuls, under whom would be aediles and quaestors. It was customary in some places for the college of magistrates to be called collectively rulers, or *archontes*, while the *duumviri* were, as Cicero tells us, and as inscriptions from other Roman colonies shew, in the habit of calling them-

[1] Ramsay, *St. Paul the Traveller*, pp. 206, 207.

selves praetors.¹ These are the names given in the Acts. Moreover, the chief magistrates of a colony, like the magistrates at Rome, were attended by lictors,² a name which would of course be quite incorrect if used of a Greek city. The officials of the city were therefore all described in the ordinary popular phraseology of the day. "The title 'praetors' was not technically correct, but was frequently employed as a courtesy title for the supreme magistrates of a Roman colony; and, as usual, Luke moves on the plane of educated conversation in such matters, and not on the plane of rigid technical accuracy."³

From Philippi, St. Paul went to Thessalonica (the modern Salonika), and there found himself, not in a Roman colony, but in a free Greek city, which possessed its own constitution, like Athens, or Tarsus, or Antioch. It had received this privilege for the part that it had taken against Brutus and Cassius in the civil wars. It kept its old constitution; it had the right of self-government in its own affairs; and the governor of the province had, under normal circumstances, no right to interfere. Now in the Acts the magistrates of this city are called *politarchs*, a name which does not appear in any other place in Greek literature, yet the evidence of inscriptions shews that its use here was perfectly accurate; an inscription of Salonika, on an arch which was demolished some years ago, tells us that it was erected when certain persons were "politarchs of the city."⁴ It is worth quoting the remarks, in this place, of Conybeare and Howson, who bring out the distinction between the two cities very well, and who, when opportunities were less than they are at present, applied to the Acts of the Apostles all the

¹ *I.e.* στρατηγοί.
² *I.e.* ῥαβδοῦχοι.
³ Ramsay, *op. cit.*, p. 218.
⁴ See especially a paper on the *Politarchs* by Dr. Burton, reprinted from the *American Journal of Theology* (1897), p. 598.

archaeological knowledge of their day: "The whole aspect of what happened at Thessalonica, as compared with the events at Philippi, is in perfect harmony with the ascertained difference in the political condition of the two places. There is no mention of the rights and privileges of *Roman citizenship*; but we are presented with the spectacle of a mixed mob of Greeks and Jews, who are anxious to shew themselves to be '*Caesar's friends.*' No *lictors* with rods and fasces appear upon the scene; but we hear something distinctly of a *demus* or free assembly of the people. Nothing is said of *religious ceremonies* which the citizens, being Roman, may not lawfully adopt; all the anxiety, both of people and magistrates, is turned to the one point of shewing their loyalty to *the Emperor*. And those magistrates by whom the question at issue is ultimately decided are not Roman *praetors*, but Greek *politarchs*."

One more observation, and we shall have finished with these towns. It is well known that the visit to Philippi is described in the first person plural, while in that to Thessalonica we get back into the ordinary narrative in the third person. Now that is usually held to mean that in the one narrative we have the evidence of an eyewitness, whether worked up or not, in the other we have not. And the further question arises, Is the author of the Acts the eyewitness who falls naturally into the first person when he is describing occasions at which he was present with St. Paul, or is he a later writer, who, in an extremely inartistic way, incorporated the fragment of a diary with other information? Now on this we have only one observation here to make. The narrative of the visit at Philippi is accurate and full of local colouring. That, it is said, is owing to the fact that the author had good material here. But when we pass to Thessalonica, we have the same evidence of local knowledge, and the same accuracy in constitutional points. Does not this suggest that we have here the work of the same hand in both cases? If St. Luke were a native of Philippi, he would know the constitution of the neighbouring city of Thessalonica; and although he was not present, his narrative based on various information that he received would be accurate; and the local circumstances would naturally become prominent. The hypothesis that the author was the same is surely more natural than to imagine two sources, both the product of authors with good local knowledge, worked up in the same style by a *tendenz* writer of the second century.

It is the purpose of these essays to estimate our debt to archaeology. It is sometimes difficult for us to realize how great that debt is, for from the earliest revival of learning onwards archaeology has been working side by side with literature to restore to us the life of the past. Much of the result of archaeological research has become part of common knowledge, and we absorb it in our classical training without realizing in the least whence it comes. Our knowledge of the worship, the religious rites, and the mythology of the ancients is largely the result of past archaeological research, a research which is continually being amplified and corrected. We may illustrate this by the episode of the disturbance in the theatre at Ephesus mentioned in the Acts. Why were our ancestors content with the translation "Great is Diana of the Ephesians," and why do we desire to substitute Artemis? The gradual extension of our knowledge, an extension in which archaeology has played a very considerable part, may be marked by three stages. The first confused the Greek Artemis with the Roman Diana, after the manner of the Roman poets. The second restores her individuality to the Greek Artemis. The third goes back behind the Hellenic covering, and reminds us that the Ephesian Artemis was an Oriental goddess who had been incorporated into Greek mythology, and identified with a Greek goddess. Coins are sufficient to remind us that the Ephesian goddess, with her multitude of breasts, was, in her origin, to be identified, not with the perfect womanhood of the Aryan Huntress, but with the Oriental personification of the reproductive force in nature, and the religion of an elder race, surviving in an Hellenic dress. The scene in the theatre of Ephesus is described in language singularly correct. The whole narrative has been illustrated by the result of discoveries made on the site of Ephesus by the authorities of the British Museum. Although they were undertaken many years ago, it is only recently that the inscriptions discovered have been properly edited by Dr. Hicks for the British Museum, and no really scientific account of the excavations has appeared.[1]

All our inscriptions remind us of the important place occupied by the worship of Artemis in the life and trade of Ephesus. This is brought out most clearly by one text often quoted, but so apposite to our purpose that it may well be quoted again: "Not only in this city, but everywhere, temples are dedicated to the goddess and statues erected and altars consecrated to her, on account of the manifest appearances she vouchsafes." There was a month which bore her name, "Artemision," and during this month "solemn assemblies and religious festivals are held, and more especially in this our city, which is the nurse of its own Ephesian goddess." These words seem almost identical with the language of the Acts: Great is Diana of the Ephesians, whom all Asia and the world worshippeth." Let us also remember that it suits well with the chronology of the Acts if we place this disturbance at Ephesus in the late spring, just during the month sacred to the goddess; "the people of the

---

[1] Hicks, *Greek Inscriptions in the British Museum*, Part II.; Lightfoot *Essays on Supernatural Religion*, p. 291.

Ephesians, considering it meet that the whole of this month which bears the divine name shall be kept holy and dedicated to the goddess," has decreed to that effect.

We need not quote more; let us look at one particular point. The Acts tells us that Ephesus was *Neokoros*, or "temple-warden," of Artemis. This was an honorary title conferred on cities, or, in some cases, adopted by them, in relation to the worship of the Emperor, and also of Artemis. Curiously enough, until recent discoveries, there was no certain evidence that it was used of Ephesus in relation to Artemis, although it was known to be used in relation to Augustus. Later discoveries have repaired the defect. "The city of the Ephesians . . . . . twice temple-warden of the Augusti, according to the decrees of the Senate, and temple-warden of Artemis,"—so the city describes itself in an inscription.

The narrative in the Acts bristles with details, and every detail might be corroborated. There is the theatre, which was the recognized place of public meeting and the centre of the civic life of the city. There is the special stress laid on sacrilege. The words "Let it be accounted sacrilege" seem to have been a most stringent form of condemnation. There are the town-clerk, *grammateus*, as distinct a feature in Ephesus as the politarch in Thessalonica or the court of the Areopagus at Athens; the assembly, *ecclesia*, of the people, or *demus*, a survival of the old Greek democracy; the *regular assembly* being a feature particularly noted in inscriptions. Add the Asiarch, the proconsul, the Roman assizes, and we get a very complete picture introducing all the leading elements of the life of the place, as archaeology has revealed them. Now our knowledge of all these details, in fact of most of the leading features of this account, is derived from inscriptions and from the discoveries made during the excavations undertaken by the British Museum at Ephesus.

These excavations produced very little that museums love, and were not conducted with any real skill; but, all the same, the results were singularly important. If we put aside a love for merely dilettante archaeology, if we have a really scientific desire for reconstructing the life of the ancient world, a regular and systematic exploration, undertaken with adequate means, of representative sites, great and small alike, in the Roman province of Asia, would fulfil our aims.

As has been implied above, there are very few points in which the Gospel narrative touches on anything in secular history that enables us to test it; but the writer of the third Gospel—a writer who, whatever opinion we may form about his work, has evidently some of the characteristics of a secular historian which the other Evangelists do not possess—has attempted to fix somewhat precisely the date of our Lord's birth and ministry; and in doing so has made statements round which much controversy has circled. It may be as well to state at once that in our opinion it may be quite possible to consider that St. Luke is a credible historian, and to attach a high value to his narrative, even though in one or two such statements he may have made a mistake. He was writing sixty or seventy years after some of the events that he recorded, and at that distance of time an error on such a point might occur in a good historian. To make therefore the accuracy of St. Luke to depend upon the result of exceedingly intricate and admittedly obscure investigations into the question of the date of Quirinius (Cyrenius) shews a great deficiency in the sense of proportions. Still less is the question of inspiration dependent on such accuracy. It is certainly not possible to say that there are no historical errors in the Bible, and to do so would imply a very mechanical theory of inspiration. But, allowing that some error or partial error may be possible in a good history, yet the value of any such work is enhanced, the greater the number of times that we find it actually correct; and if what was suspected to be a blunder is proved to be an accurate statement in St. Luke's chronology, we shall certainly think better of him, and persuade others also to think better of him.

In St. Luke ii. 1-4 a series of statements are made which, to our imperfect knowledge, are certainly difficult. It is there stated that a decree went out from Caesar Augustus that all the world should be enrolled; that this was the first enrolment, made when Quirinius was governing Syria; and that for it Joseph with his espoused wife had to go up to Bethlehem, his ancestral city, to be enrolled. The whole of this statement has been called a blunder or a fiction. Augustus, it is said, never made such a decree; if he had made it, it would not have had any force in the kingdom of Herod; even if there had been such an enrolment, it would have been absurd for any one to go as Joseph is represented as doing to Bethlehem for the purpose of enrolment; and that such a census could not have taken place under Quirinius, who was governor of Syria for the first time after the death of Herod. In fact, the whole story arises, it is said, from a confusion with a later census made under Quirinius when the Romans assumed the direct rule over Palestine.

Now, can archaeology help us here? Within the last few years a series of papyrus documents have shewn, and that certainly, that in Egypt there was held every fourteen years an enrolment of the people according to households. This discovery, which we owe to the independent work of Mr. Kenyon, Dr. Wilcken, and Dr. Viereck, has been made by Professor Ramsay the basis of a very interesting investigation.[1] He maintains, first of all, that this custom

[1] *Was Christ born at Bethlehem? A Study on the Credibility of St. Luke.* By W. M. Ramsay, M.A., D.C.L.

of a periodical census must for many reasons be dated back to the time of Augustus, the organizer of the empire. Even while Mr. Ramsay's book was in process of production new documents were discovered substantially supporting his argument. He maintains, further, that this is only an instance of what was a universal system; and that a considerable amount of evidence, partly literary, partly derived from inscriptions, shews that it prevailed in Syria. The first enrolment, he argues, must have been for the year 9 B.C.; this it was to which St. Luke refers, and thus his language speaking of it as the "first" is perfectly accurate. He goes on to give reasons which shew that the enrolment must have been made in Palestine under Herod, and that in this case it was postponed for a year or two, and probably taken in the year 6 B.C. in the early autumn. Further, political reasons, amongst others the desire to conciliate the Jews, would lead to its being taken according to families and tribes, and that this was why Joseph went to Bethlehem. He also suggests that the first rule of Quirinius in Syria, a rule of which we have evidence in inscriptions and which is generally accepted, was a special military command, and could therefore be dated earlier than was supposed possible during the reign of Herod. We cannot here examine the validity of all this structure. We may be sometimes inclined to remember the facility with which an expert chronologer can build up a system which seems quite convincing, until it is realized that half a dozen rival systems, equally convincing, exist. But at the basis of it all—and this is the importance to us—there is a new discovery, a discovery absolutely certain so far as it goes, which puts St. Luke's statement about "the first enrolment" on a quite different basis to that on which it previously stood. The corroboration of his statement on this one point will make us much less inclined to reject his evidence elsewhere, and certainly forbids us to adopt the attitude assumed by many critics that a statement in the New Testament must be wrong unless it can be proved to be right.

One more instance may be given of an illustration in the New Testament from the religious life of the day. In Rev. ii. 20 we read: " But I have this against thee, that thou sufferest the woman Jezebel, which calleth herself a prophetess ; and she teacheth and seduceth My servants to commit fornication, and to eat things sacrificed to idols." Who was Jezebel ? Can we get any light thrown on it from other sources ? The analogy of Balaam and Balak shews that the name is used figuratively. It was some woman who called herself a prophetess, who, like the wife of Ahab, was an active promoter of false religions. Now Dr. Schürer has drawn attention to an inscription from Thyatira, which seems to imply the existence in the place of a shrine of the Eastern sibyl. Such a shrine would be a centre of divination, of the sort of magic which was always most hostile to Christianity, of the sanctified immorality which was an habitual concomitant of Oriental types of religion and of the often licentious sacrificial banquets. The presence of such a shrine, as much a home of alien and novel worship as was a Christian Church, with a vigorous and interested propaganda, would be a great danger to Christianity. In the account of Pergamum, again, great light is thrown on the words of the Revelation when we learn that it was the home of the imperial cult in the province of Asia. The Apocalyptic vision is throughout a protest against the worship of the beast, that is the " Empire and Emperor, the official state religion," which was a standing menace to Christianity. When, then, we read of the Angel of the Church in Pergamum, " I know where thou dwellest, even where Satan's throne is," the passage obtains a new meaning if we learn that the throne of Satan may be interpreted as the home of imperial worship in the province, and was perhaps the great altar the sculptures of which are now at Berlin.

There are other illustrations which might be given. One of the most hotly disputed questions in New Testament introductions is that as to the locality of the Galatia of the Epistles. Was it the Roman province, and the cities of Iconium, Derbe, and Lystra, or was it the northern district? Here the evidence of archaeology is of the greatest importance; but unfortunately the epigraphic remains are at present somewhat disappointing. The Sergius Paulus of Acts xiii. 7 probably appears in an inscription of Soli in Cyprus.[1] The foundations of the temple of Jupiter before the city may still be traced outside the city of Lystra. An inscription from Malta gives us the somewhat unusual name, the First man ($\pi\rho\hat{\omega}\tau os$), for the head of the island. The study of the names at the end of the Epistle to the Romans is very much helped by the epitaphs of imperial slaves and freedmen found in *Columbaria*. We might add more; but there would be little gain. Sufficient has been done for the purpose of shewing the value of archaeology. This value is double. Archaeology brings us new material; but it also helps in the development of a new method. It has enabled us to understand the whole of the government of the empire, both local and imperial, in a manner which would have been quite impossible otherwise. It enables us to make out the boundaries and divisions of the provinces, the roads and cities, the local and imperial magistrates. It enables us to study the varied phases of popular religion. How little, apart from inscriptions, should we realize the extent and importance of the imperial cultus and of all the organizations of games and festivals connected with it! how little of the infinitely diverse

[1] Lebas and Wadd. 2779; cf. Hogarth, *Devia Cypria*, p. 114.

forms of popular worship which attempted to satisfy the religious needs of the people in an age of religious transition! Archaeology gives us all this material; but it also helps in the formation of a method. It teaches us to study the books of the New Testament and the writers of the early Church from the point of view of history. We may begin with some small point of geography or administration. We find that an inscription illustrates it. We find that an obscure reference to local religion becomes full of meaning when we ask how men worshipped their gods in Smyrna or Thyatira. Then as we go on we realize that in this way we may get light on more important questions. Do we want to know what St. Paul means when he talks of justification? Is it not better to begin with asking what are the ideas which the word conveyed when he first wrote, rather than the scholastic interpretation which has been imposed upon it? The word "sacrifice" has been transformed by Christianity; what did it mean to the first Christians? The same methods must be pursued as are followed in less important details, and archaeology may here give us some material. At any rate, a mind trained in an archaeological method will be trained to interpret a book historically, and not to use it controversially without any regard to the circumstances under which it was written or the meaning that the author intended to convey.

II. Remains in Phrygia.

IN the early history of Christianity the district of Asia Minor called Phrygia has a double interest. It has long been known as the home of a great religious movement called Montanism, or, from the place of its origin, the Cataphrygian heresy; and within recent years there have been found in it a larger number of inscriptions, claimed as Christian, than in any known part of the ancient world except Rome. As will be apparent later, there is a close connexion between these two facts: the same cause which produced the Montanist movement also caused Phrygia to be a place where Christianity early left monumental remains of itself. With one exception, which rises almost to the dignity of a controversial document, these inscriptions are not individually of very great importance; but the fact of their existence and a number of deductions which can legitimately be drawn from them enable us to do a great deal towards reconstructing the history of Christianity in the district. Literature, it must be remembered, has generally preserved for us what is most valuable; archaeology, whether in inscriptions or in papyrus documents, gives us what is commonplace and unimportant: yet the commonplace may often enable us to get a safer and deeper insight into historical questions than what is intrinsically more valuable. Any one who would describe English religious life must know a country parish as well as a cathedral or a university.

A few words must be said on the discovery of the

inscriptions. A certain number are due to older explorers, especially to Hamilton and Waddington; but by far the larger number to the energy and insight of Professor W. M. Ramsay and to the support of the Asia Minor Exploration Fund. His researches began about the year 1880, and have been continued since with the assistance of various companions and scholars. The results were first of all published in the *Journal of Hellenic Studies*, the *Bulletin de Correspondance Hellénique*, and many other periodicals. A certain number of these inscriptions were made use of by Bishop Lightfoot in his edition of the writings of Ignatius, and round some of the more important a considerable literature has grown up, De Rossi, Duchesne, Harnack, and other well-known scholars having contributed. A very interesting popular account of some of the Christian inscriptions was contributed by Professor Ramsay to the *Expositor* for the years 1888-9; and all those of Phrygia, with the exception of the north-western district, have now been collected in the second volume of the *Cities and Bishoprics of Phrygia*, where almost all the material on which the present chapter is based will be found.

The method of the following pages is to give in accurate translations a series of typical inscriptions; to bring out their meaning, avoiding so far as possible technicalities; and to test the conclusions that have been arrived at. Occasionally some things may appear far-fetched and over-ingenious in Professor Ramsay's conclusions; but in one of the most doubtful points further discovery has provided a brilliant corroboration. Substantially he has been supported by Duchesne, by De Rossi, and by Lightfoot, who have themselves helped to point out the significance of some discoveries; and the conclusions of the following pages may be accepted, the writer believes, as a sound contribution to knowledge.

The tract of country we call Asia Minor, roughly speaking a rectangular peninsula, having the sea on three sides, consists of an elevated plateau, averaging from 2,500 to 4,000 feet above the sea, surrounded by mountain systems which make it resemble a large tea-tray, and by a narrow strip of coast-land. The extreme western part of the plateau and a portion of the mountains—which towards the west are considerably broader than to the north or south—bore in ancient times the name of Phrygia. The more eastern portion of this country consists of broad, open valleys, gradually merging into the great steppe which forms the centre of Asia Minor; to the west it is more broken; it has several important mountain ranges; and its cities lie in mountain valleys, through which pass the main lines of communication. Throughout it run the two great roads which have at different periods connected the seacoast and the interior; and Phrygia has in consequence always had a double history—on the one side linked with the central plateau and the East, on the other with the seacoast towns and the Greek peoples of the West.

In the population, too, there was a double element. The basis consisted of a race Oriental in its origin and Oriental in its ideas and character; but besides this, and for the most part ruling over it, was a second race which had come from the north, bore in history the name of Phrygian, and was probably of European origin. These latter people were the more vigorous and hardy; but being a conquering minority, probably with a predominance of the male element, they would speedily intermarry with the subject population, and the native stock would, as almost invariably happens where it is not exterminated, gradually reassert itself. The history of the other nations would seem to have been largely similar. In Caria the Western influence was always strong; in Lydia the Oriental seems soon to have asserted itself. Farther to the East, up to the time of the Gallic invasion in the third century B.C., the old population, Cappadocian, or, as it is the fashion now to call it, Hittite, survived.

Side by side with the double population was a double type of worship. There was the Oriental type, the worship of the reproductive force in nature, often imaginative, often extravagant, represented by the worship of the Phrygian mother of the gods, of the Ephesian Artemis, and by many other less-known cults; it was the worship of the male and female principle—the Baal and Astarte of Syria,—often as mother and son, sometimes as husband and wife. The second type introduced by the invading race was the worship of an armed warrior. The tendency naturally was to identify the god of the conqueror with the male deity, and the worship of the country became a combination of the two types. At a later date, under Greek influence, god and goddess alike received Greek names, and added new elements to the medley called Greek mythology.

The extent of early Greek influence in these Phrygian lands cannot be estimated. Phrygia was the home of some well-known myths, and there is an obvious connexion between early Phrygian and Greek architecture. But it was at the time of the Alexandrian Conquest that Greece really asserted itself. The Greek rulers planted colonies, Seleuciad and Pergamene, such as Laodiceia and Apameia and Eumeneia; the Greek language began to spread, and Greek influence to make itself felt. The work begun by the successors of Alexander was continued by the Romans with greater system. They made little attempt to introduce Latin. Latin inscriptions are rarely found except on the sites of colonies. But Greek quickly, under their influence, replaced the older languages. By the beginning of the Christian era Phrygian had probably ceased to be spoken in all the larger towns; but it still continued in the remoter districts, and Phrygian Greek, as judged by inscriptions, is often singularly defective in grammar and orthography. The spread of Greek was probably made complete by the growth of Christianity, which was, as will become apparent, very rapid.

One element in the population remains to be chronicled —the Jewish. The successors of Alexander seem everywhere to have favoured the Jewish race, and under their auspices large settlements were founded in the more important cities of Phrygia.

The Christian remains of Phrygia come from three districts—one in the centre of the country, one in the north, and one in the south-west. Almost exactly in the centre of Phrygia, among the mountains where are the head waters of a tributary of the Maeander, is a large fertile valley, now called the Sandykly Ova. It was in Roman times the seat of five little-known cities—Brouzos, Eucarpia, Hierapolis, Thermae, and Stektorion—called the Phrygian Pentapolis. From this district come the most important of the inscriptions of Asia Minor.

The discovery of the Avircius Inscription is a romance of archaeology. Among the Lives of the Saints, contained in the collection ascribed to Symeon Metaphrastes, a late Byzantine hagiographical writer, is one that gives an account of a certain Avircius, or Abercius, who was described as Bishop of Hierapolis, in Phrygia. The life was recognized to be spurious; but it contained an epitaph written in verse, which the writer stated that he had seen on a stone near the city of Hierapolis, still existing, although injured by time. Attention was drawn to this epitaph by Cardinal Pitra, and it had seemed to many scholars, amongst others to Bishop Lightfoot, to have a genuine ring about it. " I had accepted it as genuine," the latter writes, "endeavouring to assign a place to this Abercius, as Bishop of Hierapolis, and to identify him with the Avircius Marcellus who is mentioned about this same time by an anonymous writer in Eusebius. There was, however, some slight difficulty in finding room for Abercius in the Episcopate of Hierapolis, the ground being occupied."

In 1881 Professor Ramsay, travelling in Asia Minor, found, at a place called Kelendres, in the Sandykly district, a metrical inscription, of which the following is a translation :—

> I, the citizen of a notable city, have made this tomb in my lifetime, that I may have openly a resting-place here for my body. Alexander the son of Antonius by name, I am a disciple of the pure shepherd. No one shall place another in my tomb. If he does, he shall pay 2,000 gold pieces to the treasury of the Romans, and to my good fatherland Hierapolis 1,000 gold pieces. This was written in the year 300, in the sixth month, during my lifetime. Peace to those that pass by and make a memorial of me.

This inscription dates from the year 216 A.D., the era of the province being 84 B.C. When it was first published by Professor Ramsay, he was quite ignorant of its importance. As will become apparent later, it is undoubtedly Christian, but written so as to have nothing too obtrusively Christian about it. The words "disciple of the pure shepherd" and "peace to those that make a memorial of me" would speak quite clearly to those that were intended to understand, and the expression "citizen of a notable (or select) city" was capable of a double interpretation. It is the heathen epithet gradually being transformed for Christian use.

But the interest of the inscription does not stop here. It was first published in 1882 in the *Bulletin de Correspondance Hellénique*. There it was noticed by the Abbé Duchesne, who saw at once that it was copied from the epitaph of Avircius as contained in the Life of the Saint, and that it proved that epitaph to be genuine. As will be seen, all that is purely formal in the Avircius Inscription

THIRD]   RAMSAY'S INSCRIPTIONS   369

has been copied; while in the third line "Alexander son of Antonius" has been substituted for the name of "Avircius" in a way that makes scansion impossible, and proves that the epitaph of Alexander is not the original.

In 1883 Professor Ramsay again visited the same district, and there in the bath-house at some hot springs he had the good fortune to find two fragments of the epitaph of Avircius himself. They only contain a small portion of the inscription; but that is of course sufficient to prove that it is genuine. We have now three different sources from which to reconstruct the text: we have the copy in the MSS. of the Life of the Saint—this was made after the stone had begun to decay, and it is in some places faulty; we have, secondly, the fragment of the original inscription, which has now been removed to the Lateran Museum; and, thirdly, the epitaph of Alexander. The following translation is based on what appears to be the best text; it has not seemed necessary to discuss variations which do not affect the general sense :—

> I, the citizen of a notable city, have made this tomb in my lifetime, that I may have openly a resting-place for my body. Avircius by name, I am a disciple of the pure shepherd, who feedeth flocks of sheep on mountains and plains, who hath great eyes looking on all sides. For he taught me faithful writings, and he sent me to Rome to behold the king, and to see the golden-robed, golden-slippered queen, and there I saw a people bearing the splendid seal. And I saw the plain of Syria, and all its cities, even Nisibis, having crossed the Euphrates. And everywhere I had fellow-worshippers.' With Paul as my companion I followed, and everywhere Faith led the way, and everywhere set before me fish from the fountain, mighty and stainless, whom a pure Virgin grasped. At all times Faith gave this to friends to eat, having good wine, giving the mixed cup with bread. These words I, Avircius, standing by, ordered to be inscribed; in truth I was in my seventy-second year. Let every associate who sees this pray for me. No one shall place another in my tomb. If he does, he shall pay 2,000 gold pieces to the treasury of the Romans, and to my good fatherland Hierapolis 1,000 gold pieces.

The name Avircius, or Abercius, is known in ecclesiastical history. In Eusebius' *Ecclesiastical History* (v. 16) extracts are given from the anonymous writer against Montanism. These are addressed to a certain Avircius Marcellus. The date of these extracts is not certain; but mention is made in them of a twelve years' peace to the Christians, which might correspond to the peace in the reign of Commodus. The epitaph of Avircius must be earlier than that of Alexander (A.D. 216) quoted above, which copies it, and hence the date suits that reign. A further argument for identification is that in these extracts reference is made to our "fellow-presbyter Zoticus of Otrous"; and Otrous was only a few miles distant from Hierapolis of the Pentapolis.

Avircius, then, was a leader of the Anti-Montanist party in Phrygia at the end of the second century. His home was not the well-known city on the Lycus valley, but a less-known place, Hierapolis, in a remote mountain region. He is generally called Bishop, and very probably rightly; but there is no evidence to prove it. He erected this monument openly, between the years 190 and 200, to assert the reality of his religious principles; but although the monument was "open," the language was still veiled and symbolic. It would be quite clear and intelligible to every Christian; it would contain nothing overtly Christian, and therefore nothing that would violate existing laws and customs.

"The pure shepherd, who feedeth flocks of sheep on mountains and plains" reminds us at once of Christ as the good Shepherd; and the "great eyes" represent, symbolically, His prudent care. He had taught His disciple from true and sacred books; and under His guidance that disciple had travelled everywhere east and west, to Nisibis beyond the Euphrates, and to the great city of Rome, really, as we can see, to learn the truths of his religion.

The next three lines have caused interpreters considerable difficulty. "He sent me to Rome to behold the king, and to see the golden-robed, golden-slippered queen, and there I saw a people bearing the splendid seal." Who are intended by the king and queen? Are these words to be taken literally or symbolically? The reference in the last line to the word "seal" ($\sigma\phi\rho\alpha\gamma\iota\varsigma$), and the technical word for "people," $\lambda\alpha\acute{o}\varsigma$ (laity), suggest at once that the line refers to the Christian people in Rome. If this be so, the "queen" of the preceding line naturally suggests the Christian Church, the "King's daughter who is all glorious within." There is still more difficulty about the first line. Is the king the Emperor? The mixture of symbolism should cause no difficulty. To a heathen the words would mean the Emperor, the Empress, and the Roman people; but a Christian would have much more suggested to him by them. Everywhere Avircius followed in the track which Faith pointed out to him, and the Apostle Paul was his companion. These words are abrupt; but of their meaning there can be little doubt. Avircius had been brought up on the writings and life of the Apostle Paul, and in all his wanderings the thought of St. Paul travelling the same journeys is before him, and the faith and example of St. Paul are his support. In the lines that follow we have reference to well-known Christian symbolism. The "fish" ($\iota\chi\theta\acute{u}\varsigma$) refers to our Lord, and especially to Him in the Eucharist. He is the "fish from the fountain," referring to baptism, by which alone there is access to Him. He is born of a "pure Virgin." Everywhere that Avircius goes he finds fellow-Christians; he is admitted to their religious rites, for at all times Faith gives the "mixed cup with bread." Avircius asks all his coreligionists to pray for him, and ends with the usual regulations against the profanation of the tomb.

The above interpretation, in which (in its main outline) almost all leading scholars are agreed, is based on the ordinary Christian symbolism, which is well known both from Christian literature and from the paintings and inscriptions in the Catacombs. It has the support of Zahn, Duchesne, De Rossi, Lightfoot, and Ramsay, to mention only five typical names, and is, in the opinion of the present writer, undoubtedly correct. It has, however, not been universally accepted. Ficker, in a paper published by the Berlin Academy, has attempted to prove that the inscription is really heathen, and Harnack has adopted his hypothesis in a modified form, suggesting that it is partly heathen and partly Christian, and belongs to a syncretistic Gnostic sect. Both Ficker and Harnack are learned and ingenious, but their arguments are untenable. " It is hard to say whether the scholar, who can understand this epitaph as the public testament of a priest of Cybele, shews more misapprehension of the character of second-century paganism or want of appreciation of the spirit of second-century Christianity." Professor Ramsay does not in these words put the case too strongly.

It would take too much space to discuss the question fully; but it may be stated that the external evidence such as it is, is in favour of a Christian origin. The inscription was viewed as Christian by the compiler of the Life, who apparently knew the name of Avircius from other sources. Time, place, and circumstances connect that name with the Avircius of Eusebius, who was clearly a Christian; and the epitaph of Alexander corroborates the evidence as to the religion. But internal evidence is stronger. It may be perfectly possible to discover a pagan analogy to most of the words used, a fact which is not unnatural, as Christianity did not, for the most part, invent a new language; but the combination of words and phrases, all Christian in their associations, and representing the most typical ideas in exactly the way in which we know that they were represented, is too strong an argument to be got over. The Shepherd, the laity, the seal, the fish, the pure Virgin, the bread and mixed cup, the prayer for the departed, are just what might be expected. The resemblance to heathen epitaphs at the end and the absence of too obtrusive Christian language are characteristics found in many other epitaphs, and were natural in the circumstances under which alone Christianity could then be practised.

The epitaph, indeed, fits into its proper place as a Christian document of the end of the second century. Like Melito of Sardis, like Hegesippus, like Clement of Alexandria, Avircius was one of those travellers who, in order to satisfy himself of the truths of his religion and the teaching in which he had been brought up, visited all the principal Christian Churches. Everywhere he finds the same teaching and the same religious customs. He does not tell us anything which we did not know before; we recognize his Christianity by the correspondence of his language with that of other documents and remains: but he helps to build up a testimony, which is really overwhelming, in favour of the solidarity and unity of the Christian faith in the second century.

No other inscription has been found of equal interest with the epitaph of Avircius Marcellus. The same district yields, however, some others, amongst them the following:—

Aurelius Dionoisius the Presbyter erected this resting-place in his lifetime. Peace to all the brethren.

The word for "resting-place" ($κοιμητήριον$) is only found in Christian inscriptions. This inscription may very likely be third century. A very similar inscription from the same place has "Peace to the brotherhood." Here we get one of the names by which the Christian community was known.

The next inscription, also from the same place, was copied by Hamilton, a traveller in the early part of this century :—

> Peace to all who pass by from God. I, Aurelius Alexander, the son of Marcus, of the family from Xanthus (the reading is here doubtful), for their love and beauty have erected this monument to my most sweet children, beloved of God, honoured in the peace of God. For this reason I erected the monument to the memory of Eugenia and Marcella and Alexander and Macedon and Nonna, my most sweet children, who at one moment obtained the lot of life. And whatsoever stranger is offended at this tomb, may they have children untimely born.

On the other side was read a short inscription, stating that up to this spot the burial-place was the common property of "the brethren." Here we have a text which is clearly Christian. The statement that at one moment the children "obtained the lot of life" would be alone sufficient to prove this. Pagan influence and feeling have not, however, been entirely obliterated, and the inscription ends with a curse against any one who violates the tomb, of a character which might be paralleled from many heathen epitaphs. But this does not exhaust the meaning. How does it happen that five children should die all on the same day? That they should die thus a natural death would be most unusual. It has been suggested that they were martyred. It was the custom to commemorate a martyr on the day of his death, which was designated as his birthday; and that would accord with the expression "obtained the lot of life." These five martyrs were probably not the children of Aurelius in the flesh; but he, as bishop of the Church, speaks of five of his flock who had died for their faith as his children. So in one of the Acts of the Martyrs a bishop, when asked if he had any children, replied that he had many in the Lord.

The two next inscriptions are interesting as containing the name of Avircius; they come from the same part of Phrygia, but not from the immediate neighbourhood :—

> I, Avircius, son of Porphyrius, a deacon, erected this monument for myself and my wife Theoprepia and my children.

Below is a figure, apparently of Christ as a youth, with his hand raised in the act of instructing. On either side are busts of Avircius and his wife. The art of the monument is very much above the ordinary level.

The second is headed by the letters alpha and omega (A and Ω), with the monogram ☧ between :—

> I, Aurelius Dorotheus, the son of Avircius, erected this tomb for myself and my mother Marcellina and my children and my cousins. Farewell ye that pass by.

The formula at the heading makes the Christianity of this inscription indubitable, and suggests, what experience proves to be the case, that the greeting to those that pass by is a sign of Christian origin. The date of these last two inscriptions cannot be precisely fixed; but there is nothing in them which implies a date later than the third century.

We may pass now to another district, that of Southwestern Phrygia. The cities in this district are situated for the most part in the valleys of the Maeander and its tributary the Lycos. The first we turn to is Eumeneia. It lies about twenty miles south-west of the Hierapolis district, where the Glaucus joins the Maeander, and about thirty-five miles from Colossae in the Lycos valley. This city has probably provided a larger number of Christian inscriptions than any other Phrygian city; their interest, however, lies, not in the contents of any one of them, but in the inferences which the whole collection suggests. The following is an instance. It is an inscription erected by some one whose name is lost: " to himself and his mother Meltine and his son Gaius and my brother Axlas"; it then proceeds: "It shall not be lawful to any one besides the above named to be buried in it; if any one shall do so, he will have account with the living God, both now and in the judgment day."

This expression sounds Christian, and a number of considerations shew us that it is so. It occurs with many variations; some of them are certainly Christian, and these corroborate the Christianity of others. We find "he shall give account to Jesus Christ," "he shall give account to Him that cometh to judge the quick and dead," "to the righteousness of God," "he shall receive from the eternal God the everlasting scourge," "he shall give account to the immortal God," "to the God that judgeth," "to the hand of God," "to the living God," "to the great name of God." All of these may be, and some of them must be, Christian, and all clearly belong to the same type of epitaph. The most common form is also the shortest: "He shall give account to God" (or, to the God). Then, again, this phrase is often joined with other words or expressions which are Christian; with the word for "resting-place" ($κοιμητήριον$), only used of Christian tombs; with names which are always Christian, such as Agapomenus; with words like "bishop" ($ἐπίσκοπος$), which are almost invariably Christian—certainly in such a connexion; and with other Christian symbols. But what enables us most decisively to take the formula in question as a criterion of the Christian character of the inscription is that it is never found combined with any distinctly pagan expression. Yet, although the formula is clearly Christian, it is not, in its simpler form at any rate, obtrusively Christian. The implied monotheism would always be recognized by a fellow-Christian; but there would not be anything illegal or likely to cause offence. It was probably a slight variation of a heathen formula, substituting the vague and indefinite "God" or "living God" for the local name of the deity. It would therefore exactly fulfil the purpose for which it was introduced; namely, to distinguish Christian graves without offending popular prejudice.

These inscriptions are found in various places in Southwestern Phrygia; but at Eumeneia they are particularly numerous, and belong apparently almost certainly to the third century. The few illustrations that follow will bring out one or two special points. The following is dated :—

> In the year 333 (*i.e.* A.D. 249), in the tenth month, in the fifth day of the month. I, Aurelius Moschus, the son of Alexander, constructed the tomb (Heroon) for Aurelius Alexander, the son of Menecrates, as he commanded in his will. If any one shall intrude another, he shall give account to God. A copy of this is deposited in the Archives.[1]

The next has more than one point of interest :—

> I, Aurelius Menophilus, the son of Menophilus, the grandson of Archipiades, a Senator, have erected the pile in front for myself and my son Apollonius and his wife Meltine, and Menophilus and Asclepiades his descendants, and for whomsoever else he, while alive, may be willing. If any one shall attempt to place any other in the tomb, he shall give account to Jesus Christ.[2]

The words at the end are an expansion of the monogram ⋇. This is the earliest form of the Christian monogram, giving place in the fourth century to the better-known ☧. There is a dated example at Rome in 268 or 279, and this inscription is probably of the same age as the last and belongs to a member of the same family. We notice how the Christian monogram enabled the sacred Name to be used without any illegal ostentation. We also notice that here we have a Senator in Eumeneia as a Christian; nor is this the only example :—

> Fare ye well! Aurelius Gemellus, son of Menas, a Senator, to his most sweet parents, Aurelius Menas, son of Menas, grandson of Philippus,

---

[1] *C. and B.*, ii., p. 528.
[2] *Op. cit.*, ii., p. 526.

a Senator, and Geraius, and Aurelia Apphias, daughter of Artas, his own of his own. He has buried here his brother Philippus and his father's aunt Cyrilla and his cousin Paula. Here also shall be buried his foster-sister Philete, and any one else he shall allow while alive. Whosoever shall attempt to bring in another, he shall receive from the immortal God an eternal scourge.[1]

The last phrase is curious, and seems to combine heathen sentiments and a Christian phraseology. Here we have another instance of a member of a Christian family who is a "Senator." But he is also called "Geraius." What the word means we do not know. It has been suggested that it is a synonym for Presbyter, but there is no evidence. We must be content at present to be ignorant. The word occurs in other inscriptions of the place.

The last instance we shall quote contains the title *episkopos*. The inscription is undated; but other considerations would put it early in the third century:—

Damas, the son of Dioteimus, constructed this tomb (Heroon) for his maternal uncle Metrodorus the Bishop, and his father Dioteimus, and himself. If any one shall attempt to place another, he shall pay into the treasury 500 denaria. If he shall despise this, he shall give account to the living God.[2]

The above are a sufficient number of instances of these inscriptions; but their importance lies in their number. There are more apparently Christian inscriptions dating from the third century than there are heathen. This suggests that the Christians formed a majority of the population. But not only this. Side by side with this abundance of third-century Christian inscriptions is the almost complete absence of any belonging to a later period. Is there any reason for this? Eusebius, in his *Ecclesiastical History*,[3] tells us that early in the Diocletian persecution a whole Christian city was burnt to the ground, with its people, men, women, and children, calling upon the God

---

[1] *C. and B.*, ii., p. 520.
[2] *Op. cit.*, ii., p. 521.
[3] viii. 11.

who is over all. This may have been Eumeneia itself. The fact related by Eusebius proves at any rate the wholesale character of the persecution in some places.

For an interesting coincidence we may quote Professor Ramsay's own words :—

"To one who has by the patient toil of years tracked out these Christian communities by their formula of appealing to 'the God,' it comes as one of those startling and convincing details of real life and truth that the one thing revealed about the destroyed people is that they died 'appealing to the God over all.' Unconsciously Eusebius writes, as the epitaph over the ashes of the destroyed people, the words by which we have recognized the epitaphs which they themselves habitually employed."[1]

The history of Eumeneia may now be conjecturally reconstructed. Here, as in most towns of the neighbourhood, Christianity spread early, and took a very definite hold on the people. But, at any rate after its first beginning, it was not of an aggressive character. The Christians lived among their neighbours, adhering to the law as far as they could, and doing little to cause offence. Nor was there much opposition to them on the part of their heathen neighbours. They took their place in the life of the city, and gradually the whole city, or the greater part of it, adopted the new creed. Then came the persecution of Diocletian. This was a regularly organized attempt to stamp out Christianity, and in this district it was natural that some city, perhaps more than one, should feel it with terrible severity. Some act of rebellion or defiance of the authorities may have been the cause. At any rate the fact remains, and it has left its mark on the history of the district. A whole city was wiped out. It was not merely a persecution, it was a massacre.

It will be recognized that a certain element in the foregoing

[1] *C. and B.*, ii. p. 50

account is conjectural, and it must be remembered that conjecture has a considerable part to play in archaeological history. Is it, in this case, to be accepted? Both the material and the argument, so far as space allowed, have been given that they might tell their own tale. The arguments by which the series of inscriptions are claimed as Christian seem satisfactory, and have been arrived at independently by Professor Ramsay in the *Expositor*,[1] and by M. Cumont.[2] The large number connected with one city implies a very large if not preponderating Christian population in the third century. This supports, and is supported by, the statement made by Eusebius that a whole town in Phrygia was Christian. This may not indeed have been Eumeneia; but what was true of one city would very probably be true of another. But the evidence is corroborative. The last point, the character of the Diocletian persecution or, as Professor Ramsay calls it, massacre, is a little more doubtful. It is quite true that there was one such massacre. It is true that in Eumeneia, and in other cities, the epigraphic remains of the fourth century shew a marked decline, both in numbers and in interest. But other causes may have helped, and the attempt (suggested by the analogy of recent events) to exaggerate the vigour of the persecution cannot be considered altogether successful. In isolated cases it was a massacre, but not universally.

Two very interesting, but obscure, inscriptions from Hierapolis will introduce the next topic. Hierapolis must be carefully distinguished from the less-known Hierapolis of the Pentapolis whence comes the Avircius epitaph. The Hierapolis now in question was the city mentioned in the Epistle to the Colossians, situated on the northern

---

[1] 1888, 1889.
[2] *Les Inscriptions Chrétiennes de l'Asie Mineure*, in *Mélanges d'Archéol. et d'Hist.*, 1895.

slopes of the Lycus valley, not far from Laodicea and Colossae. It was famous for its hot springs, which made it early a great religious centre and gave it a name, and for its beautiful white terraces formed by deposit from the hot water dropping over the rocks. It is known, too, to have been early a centre of Christian life in the district.

The following inscriptions are engraved partly on the side and partly on the end of a large sarcophagus on the south side of the road which leads out of the western gate of Hierapolis :—

A. This sarcophagus and the ground around it, with the pedestal supporting it, is the property of Marcus Aurelius Diodorus Coriascus, called Asbolus the Younger. In it shall be buried himself and his wife and his children. And as long as I live I shall bury whomsoever I please. But no one else may be buried in it. Otherwise he shall pay as a fine to the most holy Treasury 500 *denarii* and to the most reverend Senate 500 *denarii*. So far as thou mayest provide for thy life, O friend that passeth by, do so, knowing that these things are the end of your life.

B. I have bequeathed also to the council of the Presidency of the *Porphyrabaphoi* (*i.e.* those bathed in purple, or the purple-dippers) 3,000 *denarii* for burning the *Papoi* on the customary day from the interest thereof; but if any one shall disregard these, so as not to burn, what is left shall go to the Guild of the *Thremmata*. My wife also shall be buried here.[1]

This text is certainly enigmatical. It might seem farfetched to consider it Christian, yet that probably is what it is. M. Waddington, who first published it, suggested that it was so; and Bishop Lightfoot agreed with him. In the first volume of his *Cities and Bishoprics of Phrygia*, Professor Ramsay wrote: "Years of further experience only deepen my sense of the inconsistency between this text and the pagan inscriptions"; and in a note he adds : " I believe that the *Porphyrabaphoi* are the Christian Church directed by the council of *presbyteroi* under presidency of the *episkopos*; and that the Guild of the *Thremmata* is the

[1] *C. and B.*, i., p. 118; ii., p. 545.

charitable fund connected with the Church. The money, if not applied entirely to purposes of ceremonial, is to be used for charity."

By an interesting coincidence, since these words were written a second inscription has been published, which, as will appear, corroborates them at any rate to a certain extent:—

The tomb of Publius Aelius Glycon. .... In it shall be buried himself and his wife and his children, and no one else shall be buried there. He gave also to the most reverend assembly of the *Porphyrabaphoi* 200 *denarii* as money for crowning the tomb, to be paid to each from the interest ..... on the feast of unleavened bread. Likewise he left to the council of the *Kairodapistoi* 150 *denarii* ... on the feast of Pentecost.[1]

This inscription is clearly Jewish or Christian, at any rate not heathen, and suggests that the other likewise is Jewish or Christian. Of the two, a Christian explanation is the easier. Here we have an inscription (as we have noticed in other cases) written with the object of implying Christianity, without containing anything illegal. The formula of greeting to passers-by was modelled on the current formulae, but had a Christian tone. The reference to the presidency probably, as we have seen, means the bishop and his council of presbyters, but was not unlike language which might be used of the Senate of the city or the governing body of some of the guilds. The exact meaning of the "Guild of the *Thremmata*" is doubtful; but it implies some charitable institution, perhaps for rearing orphans, connected with the Christian Church. The funeral rites were concealed under an unknown word "*Papoi*," for which no adequate explanation has been found. The feasts have Jewish names only given them, because the religion of the Jews would be lawful. The term *Porphyrabaphoi* was a name chosen for one of the burial clubs under which the Christians, or some of them, were

[1] *C. and B.*, ii., p. 525.

organized. It was chosen because dyeing was a great industry at Hierapolis, and a guild of "Dyers" was well known. The passers-by would read it as "purple-dippers," "dyers in purple"; but the Christians would know that it meant "those who were washed in the blood of the Lamb." *Kairodapistoi* is still unexplained.

Now the above interpretation of what is obviously an obscure inscription may seem far-fetched, and no one would pretend that it is demonstrated. It is, however, important for our purpose to emphasize the corroboration which the discovery of the second inscription has given. It is part of the assumption in our investigation that the Christian inscriptions will not be obtrusively Christian, that they were not intended to give information to every one, and consequently they will often be likely to elude us. We are therefore dependent on the trained and critical insight of investigators, whose judgment, by constant practice, will enable them to detect what they believe to be a Christian ring. The discovery of the Avircius Inscription increased our respect for the judgment of those who had suspected that it was genuine; the discovery of the second Hierapolis inscription will make us more inclined to believe M. Waddington, and Bishop Lightfoot, and Professor Ramsay, when they detect Christianity in unlikely places and under strange disguises.

These inscriptions, it is claimed, present us with an account of a Christian burial society, which had adopted a somewhat strange name. Another instance is perhaps supplied by an inscription from Acmonia, a city about twenty miles to the north. It runs as follows, being engraved on three sides of a tombstone which has the form of an altar:—

A. Aurelius Aristias, son of Apollonius, purchased from Marcus Mathus a vacant piece of ground ten cubits square in the year . . .

B. promising to the neighbourhood of the First-Gate-People two workmen with two pronged picks every month and diggers in proportion.

He gave them on condition that each year they should offer Roses on the tomb of my wife Aurelia.

C. And if they shall neglect to offer Roses each year, they shall be exposed to the righteousness of God.

On the side A, in smaller and ruder letters, there is added :—

His children Alexander and Callistratus prepared the tomb for their father and mother in remembrance.[1]

Here the concluding formula, if our previous conclusions are correct, marks this inscription as Christian, and it falls into the same place as the last. At Acmonia the Christian society, or a part of it, was called the "First-Gate-People." The custom, on certain days, of adorning a tomb with roses was pagan in origin, but was early adopted by Christians. It was customary to hold a ceremony called *Rosalia* on the anniversary of saints and martyrs. Similar to this inscription is one from Apameia, at the source of the Macander, which ends with, "My farewell greetings to the beloved of God and the newly caught," alluding probably to the Christians as fish newly caught in the waters of baptism. In many places, both in Phrygia and elsewhere, we find the Christians described simply as "the brethren"; and this was the commonest name.

Now for all these curious designations there was a very good cause. Although Christianity was often free from persecution, it was always an illegal religion. Its members therefore in their corporate capacity could not hold property. Moreover, there were decrees against clubs, societies, and any such combinations. But to this there was one exception. Societies of poor persons for burial purposes were allowed. Under this pretext the Christians were enabled to organize themselves, and to acquire property in which they could be buried—a matter, of course, of great moment. But they must adopt some neutral name, some-

[1] *C. and B.*, ii., p. 562.

thing which would not expose them to the suspicions of their heathen neighbours, and could at the same time be recognized by themselves. This explains the somewhat curious names that we have found in the inscriptions just quoted. It need not, however, be supposed that there was anything very secret about the practice. Most persons would know very fairly well who the "Brethren" or the "Purple-dippers" or the "First-Gate-People" were. All that was required was that the law should be obeyed, that prejudice should not be hurt, that fanatical feeling should not be aroused. To this course the Church would gladly conform. It never courted martyrdom, and always tried to live at peace with its neighbours.

So far we have been dealing with inscriptions which do not openly profess their religion; but Phrygia has yielded a certain number of an early date which definitely proclaim themselves as Christian. Besides this fact they have little that is interesting, and need not detain us long. The first comes from the modern town of Ushak, in Central Phrygia, and is important from having a date:—

In the year 363, on the 10th of the month Pereitius, Eutyches, son of Eutyches, to his wife Tatia and his father in remembrance, being Christians, and to himself: Phellinas of Temenothyrai. . . .[1]

The rest is imperfect. The date is about the 3rd of January, A.D. 279.

The next five all come from Northern Phrygia:—

In the year 333 (A.D. 248–9).

CHREISTIANS TO A CHREISTIAN

Aurelia Ammia, with their son-in-law Zoticus, and with their grandchildren Alexandria and Telesphorus, to her husband, constructed (the tomb).

The date is a good deal restored.

[1] This set of inscriptions are taken, not from the originals, to which I had not access, but from the translations published by Professor Ramsay, *Expositor* (1888), ii., pp. 401 f.

Aurelius Zoticus, son of Marcion, to his own parents Marcion and Appe, and to his brother Artemon, in remembrance during his lifetime.
CHREISTIANS TO CHREISTIANS.

Aurelia Rufina, daughter of Trophimus, to Aurelius Alexander Domnas, her own husband, and to her children Cyrilla and Bernicianus and Aurelia and Glyconis and a second Bernicianus, in remembrance constructed (the tomb) along with her own son Aurelius Alexander during their lifetime.
CHREISTIANS TO CHREISTIANS.

Auxanousa, the consort of Andronicus, and his son Trophimus, and his cousin Lassamus during their lifetime to themselves and to Andronicus, Chreistians to a Chreistian, erected this tomb.

Aurelius Glycon to his consort Demetria and to himself while still living, and their children Eugenius and Domna and Patricius and Hypatius and Glycon and Zotikes, Chrestians to a Chrestian.

This small group of inscriptions is almost unique, for in hardly any other case do we get the name Christian plainly mentioned. One of them is dated the third century, and that was probably the period to which they all belong. When the whole population was Christian, no one would probably put the name on the tomb; it would not be a mark of distinction. The inscriptions are to all appearance early; and they all come from a country district, and not from cities, being found in a wide mountain valley of Northern Phrygia. They thus differ from those, previously given, which all come from cities. In a quiet country district the laws against Christians, which were only rarely enforced vigorously anywhere, would probably be absolutely ignored. There would be no interested officials to put them into force, and few heathen customs or observances by evading which the Christian would make himself conspicuous. These inscriptions, then, which have little that is important in their contents, being hardly more than a list of names, are valuable as evidence of the way in which Christianity might establish itself as a recognized institution in any out-of-the-way place.

One more inscription may be quoted, which may perhaps be early, and contains a definite statement of religion :—

> I, Aurelius Proclus, son of Zotikus, make this tomb for myself and my wife Meltine of the Chreistians.[1]

This was found in a field by the road about a mile from the city of Apameia, on the edge of a small dell.

A very interesting heathen inscription from the city of Acmonia (in Central Phrygia) introduces us to another phase in the contest between Christianity and Heathenism. It is inscribed on the four sides of an altar, and is in three parts :—

> A. In the year 398, and keeping the commands of the immortals. Also I am he who speaketh all things, Athanatus Epitynchanus, initiated by the noble high-priestess of the people, Spatale, of honourable name, she whom the immortal Gods honoured within and beyond the bounds of the territory of Acmonia. For she redeemed many from evil torments.
>
> The high-priest Epitynchanus, honoured by the immortal Gods. For him it was consecrated by Diogas and Epitynchanus and Tation his bride and their children Onesimus and Alexander and Asklas and Epitynchanus.

In the centre was a relief; it has been defaced, and a rude cross incised in its place.

> B. I, Athanatus Epitynchanus, the son of Pius, honoured first by Hecate, secondly by Zeus, Manus, Daus, Heliodromus, thirdly by Phoebus, the Founder, the Giver of oracles, have truly received a gift of giving oracles of truth in my native land, yea within the bounds to give laws and oracles. For all I have this gift from all the Immortals.
>
> To Athanatus Pius, the first high-priest, the father of the beautiful children, and to my mother Tation, who bore many fair children, a glorious name, namely, the first Athanatus Epitynchanus, the high-priest, the Saviour of his country, the Lawgiver.

---

[1] *C. and B.*, i., p 536.

On this side there are three reliefs: at the top, a radiated head; below, the horseman god with battle-axe on shoulder; and below him, a bust with hands folded on the breast.

C. The Immortal first high-priests, the two brothers, Diogas and Epitynchanus, the Saviours of their country, the Lawgivers.

Relief, a bird with a ring in its mouth.

D. On the fourth side there is only a relief, a siren.[1]

The date 398 of the era of the province corresponds to our year 313-314, and the inscription dates from the period just after the last Christian persecution. It is the memorial of a series of high-priests. The first of these, Athanatus Epitynchanus Pius, had been initiated into his office by a certain high-priestess Spatale. He was distinguished for the gifts he had received from the gods, the power of giving oracles and divine laws. He was known under the titles "Saviour of his country" and "high-priest." He was succeeded by his two brothers. Now we know from Eusebius that, as a final means for overcoming Christianity, Maximin had organized a heathen priesthood on the analogy of the Christian hierarchy. Each province was to have its chief priests to organize and control the priests under them, to take measures against the Christians, and to produce controversial writings. It was to this class that the priests commemorated in the epitaph belonged, and in the phraseology of the inscription we have an imitation of Christian language by this artificial revived paganism. Previously we have had to speak of Christianity concealing itself under native signs and expressions; now it is paganism in its decadence trying to gain popularity by adopting Christian customs and phrases. " Keeping the commands of the immortals " has a decided Christian sound; "I am he that speaketh all things" is almost exactly modelled on "I that speak unto

[1] *C. and B.*, ii., p. 566.

thee am He." "She redeemed many from evil torments" is what a Christian might say of conversion.

A metrical inscription from another district brings Epitynchanus before us again. From it we learn that he was a great astrologer. "He knew the unerring portents of the air, and the divine voices which speak to men beforehand of things that are, and things that are coming, and things that are to be. In many cities he gained the honours of citizenship, and left behind him sons in no way inferior to himself." He belonged to the class of heathen teachers who carried on the last struggle against Christianity. In Porphyry, in Julian the Apostate, in Hypatia, there was the same admixture of conviction and imposture, of religion and magic or astrology, of opposition to Christianity and imitation, conscious or unconscious, of the too powerful faith. The cities honoured Epitynchanus, but they ceased to be heathen.

Closely connected with the history of Christianity is the history of the Jews. The successors of Alexander seem generally to have favoured this people, and Phrygia was no exception to the rule. When they founded colonies with the purpose of strengthening their hold on the district, they introduced many Jews, and the Jewish population, in some cities at any rate, became very numerous. We have spoken several times of Apameia. Its situation and history make it one of the most important towns in Phrygia. It lay at the source of the Maeander, just where the great road from the sea reaches the interior plateau. The site had always been important, and the old Phrygian city, bearing the name of Celaenae, is well known to all readers of Herodotus. It would be wandering too far from our subject to describe the rivers and fountains which played a great part in Greek legend, to do more than remind the reader that it was the home of the legend of

Marsyas, the inventor of the flute, who challenged Apollo, the Greek god of music, and the home too of the tale of Lityerses, the son of Midas, and of other myths. We are concerned with a later, although a still interesting, phase in its history. The following inscription will introduce the subject:—

I, Aurelius Rufus, son and grandson of Julianus, erected this monument for myself and for my wife Aurelia Tatiana. No one else is to be buried here; if any one does so, he knows the law of the Jews.[1]

The phrase "the law of the Jews" does not mean the Jewish law, but the special laws of Apameia guaranteeing certain privileges to the Jewish body. It seems to imply that the Jews in this place were a large and influential body. Some evidence in literature supports this; but the most interesting is given by the coins of the city. On certain coins struck at Apameia at the beginning of the third century, under Severus, Macrinus, and Philip, there appears the type of a chest or ark, inscribed $N\Omega E$, floating on water; within it are two figures, and standing beneath it a male and female figure; on the top of the chest a raven, and above a dove carrying an olive-branch. Here we have a definite sign that the Noah legend had become a possession of the city. One of the Sibylline oracles tells us that the conical hill above Apameia, on which formerly the citadel had stood, was identified with Mount Ararat, and the city was called Apameia Cibotus, or Apameia of the Ark. How this identification came we cannot say. The name may have caused the legend, or the legend the name. Perhaps some native name, Graecized into Cibotus, suggested the legend. At any rate it is curious that a hill of a very slight elevation, much less than that of the surrounding mountains, should have been selected as Mount Ararat. But whether the Jewish legend gave the

---

[1] *C. and B.*, ii., p. 538.

name, or the name suggested the appropriation of the legend, in either case a very strong Jewish element in the population is implied—one ready to mingle with its neighbours, and not troubled with too much Jewish exclusiveness. This was traditionally the character of the Jews of Phrygia. "The baths and wines of Phrygia had separated the ten tribes from their native land," says the Talmud; and the existence of a body of Jews like this will explain how easy the rise of Jewish Gnosticism, as at Colossae, would be.

The city of Acmonia furnishes another interesting Jewish inscription :—

> The house prepared by Julia Severa. Gaius Turrhonius Claudius, who was through life ruler of the synagogue, and Lucius Lucilius and Popilius have built up at their own expense from the foundations the columns and the walls and the roof, and have provided for the safety of the doors and all the cost of the adornment. These the synagogue has honoured with a golden implement for their virtuous life and their goodwill and zeal to the synagogue.[1]

The mention of Julia Severa enables us to date the inscription to the years A.D. 60–80, a period when her name appears on the coins of the city. She was a somewhat typical character, of high birth, the descendant of kings, holding important social and political positions in more than one city of Asia, and, as we have now found, a Jewess and a patron of Judaism. Throughout Asia there were settled various descendants of the ancient rulers of the country, enjoying much social distinction; and just about this period the influence of the family of the Herods (which had wide ramifications) seems to have been considerable among this class of "mediatized" princes. At any rate it is interesting to get this evidence of the high position occupied by Jews just at the time when Christianity was first preached in the country.

[1] *C. and B.*, ii., p. 649

In the preceding pages it has been possible only to give specimens of the inscriptions of Phrygia; but the specimens have been selected as typical of different phases of life. It remains to sum up and estimate the gain to history. The question of the validity of our conclusions has been already touched upon, and the reader will largely be able from the material put before him to test the legitimacy of the reasoning. There is an element, it may be admitted, that is speculative; but it must be remembered in this case, where we are dealing with phases of life rather than the history of individuals, that the general result depends upon cumulative evidence, and is more certain than any single fact on which it depends. In some cases there may be error; in some cases further research may modify conclusions: but the general result will remain the same. These inscriptions depict to us the progress of Christianity in a remote and half Hellenized part of the empire.

The first, perhaps the main, gain to history lies in the existence of the inscriptions at all. Where so many have been preserved, the Christians must have been numerous, and have become an integral part of the population. They were not only actually but relatively numerous. From causes which we cannot perhaps certainly estimate, Christianity spread early, so as to be, not the religion of a small body of persons removed from the life of the place, but of a section of the population. Hence it influenced, and was influenced by, the character of the people. This fact connects itself at once with the other product of Phrygian Christianity—Montanism.

Montanism we know as a wild, undisciplined sect of Christianity, which had its home in Phrygia, and its chief centre at a place called Pepouza, a few miles from the city of Eumeneia, whence so many inscriptions come. In its original form its chief characteristics were the stress that it laid on the mission of the Paraclete, its belief in prophecy, and the prominence given to women in its ministrations. The prophecy, we are told, was not like the sober gift of the early days of Christianity, but wild, disorderly, and extravagant. Montanism may very likely not have been as bad as it has sometimes been presented by its orthodox opponents; but it undoubtedly shewed considerable evidence of extravagance and disorder. Now both the prominent position of women and a more or less orgiastic worship were characteristic of Phrygia. Montanism was then really the Phrygian character asserting itself under Christian forms. This was only possible where the new religion had got a hold on the people; and that happened, as the inscriptions shew, at an early date in Phrygia. Gradually, as we have been accustomed to recognize, each nation as it became Christianized contributed its elements of good and evil; Roman, Egyptian, African, Greek Christianity, all had their distinguishing features. In Phrygia earlier than elsewhere the national type appeared. At a later date Catholic Christianity overcame, or perhaps absorbed, it, by gradually adopting many native customs and ideas, by sanctifying native sacred places, and thus harmonizing the spirit of the people with that of the new faith. Of recent years there has been a great deal written about Montanism with a more or less controversial object. It has been supposed to represent primitive Christianity asserting itself against a dominant ecclesiasticism; and other rather crude ideas of the kind which are often looked upon as scientific history have been put forward. The present writer believes these theories to be entirely false. The enthusiastic, ill-disciplined Phrygian character was as well known in the ancient world as that of the Celt in the modern world. That fact, and the equally clear fact of the widespread character of Christianity in the district, are together quite sufficient to explain the movement, without recourse being had to the very unsubstantial speculation which has been largely accepted.

It is less easy to define precisely the remaining gain from these inscriptions. We cannot definitely say that many new facts concerning the character of the early Church have been given. The epitaph of Avircius exactly fits in with evidence from various other sources. It corroborates, it does not prove. The other inscriptions give illustrations of known facts rather than additions to our knowledge. Those that suggest the organization of the Church as a burial society fall in with other inscriptions from different parts of the world, to which we shall return in the next chapter. But having admitted to the full the limitations of our new material, it must be remembered that there is an immense difference between doctrines as we read them in a theological treatise, the product of the more able intellects of the day, and the same doctrines or ideas translated into the language of practical life. Illustration makes history real, and corrects the false ideals and generalizations of literature. This is the gain of any epigraphic study of a religion. We learn about it, not as it ought to be, but as it was. It is concrete, it is no longer abstract. We have pictured to us large and influential Jewish colonies, having particular influence among the "devout and honourable women." We trace the growth of a Christian community by no means insignificant in size, with a strong hold on the people, yet avoiding self-assertion, accommodating itself where possible to the prejudices of its neighbours, organized as a mere burial society under a harmless and enigmatical name. We see in Avircius Marcellus the traditional and Catholic Christianity contending with the local variety called Montanism; and we have a picture of the final struggle of a decadent paganism honouring the self-deluding impostures of Epitynchanus.

One thing more we have to emphasize: the above inscriptions were the result of exploration only, not of excavation,—of an exploration which is obliged to be only partial and occasional. Where there is one inscription above ground, there will probably be many below the surface. There is much more to be found. A few weeks' work at Hierapolis or Apameia or Colossae will yield many discoveries whenever the conditions of government make that work possible.

III. *The Catacombs at Rome.*[1]

THE Roman Catacombs constitute one of those subjects about which there is a considerable amount of inaccurate knowledge and misinformed interest. Many persons have seen them, many have read something about them, and much has been written in controversial interests which is absolutely erroneous.

It is not necessary to do more than remind the reader that the Catacombs, as many as forty in number, are subterranean burial-places in the neighbourhood of Rome, admittedly dating—in part, at least—from the earliest days of Christianity. They consist for the most part of long narrow passages, with places for the dead on either side, and occasionally larger chambers, some used for burial, some apparently for worship. They are often labyrinthine in character, and extend in some cases to a considerable depth, one story being constructed below the other. This was obviously done to economize space. Although in some cases one or two adjacent Catacombs seem to have been joined together, for the most part they

[1] I must express my thanks, in writing this chapter, to the Rev. Archibald Patterson, whose knowledge is greater on this subject than that of any English scholar. The primary authorities are of course the volumes of De Rossi, *Roma Sotterranea* and *Inscriptiones Christianae Urbis Romanae*; and the most useful English books, generally trustworthy in the archaeological part, are the works of Northcote and Brownlow. By far the best criticisms on all subjects connected with Roman Archaeology will be found in Lightfoot's *Apostolic Fathers* and Duchesne's *Liber Pontificalis*.

are separated, and the legend that there are subterranean passages connecting the whole is not only untrue, but impossible; for the Catacombs are excavated, and can only be excavated in the higher ground, which is dry, and are separated from one another by streams or low marshy ground, through which communication would be impossible.

A considerable number of other erroneous conceptions, or incorrect theories, must be disposed of as shortly as possible. In the first place, the Catacombs are definitely Christian. In one or two cases they may communicate with, or have originated in, a tomb in which heathen traces are found; in the course of investigation a non-Christian burial-place has occasionally been broken into, and one or two stones with heathen inscriptions have been found, re-used as Christian tombstones: but, with these exceptions, the whole extent of the Catacombs is definitely Christian, and the work of the Roman Christians. Then, again, they were excavated and made for the purpose for which they have been used. It has been asserted that they were really *arenaria*, or sand-pits, converted into burial purposes. That this is not so is shewn by the strata in which they have been excavated. The volcanic deposits in the neighbourhood of Rome contain certain beds of what is called *peperino*, a hard stone suitable for building purposes, and strata of a loose, friable sand, *pozzolana*, used for making the cement out of which so much of Rome has been constructed. The Catacombs do not occur in either of these, but in what is called the *tufa granulare*, a stratum easily worked, but sufficiently solid to enable passages to be formed in it, and quite useless for any other purpose. In one or two instances disused *arenaria* have been converted into burial-places, and then the arrangement and construction are quite different. The *arenaria* were made with the object of obtaining as much material as possible, and have only the support necessary to prevent the ground from falling in; in the Catacombs the passages are as narrow as possible. The cemeteries were constructed according to a definite plan by a body of professional diggers called *fossores*. The name, with the tools of office, appears in tombs early in the third century; they seem to have been organized into a guild, and incorporated to some extent in the Roman clergy. They would be paid out of Church funds, their name appeared in the "list," they would be appointed for their work probably by some religious ceremony, and might possibly be included among the minor orders. These latter, until they had ceased to be of use, were not at any time fixed in number; they varied in different places and at different times. It was only at a later time that the seven orders were definitely fixed.

Nor, again, were the Catacombs made for the purposes of concealment. It must be quite obvious that in a city like Rome excavations on so large a scale could not have been made without attracting notice; the original entrances also were not concealed in any way. At a later date in the third century, and perhaps still more in the Diocletian persecution, they were used for hiding-places. We find evidence of passages being blocked up, of new openings made, and of concealed entrances into *arenaria*. But these were not part of the original plan, and were only later measures adopted under a sudden emergency.

In a previous chapter something has been said about the methods by which Christians obtained the opportunity of burial. To those that were rich, of course, there would be no difficulties; to those that were poor the difficulties would be very considerable. These would be overcome in one of two ways. Either some rich person, who had become a convert to Christianity, would place a burial-plot, duly registered and surveyed, at the disposal of poorer members of the community, or else the Church, or a portion of the Church, registered as a burial society, would itself provide a cemetery. In either case, as the Christian community would feel itself bound to care for all its members, even the poorest, the great object would be to provide as many burial-places as possible within the area attainable, and this would lead to the particular and specially Christian form of excavation adopted: an inspection of any plan will shew that the Catacombs generally occupied a rectangular portion of ground, and that the passages in them were arranged so as to make as much use as possible of the whole space. Examples of both types are probably to be found. Cemeteries like those of St. Domitilla and St. Priscilla seem to have started, at any rate, from the burial-places of rich members of the Christian community, while that of St. Callistus seems to have belonged to the Church, and is so designated. The beginning of the official career of Callistus was his appointment in charge of "The Cemetery"; that is, the cemetery which is now known as the Catacombs of Callistus.

To the Phrygian tomb-inscriptions quoted above may now be added others from Rome and the western provinces. One from Caesarea of Mauritania tells us that "the assembly (or Church) of the brothers restored this inscription."[1] Another, also from Africa, which recorded how Euelpius, described as worshipper of the Word (*cultor Verbi*), had given an *area* for sepulchres and left a memorial to the Holy Church, tells of a certain Victor, called a presbyter, who made a burial-place for all the brethren (*cunctis fratribus*); and in Rome we have a request to the "good brothers" to prevent a tomb from being desecrated.[2] Two inscrip-

---

[1] " Ecclesia fratrum hunc restituit titulum."
[2] "Peto a vobis fratres boni per unum deum ne quis . . . titulo molestet post mortem meam."

tions may also be quoted as giving instances of burial-places set apart for members of a family; the first is certainly, the second probably, Christian. " M. Antonius Restitutus made this burial-place for those of his family that believe in the Lord." The other is stated to be erected by certain persons "for their freedmen and freedwomen, and their posterity, those belonging to my religion," and proceeds to define the extent of the burial-place. These inscriptions, added to those already given, help to bring out the importance in early days and the widespread character of this side of Church organization. It enabled the Christian community to exist as a legal body even when Christianity was an illegal religion, and to hold property for the purpose of burial; probably also in this way a legal status in other matters was acquired. All this side of Christian life has been revealed to us, and revealed entirely by archaeological research.

We must now briefly sum up the history of the Catacombs. Their construction and use began in the latter part of the first century, and to that date are referred five cemeteries: (1) the Vatican cemetery, now almost entirely destroyed to make way for the substructure of the Vatican Basilica; (2) that of St. Paul on the Via Ostiensis, also destroyed; (3) that of Priscilla on the Via Salaria Nova; (4) what is called the *Ostrianum* on the Via Nomentana; and (5) that of Domitilla and of Nereus and Achilleus on the Via Ardeatina. To the questions, How do we know the date of these? and can we be certain that that date is correct? the answer is that we find Christian tradition corroborated by archaeological signs. The names are often those of the Flavian epoch, the ornament is early and often barely Christian in character, the starting-point of the tombs is a family burying-place containing names belonging to the early imperial days, and apparently in one or two cases dates have been found, the earliest of the year A.D. 107.[1] Of the correctness of the dating in most of these cases there can be no reasonable doubt. These cemeteries, which date from the close of the first century, would largely suffice for the use of the Christian community during the second century; but we know that a certain number of others belong to that period. The most prominent is that of Praetextatus, on the Via Appia, to which must be added, apparently, those of Hermes, and of Maximus and the Jordani, on the Via Salaria Nova. It was at the close of the second century and the beginning of the third that the extension of the Christian Church in Rome began. From the days of Commodus onwards until the middle of the next century it enjoyed almost uninterrupted peace; the numbers increased; it was a period when the national worship declined, and Oriental influences prevailed. At this time we first hear of the cemeteries in literature, and find an officer appointed over them. There was some organization of course before; but we have no certain record of it. At a later date came the organization of the cemeteries under the seven deacons, and the connexion with the different *tituli* of the different parishes. The great cemetery of the third century is that of St. Callistus, with the tombs of most of the Roman Bishops during that period.

We are unfortunately singularly without information concerning the history of the Roman Church during the period of the Diocletian persecution. With the peace of the Church under Constantine the need of the Catacombs ceased, as the Christians were able to acquire land in the ordinary manner, and cemeteries above ground began; but the habit of burying in the old way survived for another century. It is computed that about two-thirds of the burials of the fourth century were still made in the

Catacombs. Old habits do not die out easily, and a further motive now prevailed. There was a desire to be buried near the remains of martyrs, and we find instances of the sale of burial-places to those who desired this privilege. But the fourth century gives us another phase in the history of the Catacombs. They became places of pilgrimage, and for that purpose were adorned and restored. Jerome and Prudentius, the one in prose, the other in poetry, tell us of their history; and Damasus, Bishop of Rome from 366 to 384, devoted himself to their adornment. Almost every cemetery shews signs of his work. Wherever there was a grave of any martyr, he made new entrances, broadened the passages, and erected inscriptions—the letters, beautiful examples of calligraphy, being specially executed by one Filocalus—recording the history or tradition of those buried there. Many of these were copied by visitors to Rome in the eighth and ninth centuries, and are preserved in libraries, for the most part north of the Alps. The originals have been found in small fragments—always distinguishable by the characters in which they are cut—and restorations are possible (as in the case of the Avircius inscription) by means of the MS. copies.

To the fourth century belong the greater number of the dated inscriptions found in the Catacombs, and to this period is to be ascribed the foundation of the various basilicas outside the walls. With the invasion of Alaric in 410, burials in the Catacombs entirely ceased, as is testified by the absence in them of inscriptions bearing a later date.[1] Thereafter the Catacombs existed only as places of pilgrimage and devotion. From time to time some of them were adorned and restored, and a certain

---

[1] Speaking precisely, only two inscriptions have been found in the Catacombs which bear dates after 410; *viz.* one of A.D. 426, the other of A.D. 454.

number of ornaments, definitely ecclesiastical in style shew unmistakable signs of their later origin.

Before passing to the historical value of the Catacombs, two further observations must be made. In the first place, we must state definitely that the archaeological conclusions of De Rossi are almost absolutely to be depended upon. Some of his historical deductions may go a little beyond the evidence; some of his copyists and followers have gone still further in controversial deductions: but as against his Protestant and other critics, his methods, his dates, and his general archaeological deductions, as they have been very shortly summarized here, are absolutely trustworthy. The second point is that we must distinguish carefully between the original inscriptions and the Roman traditions of the fourth century as recorded by Pope Damasus. The former, so far as they go, give us first-hand evidence; the latter may often contain historical information, but it is certainly in some cases confused, and is not to be absolutely depended upon. It is evident that the records of the Roman See were almost all destroyed at the end of the third or beginning of the fourth century.

The Catacombs, as has been said, date from the close of the first century, and their beginnings are connected with an interesting period in the history of the Roman Church.

According to Dio Cassius, or rather the epitome of that historian written by Xiphilinus, T. Flavius Clemens, who was consul in 95, was put to death by Domitian, and his wife Flavia Domitilla (niece of the emperor) was banished to the island of Pandateria, "on a charge of atheism and Jewish rites." Eusebius, quoting the authority of non-Christian writers, definitely claims Domitilla—whom he makes niece, not wife, of the consul—and apparently also the consul himself, as Christian; and the name of Domitilla has become well known in a Christian legend which tells us of her as the virgin martyr who preferred death to marriage, of her two chamberlains Nereus and Achilleus, and adds the story of Petronilla, the daughter of St. Peter, who had also chosen virginity even at the cost of martyrdom. Now how much of this can be supported by archaeology? The first and most important question is whether it was as a Christian, or at any rate a sympathizer with Christianity, that Flavius Clemens, the consul, was put to death. That it was so seems proved by the following discoveries. Among the oldest of the Christian burial-places was the *Coemeterium Domitillae*, on the Ardeatine Way. Inscriptions found on the spot have proved that this was situated on land belonging to Flavia Domitilla. One states that a burial-place had been given to its owner EX INDULGENTIAE FLAVIAE DOMITILLAE, "through the kindness of Flavia Domitilla"; another records a certain Tatia, who describes herself as the "nurse of seven children of the divine Vespasian and of Flavia Domitilla, niece of Vespasian," and records that the monument was erected by her kindness. This cemetery was approached by a vestibule above ground, which led down to a large *hypogaeum*, with chambers opening out of it. This vestibule appears to be of the first century, and has all the appearance of being erected by persons of wealth and distinction. Moreover, in the chambers are burial-places of those who, judging by their names, were members of the Flavian family or household. Such are φλ. cαβεινοc και τιτιανη αδελφοι (Flavius Sabeinus and Titiane, brother and sister). Here, then, we have a Christian burial-place closely connected with the imperial family, and the deduction seems to be legitimate that the statement of Eusebius (supported, probably as it is, by Dio Cassius) is correct that Flavia Domitilla was a Christian, and that it was for Christianity that her husband, the consul, suffered. Archaeology clearly strengthens the natural, but not certain, interpretation of the historical passages.

But what of the further developments of the story? Do these find corroboration in catacombs? Here the service of archaeology is different. It suggests the manner in which the legend grew. A sarcophagus bearing the inscription, "To my most sweet daughter Petronilla," recalled to a later and uncritical age the name of St. Peter. Here was evidence of a daughter of his; here was an inscription cut, perhaps, with his own hand; to this name was affixed a legend, and a cultus; a basilica was built; and ultimately the body of St. Petronilla found a resting-place in the Vatican by her supposed father, whom a later age, shocked at such a suggestion, called her spiritual father.

It is sometimes claimed that the discoveries of the Catacombs corroborate the legends as well as that which we have stated our belief to be history. This is not so. The story of Avircius presents an almost exact analogy. There the discovery of a portion of the epitaph proves to us the genuineness of that epitaph, the reality of the person, and the spurious character of the life. So, in this case, the discovery of the vault and burying-place of Flavii in a Christian catacomb definitely connects the family with Christianity; but it does not prove that the life as told by the hagiographers is genuine. The name of Petronilla in an epitaph does not prove the story of the daughter of St. Peter; it rather disproves it. The name is not derived from Petros, but from *Petronius* or *Petro*, and the founder of the Flavian family bore the latter name. The epitaph in this case also suggested the story.

It is interesting to learn that already as early as A.D. 95 Christianity had reached members of the Flavian family; but the case of Flavius Clemens is not isolated. At the same time many others, we are told, perished; among them was M' Acilius Glabrio, who was consul with Trajan in the year 91. Was he, too, a Christian? It seems so. After digging many years in the *Coemeterium Priscillae* on the Via Salaria Nova, De Rossi came at last on the oldest portions of the cemetery. Here he found a large sepulchral chamber, much resembling the oldest portion of the cemetery of Domitilla, containing, not the ordinary *loculi*, but places evidently occupied by sarcophagi. This was proved by inscriptions to be a burial-place of the Acilian *gens*. One is to an " Acilius Glabrio, son of . . . "; another contains the names of M' Acilius and Priscilla. Now we must not at once jump to the conclusion that here we have the burial-place of the consul of A.D. 91. That is not necessary for our argument. The family was a distinguished one, and had many persons of the same name. What is proved is an intimate connexion between members of the Acilian *gens* and the Christian Church; and surely it is more than a coincidence that just those Roman nobles whom we might judge from the language of historians to have suffered under Domitian on the charge of Christianity should be those whose names are found intimately connected with the oldest Christian cemeteries. Inscriptions connect for us the name of Priscilla with the Acilian *gens*, but not, so far as we know, until the second century. The name is one which was important in the early history of the Roman Church, but how we cannot say. A very reasonable conjecture suggests that the Clement who was Bishop of Rome was a freedman of Flavius Clemens, the consul; it would be interesting to connect the Priscilla of the Acts and the Epistle to the Romans with the Priscilla of the Catacombs and the Acilian *gens*, but as yet there is no historical evidence. The clue is not found. We only know that the name of Priscilla occupies a prominent position in the early history and traditions of the Roman Church.

Yet one more name of interest comes before us connected with the secular history of the first century. The historian Tacitus tells us how Pomponia Graecina, a lady of rank, the wife of Plautius, conqueror of Britain, had been accused of being guilty of "foreign superstition." Her husband was allowed to try her, she was acquitted, but the rest of her life was one of "continued sadness." Many writers have suspected that she might be a Christian; and again archaeology seems to support the suspicion. The earliest portion of the cemetery of St. Callistus is called the Crypt of St. Lucina. It may be as early as the first century. Here an inscription has been found bearing the name of Pomponius Graecinus. The coincidence is again interesting. The cemetery was probably constructed by some one of position during the first century; amongst those for whom it was used in that century was some one bearing this name, who may reasonably be considered to have been a connexion or descendant of the founders. We need not do more than mention the suggestion of De Rossi that Lucina was really the baptismal name of Graecina herself; without that, which must remain only a clever guess, the corroboration of the conjecture that Pomponia was a Christian must remain strong.

Omitting some minor points, which although interesting need not detain us, let us now inquire, What has archaeology to say to the connexion of the two Apostles St. Peter and St. Paul with Rome? Here the direct evidence, or the localities which might give direct evidence, have been destroyed. The catacombs which succeeded the reputed burying-places of St. Peter and St. Paul, and which presumably were the earliest of the Roman cemeteries, have been practically obliterated by the gigantic basilicas built on the sites. Speaking generally, archaeology here corroborates and intensifies, but does not change, the character of the evidence from literature. Literature makes it clear that there was a strong and widely held belief in the second century that St. Peter and St. Paul were the joint founders of the Roman Church, and a writer at the close of that century speaks of the "trophies of the apostles" as existing on the Vatican Hill and Ostian Way. Archaeology makes it quite clear that from the second century onwards the two apostles were jointly honoured in the Roman Church in an especial manner. From that date onwards their figures appear represented on various kinds of archaeological remains, in paintings, on sarcophagi, and on glass vessels used as chalices. The present writer has no shadow of doubt that the two apostles were connected with the Church in Rome, and believes that the tradition which holds that their relics are preserved may be quite correct (although proof is unobtainable); but the patristic evidence is not really strengthened by the monumental. This latter does not prove the fact; it only proves the belief, and literature also does that. In neither case have we (as yet) contemporary evidence; but in both the tradition is so strong that there is no real ground for doubting the fact. One more point may be added. There is a distinct tradition in the portraits preserved. They are found on glass, dating, in some cases, from an early period; and there is a large bronze plaque, probably belonging to the second century. In all these there is a distinct resemblance. St. Paul is represented (as tradition represented him) bald, St. Peter has long curling hair. St. Paul, again, always has a prominent nose and meeting eyebrows. Whether this common tradition goes back to actual portraits we cannot say. It is possible, or perhaps probable. Some attempt has been made to find significance in the fact that in some of the portraits St. Peter is on the right, in others

St. Paul. Nothing can ever be deduced from a point of that sort, as we can never really say which is the position of honour. All that is suggested by the facts is that the point was then one of indifference.

When we pass to the second century, we learn very much less history from the Catacombs. The Bishops of Rome at that time are reputed by tradition to have been buried in the Vatican cemetery, a statement which we need not doubt, but which, owing to the vandals of the sixteenth century who prepared the foundations of St. Peter's, we shall never be able to verify. But we find among Acts of the Martyrs some which contain names preserved in the Catacombs or the records of the Catacombs. Amongst these the Acts of Felicitas and her Seven Sons have been the subject of much discussion. They are a variation of a theme, which was inherited at least from Jewish days, of the martyrdom of a mother and seven sons, and the story contains many obvious blunders. An examination of early records and monuments makes it clear that the story was framed on the fact that seven martyrs are commemorated on one day; but the same records tell us that they were buried in four different cemeteries, and in one case the actual tomb—that of Januarius—has been found, and bears the characteristics of the age of the Antonines. The fact of the martyrdom of these seven is probably true; it may be that they all date from the second century, although we have not as yet the evidence which will enable us to say. The commemoration on the same day united these names together in a fourth-century list, and the Second Book of Maccabees suggested the form that the legend should take. Again we have an instance of a late story growing up out of the epitaphs and other records of an earlier age.

To the third century belongs the great cemetery of

St. Callistus, to which De Rossi devoted such infinite labour, and again our history becomes more considerable. To the first half of that century belongs the statue of Hippolytus, with the inscription upon it containing a list of his works and his Easter table. The monument is proved to be contemporary by the fact that this table would have been seen to be clearly wrong after a certain number of years, and it is not likely that an honorary statue would be adorned with an achievement which had been shewn to be valueless. The existence of this monument, by far the finest memorial of early Christianity in Rome, erected to the memory of one who, although very greatly distinguished as a writer, clearly occupied a somewhat ambiguous place in the Church and about whom tradition early became confused, is full of interest, and raises more questions than it solves.

While a body of personal admirers seem to have commemorated this anti-pope—if such he was—with a statue, the actual Bishops of Rome at that period were buried in a crypt which has been discovered, and fragments of their original epitaphs have been found there. The first to be buried in that crypt (so the records tell us) was Zephyrinus, who died about A.D. 217; the last was Eutychianus, A.D. 284: but the same cemetery, although not the same vault, contained several others. The following original inscriptions have been found in the Crypt of the Popes (as it is called): ΟΥΡΒΑΝΟC ⊣ ε[πιc], ΑΝΤεΡωC ⊣ επιc, ΦΑΒΙΑΝΟC ⊣ επιc ⊣ ΜΑΡ. (the last word being added by a later hand), ΛΟΥΚΙC ⊣ ΕΥΤΥΧΙΑΝΟC ⊣ επιc. Besides these, other epitaphs have been found in the cemetery, but not in the crypt. The first epitaph to be found was that of CORNELIVS ⊣ MARTYR ⊣ EP ⊣ who we know was buried in a separate vault, and whose epitaph is the only one in Latin. Now of course these discoveries do not increase our knowledge. We know that these bishops lived; we know which were martyrs. There is no new fact gained. But yet there cannot be any doubt that the knowledge that here we have the actual burial-places of these early bishops, and the original epitaphs, adds a vividness and reality to history which written records alone can never give.

Close to the Papal Crypt has been preserved another chamber, which was undoubtedly the burial-place of St. Caecilia. Here again we have the origin of the well-known Acts of her Martyrdom. They were undoubtedly later, and are undoubtedly unauthentic in their present form. The discovery of the burial-place of the saint does not necessarily add a particle of evidence in favour of the genuineness of the Acts. What it does prove is the reality of her existence. The time when she died is not certain; but apparently there are archaeological reasons for considering that her crypt is older than that of the Popes. De Rossi concludes that Caecilia was, as her Acts represent, a noble lady of the Caecilian gens; to her family the land belonged; some members of it were converted to Christianity in the second century; to that fact was owed the origin of the cemetery; here Caecilia, who perished under the Antonines, was buried; and here were buried many other members of her family. Probably all this may be true, and it gives the basis on which the later Acts, with their confused chronology and legendary details, were built.

We have already referred to the work of Damasus, to the labour he spent in adorning the Catacombs, and to the historical inscriptions he erected. With these we must close our survey of the historical information that the Catacombs give. The inscriptions were erected, it must be remembered, in the fourth century, by a pope who was contemporary with St. Jerome. The historical traditions of the Church of Rome at that date may be occasionally confused, but in the absence of better evidence must be quoted as being of considerable historical value. To archaeologists they have a double interest. Damasus was the first Christian archaeologist who studied the monumental remains of the early days of Christianity, and the history of his work draws our attention to another archaeological period. The epitaphs only exist *in situ* in a very fragmentary form, but northern archaeologists of the ninth and following centuries, full of eagerness to study the early records of the martyrs of the Church, have preserved for us copies made before these records were destroyed; and the northern archaeologist of the present day, who, perhaps with different ideals and methods, turns full of interest and enthusiasm to the monumental remains of early Christianity, may express his thanks to his predecessors of the school of Alcuin.

We will conclude this historical survey with some instances of the Damasine inscriptions. The following is the one in which he commemorates the death of Pope Xystus II., who was decapitated, in the reign of Valerian, in the Catacombs of Praetextatus, situated near the cemetery of Callistus, but on the opposite side of the Appian Way:—

> What time the sword pierced the tender heart of Mother (Church) placed here as ruler I taught the laws of heaven. Suddenly they came; they seize me as I chanced to be sitting in my chair; the soldiers are sent in; the people bent their necks to the sword. Soon the old man saw for himself who wished to bear the palm, and was forward to offer himself and his head, that the impatient cruelty might injure no one else. Christ who renders the rewards of life shews forth the merits of the pastor, and Himself protects the flock.

Here is another inscription, also in the Papal Crypt:

> Here, if you seek them, lie buried a great crowd of the holy:
> These venerable tombs hold the bodies of the Saints,
> Their noble souls the royal Court of Heaven has snatched away.
> Here lie the companions of Xystus who bear away their trophies from the enemy;
> Here a great band of chiefs who guard the Altars of Christ;
> Here lies buried the Bishop who lived in long peace (*i.e.* Fabius).
> Here the holy Confessors whom Greece sent us;

> Here youths and boys, old men and chaste children,
> Whom it pleased to keep their virgin purity.
> Here, I confess, I Damasus wished to lay my bones,
> But I feared to vex the sacred ashes of the Saints.

Of the Roman Bishops at the beginning of the fourth century we have singularly little knowledge, so that the following inscription is of interest. It has been put together from a few fragments of the original, from a restoration in the fifth century, and from a later MS. copy. On one side is, "Damasus, the Bishop, set up this to Eusebius, Bishop and Martyr." On the other, "Furius Dionysius Filocalus, a worshipper and lover of Pope Damasus, wrote this." The inscription is as follows :—

> Heraclius forbad the lapsed to grieve for their sins. Eusebius taught those unhappy ones to weep for their crimes. The people were rent into parties, and with increasing fury arose sedition, slaughter, war, discord, strife. Of a sudden both were banished by the cruelty of the tyrant, though the Ruler preserved inviolate the bonds of peace. He bore his exile with joy, looking to the Lord as his Judge, and on the Trinacrian shore (Sicily) left the world and life.

Here we have a poetical and probably exaggerated account of an otherwise unknown episode in the history of the Roman Church, arising, as others had done before, out of the treatment of those who lapsed in the persecution.

We will give, lastly, the inscription Damasus erected in memory of Hippolytus :—

> Hippolytus, the Presbyter, when the commands of the tyrant pressed upon him, is reputed to have remained all along in the schism of Novatus, what time the sword wounded the vitals of our Mother the Church. When, as a Martyr of Christ, he was journeying to the realms of the Saints, the people asked him whither they might betake themselves, he replied that they ought all to follow the Catholic faith. Our Saint by his confession won the crown of Martyrdom. Damasus tells the tale as he heard it. Christ tests all things.

Here we have a confused tradition of the fourth century, which became one of the sources of later legend. Hippolytus, who thirty years earlier played a part analogous to that of Novatian, is stated to have been a follower of his. But the inscription seems to preserve a tradition that before his banishment he was reconciled again to the Catholic Church—a tradition which was probably true.

Quite sufficient indication has been given of the illustrations afforded by the Catacombs to the history of the Roman Church; but more important, or certainly more interesting, is the light they throw on the life of the early Christians. Here we have from 15,000 to 20,000 inscriptions —many of them, it is true, slight and fragmentary—relating to the second, third, and fourth centuries; and to these we can add the sarcophagi, the frescoes, and smaller antiquities, especially the remains of glass chalices, which have been found in them.

It is especially the beliefs and practices concerning the departed that are illustrated, and a comparison with heathen inscriptions has suggested a number of reflections. The great simplicity of the Christian epitaphs contrasts very markedly with the character of the heathen. The latter contain generally an elaborate account of the parentage, the rank, the position of the deceased; the former are often content with the name alone. And this, it is asserted, is natural for those who looked upon themselves as sojourners in this world, and fixed their hopes on the more permanent abode in the world to come. It may be doubtful whether so much stress ought to be laid on this. There is the same shortness, simplicity, and absence of worldly information in many of the inscriptions in the *Columbaria* of freedmen and slaves, and it may well have been natural to the class from which so large a number of the Christians must have come. They had no worldly position to record. More important and more valid is the contrast afforded on the subject of belief in a future state. The prevailing characteristic of the pagan epitaph is hopelessness; but of the Christian it is hope. The one may contain beautiful expressions of personal and family and parental affection, it may be cynical or flippant, it may express resignation or a sense of wrong; it rarely expresses hope. But hope is the most prominent characteristic of the Christian epitaph. This is shewn very clearly in the new name for a burial-place which came in with Christianity, and wherever that is found it is the unconscious witness of the Christian faith,—cemetery, or *coemeterium*, the place of sleep or rest, implying always the hope of an awakening.

We will now give some instances. The most simple of all are such as the following: "Alexandra in peace." So, "To my most sweet wife, the well-deserving, in peace"; "Thou livest in peace"; "Thou shalt live in peace"; "Agape, thou shalt live for ever"; "Victorina in peace and in Christ."

A slightly different set of ideas is introduced in the following: "Regina, mayest thou live in the Lord Jesus"; "Peace to thy soul, Oxycholis"; "To dear Cyriacus; sweetest son, mayest thou live in the Holy Spirit"; "May thy spirit rest well in God"; "May God refresh thy spirit."

And yet a further circle of ideas in such as the following: "Matronata Matrona, who lived one year and fifty-three days. Pray for thy parents"; "Anatolius made this for his well-deserving son, who lived seven years, seven months, and twenty days. May thy spirit rest well in God. Pray for thy sister"; "Mayest thou be well refreshed, and pray for us"; "Mayest thou live in the Lord, and pray for us"; "Sabbathius, sweet soul, ask and pray."

Here we have three different stages. The first expresses the confident hope of a Christian, the second is an exclamation or prayer for the departed, the third is a request to those gone before to pray for us. These last two demand a few observations, as their theological importance is considerable.

Epitaphs containing these exclamations on behalf of the dead are not late, but early. We have more than one dated to the end of the third century; we have several which, although undated, from the place in which they are found, or other indications, must be assigned to an early date in the second century. Among the very considerable number of dated inscriptions later than Constantine there is not one containing these exclamations. The custom, so far from being a late introduction, is early, and prevailed at an early date. This is in accordance with other evidence. We know that the custom existed at the end of the second century from literary evidence, and we know that in the third century the Holy Eucharist was celebrated as a memorial of the dead. Moreover, exclamations such as these, on graves, were a custom inherited from Jews. The following inscriptions from a Jewish cemetery in Rome will illustrate this. Their religion is shewn by the seven-branched candlesticks with which they are adorned. "Pardos Sabeina .... who lived sixteen years. May her rest be in peace (or, Her rest is in peace)." Another is to a certain Alexander, of whom it is said, "May thy sleep be among the just."[1] In both these cases the language is ambiguous, as it is so often in Christian epithets; but there is no real ambiguity, as this expression "Mayest thou rest among the just" survives to the present day among the Jews, and is used by them as an exclamation.

It is not possible to speak so definitely, perhaps, about the date of those inscriptions in which the departed are

---

[1] These, and some other inscriptions, have been copied from a small collection, the property of Pusey House at Oxford, but at present in the hands of the donor.

asked to join in prayer; but there is no reason for placing them late. Some would naturally be put early, as, for example, those written in Greek. It must be noted that this custom of "invocation of saints"—if it be called so—is not that of "invoking" only those of special sanctity, but of calling on those near and dear to offer up prayers on behalf of the living. It is the form in which the custom prevails among numbers of Eastern Churches to the present day, and is in accordance with the early belief of the solicitude of the departed for those still living. We may notice that in both these cases we have the theological belief of the day translated into popular language and custom. It is that, rather than controversial interest, which gives them their value.

Before we conclude our account of the inscriptions, we must notice two things, their bad grammar and spelling, and the fact that so many of them are in Greek, or, still more curious, Greek written in Latin letters. This corroborates other evidence, to the effect that the Roman Church was for two centuries largely Greek, and that although there were, as we have seen, exceptions, its great hold was on the lower classes of the population.

More interesting for the most part than the inscriptions are the paintings of the Catacombs. These date in some cases from the earliest periods, and, at any rate in their beginnings, were influenced both in design and treatment by contemporary heathen art. The earliest Christian artists, or artists of Christian tombs, must have been trained in heathen traditions, and these would only gradually be modified. To this influence must be traced the addiction to scenes representing the vine and vintage, which easily found a home in Christian symbolism; the figure of Orpheus, a type, first to the heathen and then to the Christian world, of the Resurrection; and probably the Good Shepherd, which, perhaps modelled on a heathen statue, became the most favourite of all designs. But quite early a definite cycle of Biblical and symbolical pictures developed, which centred for the most part in two or three leading ideas.

The Biblical scenes represented are hardly those which would be expected. They mainly come from the Old Testament, and most common of all are paintings of the stories of Jonah and Daniel. Both are symbolical of the resurrection from the dead, and both might prove an incentive to the Christians in the trials of persecution. The Ark of Noah seems to have represented the salvation in the Christian Church, the Flood being associated in various symbolical ways with Baptism. Moses striking the rock and the sacrifice of Isaac were other ideas belonging to the Old Testament. In the New Testament the chief types selected were the Adoration of the Magi and the Resurrection of Lazarus.

To Biblical subjects must be added a large cycle of symbolical designs such as the anchor, the lamb, the dove, the ship, the meaning of which in each case is fairly obvious, and, most constant and characteristic of all, the fish. It is well known how very early some ingenious Christian discovered that the initial letters of the titles of our Lord—'Ἰησοῦς Χριστὸς Θεοῦ Υἱὸς Σωτήρ, i.e. "Jesus Christ, the Son of God, the Saviour"—formed the word ἰχθύς (fish). The literary habits of the time, perhaps some little desire for secrecy, a feeling of reverence which shrank from expressing too openly the most sacred things, and which pervaded so much of early Christian life—all these combined to make the name attractive, and, once adopted, its symbolism lent itself to a large cycle of Christian teaching. It would particularly connect itself with the two great Christian ideas of Baptism and the Eucharist, for through all the symbolism and paintings of the Catacombs there is a strong sacramental element. The fish represented both Christ and His disciples; the water in which it swam might be the waters of baptism; the feeding of the five thousand with the fish and the bread brought together the type and the antitype in one representation. The Christian feast—an *agape* or Eucharist, for we cannot clearly distinguish them—is generally represented by a typical number of seven Christians, and before them are baskets of loaves and two fish. The imagery once started was capable of very great variation; doctrine might suggest symbolism, and symbolism doctrine. We know how in the Fathers wherever water or bread or wine or the grape is mentioned there Baptism or the Eucharist is found. Symbolism never desires to be consistent or logical. It only becomes untrue when it is developed into a system, and in the Catacombs the reality of the sacramental life of the Church is clear and conspicuous. From them, as from the Fathers, we learn how the great ideas of the washing in Baptism and of the communion with Christ in the Eucharist penetrated the whole of the Christian life. They were not additions to it, as they are so often with us; they lay at the root of it. So much the Catacombs prove. But when we ask what particular doctrine they taught, we are in a region of thought that they do not touch. Their evidence cannot be used, for symbolism can always be interpreted just in accordance with our *a priori* ideas.

The reference to the fish symbol will suggest the quotation of one more inscription, which, although not belonging to the period to which we have limited ourselves, and not from Rome, harmonizes exactly with this circle of ideas. It is the inscription of Autun, found there in the year 1839, and first published by Cardinal Pitra. It dates probably from the fifth century, to which time it carries on the symbolism of an earlier age, and unfortunately some lines give considerable scope for conjectural restoration. It must be perfectly obvious that evidence can never be based on a restoration, however probable or ingenious, which exceeds a few letters. The following is a translation of the first and last portion of the inscription, where the reading is fairly certain :—

> Offspring of the Heavenly Ichthys, see that a heart of holy reverence be thine, now that from Divine waters thou hast received, while yet among mortals, a Fount of life that is to immortality. Quicken thy soul, beloved one, with ever-flowing waters of wealth-giving wisdom, and receive the honey-sweet food of the Saviour of Saints. Eat with a longing hunger, holding Ichthys in thine hands. . . . . Aschandius, my Father, dear unto mine heart, and thee, sweet mother, and all that are mine. . . . . Remember Pectorius.[1]

We have had throughout to touch very cursorily on many points which have aroused great controversial interest, and have not been able to deal with any of them with a proper degree of thoroughness. We have wished to suggest certain principles of dealing with the evidence. In the first place, the Catacombs add little or nothing to the evidence of the Fathers; they present it only in another form. We may, or we may not, approve of prayers for the dead; but the Fathers teach it, and the Catacombs suggest it. We may doubt whether St. Peter visited Rome; but the Catacombs and Fathers both imply that it was the fixed belief of the Roman Church at a very early age that he did. The Catacombs shew how large a part Baptism and the Eucharist played in the early Church; but so do the Fathers, from Hermes and Ignatius onwards. In the second place, much that is in the Catacombs, being symbolical, can be interpreted just in accordance with the prepossessions with which we approach such symbolism. There is no doubt that we have early pictures of the Virgin and Child, but they never occur except as a part

---

[1] I have taken, for convenience, the translation by the Rev. W. B. Marriott, in *The Testimony of the Catacombs*, p. 119.

of Biblical scenes; one writer can lay stress only on the positive evidence, another only on the negative. And then, thirdly, modern controversial questions largely turn on distinctions which were not present in the mind of the early Church. To any such, an answer dragged out of inscriptions which are often imperfect, out of paintings which are symbolical, which need restoration or interpretation, must necessarily be very uncertain. It is not as controversial documents that the Catacombs are valuable. It is to take us out of controversy. It is because they represent to us the life, or rather a phase of the life, of the early Church. They translate theological expressions into the language of popular life. Their very existence is a striking fact. They exhibit to us the Christian Church, with all its care for the dead, transforming the funeral customs and the methods of burial of the people. They exhibit to us its abiding faith in the Resurrection, its intense concentration of mind on the Person of its Redeemer, its life permeated by the symbolism of the two great Sacraments. We can study them, catching at any controversial point which tells in favour of our views, or laboriously proving that everything with which we disagree must be late; or we can allow our minds to be concentrated, as those of the makers of the Catacombs were, on the great Christian ideas of the continuity of the Christian Church, the resurrection of the dead, the reality of the spiritual life in Christ, and the communion of saints.

We have reviewed in these three chapters the evidence of archaeology as affecting the history of Christianity. We have tried to emphasize two points about archaeology throughout. The first is, that it is of great value to the historian; the second, that it is apt to be disappointing to the controversialist. It will sometimes prove a certain amount, but it will never go quite as far as the latter wishes.

But if we are content to ask, not how it will help us in modern points of dispute, but how it will help us to learn the early history of Christianity, its service is very great. It translates the history into life. It enables us to study the environment in which it grew up, and the books of the Bible in the light of that environment. It shews us the early Christian dwelling in the world, influenced by it, changing, but only gradually, the customs and habits which he inherited. It suggests the proportion in which he held the Christian faith. Its tendency is constructive, and not destructive. It supports, on the whole, the literary evidence. It shews the intense reality with which the earliest Christians held the most transcendent doctrines of their faith; but on the actual evidence for their doctrines, the life and death of the Redeemer, it is silent.

INDEX

The figures in italics refer to the footnotes only.

AAHMES, 172
Abdi-khûba, governor of Jerusalem, 73
Abel-beth-maacah, 99
Abercius Inscription, the, 367-373
Abraham, 35, 38, 45, 83
Abu-Habba, 102, 122
Abu-Shahrein, 20
Academy, the, 141
Acbatana, 200, 201
Accad, *29*
Acco, 69, 73
Achimit, 103
Achshaph, 70
Acilius Glabrio, 406
Acmonia, inscription from, 383, 387, 391
Acropolis, Athens, 256, 257-261; fragments of vases at, 274
Actisanes, 194
Acts of Felicitas and her Seven Sons, 409
Acts of the Apostles, 338, 348-356
Acts of the Martyrs, 409
Adam, 22
Adar (Saccuth or Siccuth), Assyrian god of war, 23, 140
Adar, month of, 109, 125
Addison, Joseph, 330
Adrammelech, 109
Aegean, discoveries, 228 *et seq.*; civilization, 237-241; influence on Rome, 304
Aegina pediments at Munich, 277
Aeginetan Treasure in British Museum, 252
Africanus, 164, *170*
Agadè, 211, 213
Agamemnon, 225
Agamtânu (Ecbatana), 124

Agapomenus, 376
Agoracritus, 282
Ahab, 80, 88, 90, 93, 94, 118, 360
Ahaz, 16, 99, 118
Ahimelech, 83
Aijalon, 87
Akaba, gulf of, 65
Akerblad, Swedish Orientalist, 156
Akkad, 124
Alaric, 403
Alcamenes, 281
Alcuin, *412*
Aleppo, 6, 85
Alexander, epitaph of, 369, *372*
Algiers, 310
Alisphragmuthosis, 171
Altaku (Eltekeh), 106
Amalek, 92
Amanus, 37
Amar, land of, 74, 83
Amasis, king of Egypt, 117, 179, 181
Amen (or Amon), supreme god of Thebes, 56, 87, 113, 140
Amenemhet I., 55
Amenemhat II., 169
Ameni, governor of the "nome of the Gazelle," 50
Amenôphis, 64, 70-72, 171
American Journal of Theology, *17*, *352*
American University of Pennsylvania, 32, 40, 142, 213, 214
Amil-Marduk (Evil-merodach), 120
Ammenemes (Amenemhat II.), 169
Ammisatana, 40, 72
Ammi-zaduga, 27
Amon (or Amen), supreme god of Thebes, 56, 87, 113, 140
Amorgan cemeteries, the, 227
Amorgos, 242

INDEX

Amorites, 40, 73, 75, 83, 85, 86
Amosis, 173
Amphipolis, 350
Amraphel, king of Shin'ar, 39, 44
Amurru, *see* Amorites
Anab, 70
Anastasi I., Papyrus of, *70*
Anath, goddess, 139
Anathoth, 140
Ancyran Monument, the, 313
Annalistic tablet of Cyrus, 122, 123
Anshan (Anzan), the home of Cyrus, 124-126, 128, 201
Anshar, 11
Antennae, 303
Anti-Montanists, 370
Antiochus Soter, 196
Antiquity of man, 32-34
Anu, 11, 23
Anunnaki, 14, 25
Apameia, 366; inscriptions from, 384, 389, 390
Aperiu (Hebrews ?), *56*
Apollo Belvedere, 277
Apollo, challenged by Marsyas, 390
Apollo, temple of (Rome), 320
Appêden (apadâna), Persian for palace, 141, *142*
Apries (Hophra), 178, 179, 183
Aquincum, 325
Arabia, 5, 6, 81, 219
Arad, 88
Aramaeans, 37, 133
Aramaic dialect, 5, 6
Aram-Naharaim, 37, 84
Ararat, land of (Urartu or Armenia). 110, 142
Ararat, Mount, 390
Arbakes, 198
Arbela, 124
Arcadia, 265
Archaeology, bearings of, on O.T. narratives, 66-68, 130, 143 *et seq*.; and scholarship, 255
Architecture in Greece, 285
Ardoch, 313
Arenaria, 397
Aretas, 135
Arezzo in Etruria, 326
Argive pottery, 271

Argolid, the, 229, 233
Argos, 282
Arioch (Eri-aku), king of Ellasar, 20, 40
Aristophanes, 276
Aristotle's *Constitution of Athens*, 291
Arles, 327
Armenia, 110, 140, 142, 219
Arminius, 314, 330
Arnaud, 81
Arnon river, 90
Artaxerxes I., 142
Artaxerxes II., 141
Artaxerxes Mnemon, 196
Artemis, 354-356
Aruru. 23
Arvad, 93, 105
Aryans, 211
Asclepius, 264
Asenath, 52
Ashdod, 102, 103, 105, 107
Asher, tribe of, 70
Ashkelon, 73, 104, 105
Ashtaroth, 69
Ashtart (Ashtoreth), 92, 138
Ashteroth-karnaim (Astr-tu), 69
Ashtor, 92
Ashtor-Chemosh, 92
Ashtoreth (Ashtart), 92, 138
Asia Minor, 219, 310, 365
Asia Minor Exploration Fund, 364
Asshurbanipal, 28, 30, 42, 47, 112, 113, 141, 143, 203, 212
Asshurnâsirabal, 84
Asshur (now Kal'at-Sherkat), city of, 30
Asshur, supreme god of Assyria, 11
Assyria, archaeological results yielded by, 4; inscriptions from, 28; monuments of, 92; Israel tributary to, 96; chronology of Books of Kings corrected by inscriptions from, 118; tales of, 197
Assyriology, science of, 155; accepted name for study of Euphratean civilization, 196; its influence, 218
Astarte, 366
Astr-tu (Ashteroth-karnaim), 69
Astyages, 124, 200, 201
Athanatus Epitynchanus Pius, 388

INDEX 425

Athena, 258
Athenaeus, 192
Athens, 229, 256-261; excavation of private houses at, 287
Atiu river, 60
Atlas of Ancient Egypt, 62
"Atreus," "Treasury of," 224
Attica, 229, 231, 244
Attic art, knowledge of early, 278-280
Atuma (Etham or Edom), 61
Augusta on the Mosel, 321
Augustus, 308, 313, 317, 319, 320, 322, 329, 330, 356, 358
Aurelius Alexander, 374
Aurelius Dorotheus, 375
Authority, Hebrew, 3-152; Classical, 155-331; Christian, 335-422
Avaris (Het-Wart), city of, 170, 172
Avircius Marcellus (or Abercius), inscription of, 367-373
Avva, 101
Azaga-Bau, 199
Azariah (Uzziah), 98
Azuri, king of Ashdod, 103
Azuru, 106

BAAL, 139, 366
Baal-zephon, 57, 61
Baba, 50
Babel, tower of, 32
Babylon, 14, 30, 101, 108 *et seq.*; first dynasty of, 29; under Nebuchadnezzar, 119; buildings of, 120, 121; prophets of the Exile on, 120; conquered by Cyrus, 120-123
Babylonia, archaeological results yielded by, 4; antiquity of civilization in, 7, 29, 30, 33; deities of, 10; cosmogony of, 15; mythology of, 21; inscriptions from, 28; Herodotus on, 195-206; Diodorus on, 196-198; kings of, 212
"Babylonian Chronicle," 97, 109
Babylonian Epic, differences between Book of Genesis and, 14, 22
Bacchylides, 276, 291
Baden, 330
Bahr el Ghazâl, 189

Bahu the goddess, 20
Bairest, 53
Bakers, Egyptian, 48
Bakhtan, 175
Balaam and Balak, 360
Bali-zapuna, 61
Bardiya (Smerdis), 180
Bashan, 71, 73
Bau-ellit, 199
Bazu, 46
Beauvois, E., *Antiquités Premycéniennes*, 227
Bedawin, 51, 54, 57
Behistun inscription, the, 159, 180, 200, 203, 207
Bekhen (towers), 58
Bel, 12, 23, 26, 121, 122, 124, 129
Belbeis, 53, 60
Belîkh, 37
Bel Melodach, 206
Belshazzar, 122, 123, 126
Beluchistan, 211
Benê-barak, 106
Ben-hadad, 93-95
Beni Hasan, 174
Berenike, 156
Berosus, 12, 22, 196, 216
Beth-anab, 70
Beth-anath, 69, 140
Beth-anoth, 88, 140
Beth-dagon, 106
Beth-el, 70
Beth-horon, 87
Beth-lehem, 47
Beth-sha-el, 70
Beth-shemesh, 131
Beyrout, 70, 73
Biblical chronology, 32-35, 118, 119
Biblical cosmogony derived from Babylonia, 9, 15-17
Biblical World, 62
Bickell, Professor, 342
Birrens, 313
Birs Nimroud, 31
Biruti (Beyrout), 70, 73
"Bitter River," the (or Persian Gulf), 108
Bit-Yakin, 108, 109
Black Obelisk, the, 94
Blass, 350

INDEX

Blinkenberg, Dr., 227
Bliss, Dr. F. J., *A Mound of Many Cities*, 74, 75
Boekch, 289, 309
Boghaz Keui, 85
Bologna, 304, 305
Bonn on the Rhine, 312, 314, 329
Borchardt, *165*
Borghesi, 309
Borsippa, 31, 43, 115, 121, 122
Bosnia, 310
Bouriant, M., 343
Breasted, *62*, 63
Brick-making in Egypt, 56
Brigetio, 325
Britain, Roman defences in, 328
British Association Address, *240*, *252*
British School at Athens, 228
Brouzos, 367
Brownlow, *396*
Brugsch (*Steininschrift und Bibelwort. History of Egypt*), 50, 52, 55, 56, *57*, 60, 61, 62, *84*
Brunn, 272, 284
Brutus, 352
Buckhardt, 85
Buda Pest, 325, 331
Bul, month of, 137
Bulletin de Correspondance Hellénique, 364, 368
Bunsen, 168
Burnaburiash, 72
Burnouf, 159
Burton, Dr., *the Politarchs*, *352*
Butlers in Egypt, 48
Buto, 184
Buz (Bazu), 46
Byblus, 136

Caelius, the centurion, 314
Caesarea of Mauritania, inscription from, 399
Caesarea Philippi, 339
Cain, 22
Calach (now Nimroud), 30
Calleva (Silchester), 312
Calneh, *29*
Cambyses, 179, 203, 204
Camulodunum (Colchester), 323
Canaan, 72, 74

Canaanites, 16, 28; allied with Hebrews in language, 76
Canina, 310
Canopus inscription, the, 48, 49
Caphtor (Crete), 46
Cappadocia, 85, 219
Caracalla, 321
Carchemish, *71*, 83-85
Caria, 236, 365
Carnuntum, 312, 324, 331
Carthage, inscriptions from, 76, 139
Cassite dynasty of Babylon, 29, 72
Cassius, 352
Castellazzo di Fontanellato, 302
Catacombs at Rome, 396-421
Cataphrygian heresy, the, 363
Catiline, 320
Celaenae, 389
Chabas, 48, 56
Chabiri, the, 73
Chalcis, 270
Chaldaeans, *36*, 108, 122, *127*
Champollion, Jean François, 4, 156, 157
Charu (the Horites), 63
Chebar river (Kabaru canal), 143
Chedorlaomer, king of Elam, 42, 44
Chemmis (Ekhmim), 188
Chemosh, national god of Moab, 89, 91
Chephren (Khafra), statues of, 176
Cherubim, 19
Chester, 313, 314
Chesters, 313
Cheyne's *Isaiah*, *108*
Chierici, 302
Chislev (Kislev), month of, 125
Chiun, Assyrian name of Saturn, 140
Christian Authority, 335-422
Christianity, the gain from archaeology to, 335 *et seq.*
Chronicles, Books of the, 114
Chronology, Biblical, 32-35, 118, 119
Church, the Early, 335-362
Cicero, 319, 351
Cimon, 259
Cities and Bishoprics of Phrygia, 364, 377-382, 384, 387, 388, 390, 391
Classical Authority, 155-331
Classis Flavia Pannonica, 324

Claudius, 317, 322, 329
Clazomenae, 268
Clement of Alexandria, 373
Clinton, Mr., 198
Cockerell, Mr., 285
Coins and gems, Greek, 288, 289
Colchester, 323
Colonies, Roman, 322-325
Colossae, 375
Commodus, 319, 370
Comptes Rendus de l'Acad. d'Inscriptions, 40
Congo, dwarfs of the, 189
Constantine, 327, 401
Constantinople, 321
Contemporary Review, 62, *133*
Coptic, 156, 158
Corinth, 229, 270
Corn-tax, Egyptian, 49
Corvée, the, 55
Cosmogony, Biblical, 9, 14-17; Babylonian, 9-14
Crassus, the banker, 319
Creation, tablets relating to the, 9 *et seq.*
Crete, 46, 229, 231, 233, 290
Criticism, modern, and archaeology, 66-68, 143 *et seq.*
Critius, 284
Crum, Mr., 64
Ctesias, 196, 197
Cuneiform inscriptions, 3, 158
Cush (Kash, Kesh, or Kush), 28, 29, 110, 111, 113, 114
Cuthah (Kutu), *36*, 101, 102
Cyaxares, 198
Cyclades, 228, 230, 242
Cylinder-Inscription of Cyrus, 122, 128
Cyprus, 112, 138, 229, 268, 361
Cyrenius, 357-359
Cyrus, 120, 122, 124-126, 128, 200, 201, 207
Cythera, 235

DACIA, 327
Dad'idri of Damascus (Ben-hadad II.), 93, 95
Daîn-Asshur, 140
Dali (Idalion, Idail), 138
Damascus, 93, 95, 96, 99, 100

Damasus, bishop of Rome, 402, 403, 412, 413
Damophon of Messene, 282
Daniel, Book of, 122, 126
Danube, 312, 328
Daphnae, 184, 268
Darius, inscription of, 159, 180; stelae of, 184; capture of Babylon by? 202; ancestry of, 207
Darius the Mede, 127
David, the *corvée* introduced by, *56*; and the Moabites, 90
Dead Sea, 88, 90
Debir, 70
Decian persecution, the, 347
Deioces, king of the Medes, 200
Delitzsch, Friedr., *Das Bab. Weltschöpfungsepos*, *10, 12, 13, 20, 124*
Delos, 286, 288; inscriptions found at, 290; excavations at, 311
Delphi, 227, 229, 287; excavations at, 262; inscription from, 291
Delta, Aegean pottery in the, 229
Deltaic records, destruction of, 183
Deluge, Babylonian story of the, 22-27
Demeter, 264
Derbe, 361
De Rossi (*Roma Sotterranea. Inscriptiones Christianae Urbis Romanae*), 364, 372, 396, 403, 406, 410, 411
De Sacy, 156
De Vogüé, 5
Dethabar, Persian for judge, counsellor, etc., 142
"Devote," to, 92
Dhibân (Dibon), 88
Diakku, 200
Diana of the Ephesians, 354, 355
Dibon, 88
Dictionary of the Bible, 20, 47, *64*, *71*
Dieulafoy, M. (*L'Acropole de Suse. L'Art antique de la Perse*), 129, 142
Dijon, 327
Dio Cassius, 403
Diocletian persecution, the, 378, 379, 401
Diodorus, 161-163, 165, 166, 168, 181,

428 INDEX

185, 194, 195; his Assyrian tales, 197 *et seq.*
Dipylon Gate, Athens, 244, 270
Doclea in Montenegro, 312
Dodecarchy, the, 163, 178
Domitian, 318, 320, 329, 403
Domus Augustana, 320
Domus Tiberiana, 320
Dorian invasion, 269, 271
Doric architecture, 286
Dörpfeld, Professor, 285, 287
Dreams, weight attached to, in Egypt, 48
Driver, Dr. S. R., *Sermons on the O.T.*, *17*; articles in *Guardian*, *45, 73*; his volume on *Isaiah* in the "Men of the Bible" Series, *108, 119*; *Introduction to the Literature of the O.T.*, *115*; on Nabonidus' inscription, *197*
Duchesne, Abbé, 364, 368, 372; *Liber Pontificalis*, *396*
Dummler, 228
Dungi, 36
Dupsar (tiphsar), scribe, etc., 141
Dur-Yakin, 109
Dushara (Nabataean god), 134, 135
Dyers, guild of, 383

EA, 11, 23, 26
Eabani, 23
Ebers, Professor, 48, 52, 55, 61
Ecbatana, 124
Eden, 19
Edfu, 48
Edom, 47, 61, 65, 105, 133, 135
Egina, 229, 231
Egypt, archaeological results yielded by, 4; antiquity of civilization of, 7, 33 *et seq.*, 209 *et seq.*; exploration in, 33; border-forts of, 57; the evil genius of Palestine, 103; Esarhaddon's conquest of, 110; invaded by Nebuchadnezzar, 117; classical historians of, 161; Herodotus' account of, 162-195; Manetho's, 164-173, 177; Diodorus', 162, 166-168, 181, 185, 194, 195; Cambyses in, 179-181; discoveries of Aegean pottery in, 229

Egypt Exploration Fund, 54, *62*
Egyptian writing, forms of, 3, 155; words in the O.T., 142; chronology, 214
Egyptology, science of, 155; excavation the latest development of, 208; its influence, 218
Ekhmim (Chemmis), 188, 343
Ekron, 104, 106
Elah, 99
Elam, 23, 28, 30, 41-43, 112, 124-126, 201, 219
Elbe, the, 329
'El 'Elyon, *73*
Elephantine, 188
Eleusis, 229, 263
Elgin marbles, the, 277
El Kab, 48, 50, 172
Ellasar, 40
El Makrizi, Arabian historian, 50
El-'Öla, 134
Eltekeh (Altaku), 106
Elul, month of, 135, 136
Encyclopaedia Britannica, 156
Ennugi, 23
Enoch, Book of, 343
Ephah (Khayâpâ), 46
Ephesus, 277, 354, 356
Epidaurus, 264, 282, 286, 291
Epigraphy, a democratic science, 313
Epistle to the Romans, 361
Epitaphs in Roman Catacombs, 415, 416
Eponym Canon, 118
Erech, 14, 23, 29
Erechtheum (Athens), 258, 260, 261
Erechtheus, 258, 260
Eretria, 270, 286
Eri-aku (Arioch), 20, 40, 43
Eridu, 19, 20, 41
Erman, *Life in Ancient Egypt, 48-51, 56, 57, 60, 70, 71*
E-sagil, temple in Babylon, 14, 121
Esarhaddon (Asshur-ah-iddin), 28, 30, 46, *108*, 109, 214; his conquest of Egypt, 110
E-shara, 12
Eshmun'azar, inscription of, 136-138
Esther, 129

INDEX

Etham, 57, 61, 65, 68
Ethanim, month of, 138, 139
Etruria, 303
Etruscan, 233; vases, 274-276; influence on Rome, 304-306
Eucarpia, 367
Euelpius, 399
Euganeans, 301
Eumeneia, 366; inscriptions of, 375-379
Euphratean civilization, 210; chronology, 213
Euphrates, the, 14, 19, 36, 85, 102, 126; valley of, 195 *et seq.*
Euphronius, 274, 276
Euripides, 267
Europe, debt of, to Mycenae, 253
Eusebius, *Ecclesiastical History*, 339, 346, 369, 378, 388, 403, 413
Euting, *Nabat. Inschriften*, 6, 134
Eutychianus, bishop of Rome, 410
Evans, Arthur J., 227, 237, 240, 252, 310
Evetts, *141*
Evil-merodach, *120*
Exodus, Book of, 54-68; date of the, 62, 64
Expositor, the, *45*, 364, 385
Expository Times, the, *27*
Eyuk, 85
Ezekiel, 19
Ezem, 88
E-zida (temple in Borsippa), 121
Ezra, 112

FAKOOS, 54
Falerii, 303, 307
Famines in Egypt, 50
Farrar, Dr., 344
Fayûm (Faiyûm, Fayoum), the, 190, 229, 231, 342, 349; Papyrus of, 346
Ficker, 372
Filocalus, 402, 413
"First-Gate People," 384, 385
Flavia Domitilla, 404
Flavian dynasty, 320
Flavius Clemens, 403, 406
Forum, Rome, excavations at, 310
Fossores, 398

Frazer, J. G., *Pausanias*, *226*, 236
French Archaeological Mission at Cairo, 343
Friederichs, 284
Furtwängler, Professor, *Masterpieces of Greek Sculpture*, 285

GAD, 47, 90
Galatia, 361
Galilee, 99
Gallio, 322
Gaulish art, 328
Gauls, the, 305, 326
Gaumata, 204
Gaza, 70, 73, 87, 98, 107
Gazza, 43
Gebal (Byblus), 70, 100, 136
Gems and coins, Greek, 288, 289
Genesis, Book of, 9-54; difference between Babylonian Epic and, 14, 22; chronology of, 34; teaching of monuments respecting, 44; Palestinian topography of, 148
Germany, excavations in, 312
Gesenius, *Monumenta Phoenicia*, 5
Gezer, 63, 69, 73
Ghiaur Kalessi, 85
Gihon river, *19*
Gilead, 46
Gilgamesh (Izdubar or Gisdubar), 23, *29*
Gimirrai, 28
Gisdubar, *23*
Gladstone, W. E., 222, 224
Glaser, Ed., 6, 81, 82
Glaucus river, 375
Gobryas (Gubaru), Cyrus' general, 125-127, 202
Gomer (Gimirrai), 28
Gortyna in Crete, 290
Goshen, 52-54, 68
Gospels, Synoptic, 342, 343
Goyim, 43, 44
Gozan, 102
Gracchi, the, 308
Granaries in Egypt, 49
Gray, G. B., 45
Great Sea, the, 96
Greece, 161, 164; survivals in historic, 243; travelling in, 256;

430 INDEX

dark ages of, 269-272; early pottery, 271; Mycenaean traditions in, 272; vase-painting, 273-276; sculpture, 277-285; architecture, 285; theatres and private houses, 286-288; coins and gems, 288, 289; inscriptions, 289-291; mythology, 292-294
Greek and Roman history compared, 296
Greek Archaeological Society, 225, 264
Greek Revenue Papyrus, the, 190
Grenfell and Hunt, *Oxyrhynchus Papyri*, 344
Griffith, F. Ll., *56, 63*
Grotefend, 4, 158
Grote, George, 217
Guardian, the, *29, 45, 73*
Gubaru (Gobryas) Cyrus' general, 125-127, 202
Gudea, king of Lagash, 37
Gunkel's *Schopfüng und Chaos*, 10, 16
Guti, Gutim, 41
Gyolbashi, 282
Gythium, 235

HABOR river (now Khabour), 37, 102
Hadad, Syrian god, 131, 132
Hadadezer, *93*
Hadrian, 317, 321, 324, 329
Hadrian's Wall, 313, 328
Hagen, *124*
Halévy, 6, 81
Hallstatt graves, the, 245
Hamah, 85
Hamamat quarries, *57*
Hamath, 93, 98, 100, 101, 123
Hamilton, Mr., 364, 374
Hanno, of Gaza, 100
Hapharaim in Issachar, 87
Haran (Kharran), 35, 37, 38
Hârithat (Aretas), 135
Harnack, *Texte und Untersuchungen*, *342*, 364, 372
Hastings, *Dictionary of the Bible*, 20, 47, *64, 71*
Hat-hor, 49
Haupt, Professor P., translation of Schrader's *Cuneiform Inscriptions and the O.T.*, *24*; *Beiträge zur Assyriologie*, *124*
Haurán, 95
Haynes, Mr., 33
Hazael, 95
Hazo (Hazu), 46
Hazor, 70, 99
Head's *Historia Numorum*, 289
Hebrew Authority, 3-152
Hebrew Civilization, 7
Hebrews, allied with Canaanites in language, 76
Hebron, 83, 86
Hegesippus, 346, 373
Heliopolis, *56*, 59, 188
Helisson excavation at Megalopolis, 265
Hellenic civilization, 250
Hellenium, 184
Hellig, Dr., 237
Heracles, exploits of, 278
Heraeum, American excavations at the, 269, 271, 282, 286
Hermes Cemetery, the, 401
Hermon, 86, *95*
Herod, 358, 359
Herodotus, 100, 126; his account of Egypt, 161-195; his list of kings, 164-168; his ignorance of ancient events, 168; confuses Assyria and Babylonia, 195; on rise of Median power, 200; Apameia, 389
Herondas, 291
Hesiod, 242
Hezekiah, 104, 107, 109, 118
Hicks, *Greek Inscriptions in the British Museum*, *355*
Hiddekel (the Tigris), 19
Hierapolis, 367, 370, 382
Hierarchy, the Egyptian, 49
Hieron of Epidaurus, the, 265
Hilprecht, Professor, 29, *33*, 143
Hincks, Edward, 159
Hippolytus, 410, 413
Hissarlik, mound of, 222, 226, 228, 230, 231, 244
Hittites, 28, 30, 71, 72, 83-86, 133, 366; land of (Hatti), as general term, 84, 96, 105, 111; hieroglyphs of, 219

INDEX

Hivites, the, 86
Hogarth, D. G., *Devia Cypria*, 361
Homer, 234, 236, 238, 242, 245-250, 267, 272, 291
Hommel, Professor, *Ancient Hebrew Tradition*, 13, 19, *38*, 43, *63*, 145
Homolle, M., 280
Hophra (Apries), 178, 179, 183
Hoppin, Dr. J. C., *269*
Horace, 330
Horapollo, *Hieroglyphics*, 195
Hor-em-heb, 51, 194
Horites, the, 63
Hormuzd Rassam, 102, 122
Hort, Dr., 343, 349
Hortensius, 319
Hosea, Book of, 97
Hoshea, 98-100
Housesteads, 313
Humbaba, 23
Huxley, Professor, *Essays on Controverted Questions*, 27
Hyksos, 51, 58, 170-173
Hypatia, 389

Ialyssus, 221
Iaoudhammelouk, 87
I-barra, temple of, 102
Ibleam, 69
Iconium, 361
Idalion, 111, 138
Idiglat (the Tigris), 19
Ignatius, 364
Ijon, 99
Illyrians, 301
India, 211
"India House Inscription," of Nebuchadnezzar, 120
Inscriptions, their value and importance, 289-291, 313-315, 337, 394
Intaphernes, 204
Inuhsamar, 44
Irchulini, king of Hamath, 93, 94
Is (Hit), 205
Isaiah, 99, 100, 103, 107, 121, 129
Isis, 49, 194
Ishtar, 25, 110, 249
Ishtuvegu (Astyages), 124. 200, 201
Israelites, religious system of, 7, 16; traditions of fortified cities, 75; their relations with Assyrians, 80; deported to Assyria, 101
Israel, mention by Merenptah of, 62-65; *v.* Syria, 94; tributary to the Assyrians, 96; Tiglathpileser's invasion of, 99
Issachar, 87
Isyllus, 291
Italian exploration, 300
Italy, 229; prehistoric, 300
Ithaca, 222
I-ulbar temple, 102
Ivory couches, 96, 107
Ivrîz, 85
Izdubar, *23*

Jablonski, 162
Jacob, 51
Jamneia, *63*
Jamutbal, 41
Janoah, 99
Jastrow, Morris (*Religion of Babylonia and Assyria. The Original Character of the Hebrew Sabbath*), *10*, *17*, *20*, *23*, 31
Jauhazi (Joahaz) of Judah, 100
Javan (Yavan), 28
Jebel Mûsa, 65
Jebel Serbâl, 65
Jehoash, 96
Jehoiachin, *120*
Jehoram, 83
Jehoshaphat, 94
Jehu, 94, 95, 118
Jensen, P., 86
Jerabis, 85
Jeremiah, 114, 117
Jeroboam, 88, 96, 97
Jerome, 402
Jerusalem, *46*, 73, 87, 107; date of destruction of, 119
Jews, return under Zerubbabel of, 120; re-established in Palestine, 130; in Phrygia, 367; history of, 389
Jezebel, 360
Joahaz, 100
Job's Stone, *71*
Joppa, 69, 70, 73, 106
Jordan, 87, 90.
Jordani, cemetery of the, 401

Joseph in Egypt, 47-51, 66, 67
Josephus, 170, 171
Journal of Hellenic Studies, 364
Judah, 80, 99; invaded by Shishak, 87; invaded by Sennacherib, 104-107
Julian the Apostate, 389
Julia Severa, 391
Julius Caesar, 308, 317
Justin Martyr, 339

KABARU Canal, 143
Kadesh, 65, 84, 86
Kairodapistoi, 383
Kaiwan or Chiun (Saturn), 140
Kal'at-Sherkat, 30
Kaldû (Chaldaeans), 36
Kanâan, 58
Karabel, 85
Karal, 131
Karkar, 93
Karnak, 58, 69, 87
Kasdim (Kaldû, Chaldaeans), 35
Kash, 28
Kasr Bint-el-Yehudi, 117
Kasshu, 29
Kaushmelek of Edom, 100
Kedar (Kidrai), 46, 47
Kedesh, 99
Keilah, 87
Kelendres, 368
Kemur, 57
Kenyon, Mr., 358
Kesem, 53
Kesh, 28
Khabour river, 37, 102
Khafra (Chephren), statues of, 176
Khalman (Aleppo), 93
Khammurabi, 27, 29, 39, 40, 42, 44, 72, 212
Khayâpâ, 46
Khetem, a fortress, 58, 61
Khnemhetep, 174
Khons, 175
Khufu, the cartouche of, 174
Kidrai, 47
King, L. W., *Letters and Inscriptions of Hammurabi*, 43, 44
Kings, Books of, 80; chronology corrected by the Assyrian inscriptions, 118

Kiriath-sopher, 70
Kition, Kittim, 138
Klein, Dr., 88
Kouyunjik, 104
Krall, Professor, 170
Kudur, 41. 42
Kudurmabuk, 41, 43, 45
Kudurnuchgamar, 44
Kûrash, *see* Cyrus
Kurdistan, 44
Kush, *see* Cush
Kutha, 115
Kutu (Cuthah), 103

LABASHI-MARDUK, 120
Labynetus, 199, 202
Lachamu, 11
Lachish, 73, 75, 107
Lachmu, 11, 47
Laconia, 229
Lagamar (or Lagomer), 42
Lagash (now Telloh), 33, 37, 40
Lakes, the Bitter, 57
Lambaesis, 312, 331
Lanciani, Professor, 311
Land-tenure in Egypt, 51
Laocoon, 277
Laodiceia, 366
Larnaca (Kition, Kiti, etc.), 138
Larsa (now Senkereh), 35, 40
Latium, 301, 306
Layard, Sir A. Henry, *Nineveh and its Remains*, 3, 30, 94; the Kouyunjik bulls, 104
Leake, Mr., 291
Lebanon, cedar-wood rom, 37, 86, 121
Lebas and Wadd., 361
Lehmann, 213
Lenormant, 20
Leviticus, 76, 78
Libyans, the, 62
Lightfoot, Bishop (*Essays on Supernatural Religion. Apostolic Fathers*), 355, 364, 367, 372, 383, 396
Little Zab, 25, 44
Lityerses, legend of, 390
Lobeck's *Aglaophamus*, 264
Lock and Sandy, *Two Lectures on the "Sayings of Jesus,"* 344

INDEX

London Society of Antiquaries, 312
Lugal-zaggisi, 29, 33, 40, 72
Lycaonia, 85
Lycia, 282
Lycos, 375
Lycosura, 282
Lydia, 306, 365
Lystra, 361

MACCABEES, Second Book of, 409
Macedonia, 349
Machpelah, cave of, 83
Mackenzie, 228
McLennan, 293
Macrinus, 390
Madâ (Madai, Medes), 28
Maeander river, 367, 375, 389
Magians, the, 206
Magnesia, 286
Mahanaim, 87
Mainz, 330
Makârib, priest-kings, 82
Makkedah, 87
Maktl, 61
Malta, 361
Manasseh, 111, 112, 114–116
Manatt, *Mycenaean Age, 226*
Manetho, *51*; list of Egyptian kings, 164–169, 215, 216; his account of the Hyksos, 170
Mannai, Minni, 142
Mannhardt, 293
Marduck (Merodach), supreme god of Babylon, 10, 11, 13, 14, 109, 120–122, 127–129
Marib (Mariaba), 82
Mariette, 221
Marriott, Rev. W. B., *Testimony of the Catacombs, 420*
Marseilles and the Carthaginian inscription, 76
Marsyas, legend of, 390
Martigny, forum at, 325
Martu, or the West Land, 39–42, 72, 105, 123
Marzabotto, 305, 306
Maspero (*Dawn of Civilization. Revue Archéologique. Struggle of the Nations. Transactions of the Victoria Institute*), 20, 37,
39, 46, 55, 57, 58, 61, 63–65, 69, 71, 84, 86, 87, 88
Maximin, 388
Maximus, cemetery of, 401
Meda'in Salih, 6
Medes, 197; Herodotus on the, 200; rise of their power, *ibid.*
Medum, 174
Megalopolis, excavations at, 265, 286
Megiddo, 69, 70, 73
Meissner, 29
Melchizedek, 45, *73*
Melito of Sardis, 373
Melos, island of, 228, 231, 242
Memphis, 59, 175, 185, 188
Menahem, 97, 118
Menander, 267
Menes, first historical king of Egypt, 33, 164, 185
Mentiu, nomads, 51
Merenptah, 51, 58, 61, 80; Israel mentioned by, 62–65
Meris, 349
Merodach, *see* Marduk
Merodach-baladan (Marduk-abaliddin), king of Babylon, *36*, 108, 109
Meroe, 189
Mesha, king of Moab, inscription of, 6, 88–90
Meshech (Musku), 28
Mesopotamia, 37, 38, 71, 84, 102, 218, 268
Methushael, *22*
Meyer, Ed., 125, 215
Migdol, 57, 61
Miletus, 270, 277
Minaean inscriptions, 6
Minni, Mannai, 142
Minos, 233
Misphragmuthosis, 171
Mitanni, 71, 84
Mithraism, 331
Mitinti of Ashkelon, 100
Mittheilungen aus dem Orientalischen Sammlungen, 110
Mizraim (Egypt), 147
Moab, 5, 89–91, 105
Moabite Stone, 88
Moeris, 164

28

Mommsen, Theodor, *Corpus Inscriptionum Latinarum*, 309, 312, 313
Montanism, 363, 392
Montelius, Dr., 252
Montenegro, 312
Morgan, M. de, 33
Mosel river, 327
Moses, 16
Mugheir (Ur), 122
Müller, D. H., *Die Altsemitischen*, etc., *133*
Müller, W. Max, *Asien und Europa*, etc., 46, 70, 74, *87*
Municipia, 322-325
Municipium Aelium Carnuntum, 325
Musku, 28
Muzuri, *101*
Mycenaean art, etc., 234-242, 267-269; civilization, the Homeric Epics inspired by, 251; pottery, 270
Mycenae, Schliemann at, 223; the Circle-graves, 225; Homer and, 245-250; Europe's debt to, 253
Mycerinus, 176
Myekphoris, 190
Myres, J. L., *227*
Myron, 284
Mythology, study of, 292-294

NABATAEAN inscriptions, 6, 134, 135
Nabo-balatsu-ikbi, 199
Nabo-kin-akhi, 123
Nabo-na'id, last king of Babylon, 38, 102, 119, 120, 123, 125-127
Nabonidus, inscription of, 197, 199, 202, 213
Nabopolassar, *36*, 121, 197, 198
Nachrima, Naharina, Narima, 37, 84
Nadintu Bel, 204
Nagada, 33
Nahor, 46
Nahum, 92, 112, 119, 140
Nannar, the moon-god Sin, 36
Naphtali, 99
Narâm-Sin, 33, 40, 211, 213
Narce, 303
Naucratis, 184, 190, 257, 268
Naville, M., *Recueil de Travaux*, 48, 52-55, 61, *63, 64*

Naxos, 227
Nebo, 92, 121, 122, 124, 129
Nebuchadnezzar (properly Nebuchadrezzar), 31, *36*, 199, 202; his inscription, 116, 120; his invasion of Egypt, 117; his buildings, 120, 121
Necho, 178
Nectanebo, 53
Nehemiah, 129
Nereus and Achilleus, cemetery of, 400, 404
Nergal, 36, 93, 102
Neriglissar (Nergal-shar-uzur), 120
Nero, 318, 329
Nerva, 319
Nes-Hor, 117
Nesiotes, 284
Neumagen on the Mosel, 327
New Testament narrative, illustrations of, 360
Newton, Sir Charles, *Art and Architecture*, 225, 289, 338
Nibby, 310
Niebuhr, 158, 217
Niffer, 32
Nile, 49; valley of the, 34, 162
Nilotic civilization, 210
Nimrod, 29
Nimroud, 3, 30
Nineveh, 3, 29, 30; fall of, 119, 197
Ninus, 197
Nippur (now Niffer or Nuffar), 14, 32, 33, 40, 142, 143, 213, 214
Nisan, month of, 123, 125, 135
Nisaya, 204
Nisibis, 370
Nisin, 41
Nitetis, 179
Nitocris, 164, 199
Nizir mountain, 25
No (Thebes), 113, 114, 140
Noah, 22, 390
Nöldeke, Professor, 77, *135*
Northcote, *396*
Northern Phrygia, inscriptions from, 385
Novatian, 414
Nuffar, 32

INDEX

OLYMPIA, excavations at, 262, 281, 282, 285
Omri, 80, 89, 91, 94; "land of," 95, 96, 98, 101
On, *see* Heliopolis.
Ono, 69
Opis, 125, 202, 205
Orange, theatre wall of, 331
Orchomenus, 236
"Orient-Comité," German, 110
Orontes, 74, 84, 85
Oropus, 286
Orsi, Dr., 230
Osiris, 193, 194, 217
Osnappar, *see* Asshurbanipal
Ostia, 331
Ostrianum Cemetery, 400
Osymandyas, 194
Otrous, 370
Oxyrhynchus, 336, 344

PADI, king of Ekron, 106
Padua, 306
Paembasa, 60
Paeonius, 281
Paheri, 48
Paintings and symbolism in Roman Catacombs, 417-419
Pa-Kan'ana, 58
Palatine, the, 303, 310, 319-321
Palestine, its state before the Exodus, 68-76; Egypt the evil genius of, 103; Jews re-established, in, 130; its topography in Book of Genesis, 148
Palmyra, inscriptions from, 5, 135, 136
Panammu, 131, 132
Paneas (Caesarea Philippi), 339
Pannonia, 327
Papias, 346
Papoi, 382
Papremis, 186, 190
Papyri, discoveries in Egypt of, 291, 341, 344, 347, 348
Papyrus, Anastasi I., 70; Turin, 214; the Fayoum, 346; Greek Revenue, 190
Paradise, story of, 21
Pa-Ramessu Meriamun, 55

Parma, 302
Parnassus, 263
Pâr-napishtim, 23-26
Paros, 227, 241, 279
Parthenon, Athens, 258, 260, 285, 286
Patêsi, a priest-king, 30
Pathros, *111*
Patterson, Rev. Archibald, *396*
Paturis (Pathros), 111
Pausanias, 222, 224, 225, 281
Pekah, Assyrian for governor, 141
Pehlevi, 142
Pekah, king of Israel, 99, 118
Pelasgians, 237, 243, 244
Pelasgic Wall, Athens, 258
Peloponnesus, 243
Pelusium, 186
Pennsylvanian Expedition, 32, 40, 142, 213, 214
Penrose, Mr., 285
Pentateuch, the, 9-79; dates of, 32; criticism of, 146
Pentaur, 84
Pentelic marble, 279
Perath, *see* Euphrates
Per-Bairest, 53, 60
Pergamum, 283, 360
Perrot and Chipiez, *History of Art*, 226
Perrot, M., 250
Persia, 161, 201; dynasty of, 177; royal records of, 196
Persian Gulf, 19, 20, 108
Petersen, Professor, 227
Petra, 135
Petrie, Professor Flinders (*Egyptian Tales. Syria and Egypt in the Tell el Amarna Letters. Tanis*), 33, *48*, *51*, 55, 57, 62, 63, *72*, 74, 117, 210, 215, 229, 231, 239
Petronilla, 405
Pfahlgraben, 330
Phakusa, *53*
Phaleric ware, 271
Pharaoh (the Egyptian Per-âa), 48, *68*, 103, 140
Phidias, 266, 274, 281
Phigalia, 277
Philip, 390

Philippi, 349-353
Philistines, the, 46, 102, 103
Phoenicia, 74, 85, 104, 268
Phoenician inscriptions, 5, 118, 136-139; art and influence of, 235-238
Phraortes, 200
Phravartish, 200
Phrygia, 85; remains in, 363-395
Phylákopi, 228, 231
Pigorini, 302
Pi-hahiroth, 57, 61
Pinches, T. G. (*Records of the Past. Transactions of the Victoria Institute*), 14, 20, 29, 42, 97, 108, 109, 122, 141, 195, 198
Pindar, 262
Pir'u, *101*
Pishon river, *19*
Pisistratus, 258, 278
Pithom (Pi-Tum), 54, 61, 65, 68, 185
Pitra, Cardinal, 367
Pius, 329
Plato, 267, 291
Pliny, 162
Plutarch, *De Iside et Osiride*, 162, 195, 217
Pola, 331
Polychrome Bible, the, *108*
Polyclitus the Younger, 265, 267
Pompei, excavations at, 311, 331
Pomponia Graecina, 407
Pont du Gard, 331
Popes, Crypt of the, 410, 412
Porphyrabaphoi, 382
Porphyry, 389
Potiphar, Poti-phera, 47, 52
Po Valley, the, 302
Praetextatus Cemetery, 401, 412
Praxiteles, 267, 282
Prophets, their writings illustrated by inscriptions, 81, *100*, 103, 107, 108, 111, 120, 121, 126, 129, 130, 136-143
Prosopis, victory of, 62
Prudentius, 402
Psammetichus, 117, 163, 164, 176, 177
Ptah, his shrine at Memphis, 185
Ptolemy, 156, 162, 190; and Cleopatra, 157; his canon of the Babylonian kings, 196, 212, 216
Pul, king of Assyria, 97
Purat, *see* Euphrates
"Purple-dippers," 383, 385
Pyramid texts, 57
Pythagoras, 267

QUINTILII, the, 318
Quirinius (Cyrenius), 357-359

RA, the sun-god, 52, 54
Raamses, city, 55, 68
Rabbith in Issachar, 87
Rab-saris, Assyrian court dignitary, 140
Rabshakeh, Assyrian military officer, 141
Rainer, Archduke, 342
Rameses, land of, 54
Rammân (Rimmon), 25, 93, 140
Rammanu-nirâri II., 197
Rammanu-nirâri III., 96, *103*
Ramoth in Gilead, 94
Ramsay, Professor W. M. (*St. Paul the Traveller. Was Christ born at Bethlehem?*), 291, 310, 350, *351, 352*, 358, 364, 368, 369, 372, 379, 383, *385*
Ramses II. (the Pharaoh of the Oppression), 52, 54, 55, 60, 62, 69, 71, 74, 83, 194; his treaty with the Hittites, 84
Ramses III., 46, 48, *56*, 69, 84
Ramses IV., *57*
Raphiah, 100
Rassam, Hormuzd, 102, 122
Ravenna, 321
Rawlinson, Sir Henry, *Inscriptions of Western Asia*, 4, 17, 44, 158
Regensburg on the Danube, 312, 329
Rehob, 69
Rehoboam, 75, 80, 87, 130
Rehoboth-Ir, *29*
Rekhmara, 56
Remaliah, 99
Renaissance, the, 254
Resen, *29*
Resheph, Phoenician fire-god, 131, 138

INDEX

Reuben, 90, 91
Revue Biblique, 27
Rezin, king of Damascus, 99
Rhamnus, 282
Rhampsinitus, 162, 176
Rhind Lectures at Edinburgh, *252*
Rhine, 312, 328
Rhinocorura, 194
Rhodes, 221, 268
Riaku (or Eriaku), 20, 40, 43
Rimmon (Rammân), 140
Rim-Sin, *40*
Romans, epistle to the, 361
Rome, its history compared with Greece's, 296 ; its growth, 303 ; the Republic, 307; birth of the Empire, 308; progress of exploration, 311 ; its inscriptions, 313 ; its Empire compared with that of India, 315; imperial system and officials, 317 ; the Palatine, 321; colonies, 322, 323; uniformity of the Empire, 325 ; archaeology and art, 327 ; frontier defences of, 328, 329 ; Catacombs at, 396-421
Rosa, 310
Rosalia, 384
Rosetta decrees, 48
Rosetta Stone, 156
Ryle, Professor, *Early Narratives of Genesis*, *17*, 31, *35*

SABAEANS, 6, 81
Sabako, 100, 111
Sabbath, the, an institution of Babylonian origin, 17, 18
Sacculh or Siccuth (Adar), 140
Sacrificial camp of the Phoenicians, 76-79
Sa'diyeh, *71*
Saft el-Henneh, 53
Sagan (deputy, prefect), 141
St. Caecilia, burial-place of, 411
St. Callistus, cemetery of, 399, 401, 407, 410
St. Domitilla Cemetery, 399, 400, 403, 404, 406
St. Lucina, crypt of, 407
St. Luke, 354 ; accuracy of, 357-359

St. Matthew's Gospel, 344
St. Paul, 349, 352, 353, 371 ; his connexion with Rome, 407, 408
St. Paul Cemetery, the, on the Via Ostiensis, 400
St. Peter, gospel of, 343, 346; apocalypse of, 344 ; his connexion with Rome, 407, 408
St. Priscilla Cemetery, 399, 400, 406
Sais, 6, 179, 182, 183, 186, 189
Saite dynasty, 177, 182
Sakama (Shechem), mountain of, 70
Salaman of Moab, 100
Salatis, 170
Salm of Hagam, 134
Salmshezeb, 133, 134
Salonika, 352
Samaria, 83, 95, 99, 101 ; fall of, 118
Samian ware, 326
Sammuramat, 197
Sâmtu, 19
Samuel, Book of, 114
Sandykly Ova, 367
Sanibu of Ammon, 100
Santorin islands, 221
Sardanapalus, 198
Sardaurri, 142
Sardinia, 229
Sargon, 28, 30, 33, 40, 45, 46, 72, 82, 84, 100-103, 108, 109, 143, 200, 211, 213
Sarludâri, 105
Sarzec, M. de, *40*
Saturn (Chiun or Kaiwan), 140
Sayce, Professor (*Verdict of the Monuments. Early History of the Hebrews. Patriarchal Palestine*), 15, 16, 18-20, *27*, *31*, *33*, *39*, *44*, 46, 47, *50*, 65, 68, *69*, *70*, *76*, *85*, *93*, *104*, *115*, 126, *127*, *145*, 146, 147, 149, 150, 189
Scheil, Father, 44
Schliemann, Henry, 220 *et seq.*
Scholarship and architecture, 255
Schrader (*Cuneiform Inscription and the O.T. Keilinschriftliche Bibliothek*), 18, *23*, *93*, 97, *127*
Schuchhardt, Dr., *Schliemann's Excavations*, *226*
Schürer Dr., 360

Science Progress, 227
Scopas, 267, 282
Sculpture in Greece, 277-285
Sehêl, 50
Selbie, J. A., 27
Seleucidae, 136
Semiramis, 185, 197, 199
Semites, the, 13, 211, 235, 240, 249
Senefru, pyramid of, 174
Senir (Hermon), 95
Sennacherib, 30, 75, 104-107, 109, 118, 140, 203
Sepharvaim, 101, 102
Septimius Severus, 321, 325
Septuagint, the, 32
Serbonis, Lake, 194
Sergius Paulus, 361
Servius, 308
Sesostris, 162, 169, 185, 194
Seth, 22
Seti I., 58, 69, 71, 74, 83
Seti II., 60
Sevè, 100, 101
Severus, 390
Sextus Quintilius Valerius Maximus, 319
Shabaka (Sabako), 100, 111
"Shades," the, 137, 138
Shaknu, *see* Sagan
Shallum, 97
Shalmaneser I., 30
Shalmaneser II., 28, 84, 93-95, 108, 140
Shalmaneser IV., 100
Shamash, Shemesh, the sun-god, 23, 102, 131, 135
Shamash-shum-ukin, 115
Sharezer, 109
Sharhana, siege of, 173
Sharkiyeh, 54
Sharuchen, 69
Shashang, 87
Shasu (or Bedawin), 51, 58, 61
Shaving, a custom in Egypt, 49
Sheba, 30, 81, 82
Shebat, month of, 42
Shechem, 70
Shepherds in Egypt, 50
Shin'ar, Hebrew name for Babylonia, 39

Shishak, king of Egypt, 52, 87, 88
Shoham, or onyx stone, 19
Shunem, 87
Sib'u, 100
Siccuth, 140
Sicily, 229, 231
Sicyon, 286
Sidon, 137; sarcophagi from, 283
Sidonians, 235
Sihon, 73
Sikayauvatish fort, 204
Silchester, 312
Simon Magus, 339
Sin, the moon-god, 36, 38, 123
Sinai, 57, 65
Sinuhit, 57, 61
Sippar, 102, 115, 122, 125
Sippara, 202
Sirmium on the Save, 321
Sivan, month of, 109
Smerdis, 180, 204
Smith, George, *Chaldaean Genesis*, 9, 15-18, 22, 31; *Assyrian Discoveries*, 103; *The Assyrian Eponym Canon*, 118
Smith, Professor G. A., *Historical Geography of the Holy Land*, 148
Smyrna, 85, 362
So, 100, 101, 111
Socho, 88
Society of Dilettanti, 263
Solomon, 56, 81
Solway, 329
Sopt, the god, 53
Soracte, Mount, 303
Spain, 229
Sparta, 298
Spatale, 388
Spata tomb, 231
Spiegelberg, 62, 63
Statilius Sisenna, 320
Steindorff, 52, 63
Stektorion, 367
Strabo, 81, 82, 162, 185
Strassburg, 330
Strassmaier, 127
Stuart, Mr., 285
Succoth, 57, 61, 68
Suez, isthmus of, 57
Sulla, 307

INDEX

Sumerians, the, 13
Sun-pillars, 135, 136, 139
Susa, 112, 129, 141, 142, 211
Symeon Metaphrastes, 367
Synoptic Gospels, 342, 343
Syra, 241
Syria, 83, 94, 98, 219

TAANACH, 69, 87
Tabali, 28
"Table of Nations," 27
Tabnith (king of Sidonians), 137, *138*
Tabularium, Rome, 307
Tacitus, 298, 407
Tahpanhes, 117
Tale of the Two Brothers, 48
Tamassus, inscription of, 138
Tammuz, a god, 20, 124, 140
Tanis (Zoan), 55
Tanith, patron goddess of Carthage, 139
Tarku (Tirhakah), 111, 113
Tartan (*turtanu*), 140
Tatia, 404
Taylor, Colonel, 36
Taylor Cylinder, the, 104
Tel el-Amarna letters, 16, 70-74, 76, 83, 146
Tel el-Kebir, 53
Tel Ibrahim, 102
Tell Defneh, 117
Tell el-Hesy, 74, 75
Tell el-Maskhuta, 54
Telloh, 33, *40*
Têma, inscription of, 133, 134
Terah, 35
Terramare, 302
Tethmosis, 171
Teufelsmauer, 330
Tevâ, 124, 127
Thamugadi, 312
Theatres, excavation of Greek, 286
Thebaid, the, 170
Thebes, 48, 56, 62, 113, 140, 175, 185, 188, 229
Theku, 58, 61
Themistocles, 259
Therasia, 231
Thersilion of Epidaurus, the, 265
Thermae, 367

Thessalonica (Salonika), 352, 353
Thessaly, 229
Thoricus, 229, 231
Thothmes I., 71
Thothmes II., 71
Thothmes III., 56, 58, 69, 83
Thremmata, guild of the, 382
Thucydides, 236, 298
Thummosis, 171, 173
Thureau-Dangin, M., *40*
Thyatira, 360, 362
Tiâmat, 10, 11
Tiberius, 320, 329
Tid'al, 43, 44
Tiglath-pileser, 28, 46, 84, 97-99, 108, 118, 132, 133, 142
Tigris, the, 14, 19, 124; valley of, 195 *et seq.*
Timaus, king of Egypt, 170
Tiphsar (dupsar), scribe, etc., 141
Tirhakah (Tarku), 111, 113
Tiryns, 229, 231, 236, 249
Tithonus, 198
Tomkins, Mr., *The Age of Abraham*, 47, *69*
"Tongue" of slander, 131
Toser, king, 50
Trajan, 319, 321, 329
Tralles, 286
Transactions of the Victoria Institute, 20, *42*, *69*, *87*
Travels of a Mohar, The, 69
"Treasury of Athens," 224
Troad, the, 222
Troy, 222, 231
Tsountas, Dr., *Mycenaean Age, 226*, 227-229
Tubal (Tabali), 28
Tudchula, 43, 44
Tum, 54
Tunis, 310
Turin Papyrus of Kings, 168, 214
Turtanu, 101, 140
Tylor, 293
Tyne, 329
Tyre, 70, 73, 236
Tysdrus, 331

Ukinzir, 97
Ulai, the, *112*

INDEX

Umman-manda, 43, 128, 197, 200
Ur, 35, 36, 38, 123
Urartu, *see* Armenia
Ur-bau, 36
Urd-amani (Rud-Amôn), 113
Uriah, 83
Uruk (Erech), 23, 29, 36
Urusalim (Jerusalem), 73
User, mountain of, 70
Usertesen I., 50, 57
Ushak, inscription of, 385
Ussher, 32
Uza-hor-ent-res, 179
Uzziah, 98

VALERIAN, 412
Vaphio in Laconia, tomb of, 229, 231, 235
Varhely, 331
Varus, defeat of, 329, 330
Vase-painting in Greece, 273
Vatican Cemetery, 400
Venus dei Medici, 277
Vespasian, 318, 320, 323, 324, 329, 404
Victor, 399
Vienna, 312, 325
Viereck, Dr., 358
Villas, Romano-British, 313
Vindobona, *see* Vienna
Virgil, 301
Vitruvius, 287, 288

WADDINGTON, M., 364, 383
Wady Brissa, 202
Wady Mûsa, 135
Wady Rummein, 37
Wady Tumilat, 57, 185
Waldstein, Professor, 269
"Wall" of Egypt, 57
Warka, 29
Wellsted, 81
Westcott and Hort, *Greek Testament*, 349
West Land, the, 65, 105, 115
Wiedemann, *Religion of the Ancient Egyptians*, etc., 49, 117, 192

Wilbour, 50
Wilcken, Dr., 358
Wilkinson-Birch, *Ancient Egyptians*, 48, 56
Winckler, 16, 36, 39, 74, 101, 103
Wood, Mr., 135
Wordsworth's *Greece*, 255
Wright, Dr. W., 85
Württemberg, 330

XENOPHON, *Cyropaedia*, 201
Xerxes, genealogy of, 207
Xiphilinus, 403
Xystus II., pope, 412

YÂNÛH, 63
Yasna, the, 159
Yavan (the Greeks), 28
Yenoam (Yânûh or Jamneia), 63
Young, Thomas, 156

ZAHN, 372
Zaphenath-pa'aneach (Joseph's Egyptian name), 52
Zarephath, 70, 105
Zaru (Egyptian fathers), 58, 60
Zechariah, 97
Zedek, 105
Zeitschrift für Assyrologie, etc., etc., 52, 62, 76, 135, 141
Zend-Avesta, 159
Zephaniah, 119
Zephyrinus, bishop of Rome, 410
Zerubbabel, 120
Zidon (or Sidon), 70, 73, 104, 136, 138
Ziggurat, 31, 36, 121
Zimmern, 10, 12, 20, 37, 43, 76
Zinjirli, inscriptions from, 6, 110, 131, 133
Ziribashani, 73
Zoan (Tanis), 55
Zoroastrians, 206
Zoticus, 370
Zumur (Zemar), 73
Zurru (Tyre), 73

www.ingramcontent.com/pod-product-compliance
Lightning Source LLC
Chambersburg PA
CBHW022133300426
44115CB00006B/166